ESSENTIAL PRUNING TECHNIQUES

ESSENTIAL PRUNING TECHNIQUES

Trees, Shrubs, and Conifers

by

George E. Brown

Revised and enlarged by

Tony Kirkham

With photography from Andrea Jones
(Garden Exposures Photo Library)

And a new foreword by Hugh Johnson

TIMBER PRESS · PORTLAND, OREGON

This work incorporates portions of *The Pruning of Trees, Shrubs and Conifers*, first published in 1972 by Faber and Faber Limited, copyright © 1972 by the estate of George E. Brown.

With photography from Andrea Jones (Garden Exposures Photo Library). Photo and illustration credits appear on page 386.

Published in 2017 by Timber Press, Inc.
The Haseltine Building
133 S.W. Second Avenue, Suite 450
Portland, Oregon 97204-3527
timberpress.com

Printed in China
Text and cover design by Anna Eshelman

Library of Congress Cataloging-in-Publication Data

Names: Brown, George E. (George Ernest), 1917–
    1980, author. | Kirkham, Tony, author.
Title: Essential pruning techniques: trees, shrubs,
    and conifers / by George E. Brown; revised and
    enlarged by Tony Kirkham; with photography
    from Andrea Jones and a new foreword by Hugh
    Johnson.
Other titles: Pruning of trees, shrubs and conifers
Description: Third edition. | Portland, Oregon:
    Timber Press, 2017. | "This work incorporates
    portions of The Pruning of Trees, Shrubs and
    Conifers, first published in 1972 by Faber and
    Faber Limited ... by the estate of George E.
    Brown." | Includes bibliographical references and
    index.
Identifiers: LCCN 2016017684 | ISBN
    9781604692884 (hardcover)
Subjects: LCSH: Trees—Pruning. | Shrubs—Pruning.
    | Conifers—Pruning. | Pruning.
Classification: LCC SB125 .B762 2017 | DDC
    635.9/7642—dc23 LC record available at https://
    lccn.loc.gov/2016017684

A catalogue record for this book is also available
from the British Library.

CONTENTS

Foreword by Hugh Johnson
6

General Principles
of Pruning
8

Specific Pruning Advice,
Abelia to Zenobia
50

Organizations and Products
384

References and Further Reading
385

Photo and Illustration Credits
386

Index
387

Foreword

I didn't meet the famous George Brown, though I bought his book when it came out in 1972—the very year I was writing my own first tree book. I'd like to say that all the thousands of trees I've planted since have impeccable form, growing straight and tall, thanks to his advice. And that all the shrubs I've been responsible for are the ideal size and shape and flower to their maximum every year. Tree (and shrub) growing is not that simple, even with the best advice, hallmarked Kew.

Most people, I fear, just stick plants in the ground and hope for the best. They rely on their inherent nature (as described on the label), their inherited pattern of growth and even, in many gardeners' cases, believe any interference (they'd call pruning "interference") is some kind of crime against nature. I have a neighbour who would no more take her secateurs to a shrub than to a cat. The result? Her garden looks great from above, from our bathroom, where all the lively growth is and flowers appear. From ground level it is a lightless jungle full of dead twigs and branches. (She likes it that way.)

George Brown's book has been the standard work for 44 years. Have trees changed? Isn't an oak still an oak? Yes, but our knowledge moves on. Our expectations and tastes change. The sum of professional experience grows. Kew is a world HQ of experimental plant science—and that includes the best way to grow trees, shrubs . . . everything. If you think tree growing is a leisurely affair where nothing changes, you haven't come across Tony Kirkham. He is responsible for all the 14,000 trees and shrubs in Kew Gardens, and the head of its horticultural services. Can you imagine a crowd following a man with a pair of secateurs and a little saw round Kew Gardens, straining to see every snip and hear every word? That is Tony's public, in the gardens and on television. He doesn't disappoint. He pioneered root aeration, reinvigorating ancient (and even fallen) trees. He researched the best shape of planting hole (square and shallow).

There are general principles about planting and pruning which won't change. They are based on the inherent nature of plants, above all their search for the light. Trees express their nature in developing leaders, shoots that seize the authority, as it were, become boss, and suppress (or try to suppress) rivals for the top slot. Shrubs are more team players, sharing out the hormones among their many points of growth. Rule one in pruning is to understand what the plant is trying to do and either help it on its natural way, or give it other instructions.

So every tree or shrub has a growth-programme you could call an in-built agenda, and they are all specific—different, that is, for each species. Hence the huge value of the unique second half of this book, where the experience of many years at Kew pays off, plant by plant. Tony Kirkham is direct and economical; you get the essentials, clearly set out.

The most obvious difference between this edition and its predecessors is the illustrations, which make turning its pages like a walk through the ideal arboretum on a fine day—which in a sense it is. Andrea Jones has photographed almost everything at Kew; for clarity and relevance her pictures can't be beaten. I'm not sure that such details of precise pruning operations by an expert (that's Tony) have ever been published before—nor of the structural details of trees (branch collars, for example) that need informed explanation. There are pictures, for good measure, of fat-headed blunders where trees have been ruined by ignorance of their natural behaviour. If you doubt for one moment the need for this book, look at the picture on page 31.

Blurb-writers are always claiming that the book in hand is a game-changer, but Kirkham's update of Brown is the real deal.

—HUGH JOHNSON

General Principles

of

PRUNING

Pruning is an important part of the gardener's or arborist's operations to regulate and control growth and encourage flowering and fruiting on ornamental trees and shrubs and in particular fruit trees. With correct and well-placed pruning and training in a plant's early years, the ultimate shape and form is determined for the rest of its life.

Why Prune?

The question which is often asked is why pruning should be needed in the garden, as it does not occur in nature; however, this is not absolutely true. Many tree species will shed twigs in their natural habitat (a process known as abscission), and many other factors in a natural environment—readily available light or shade, browsing mammals, soil type, microclimates, weather conditions—affect the growth of plants. In nature, when a tree or shrub is left to its own devices and not interfered with by secateurs (hand pruner or loppers) or the saw, the resulting form and habit does not always highlight the special ornamental attributes of the species or improve the longevity and health of the specimen. Growth may be typical of the species, but under natural conditions, plants are often found in balanced ecological communities and in direct competition with other, often larger plants. The larger plants frequently overpower the weaker, which will die unless they adapt to these conditions. This is not so in the garden, where the weaker plants may be protected by the gardener's pruning the stronger subjects to restrict their overall size, be they trees or shrubs.

As they grow toward maturity, many trees and shrubs accumulate dead twigs and branches; these are best removed, as they are unsightly and may hinder the development of the plant or harbour harmful pests and diseases. Diseased wood should also be cut out during any pruning operation: one of the golden rules of pruning (before any pruning for form is carried out on a plant) is to remove the four Ds—dead, dying, diseased, and damaged. Then formative pruning can begin with the pruner knowing what living material is left to be used as a framework.

Most plantings are made with a definite type of tree or shrub, which from experience is considered the most suitable form of the particular species or variety. Their training to these forms often involves the adoption of a pruning system that may take several years to complete. The need for these forms has been universally recognized for generations, and British Standards (BS) and American National Standards Institute (ANSI) publications lay down very definite sizes and types for the nursery stock of many common species and varieties.

In many cases shrubs grown for their floral display are special varieties or cultivars, which have flowers distinct from the species (e.g., they are larger, or differently coloured) and which do not occur under natural conditions. Annual pruning is a necessary part of their cultivation if the required standards of growth and flowering are to be maintained. Without it and a complementary feeding and watering regimen, growth may be weak and the flowers small, though in some cases, depending on the genus (e.g., *Rhododendron*, *Lavandula*, *Rosa*), all that is needed is the systematic removal of seedheads or fruits. Some trees and shrubs require regular, annual formal pruning to stimulate flowering spurs for the production of fruit.

Only with good pruning and training can the form and beauty of trees and shrubs in summer and winter be fully realized. Good training and growth in particular show up very plainly with deciduous subjects in winter. A well-balanced plant improves most surroundings and helps to provide a restful scene for the mind and eye, but a badly mutilated tree or shrub is depressing and, in a modern urban setting, may be seen by thousands.

Pruners must have a thorough knowledge and understanding of the attributes, growth, and flowering habits of the plants they are pruning and of the effects likely to be produced by the operation. So the questions that we pruners must ask ourselves before we even attempt to carry out any form of pruning are these: what are we trying to achieve? and what do we want to gain from pruning? If we don't know why we are pruning and what we are expecting, then we will be unable to identify the type of pruning that needs to be done, and the end result will most likely be the wrong outcome—a ruined plant and a waste of our valuable time that could have been better spent in the garden. The main reasons and objectives for pruning are as follows:

- To develop a strong framework for the future (formative pruning).
- To continue to develop a strong framework and leader (corrective formative pruning).
- To maintain or improve flower display and fruit production.
- To restrict plant growth, including correcting a plant's size or improving its balance.
- To remove the four Ds: dead, dying, diseased, and damaged wood—all of which can be dangerous—for safety reasons and disease prevention.

Formative Pruning

Pruning and training trees in their early years is time well invested, as a few minutes' work in the first one or two years will mean a strong, well-shaped tree with no potential weaknesses later on in life. There is nothing worse or more demoralising than planting a tree, watching it grow toward maturity, making a fine specimen, and then in a single breath, the tree splits in half or a main scaffold branch detaches from the trunk and ruins the fine shape, rendering the tree unsafe, ultimately needing removal. Such minor surgery is also better for the tree: it's better to remove an unwanted branch in the early years with a sharp pair of secateurs, leaving an insignificant round wound, than to have to remove it several years later with a handsaw, leaving a larger-diameter wound. That's still far better, however, than having to remove that very same branch with a chainsaw 25 years later, leaving a much larger wound that may not heal over satisfactorily, ruining the aesthetic beauty of the tree and increasing the chances of invasion from harmful wood-decaying organisms. So don't be afraid of getting in there early with the secateurs and sorting out an unruly specimen.

Formative pruning on a young *Diospyros virginiana*: "Look twice; cut once."

One of the first tasks of formative pruning is to remove any crossing branches that if left to develop will rub against other branches and disfigure the tree. Any branches that are overextended and likely to unbalance the crown should be trimmed back to a suitable healthy growing point. While doing all this, any dead branches or twigs should also be pruned out, and any unnecessary branches cluttering the centre of the crown should be thinned out to keep an open centre. Keep an open mind throughout the process; think about what you are doing, and of the tree's appearance and structure in future years. Take stock of what you want to achieve ultimately, and study the subject's form and shape before making that rash decision and making the pruning cut. "Look twice; cut once" is a good general rule that should be adhered to, as once it's pruned off, it cannot be put back—and a good, young tree may take many years to recover or even be ruined.

With decurrent trees, where there is multi-branching from the top of the main stem, it may be necessary to thin these main lateral branches (to create an evenly balanced canopy) and to thin the ends of the branches (to prevent early lions-tailing). Dead and broken branches, nursery snags from careless pruning of the main branch framework, and any crossing or rubbing branches should also be removed at this stage.

Where excurrent trees are concerned, the single central leader gives a stronger tree that is more likely to be mechanically sound, for, as the large tree reaches maturity, the huge weight of the branch system is evenly spread over a large number of lateral branches. These also tend to grow away from the central trunk more or less at right angles and are therefore strongly attached and less likely to be a problem in later life.

Sometimes—through damage to the main shoot caused by cold winds or frost, mammal damage, or insects—two or more rival leaders can develop. If there are just two, this is referred to as a forked or twin leader. *Fagus*, *Pseudotsuga*, and *Pinus* species, in particular, often split up into

Pseudotsuga menziesii showing forked or twin leaders in a young tree.

Close-up of the twin leaders on a *Pseudotsuga menziesii*.

Quercus nigra before pruning with three leaders; a standard (i.e., one leader) is required of this specimen.

Close-up of the three competing leaders.

Stopping two competing leaders on a *Quercus nigra*.

After pruning, with one leader retained.

Crown or skirt lifting a *Tilia chinensis* to produce a standard from a feathered tree.

several rival leaders or codominant stems. These should be reduced to one at an early stage—this condition should never be allowed to develop.

Rival leaders develop into very large main and ascending branches. Thus the weight is carried by two or more codominant branches or stems that are comparable to mature tree trunks in size. Such a tree may well be furnished with the branches symmetrically placed, but they will be on only one side of each of the forked leaders. As codominant stems develop, they trap included bark, especially in tight ("V") crotches, forming a structural weakness at the point of attachment and, as the branches extend, the leaders are pushed apart leaving the centre open. In addition, there will be a narrow angle (or V crotch) between the central leaders, which is a weak form of attachment. This is a serious condition when a large tree may be exposed to strong winds: a major part of the tree may be lost by one clean split, causing an irreparable tear down the main trunk. Even a small crack in the crotch from the inner core to the outer bark will cause a further weakness, which will become worse as air and water cause rot and decay and the canopy gets heavier with further growth.

Rather than completely removing the competing leaders, depending on the species, it is also good practice to stop them by pruning out the growing tips, weakening their vigour, so that the remaining leader will become dominant. This practice, which leaves no pruning scar on the main trunk, can also be done on established trees with rival leaders.

A standard tree (i.e., with one main leader) is created as part of formative pruning by taking a feathered tree (see illustration on page 000) with a strong central leader and merely clearing the trunk of lateral branches up to the required height; this is a form of crown or skirt lifting. For the pruner, who should have a good idea of where the skirt of the lower canopy should be, this is an opportunity to identify which branches will be the first, lowest permanent scaffolds that will remain on the tree into maturity. Any temporary branches below these permanent scaffolds should be removed, back to the parent trunk.

Removing suckers from the rootstock of a grafted birch cultivar.

The loss of the leader with some dieback in *Aesculus indica*.

Using a sharp handsaw for corrective pruning in the upper crown of the young *Aesculus indica*.

Using secateurs for cleaning up the trunk of lower branches on the same tree.

Using a pruning saw for corrective pruning on the trunk of *Aesculus indica*.

Finally, during formative pruning, any unwanted suckers from the rootstock of a grafted tree should be removed, as these will not come true to the cultivar being grown for its special attributes.

Corrective Formative Pruning

Following the planting of a tree in its permanent location in the garden, the growth of the tree could be checked by transplanting shock, winter cold damage, insect or mammal damage, and many other environmental factors. It is very important to carry out any corrective pruning work as soon as possible to ensure a tree with a good framework and form is produced, not to hope that the tree will correct itself without any help. One of the important parts of this type of pruning is to encourage a new leader if the original one has been lost. Sometimes this may mean pruning back the leading stem quite hard, beyond any damaged tissue, in order to guarantee no further dieback into the trunk. This stem should be pruned back to a strong, healthy lateral branch or upright shoot that has the strength and growth habit to take on the new role of leading shoot and take the crown higher. If the stem is too thick for the secateurs, a good-quality sharp saw is best used for a clean cut that will callus over evenly.

Even when a tree has established and grown away, its upper crown out of reach from the ground, it is still worth pruning out any unwanted branches to increase the chances of a stronger framework with fewer problem branches developing in the following years. This may mean

The tree we are aiming for, by carrying out the corrective pruning at this early stage.

Using long-armed secateurs to prune out-of-reach branches on a *Quercus georgiana* to encourage a tree form.

using special ladders to access the crown, but this is not always possible and is not a preferred option on undulating lawns or beds for safety reasons. In such cases, the use of long-armed secateurs or a pole saw is a much safer option.

Pruning for Flowers and Fruit

For this aspect of pruning to be fully effective, correct timing is very important, for the growth and flowering habits of shrubs in particular must be taken into account when deciding when to prune. This will be found to vary with position and locality and with such other varying conditions as soil type, rainfall, and exposure to wind and sunshine. Shrubs may be placed in three groups, according to their flowering habits.

Group 1. Shrubs that flower on the current season's wood or growths. Generally, these subjects flower in the middle or toward the end of the growing season, the earlier part being spent producing growth from buds that have rested during the winter on the previous year's shoots or on older wood. With hard pruning, the number of buds or growths that can develop will be reduced and, as a result, extra vigour will be forced into the remainder. For example, if *Buddleja davidii* is left unpruned, the result is a large number of smaller flower trusses, whereas if pruned hard, the reduced number of growths that develop produce much larger trusses of flower. The pruning is, in this sense, a form of thinning. The timing for this hard pruning is important, for if it is left too late, growth will have developed only to be wasted when it is subsequently pruned off. With shrubs that are treated in this way and which are not fully hardy, wait until the severe winter weather ends, when the overwintering buds begin to come into life and break out from the living wood in the spring. In this way the top growth is left for protection during the winter period, and it can easily be decided just where to make the cuts in the spring. If it is necessary to cut evergreen shrubs during the winter period, the collections should be light and as evenly spread as possible.

Group 2. Shrubs that flower on the previous year's wood. Many of the hardy deciduous shrubs are in this group. They can be subdivided into two main classes, based upon their period of flowering: those that blossom really early, often before leaf or growth is produced, the flower buds opening directly upon the older wood (e.g., *Forsythia*); and those that flower later, producing short laterals during the spring and flowering from these in the early summer (e.g., *Philadelphus*).

Many shrubs in these two classes benefit from annual pruning, when wood may be cut out immediately after flowering, allowing the maximum period for the young growths to develop in the extra light and air, but the extent of this varies with the plant and the season. With forsythias, for example, some form of annual pruning after flowering is beneficial, while no pruning at all is needed with *Daphne mezereum*. This cutting out of the older wood with forsythias and similar subjects that respond vigorously can be looked on as a means of retaining vigour. Another example is the *Cytisus* hybrids, which may be cut back as the flowers fade and by this method spared the effort of producing heavy crops of seeds. Instead, this energy is put into developing growth. There are many other examples to be found in the A to Z of this book.

Group 3. Shrubs that produce flowering spurs on the older wood. These spurs normally develop from year to year and are found even on the really old wood of the main branches, for example, among trees and shrubs in the Rosaceae (e.g., *Malus*, *Pyrus*, *Prunus*). Flowering may not be confined to the spur systems, for it sometimes occurs on the previous year's wood as well (e.g., *Chaenomeles*). Normally, a free-growing shrub of this group needs little if any pruning; instead, shoot production in the early years followed by spur formation results in the achievement of a balance between growth and fruiting. In confined spaces, where some form of training is necessary, stopping growth rather than pruning may give better results. Stopping during the growing season provides a check to growth and in this way encourages good spur formation and flowering.

Pruning to Restrict Plant Growth

Restricting plant growth, both size and spread, can improve a plant's balance and access under the crown. An overextended branch may spoil the general outline of a symmetrical crown. Pruning may also be necessary to prevent a shrub from overgrowing a weaker neighbour or from growing over onto a path, restricting access. A crossing branch may shut out light and air from the centre of the shrub, or may be growing down on other branches to spoil the general shape. Note, however, that certain shrubs (e.g., *Poncirus trifoliata*, *Paliurus spina-christi*) have a tangled growth, and it would spoil them to train them too severely; it cannot be

Using a pruning saw to prune out dead wood from inside the crown of a young *Acer griseum*.

overemphasized that it would in fact be a painstaking waste of energy to attempt it. A further example is provided by many of the heathers (*Erica* or *Calluna*), which need an annual pruning, as they would otherwise become too tall and leggy—characteristics that might prevail in their natural habit but that would be out of character in the garden; not only that, but garden soil tends to be rich in comparison to that of moorland or heath, contributing to leggy unnatural growth.

Pruning Out the Four Ds

Before beginning any pruning exercise on a tree or shrub, the pruner must follow the principle rule of good pruning and first remove dead, dying, diseased, and damaged branches. The pruner then knows that all the branches left are healthy, sound, and can be retained or used as part of the main framework when training or for furnishings. This pruning operation (also known as "cleaning out a canopy") can be done purely to tidy up a messy crown or as a proactive approach to safety, removing dead wood before it falls out, making a mess on the ground or injuring someone.

Pruning can also be regarded as one of the means of control or defense in the fight to prevent the spread of pests and diseases, but the effectiveness of this method will obviously be influenced by many factors and is limited to those pests and disease that can be controlled by pruning. When removing a diseased branch, prune back beyond the infection, pruning out stained wood into healthy wood.

Pruning out branches infected with fireblight (*Erwinia amylovora*) on a susceptible tree.

Hygiene plays an important part in pest and disease control. Dead or diseased arisings should be cleared away from the trees and shrubs and, if possible, destroyed by composting or burning. With bacterial diseases and some others, disinfect all pruning tools after each cut and certainly when working between individual trees; otherwise, infection can be spread from diseased trees to uninfected specimens.

Following the pruning of a deciduous hedge (e.g., *Carpinus betulus*, *Fagus sylvatica*), some of the smaller branches that weren't pruned back to live buds can die back and become infected with coral spot (*Nectria cinnabarina*). Where pests and diseases can affect trees through a pruning operation, or when pruning can control specific pests and diseases, it is mentioned in the A to Z for each specific plant.

Cultivation

Good-quality, accurate pruning by a knowledgeable pruner, no matter how skilled, will not compensate for poor growing conditions. Firstly it is important to understand the needs of a plant and select the right plant for the right situation in the first place; in the A to Z we have provided a breakdown of the cultivation requirements of the various genera.

Once a plant has been selected, the right size and type of nursery stock needs to be purchased and then planted correctly in the garden, giving it a good start in its new position. Follow this list of key planting principles for successful establishment of any tree or shrub.

Always use **good-quality, healthy nursery stock** with a good, strong, well-balanced shape. And don't forget the root system: this is the engine of the tree or shrub, and because it's covered up in a container or root ball, we often ignore it. Check the roots are alive, not circling or pot-bound, and that lots of new, healthy, fresh fibrous roots are present. Don't be afraid of knocking a tree or shrub out of its container in the nursery to inspect them or ask the nurseryman to see them.

The **planting hole** should be shallow, one spit of a spade deep or slightly deeper to accommodate the root system if large nursery stock is being planted. More effort should go into the width of the hole rather than the depth; the hole should be as wide as possible, ideally 1.5 metres (5 ft.) across, allowing the new roots to anchor and grow outward in their search for water and nutrients. At Kew we have found the best-shaped hole to be square; the four corners are the weakest part of the hole and allow the roots to break out into the surrounding soil easily, creating a natural, balanced spread.

No compost or organic matter should be added, as this tends to dry out quickly, shrinking, and is very difficult to rehydrate (or the soil slumps when wet). The tree should start in the soil that it will grow in for the rest of its life.

Soil ameliorants (e.g., tree planting mycorrhizae) can be used to aid establishment. These can be bought in many good plant nurseries and garden centres as a commercial product, dried in sachets; follow the manufacturer's recommended application rates. To ensure success, sprinkle the inoculant as close to the roots as possible during the planting operation. The result is mycorrhizae, symbiotic relationships between trees and mycorrhizal fungi, which combine to boost a tree's ability to cope with drought and pests and diseases.

The **planting operation** is critical to successful establishment; the tree must be handled carefully and the root system not allowed to dry out

A selection of high-quality nursery stock, growing in Air-Pots, ready for planting.

before and during the planting. Planting depth is of key importance—getting this wrong will result in a dead tee. The tree must always be planted to where the trunk meets the root system (also known as the root crown or nursery mark). Too deep, and the tree will sulk and refuse to grow; death can take many years.

The soil **backfill** should be firmed evenly around the roots with the sole of the boot as it is placed back into hole.

Staking and support systems should be used only when they are needed; we often stake or overstake for the sake of it, and this is often detrimental to the health and development of the tree. If a stake is needed, use an appropriate, round, treated tree stake and adopt the correct technique (short staking, oblique staking, or crossbar staking). Use a single tree tie with buffers to secure the tree to the stake(s), not wire, pantyhose, or string, which can cut into the trunk. Don't forget young

trees need to sway and move with the wind to encourage well-balanced anchor roots and to increase the incremental growth on the trunk to support the developing crown. This is known as seismomorphogenesis. If the tree is smaller than the stake and needs support, then use a stout cane with soft, plastic tying tube as a means of securing it to the tree.

The final part of the operation is to **mulch** the surface of the tree planting hole with a good organic compost to about 10 cm (4 in.) deep, keeping it away from the root crown. This will prevent competition from weeds and harness moisture in the soil. The mycorrhizae will also draw on this material as it needs it and give it back to the tree.

Aftercare must not be forgotten or neglected until the tree has reached independence. Watering must be done before the tree shows signs of stress, mulch levels maintained, tree ties adjusted, and any staking removed after 12 months.

Planting the Kew way—wide, square, shallow hole and no compost.

Getting the planting depth correct is vital to successful cultivation.

A young *Liriodendron chinense*, recently planted, without any form of support.

Tree-watering bags being used for regular irrigation of newly planted trees.

Tree Forms and Shapes

When selecting a tree for a space, an understanding of tree form is important and will reduce or eliminate the need for any pruning due to the lack of surrounding space once established. Keeping the form in mind will also help the pruner with pruning techniques suited to the individual tree.

A **feathered tree** will have a good, strong, well-defined prominent leader running straight up through the young tree and be well furnished with evenly spread and balanced lateral growths along the complete length, right down to the ground; the dimensions will vary considerably, depending on the species. Once established, the lower skirt can be raised to the desired height by pruning the lower branches off back to the trunk; alternatively, the lower branches will be shed naturally by the tree as they become shaded out by the crown. *Liquidambar styraciflua* and *Nyssa sylvatica*, for example, grow well as feathered trees. The one important advantage with this type of tree is that it is very well balanced down the trunk and therefore easier to stake (or even not to stake), as it is not as top-heavy as the excurrent standard.

An **excurrent tree** is a standard with a well-defined central leader running up through the centre of the tree. They usually make the large shade trees, with a balanced crown on a length of clean trunk that is strong, tapered, and reasonably straight. Ginkgos and red oaks are good examples of excurrent trees.

A **decurrent tree** is a standard with a branching head. These trees naturally have a main central trunk with an evenly balanced head of several main branches dividing in the lower crown, with no main branches crossing through, or they can be cultivated by removing the main leader early in the nursery and encouraging a multi-branched crown. Standards with branching heads are usually grown for the smaller trees (e.g., crab apples, hawthorns, cherries) and for larger trees that are susceptible to frost damage and lose their leading shoot in early life (e.g., *Aesculus hippocastanum*, *Quercus robur*, *Paulownia tomentosa*).

Some decurrent trees (e.g., *Zelkova serrata* and some of the cherry cultivars) have a **vase-shaped** crown, with upward- and outward-growing branches producing a crown that quite literally resembles the shape of a vase, hence the term. An advantage of this form in trees is a higher upright skirt, eliminating the need for crown lifting to increase planting space or access under the tree. The cultivars of some species with a narrower upright form will produce tighter forks in the branch system with included bark at the branch attachments, which can be a weakness in the tree's structure in later life.

A **fastigiate tree** (also known as pyramidal or columnar) is a tree with upward-growing branches. The branches point up and are erect, almost parallel to one another. This gives fastigiate trees a distinctive look, and some gardeners or arborists like to plant them where space is limited but a tall tree is still desired. *Populus nigra* 'Italica' and *Prunus* 'Amanogawa' are examples of fastigiate trees.

Hawthorns are a typical decurrent tree; here *Crataegus laevigata* shows the short trunk with a low, wide-spreading, rounded crown.

Liriodendron chinense grown as a feathered standard with the lower branches retained to the ground.

An excurrent tree, *Ginkgo biloba*, showing the tall, straight, tapered trunk and still maintaining a leader.

A typical vase-shaped form, flowering cherry *Prunus* 'Asano'.

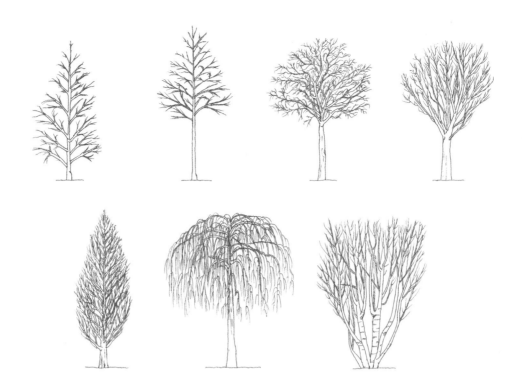

Tree forms and shapes. Left to right: (top) feathered, excurrent standard, decurrent standard, vase-shaped; (bottom) fastigiate, weeping standard, multi-stemmed.

A **weeping standard** is a well-grown tree with pendulous branches on a straight trunk and a minimum height of 1.75 metres (5.5 ft.) from ground level to the lowest branch. Some trees are top-worked, grafted on the top of a trunk in the nursery and grown mushroom-shaped (e.g., *Salix caprea* 'Kilmarnock'). Naturally weeping types include *S.* ×*sepulcralis* var. *chrysocoma* and *Betula pendula* 'Tristis'.

A **multi-stemmed tree** has two or more main stems, not necessarily uniform in height or girth, originating at or near (above or below) ground level from one root system. Trees produced in this way are naturally found suckering at the base, or can be made to produce several stems by cutting back hard. They are usually measured by overall height from ground level, and the stems may be of varying sizes. Birches (*Betula*), a popular multi-stemmed tree, can be grown as a feathered specimen with the lower feathers retained or cleaned up to show a clear stem and the main attributes.

Betula albosinensis, one of the best birches for bark effect, trained as a multi-stemmed tree.

The popular weeping willow *Salix* ×*sepulcralis* var. *chrysocoma* is a perfect example of a weeping standard.

Tools and Equipment

One of the most important factors for successful tree and shrub pruning is having the right tools and equipment for the job, and it is well worth investing in quality tools, maintaining them, and sharpening them correctly. This will make all pruning operations much easier and give a better finish and outcome to the plant; more importantly, a blunt saw or secateurs will themselves be damaged as well as damaging the retained plant tissue by leaving tears or crushed stems.

Secateurs or pruning shears. There are two types that are used for pruning, the anvil and the bypass types. The anvil types work on the principle of a sharp blade cutting down onto an anvil or bed, but often the problem with these is the blade isn't sharpened regularly enough and too large a branch is cut and the branch is crushed between the two, bruising the tissue left, rather than leaving a clean cut. In bypass secateurs, a sharp curved blade bypasses a curved cutting plate, cleanly severing the branch without much effort. The Swiss-made Felco 2 is the world's most popular bypass secateurs. It is ergonomically designed for the right-handed pruner; Felco 9 is designed for the left-hander. Most pruners try to cut too thick a diameter of branch with secateurs; branches of no more than 1 cm (0.5 in.) diameter should be cut with secateurs—thicker than that, and a pruning saw should be used instead. There is also a right and wrong way to use secateurs. When shortening a stem to above an eye or bud (rose pruning, for example) or removing

a branch from the trunk of a tree, the cutting blade should be against the piece of stem or wood being left. If used the wrong way around, the cut will not be close enough to the tree for a good, clean cut, and a short protruding snag will be left. Secateurs should always be kept in a purpose-made holster for ease of carrying between jobs and to protect the cutting parts of the tool and the pruner.

Pruning saws. The importance of having a good handsaw cannot be overemphasised, and a proper pruning saw specifically designed for cutting through green wood should be used over a general carpentry saw. Modern handsaws have a curved or straight blade of varying widths and lengths, with a pull-cut action; they are durable, lightweight, and very sharp, leaving a high-quality finish to the final cut, and the blade can access into most narrow-angled attachment points on the parent branch for the perfect final cut.

The sharpest of the saws is the Silky, Japanese tri-edge blade, with teeth that have three razor-edged facets that cut very smooth: they leave the surface wound as though a plane had been used, and they come in a variety of blade shapes, lengths, and shapes to fit all pruning jobs. The "Pocket Boy" folding pruning saw fits nicely into a pocket; it is a good idea to carry it routinely, so you always have a saw to hand. Despite the shorter blades, it can still cope with relatively large-diameter branches, leaving the same, perfect cut. With all these saws it isn't possible to sharpen them, but replacement blades are available. Most pruning saws come with a scabbard made from a variety of modern materials, which makes carrying a saw between trees much easier and safer.

A set of pruning tools—including Felco 2 secateurs, diamond sharpener, Silky folding saw, and Fanno pruning saws—suitable for most aspects of general pruning work.

The correct way of using secateurs to prune off a small branch back to the parent branch of *Liriodendron chinense*, with the cutting blade against the trunk.

Long-handled loppers and pole pruners. Long-handled loppers (or "parrot bills") are basically a heavy-duty anvil or bypass secateur with extended arms for that extra reach and leverage to help the pruner access the inside of a shrub. Too often, they are used incorrectly to tackle the removal of branches that are too large a diameter for the secateurs, leaving an untidy, torn or crushed wound when a sharp saw should have been used to better effect. They are ideal for removing the old congested wood from inside thorny shrubs (e.g., *Rosa*, *Berberis*, *Rubus*), so that the pruner has access to the interior of the shrub and can see what needs pruning. As a rule of thumb for final cuts, if the secateurs cannot cope with the branch diameter, then the handsaw should be used.

Pole pruners consist of a cutting unit (on an extendable pole) of either bypass or anvil secateurs, which are operated by a trigger at the operator's end of the pole. They are ideal for pruning those small branches that are out of reach, without using ladders. Due to the distance of the pruner from the cut, the accuracy isn't too precise and snags or tears can be left; however, for young, vigorous trees, these will soon grow over or grow out.

Using long-handled loppers on a rose to remove older growths before pruning begins.

Tool Maintenance

Maintenance is vital, both during and after pruning jobs. Saws and secateurs should be kept sharp and re-sharpened, preferably before the cutting edge goes dull. An oil stone or a small diamond sharpener that can be carried in the pocket will maintain a good edge and if the blade is damaged beyond sharpening, a new replacement bade can easily be fitted. Regular cleaning with a solvent or WD40 will remove any buildup of gums and conifer resins following pruning, and a drop of oil will prevent rusting and sticking. Give tools a wipe over with a cloth to draw out any moisture in the working parts before putting them away.

Cleaning and sterilizing tools. More and more, outbreaks of relatively new fungal and bacterial diseases affect our treescape; these include sudden oak death (*Phytophthora ramorum*), chalara dieback of ash (*Hymenoscyphus fraxineus*), chestnut blight (*Cryphonectria parasitica*), and canker stain of plane (*Ceratocystis fimbriata* f. *platani*). As well, there remain the ones that have been with us for quite a while, such as fireblight (*Erwinia amylovora*) and cornus anthracnose (*Discula destructiva*).

Infection can be spread from an infected tree to an unaffected tree by using contaminated pruning tools; it is therefore essential when working on infected trees to thoroughly clean and sterilize them before moving on to another tree (and for certain diseases, it can be helpful

A set of pruning saws (from right to left): the old framed bow saw, 2 × Silky pruning saws with scabbards, 2 × Fanno Grecian saws with open and closed handles and scabbard, and at top 2 × Silky "Pocket Boy" folding saws.

Sharpening secateurs with a diamond sharpener.

Using rubber-coated canvas gloves when pruning *Rubus cockburnianus*.

to sterilize between cuts, not just between plants). One part household bleach diluted in nine parts water is effective for soaking tools but is toxic to plants and corrosive to tools. Better still, wipes soaked in bleach are now available; these can be used to target the cutting blades without splash. Wiping tools with a cloth soaked in industrial methylated spirits (denatured alcohol) between trees or soaking tools in the same at the end of the day will also help to prevent the spread of infectious diseases between trees. Apply a drop of oil to the moving parts after sterilizing to prevent corrosion.

Personal Protection

Several subjects can cut, scratch, or irritate the pruner. Wearing some form of personal protective equipment (PPE) will help reduce your potential for contact with these specific plants. Tough leather or rubber-coated canvas gloves or gauntlets should be worn when pruning plants with thorns, prickles, or spines (e.g., *Rosa*, *Berberis*, *Rubus*) to protect your hands from cuts and scratches.

Some plants have sap which affects the skin, making it excessively sensitive to strong sunlight. Contact with the plant's sap followed by exposure to sunlight can result in very severe, localised blistering and long-lasting skin dermatitis. Latex or rubber gloves must always be worn when pruning shrubs with toxic sap (e.g., *Euphorbia*, *Ruta*, *Rhus*). It is also important to wash your hands well immediately after pruning

with soapy water to ensure no residues of sap remain, as these could affect the skin later. Pine resin is more difficult to remove; white spirit (mineral turpentine) should do the trick.

Eye protection (e.g., safety glasses or goggles) can be worn to prevent thorns or chips of branches damaging the eyes while pruning.

Timing of Pruning Operations

A majority of deciduous trees and shrubs are pruned during the dormant season, between autumn and spring—which is when it would happen in nature, following snow, ice, and strong winds. This is also a useful period for the pruner, as with no leaves attached the framework of the tree can be easily seen, helping to identify the perfect position of pruning cuts. Once the plant begins to grow the following spring, the wounds quickly heal. Despite this rule, any minor pruning to remedy broken branches, restrict vigorous growth, etc., can be carried out at any time during the year.

The susceptibility of certain plants to certain diseases can be exacerbated if the plant is pruned at the wrong time. Cherries, apricots, and plums are all susceptible to silver leaf (*Chondrostereum purpureum*). The spores of this airborne fungus are released from the bracket-shaped fruiting bodies found on dead branches under damp conditions. These spores infect healthy branches through wounds—including pruning cuts—and the fungus grows down into the wood, killing it and producing a dark

Pinus pinea with fresh wounds after pruning to lift the crown, already weeping resin to naturally seal the cuts.

Pruning cut on a *Morus nigra* bleeding a very sticky, milky sap in early spring.

Laying cool-culture grape vines ('Schiava Grossa', 'Buckland Sweetwater', 'Mrs Pince's Black Muscat', 'Foster's Seedling') on the glasshouse floor to enable the sap to run.

stain. Bacterial canker of cherry (*Pseudomonas syringae* pv. *morsprunorum*) can also enter through pruning cuts, especially during winter when trees are dormant, so the best time to prune is summer, preferably before midsummer, when the fungi are less active.

The red oaks (particularly *Quercus rubra*, *Q. coccinea*, *Q. palustris*, and *Q. velutina*) are very susceptible to oak wilt (*Ceratocystis fagacearum*); infection most commonly follows an injury, including pruning activities on trees. Insects are attracted to the fresh pruning wounds and transmit the spores of the disease to recently pruned healthy trees during the warmer months of late spring and early summer; and within one or two months of coming into contact with the infection, the tree will inevitably die. Not pruning during this period will greatly reduce the chance of infection in areas where the disease is present.

When pruning large branches from large trees, where a large scar will be left, autumn should be avoided. The reason is twofold: this is the time when trees are concentrating and using their energy reserves to shut down and cannot redirect them to healing, and this is the time when the spores of disease and decay causing fungi are more active and likely to infect otherwise healthy trees.

Unlike deciduous trees, broadleaved evergreens are best pruned before new growth starts in spring, or during the semi-dormant period of midsummer; however, dead, diseased, or damaged branches can be pruned out at any time.

The random-branched conifers (e.g., *Cupressus*, *Thuja*, *Chamaecyparis*) should be pruned in early spring or midsummer, so that new growth hides the pruning cuts. Pines and other whorled-branched conifers (e.g., *Pseudotsuga*, *Abies*, *Picea*) should be pruned in early to late spring as the candles appear; sap will weep out and naturally seal the cut surface.

Several subjects, particularly some of the deciduous trees, are prone to "bleeding" or "sap leakage"; they can bleed copious amounts of sap if the wounds or pruning cuts are made in late winter/early spring, just when the flow of sap begins to make its way to the tips of the branches. This is when the tree becomes active, in preparation for bud development and growth that takes place in the early part of the year. Once bleeding or sap leakage has started from a wound, it is difficult (if not impossible)

Branch with alternate buds showing the correct positioning of a pruning cut just above an outward-facing bud.

Branch with alternate buds after the pruning cut is made.

Branch with alternate buds showing where not to position a pruning cut.

Incorrect pruning of this branch with alternate buds has left a snag.

to stop until the tree breaks into leaf, at which time the flow which is being lost is taken by the developing growth, keeping the pruning wound dry. With this in mind—avoid pruning live branches of deciduous trees during the weeks before bud break, especially in those subjects that bleed badly, such as birches (*Betula*), maples (*Acer*), hickories (*Carya*), mulberries (*Morus*), and walnuts (*Juglans*).

It is unusual for a tree to be killed by excessive bleeding, but in severe cases it may cause considerable dieback on the ends of the branches. Grape vines (*Vitis*) are a good example of a climber that bleeds badly if it is pruned too late in the dormant period. Best practice with these vines is to spur them back annually to the main rod system in early winter. If a late pruning causes bleeding, reduce the loss by lowering the vine to the horizontal, until the buds break; lowering the rods in spring is accepted as standard practice to encourage the buds to break evenly. But the best practice of all is to prevent the need for corrective measures, by pruning at the correct time of the year for the specific genera.

A general guide for the timing of shrub pruning is that shrubs that bear flower buds on the previous year's growth (e.g., *Forsythia*, *Philadelphus*, *Syringa*) should be pruned after flowering. Shrubs that bloom on the current year's wood (e.g., *Buddleja*, *Rosa*, *Symphoricarpos*, *Hypericum*) should be pruned in early spring before bud break. This general rule does not apply when doing renovation pruning.

Pruning Cuts

Any cut or wound made on a woody stem that is growing actively and is healthy brings about a natural healing response—the result of a reaction to the wounding by the meristematic cells, which then divide very rapidly, especially during the growing season. These cells, which form a tissue referred to as cambium, are in a continuous cylinder just beneath the bark. By rapid division, they form a circle of raised tissue; and by continuous growth and division on the inside of the circle, the healing growth or callus moves over the bare face of the wound, which, as a re-

sult, gradually becomes smaller. Healing is a gradual process, the rate being directly related to the vigour and health of the tree or shrub. If this wound is untidy or jagged, the cambium may not be in a continuous circle and healing will take a lot longer.

As healing continues, the outermost layer of cambium forms a protective tissue or cork, a change that is brought about by the accumulation of a fatty substance called suberin on the walls of these cells. This layer of cork functions in exactly the same way as the surrounding bark, but the healing tissue will always remain distinct throughout the life of the tree or shrub. Sometimes when a branch is removed, epicormic shoots proliferate from the cut surface. These may need thinning out or may be removed entirely, as often as is necessary, at a later stage.

Selecting the Cut's Position

The position of the pruning cut needs to be selected very carefully; the pruner must ensure that the living tissue is preserved and maintained in the region of the cut by any growth present and any future growth, and that the general visual appearance of the tree or shrub is not spoiled by the pruning operation. The choice is governed by the following considerations.

If dead wood is being pruned out, the pruning cut must be made back to sound living tissue; the final cut must not cut into the branch collar, if it has grown along the dead branch, as good callus formation and healing is only possible from sound wood behind the collar.

It is essential that the cut is made at a point close to a branch or bud. Careless pruning often results in a length of stem being left projecting beyond this point. This piece of stem (or snag) will in the course of a few months die back to the tissue in the region of the nearest bud or branch, and the healing over of the cut surface will be delayed; but more often, the cut never heals because of the length of the snag. Following pruning, air and moisture combine to bring about the colonization of coral spot and other fungal infections, and on snags of larger-diameter branches,

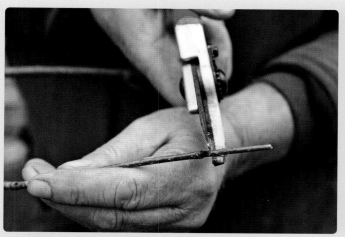

Branch with opposite buds showing the correct positioning of a pruning cut just above a pair of buds.

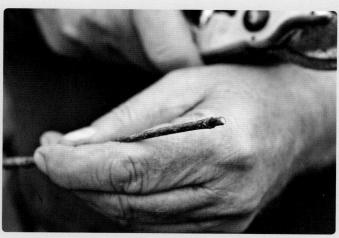

Branch with opposite buds after the pruning cut is made.

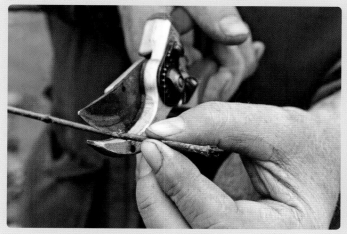

Branch with opposite buds showing where not to position a pruning cut.

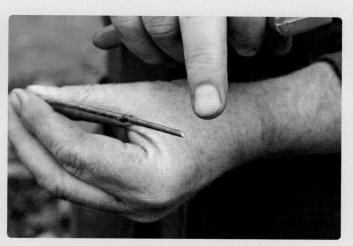

Incorrect pruning of this branch with opposite buds has left a snag.

the decay process will have extended into the heartwood and a cavity will be formed, which may shorten the life of the tree or shrub and produce a potential weak structure.

Some shrubs that regenerate freely, often from the base, can safely be cut back to older wood despite the fact that no buds may be visible; should a snag be evident at a later date after new growth has broken out, it can be removed before extensive rotting occurs. It may even break off with a slight tap from the back of the saw. As a general rule, snags are more likely to lead to trouble if they occur on trees and shrubs that have a permanent framework, rather than on those that grow quickly and regenerate freely (e.g., *Rubus cockburnianus*, which produces canes from ground level and has a life of only two seasons). The snags that are left after the old canes are cut off are not a real danger as they die off naturally.

Pruning Back to a Bud

When pruning small trees or shrubs with secateurs, it is important to select a strong, healthy bud to prune back to. The buds are arranged along the stem at regular intervals either alternately (one on one side of the stem and one on the other, further along) or opposite (one on each side of the stem directly facing one other).

For **alternate buds**, an outward-facing bud should be selected to encourage an open structure of branches and the cut made just above the bud—but not so close that there is a possibility of damaging the bud itself. A general guide is the cut should be just above the tip of the bud, not quite touching, and at a slight angle (about 30°) running away from the bud. This angle prevents any water from collecting on the end and around the retained bud and starting a rot.

Do not cut into the bud or leave a long snag from the bud, with no bud or leaf available to draw the sap to the end to form callus, or you risk dieback and infection from coral spot.

For plants with **opposite buds**, the pruning cut should be just above the pair of buds, with a horizontal cut being far enough away from the buds, so that no damaged is caused, but close enough to avoid leaving a snag that, as with alternate buds, can begin to die back.

Again, do not cut into or too close to the pair of opposite buds. Neither should you prune too far away, leaving a long snag that will eventually die back to the bud and possibly beyond it, into sound wood.

Removing a lateral branch with secateurs back to the parent branch.

Lateral pruned back to parent branch.

The position of the secateurs showing where not to prune; a cut made here would leave a snag.

This snag, the result of an incorrect pruning position, will die back to the branch.

Removing a Branch with Secateurs

Small lateral branches should be pruned back to a sound, healthy side shoot or the parent branch or trunk rather than leaving a snag or blunt end. A blunt end or snag will be unable to pull sap to the end to generate callus, and the retained snag will begin to die back. This dieback can continue into the sound healthy parent branch and decay will set in, potentially weakening the branch. It is easier, better for the tree, and much more pleasing to the eye for the small branch to be removed back to the trunk.

Removing a Branch with a Handsaw

With a light branch, it will be easier and less damaging to the tree to take the weight with the free hand as the cut is made, but this is not always possible with slightly heavier or longer branches, when you are crouched under the canopy of a tree. If a cut is made directly through the top of the branch without an undercut, there is the possibility that the branch will break before sawing right through, and there is always the possibility, depending on the species and weight of the branch, that it will tear back through the inside of the branch to the attachment point and thence into the parent branch or

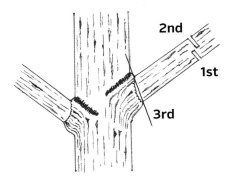

The "3-cut method" of removing a branch.

trunk. This not only disfigures the tree but will also prevent the cut from callusing over as well as being a potential entry point for any damaging wood-decaying fungi.

When removing any branch, it is good practice to use the "**3-cut method**" to avoid the possibility of the branch tearing on the underside.

Stage 1. Using a handsaw to make the undercut of the "3-cut method."

Stage 2. Using a handsaw to make the second cut, the top cut of the "3-cut method."

Stage 2. The removed branch showing the step cut on the branch end.

Stage 3. Positioning the saw for the final pruning cut on the right side of the branch bark ridge at the attachment point.

Stage 3. Removing the branch with a good, sharp handsaw.

Stage 3. A clean wound with the branch bark ridge and collar still intact.

The "A" cut; note the end face resembles the shape of the letter A, hence the name.

Stage 1. The first cut is the undercut, which should be 20 to 30 cm (8 to 12 in.) away from the final cut. Cut through one-third to half the diameter of the branch being removed, or until the blade of the saw starts to bind under the weight of the branch.

Stage 2. The second cut is the top cut, which should be about one-third the diameter of the branch being removed and away from the undercut, toward the tip end of the branch. Never try to line up the two cuts, as they will never meet (nor is there any need for them to). Once the cuts are made, the branch will break off cleanly, leaving a step cut on the end of the branch.

Stage 3. The third and final cut is to remove the snag that is left back to the parent branch or the trunk of the tree; the cut should be in one clean plane from top to bottom. As the weight of the branch has been removed, this snag can easily be held to hold any weight so that it can be sawn right through with no risk of tearing.

Occasionally it will be necessary for the piece of branch to remain attached until the pruner can snap it away. An "A" cut for the top cut is made with the saw, and then instead of making a horizontal cut parallel to the undercut, an inverted "V" is made, which holds in position until snapped off. This is a useful type of cut where a length of branch needs to be removed in small sections while being held to prevent its dropping and causing damage to plantings or buildings under the tree.

Target Pruning

In nature, as the crown of a tree becomes denser, filled with healthy leaf growth, the light levels in the inside of the canopy are reduced, and the interior branches, which grow from the main trunk, are shaded out and begin to decay. First the branch loses the bark; the sapwood quickly rots, and then the heartwood begins to degrade, reducing the diameter of the dead branch. The healthy tree naturally begins to respond to this condition at the attachment point to the tree, where the branch joins the trunk; the branch collar swells to encompass the branch, sealing the union to prevent the invasion of fungi. The more the branch breaks down and decreases in diameter, the greater the swelling—until the dead branch is aborted, falling away. Eventually the wound is totally covered in new

Natural pruning on *Quercus robur*. The branch collar can easily be seen, enveloping the branch of dead wood.

The branch bark ridge and the concentric rings of the branch collar can clearly be seen on the trunk of this tree. Following the removal this branch, both the branch bark ridge and branch collar should remain intact and visible, and the wound should be a perfect, small-diameter circle.

bark and sealed to the elements. To preserve the biological benefits of the tree's natural defense mechanism and emulate nature (who often knows best), we, the pruners, have copied the way she naturally prunes off branches; this is known as target pruning.

To understand target pruning, the pruner must be able to recognize two important areas on the trunk and branch attachment point: the branch bark ridge and the branch collar.

The **branch bark ridge** is created by the tree where the bark of the circumference of the main trunk or parent branch meets the bark of the circumference of the branch that joins it. These two sets of bark meet at differing angles and push up into a ridge, and as the two branch and trunk circumferences increase in diameter, so the ridge becomes greater and more pronounced, varying in visibility depending on the tree species. They are often described as resembling a Fu Manchu moustache and can remain as a scar on the bark of the trunk for many years after branch removal and after the wound has totally callused over, particularly on beech and maples.

Adjacent to the branch bark ridge and more pronounced on the underside of the lateral branch is a swollen area called the **branch collar**. This is created by the tree from internal tissue in the main trunk where it meets the internal tissues of the lateral branch; it consists of vigorous cambium cells that are more resistant to disease and used by the tree to make callus to cover and seal over the wound.

In target pruning, the final cut is made just outside the branch collar, which is clearly identified by the branch bark ridge. Neither of these raised areas should be damaged or removed by pruning operations, as they contain parent branch or trunk tissue. This reaction zone left on the tree has the ability to compartmentalize the wound created and produce tissue, known as callus, that will eventually cover (occlude) the wound. The angle of the cut also depends upon the nature, thickness, and mechanics of the main stem, but the cut is always at a consistent angle, enough to allow rainwater to runoff rather than being allowed to soak into the exposed wood. The point to remember is a fine one: while

The branch bark ridge and branch collar are both very pronounced and visible on this maple. The target pruning position for the saw is very obvious and clear to the pruner.

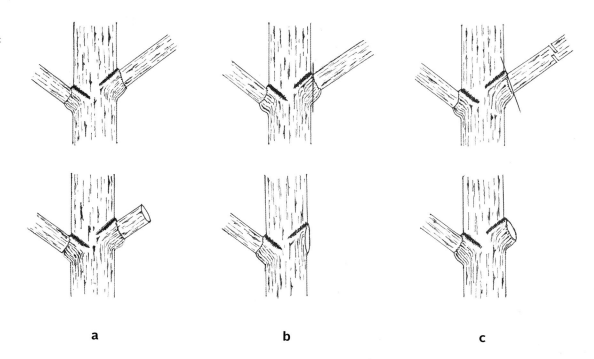

The correct and incorrect positions of pruning cuts, left to right: a) Incorrect position of final pruning cut (leaving a long snag); b) Incorrect position of final pruning cut, made too close to the trunk or parent branch (flush cutting); c) Correct position of the final cut (target pruning) just beyond the branch bark ridge and branch collar, leaving a sloping, round wound.

a   **b**   **c**

the general aim is to make the cut close to the stem (but away from the branch collar), the need to keep the wound as round and as small as possible is also important. At the same time the position of the strengthening tissues or wood needs to be considered when making that final cut.

A final pruning cut in line and close to the main trunk or branch will cut through some of the tissues supporting the remaining wood, with a weakening effect both structurally and physiologically; this is known as **flush cutting**. The wound left on the main trunk or branch will be long, oval or egg-shaped, and far larger in exposed area than a target-pruned cut, with dead spots (with little callus development) at the upper and lower ends of the cut. This final position cut is incorrect and should be avoided at all cost.

Good callus on an ash, following perfect target pruning.

For target pruning, when making the correctly positioned and angled final pruning cut, the blade of the saw should be just resting against the branch bark ridge on top of the branch and the blade angled to exit the branch at the bottom of the branch on the branch side of the branch collar, without cutting into this swollen tissue. This will leave a circular

The branch collar clearly seen as a series of concentric rings on a small-diameter branch. This young *Acer pensylvanicum* is too small to develop the branch bark ridge.

Shortening a small branch using secateurs.

Incorrect pruning position.

Snag left from incorrect pruning position.

Correct pruning position.

Finished cut, back to a healthy lateral side branch.

Shortening a larger branch using a pruning saw.

The diameter of this dead/damaged branch end is too large for secateurs.

Using a pruning saw to make the undercut.

Using a pruning saw to make the top cut.

Final cut to remove the dead branch end.

The finished cut with the lateral branch in natural flowing position, taking on the new role, drawing sap along to the end.

How not to prune a mature tree. It is bad for the plant, unsightly, and unnecessary—the picture says it all!

wound instead of an egg-shaped cut and will be relatively small compared to a flush-cut wound.

Some of the points and considerations just given may prove to be mutually conflicting, but with actual practice and experience there should be little difficulty in deciding where and how to make the cut in each particular case.

Shortening a Branch End

The tips and ends of low lateral branches can be damaged by machinery or grazing animals, and the subsequent necessity of shortening branches back to a healthy growing point is inevitable. There will also be a need to reduce the length of branches that have overextended or have unbalanced the symmetrical form of the canopy. It is important that these be pruned back to healthy growth and a strong lateral side shoot, which will have the ability to take on the role of the branch end. This will also leave a natural branch end with furnishing that looks aesthetically pleasing, rather than a blunt snag or stump end.

Tree Paints or Wound Dressings

When a large branch is removed and a pruning wound is made, a considerable amount of heartwood is exposed which, in the case of the larger-diameter stems and branches, has become hardened to give mechanical strength to the branch. This remains healthy and perfectly preserved, provided the tree is in a healthy condition and is able to combat harmful pests and organisms.

In the past, protective wound sealants or tree paints were applied to the exposed wound immediately after cutting, to protect it from air, water, and spores of destructive decay fungi and accelerate callusing and wound closure. These paints were usually bitumen- or latex-based, waterproof sealants of a pliable, non-cracking nature, occasionally with fungicidal properties—but they also killed non-harmful organisms and too often they sealed in the microorganisms behind the paint. Research has shown that these dressings rarely prevented insect or disease infestations, and the microclimate created behind them hid a multitude of problems. Decay often went unnoticed, sealed in behind the painted barrier; serious cavities soon developed. Besides encouraging faster decay, these paints had the negative effect of limiting the production of callus formed by the tree's own defense barrier, which is encouraged by accurate target pruning. It is now recommended that no wound dressing or tree paint be used.

Pruning a Mature Tree

Before any work is carried out on a tree, it is important to check with the local planning authorities to see if the tree is in a Conservation Area (CA) or has some form of protection on it, such as a Tree Preservation Order (TPO); fruit trees are now exempted from the latter. If it is or has, you will need permission to fell it or even remove a branch from it. Also check with your neighbour, especially if the tree is a boundary tree or actually in your neighbour's garden.

The pruning of mature trees is a skilled job and should be carried out only by professional arborists who are trained to climb and have all the necessary tools, equipment, and relevant insurance to carry out the work safely and successfully to industry standards.

Seek professional advice from an arborist. The reasons for pruning trees may be obvious—large dead or hazardous branches over a garden with children, low overhanging branches blocking access, a dense crown creating a lack of light to a property, overextending branches in the upper crown, or an unhealthy-looking tree with visible dieback in the canopy—but the arborist will inspect the tree, determine why the tree needs pruning, and select the relevant branches that will be removed, shortened, or thinned to meet the desired objectives. Various types of pruning operations are carried out on mature trees by skilled arborists, as follows.

Cleaning out and deadwood removal. This is the removal of any dead, damaged, or diseased branches from the crown, along with any unwanted items, such as nests or climbing plants, particularly ivy, which once established creates a large amount of weight on the main trunk and scaffolds and hides a multitude of hazards in trees. Any obvious structural defects, including split or decayed branches or storm-damaged broken branches, will also be removed during this exercise. In natural areas where the preservation of biodiversity is important, dead wood can be kicked off by the arborist; alternatively, a peg of dead wood is left attached to the parent branch or trunk, as habitat for various insects, birds, and fungi.

Crown lifting. Sometimes referred to as skirt lifting, the removal of the main lower scaffold or lateral branches is a means of improving ac-

Crown lifting, before and after pruning operation.

A young *Quercus velutina* before crown lifting.

Crown lifting *Quercus velutina*.

The finished *Quercus velutina*, crown lifted and balanced.

cess for pedestrians and vehicles. Too, it allows more light to penetrate the canopy of a tree: there may be plants nearby whose culture and well-being is important enough to warrant the removal of the lower branch system.

Often the best time for this operation is during the late summer, as the branches are weighed down with foliage at this time, giving a better picture of the extent of the problem. Another advantage is that callus formation can start before the winter sets in.

Removing branches at the main trunk is straightforward; any main scaffolds should be target pruned back to the trunk. To successfully raise the crown of a tree lightly, the laterals growing down from the main scaffolds can also be removed back to the parent branch, retaining the lower main scaffolds. The crown and the tree as a whole must be left well balanced, both in appearance and in weight, so a branch removed on one side means that some balancing might be needed on the other. This operation is best done over a period of time rather than in one go, until the desired result is found. Staggering the operation also reduces the amount of stress placed on the tree.

It should be noted that the term "lifting" is generally thought of as applying only to mature trees, but this operation may also be undertaken on young specimens as part of their formative pruning and training.

Crown thinning. Crown thinning is a pruning operation to remove selected branches (including crossing, weak, and dead branches) and epicormic growth throughout the crown to reduce the overall density of foliage, without affecting the overall shape of the crown. The reasons for crown thinning are as follows:

- To allow light to penetrate into and through the crown, which can be an advantage where there is heavy shading—for example, near a building, to allow sunlight to reach windows; or over plants that are considered valuable and which need more light.
- To reduce wind resistance, which may be important to a tree that has a weak branch or root system, by reducing the wind-sail effect and leverage on a large canopied tree.
- To reduce the weight of main scaffolds and branches, which will also help a weak or wide branch system.

Crown thinning, before and after pruning operation.

The branch system should be thinned evenly over the entire tree, and care must be taken not to over-thin, as this will reduce the tree's ability to photosynthesize. An arborist will not remove more than 25% of the tree's foliage at any one time; the removal of too much leaf area puts the tree under stress, which can induce epicormic growth.

Lateral branches from the scaffolds must be removed during the thinning exercise evenly from the main trunk out to the edge of the canopy in order not to create the effect known as lions-tailing. Lions-tailing places too much end weight on the tips of the limbs, which will result in a weakened structure and eventual branch failure.

Crown thinning is generally confined to deciduous trees. It is seldom necessary or desirable to treat broadleaved evergreens or conifers in this manner.

Crown reduction. This, the reduction of the tree's overall dimensions in both height and spread, is done by shortening branches, the pruning cuts being carefully positioned just above a strong lateral branch growing in the right direction. Crown reduction should be the last resort, as it places a large amount of stress on a tree. It is carried out over the entire main branch system if need be, with the result that the tops of leading branches are taken away. Selected laterals form the outline to the crown. It is important to maintain a balanced appearance and condition.

Crown reduction, before and after pruning operation.

Where the pruning is extensive, this is obviously a drastic treatment, but it is justified where the branch system is considered to be inadequate for the full height and weight to be carried, or where the tree as a whole is failing in health and has, as a result, become "stag-headed" (i.e., the appearance of a tree following the dieback of the crown: the name is after the similarity of the dead branches to a pair of deer's antlers). Good plant health care programmes should always form the basis of crown reduction work, and a more definite decompaction and watering regimen may be necessary as a means of overcoming the condition of poor health.

Crown renovation or renewal. Following the reduction of major scaffolds or branches, the tree often produces lots of vigorous epicormic shoots from dormant buds along and at the ends of the pruned branches. After five years' growth, these shoots will start to make substantial-sized branches and if desired a new crown can be made by selectively thinning these branches and retaining the strong, healthy ones. These will over time form a new crown framework, provided the tree is healthy and able to make strong attachments at the pruning wounds. Crown renovation is usually carried out on trees that have been badly pruned or heavily crown-reduced in the past or on old pollards that have been allowed to grow out into full-sized trees.

Reverted green branch on *Castanea sativa* 'Variegata' will need removing.

Epicormic shoots, one year's growth, on the base of *Tilia ×europaea*.

Pruning Reversions

Many species have variegated cultivars, with white, gold, or silver markings on the green leaves. Most such cultivars arise from natural sports or naturally occurring mutations of the green-leaved type, and just as the green leaves turned variegated, they can revert back to the original plain green foliage. *Acer platanoides* 'Drummondii', for example, is very unstable and prone to reversion, as is the shrub *Elaeagnus pungens* 'Maculata'. Any green shoots that appear on a variegated subject should be removed as soon as they are seen and, as with disease, they should be removed well back into variegated leaves.

Similarly, cultivars grown for their cut or feathery leaves (e.g., *Fagus sylvatica* var. *heterophylla* 'Aspleniifolia') can also revert to the normal-leaved foliage; when these reverted branches are seen, they should be pruned out.

Pruning Epicormic Shoots

Epicormic shoots (or water sprouts) are strong shoots that spring directly from the main branches or the trunk. They may spring from adventitious buds that form in places other than the meristem, but most

A very old leggy *Viburnum tinus* with dead wood and dieback, flowering at the top where it goes unseen.

Hard pruning the *Viburnum tinus* to a low framework with healthy wood.

Finished for now. The hard pruning of the main group can be staggered over a period of two or three years.

often they originate from dormant buds, which grow a small amount each year but remain latent inside the bark layer unless activated by an extra supply of food as a result of an injury higher in the branch system, such as heavy pruning, drought, or root damage and stress. The removal of a limb, even though the cut is made close to the main stem, may result in a flush of epicormic shoots around the wound; as these are removed, more appear, and there seems to be no effective or permanent control. All that can be done is to cut them back from year to year during the dormant season. If they are left, they increase in length and take vigour from the crown itself, even possibly cause it to die back, particularly in a drought season. An annual flush of these growths may also appear on the trunk of some trees (e.g., *Tilia*), even down to the base; these should also be pruned back as hard as possible to the trunk with a sharp saw or secateurs. Most epicormic shoots, if left to develop and mature on a branch or trunk, can be weakly attached, at least for the first five to ten years, as they grow from inside the bark and are not part of the overall integrity of the structure of the tree, so care must be taken when selecting and thinning them out to create a new branch framework.

Pruning Suckers

Sucker growths spring from roots or stem tissue below ground level, either from or in the region of the root system. They should be taken off cleanly and as close as possible to the point of origin on the stem. It may be necessary to scrape the soil away to reach the bases of the sucker shoots. The exposed piece should be wiped free of soil with a cloth, so that the secateurs or knife do not come into contact with grit, which may spoil the cutting edge. Trees that are prone to producing suckers include *Pterocarya fraxinifolia*, *P. ×rehderiana*, *Rhus typhina*, *Sequoia sempervirens*, and of course grafted fruit trees and hybrid roses, which send up suckers from their rootstocks.

Hard Pruning

Most often, a key principle of good pruning technique is to leave a plant looking like it has never been touched, with a natural shape. Certain shrubs, however, need to be hard pruned annually to bring out their best attributes—a valid reason, to be sure. Never should hard pruning be simply a lazy way of maintaining a shrub and keeping it within its bounds, with minimal input.

Half-hardy subjects (e.g., *Fuchsia magellanica*) are cut back annually in the spring when the danger of late frosts is past and as new growths breaks out from the older wood. Some shrubs respond to annual hard pruning in early spring, back to a low framework, with an improvement of flowers, foliage, or coloured stems (e.g., *Cornus alba* 'Sibirica'). Others respond to hard pruning by producing adventitious buds or the development of dormant buds from the older wood; such treatment is often followed by an improvement in shape—another good reason for doing this.

The nature and severity of the pruning will depend upon necessity and the ability of the plant to react favourably. Plants that do respond readily and are tired, leggy, or completely out of shape may be cut right back, almost to ground level, as an alternative to a gradual shortening back over a period of time. Many evergreens (e.g., *Taxus*, *Buxus*, certain viburnums) will do this successfully. The timing for this drastic hard pruning varies, but with most responsive deciduous subjects, the work may be carried out during the dormant season—although if there is a danger of bleeding, it should be completed before mid-winter. Evergreens, on the other hand, should not be cut back during the winter; their hard pruning is best carried out in late spring, after the danger of late frosts is past. Otherwise the young growths can be damaged and the root systems checked when there is no foliage to feed them. Conifers in particular suffer from winter pruning. There is the possibility that hard pruning, carried out annually, drains the soil of nutrients; it may be necessary to carry out soil improvements by feeding and mulching.

The occasional hard cutting back of amenable shrubs also helps to correct any poor pruning that has been carried out in the past; it can be fol-

Natural root plate mulching: this buckeye is signalling where it would like to be mulched—to the dripline.

A mature cedar mulched out to the dripline, following nature's request.

lowed up with normal pruning practice once new growth has been made.

The new growth that follows hard pruning will usually hide the large, ugly cuts that have been left behind on the old wood or stumps of the shrub.

Aftercare

Any form of pruning, however large or small, however skilled, can be stressful to plants. They will need to eat into their energy reserves to heal over pruning wounds and overcome the effects of losing a percentage of leaf material, which is so vital to photosynthesis. To keep a plant in good health and stress-free, it is important to help the plant by applying a well-balanced fertilizer of nitrogen, phosphorus, potassium, and trace elements during the early part of the growing season. Don't do this too late, or the soft regrowth that is generated can be damaged by winter cold.

At Kew, we mulch around trees and shrubs with composted woodchip. This prevents competition from weed growth and harnesses any soil moisture, making it available to the plant during dry periods, while at the same time supplying organic matter as a natural food source to the plant when it wants it.

A mulched circle to the dripline of the tree helps forestall compaction over the root plate by grass-cutting machinery and keeps maintenance vehicles from getting too close to the trunk and potentially damaging it from impact. The lower crown or skirt of the tree can also be left to develop low instead of having to keep lifting it for access, ultimately making a lollipop tree. A more natural appearance is retained with a low skirt, and the ornamental foliage and flowers are held at eye level for easier viewing.

Fruit Tree Forms

If apple trees grew on their own roots, they could make a tree 5 to 6 metres (15 to 20 ft.) high, and pear trees could be even taller. Such large trees, though they may look "in place" in a traditional country orchard, are far too large for most domestic gardens, and are not very productive, either: since most of the fruits are usually out of reach, they are difficult to harvest. For this reason, most fruit trees are grafted onto the roots of another tree of a related species. These rootstocks are used to create fruit trees of varying degrees of vigour which can be grown successfully in a restricted space or trained to a specific form; as well, they have been bred for pest and disease resistance and strong anchorage of the mature tree. Apples have the largest range of traditional rootstocks; most pears are grafted onto a quince rootstock, which are easier to propagate than a pear rootstock but compatible with the cultivars of pear.

Most apple and pear cultivars are best planted as a maiden tree, which has been grown for one full year after the scion/cultivar has been grafted onto the rootstock. It will have a straight main stem, apart from a slight kink at the graft union, with no lateral branches. Alternatively, it can be planted as a feathered maiden, which has some lateral side shoots attached to the main stem.

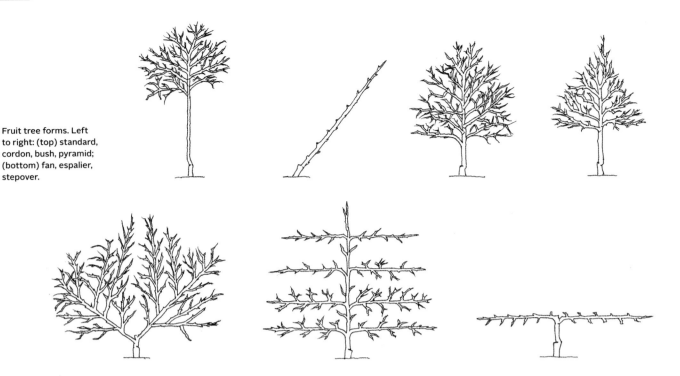

Fruit tree forms. Left to right: (top) standard, cordon, bush, pyramid; (bottom) fan, espalier, stepover.

Bush trees are the traditional and most popular form for growing apple trees, as they are easy to maintain and bear fruit at an early age. They have an open-centred crown on a short trunk up to 1 meter (3 ft.). The final ultimate height is 2 to 5.5 metres (6 to 18 ft.), depending on which rootstock is used, making them easy for anyone to harvest the fruit. **Standard** trees are larger than the bush form, with trunks of 2 metres (6 ft.) or higher. They can reach an ultimate height of 8 metres (26 ft.) and a similar width and will eventually produce high yields of fruit, but, being large trees, are not easy to maintain.

Training Fruit Trees

Young apple and pear trees need good formative pruning to create an attractive, long-lived, easy-to-manage, productive garden specimen, with a balanced branch system. Pruning is not difficult and taking the time to get it right in the early years should lead to fewer problems later on. When training newly planted bush or standard apple or pear trees, always use the best sharp secateurs and a clean, sharp pruning saw, *not* a carpentry saw. Formative pruning can also be used for training half-standard and standard apple trees, the only difference from the normal bush tree being the crown is developed on a taller clean trunk of 1.2 to 1.5 metres (4 to 5 ft.) for a half-standard and 2 to 2.1 metres (6 to 7 ft.) for a standard.

The aim of early formative pruning is to create an open goblet shape with a framework of four or five main branches to allow sunshine to penetrate the centre and increase air movement to reduce the risk of disease. The pruning methods presented here are suitable for the training of one- and two-year-old apple and pear trees. It is important not to let the tree develop any fruit in the first or second year; if any are seen, they should be removed immediately.

Year 1 (for a maiden tree with no feathers or less than two side branches). Any time after planting (but before the buds break in spring), prune the single stem with no side shoots to a bud around 75 cm (2.5 ft.) above ground level, leaving three or four healthy buds below. This

pruning will stimulate the production of strong vigorous shoots, which will develop into the primary branches that will be selected to form the new crown. The young maiden that you planted will also most probably be bare-root (i.e., not in a container with soil around the roots), and reducing the height will help the tree to establish a new root system to support the upper part of the crown without placing stress on the rest of the tree. This form of maiden will need a year to catch up with a planted feathered maiden.

Year 1 (for a feathered maiden with three or more side branches). In the first year after planting, cut back the central stem just above a wide-angled, strong side shoot, approximately 75 cm (2.5 ft.) from ground level, ensuring three or four evenly spaced branches remain below. These branches need to be shortened by one-half to two-thirds, cutting just above an outward-facing bud; remove any remaining lower branches.

Bush-form *Malus domestica* 'Duck's Bill' (apple), pruned to open up the tree's centre.

Year 2 (for maidens with no feathers). Following planting, the first pruning, and the first full growing season, the tree will have produced a very strong new leading shoot. If this topmost leading shoot is too strong and dominant, it will need removing completely, cutting back to just above a wider-angled side branch. If a standard fruit tree is wanted, then this leading shoot should be retained and encouraged to the desired height of the trunk before it is removed.

Select the best three to five lateral branches to form the main framework of branches and remove any others. Shorten the selected branches by half, cutting just above an outward-facing bud to encourage the formation of a goblet-shaped branch structure with an open centred crown. If a branch is too horizontal, prune back to an upward-facing bud and steer the new branch system in the direction you desire. Any lower branches should be target pruned back to the trunk to leave a clean stem.

Year 3 (second year for feathered maidens, third year for maidens with no feathers). Shorten the previous year's growth on the main primary branches by one-third, cutting just above a healthy outward-facing bud, leaving about eight to ten branches to form a permanent framework. The primary side branches growing from the main trunk should be left unpruned, but if they are in the way, crossing, or growing toward the centre of the tree, they should be removed, and the remaining branches lightly thinned out if they are overcrowded. Any strongly upright shoots that develop at the top of the tree should be removed.

Pruning back to a strong bud on an apple tree with sharp secateurs.

Pruning Established Fruit Trees

Once established, apple and pear trees trained as freestanding bushes or standards are best pruned every winter (during the dormant period) to ensure a good cycle of fruiting wood. Trees that are not pruned become less productive and the crown congested with old branches.

Winter pruning. When carrying out winter pruning for bush and standard apple and pear trees, it is important to always use sharp secateurs to make the pruning cuts, to avoid tearing and damaging the bark; never use long-handled loppers for the final cuts, as these will definitely bruise and damage any retained tissue, which will lead to infection and dieback. Prune just above and with the cut sloping away from a bud; the bottom of the sloping cut should be just above the base of the bud. Once in full pruning mode, there is a temptation not to be very accurate with the pruning cuts, but take some time positioning the cut with the secateurs and try not to leave too long a snag above the bud or make a long sloping cut and a wound with a larger surface area than necessary, which will both potentially lead to infection and dieback.

The first operation is to remove any crossing, rubbing, weak, dead, dying, diseased, and damaged branches from the framework of the tree. You are then assured that all remaining branches can be used for the framework if needed.

Shorten the previous year's growth on each main primary branch by about one-third to an outward- or upward-facing bud. This will encourage the development of new branches and spurs while simultaneously maintaining a good shape. Any young laterals can be left unpruned so that they can develop fruit buds in the following year; however, if they are crossing or the growth is too crowded, they can be removed. Strong

Close-up of a flowering spur/bud on an apple.

shoots longer than 15 cm (6 in.) that are growing into the centre of the tree should be pruned out.

On older established trees where spur systems have become cluttered and congested, it may be necessary to remove or thin them out, always removing the spurs on the underside of the branches, where the developing fruit will not receive enough light and therefore be smaller.

If an apple or pear tree has been neglected and unpruned for several years, open up the centre of the tree by pruning out any larger branches back to their parent branch or trunk (attachment points) with a sharp pruning saw; this operation may require one or two years' work, depending on the size and number of branches that need removing. At the same time reduce the overall height and spread of any branches that have grown too long and large by reducing them back to a vigorous outward- and upward-facing lower side branch, making sure this lower branch is at least one-third of the diameter of the branch being removed and not an epicormic shoot.

Pruning over-vigorous fruit trees. If the fruit tree is over-vigorous, sending out an excessive amount of growth each year, it will be necessary to also carrying out some pruning in early to late summer. Summer pruning depletes the tree's resources and will help to reduce its vigorous growth. This is done in addition to winter pruning and is different from the next technique, summer pruning, which is carried out on restricted forms of fruit trees.

Summer pruning. This is the main type of pruning for restricted forms of apple and pear trees (i.e., cordons, espaliers, fans, pyramids, and stepovers). It allows sunlight into the branching to ripen the fruit and ensures a good crop of fruits in the following year by encouraging the development of fruiting spurs. Timing is important and a knowledge of the local climate will determine the exact date, but a general guide is to prune when the young shoots on the lower branches are beginning to ripen and stiffen. If done too early, there is always the possibility of new secondary growth developing, which will defeat the object of summer pruning—not to mention that the new growth may not ripen enough before any winter cold. Pears will be the first to be ready for pruning, and apples a week or two later.

Summer pruning involves cutting back the new stiff and woody young shoots that are over 20 cm (8 in.) long and are attached to the main stem or the primary lateral branches to allow sunlight to reach the ripening fruit. They should be cut back to three or four leaves or buds from the attachment point. Do not prune new shoots that are less than 20 cm (8 in.) long, as they usually terminate in fruiting buds.

Cut back new shoots that are growing from existing side shoots to one leaf or bud above the basal cluster and remove any upright, vigorous growth completely. Any secondary growth that occurs after summer pruning can be safely removed in early autumn.

Prune laterals (side shoots) longer than 30 cm (12 in.) by half, to 15 cm (6 in.), all over the tree to encourage fruit bud formation; spread the pruning out over a period from mid- to late summer, pruning the branches that have stopped growing and have formed a strong terminal bud. Do not tip-prune all the laterals, only the more vigorous ones.

Renovation pruning. Apple and pear trees, even with regular winter pruning, are very likely to become larger and possibly too large for their position, taking away light and moisture from the rest of the garden and

Flowering spurs on *Pyrus communis* 'Doyenné du Comice' (pear).

making the harvest difficult. There will be a need for some form of renovation pruning, which is best timed between autumn and spring (during the dormant period).

First, decide how large the tree will be after pruning has finished, bearing in mind the type of rootstock the fruit tree is grafted onto. Badly neglected trees should be reduced to the desired height over a period of two to three years, never removing more than 25% of the canopy in any one year, to prevent excessive regrowth.

To reduce the overall height of the tree, selectively prune to horizontal-growing branches at staggered heights, thinning out cluttered branches at the same time. Prune all the upright-growing shoots in half. Take your time and as with any formative pruning, look twice (to determine where the tree should be cut back to, to retain as natural a shape as possible) and cut once.

A heavily pruned tree will send out many epicormic shoots during the following summer, and these will need removing. Between late spring and early summer, thin any fruit down to one fruit per cluster and space the clusters 15 to 25 cm (6 to 10 in.) apart; this ensures that the remaining fruit will make a harvestable size.

With very old neglected trees, it is important to try to avoid removing lots of large scaffold branches; that would leave lots of large pruning wounds, which are unlikely to callus over and will possibly decay back into the trunk. Look at the tree and see if a smaller branch can be pruned out, leaving a similar overall effect and smaller pruning wounds, taking care not to leave blunt ends or long snags.

Fan-trained *Prunus domestica* 'Oullins Gage' (plum).

Cordon-trained apple trees, including *Malus domestica* 'Discovery'.

This form of heavy pruning will also reduce the fruiting of tip-bearing and partial tip-bearing apple varieties (e.g., 'Bramley's Seedling', 'Pink Lady', 'Discovery') until the tree regenerates new material, as most of the fruiting wood will be removed, but it will be a long-term investment.

Restricted Fruit Tree Forms: Pyramid

Pyramids are similar to the bush form, but the main leading shoot is allowed to maintain its dominance, resulting in a symmetrical, pyramidal shape to 2 metres (6 ft.) high with a spread of 1.5 metres (5 ft.). These are a useful form of fruit tree to grow in a small garden as a single specimen; they can be very productive and are an attractive feature.

In the winter of the first year, cut back the leader of the maiden apple or pear tree to just above a bud at about 50 cm (20 in.) above soil level. In the winter of the second year, cut back the new growth on the main leader to about 20 cm (8 in.) to a bud facing in the opposite direction to the one chosen in the previous winter and remove the feathers up to 45 cm (18 in.) from ground level. Then prune all the laterals to an outward-facing bud about 20 cm (8 in.) and any side shoots on these laterals to 15 cm (6 in.) long.

During late summer of the third year, prune the current season's growth on the main branches to a downward-facing bud five leaves along the branch, the side shoots on the main branches to three leaves, and any secondary side shoots or flowering spurs back to one downward-facing bud.

For an established pyramid, further summer pruning is done to downward-facing buds, retaining a pyramidal form, and once the tree reaches 2 metres (6 ft.), prune the leader to 1 cm (0.5 in.). Any congestion or crossing branches should be treated in exactly the same way as for a bush or standard by thinning to allow some sunlight into the centre of the tree.

Restricted Fruit Tree Forms: Fan

This form, typically around 2 metres (6 ft.) high and grown against a sunny wall, features a short central trunk with several radiating branches growing fanwise from the crown. Horizontal wires starting 40 cm (15 in.) from the ground need to be fixed to the wall to train and tie in stems to; position these wires 15 cm (6 in.) apart, roughly two brick courses.

Plant a maiden or a feathered maiden at the base of the wall, central to the wires. Where a maiden is planted, cut back the main stem in spring, to about 40 cm (15 in.) from ground level, leaving three strong buds. In summer, erect two garden canes at 45° angles, and tie in the two branches (the arms) that have formed from the buds on either side. Any shoots that have developed on the trunk must be removed. In the second spring, reduce the two arms by two-thirds to an upward-facing bud and remove any shoots on the trunk.

Where a feathered maiden is used, the same process is carried out, but we miss a year out as the two arms are already formed and tied in to the canes.

In summer, select four shoots from each arm: one at the tip to extend the existing arm, two spaced equally on the upper side and one on the lower side. Tie them in at about 30° to the main arm so they are evenly spaced apart, using garden canes attached to the wires; rub out any shoots growing toward the wall and prune back any others to one leaf.

In the following spring, prune back each of the four branches on each side by one-third, pruning to an upward-facing bud if possible. During the remainder of the growing season, tie any new growth from the tips of these branches into the cane and wire framework to extend the main branches; any side shoots that develop, where there is space within the framework, can be tied in.

Restricted Fruit Tree Forms: Cordon

Cordons are single-stemmed trees suitable for all varieties of apples and pears. They can be planted in an upright position but are more commonly planted at an angle of 45° to attain a longer stem while still keeping the fruit at easy picking height. Fruiting spurs are encouraged to form along the stem, and any side branches are removed by pruning. Cordons take less space and crop earlier than most other forms, so more varieties can be planted into a small space, but yields are smaller per tree.

To start a cordon, plant a maiden tree or pretrained cordon at 45°, tied into a 45° angled cane, which is firmly attached to horizontal wires.

Pruning takes place in late summer, when new side shoots growing from the main stem are cut back to three leaves. Shoots produced from these lateral branches are cut back to one leaf beyond the basal cluster of leaves to create flowering spurs. This summer pruning, often carried out while the fruits are still on the tree, will force the tree to produce flower buds in the following spring.

Winter pruning (thinning) congested growth on apple cordons using secateurs.

Espalier-trained *Pyrus communis* 'Merton Pride' (pear).

Espalier-trained *Malus domestica* 'Ribston Pippin' (apple), half-pruned in March.

Cordon-trained (single "U") *Pyrus communis* 'Joséphine de Malines' (pear).

Winter pruning when the tree is dormant involves thinning out congested laterals and cutting out any really old ones that are failing to produce fruit. This exercise allows more air to circulate, improving the health of the tree, and encourages productive new growth as a replacement for the unproductive old growth. The only other pruning necessary is to prune back the main stem when the tree has reached the desired height. Any new growth at the end of the stem is cut back to just one leaf each spring.

Cordons can also be grown successfully as a single "U" cordon or a double "U" cordon, making them a very decorative specimen and ideal for growing against a wall for easy picking.

Restricted Fruit Tree Forms: Espalier

This a common style, not only for apple and pear trees but for many other fruit and ornamental trees and shrubs. Espalier-trained fruit trees consist of a central vertical trunk with three or four horizontal branches on each side trained against a wall or grown as a freestanding two-dimensional tree.

Initially, winter prune the main stem to a bud at the height of the first horizontal wire of a series of three or four wires at 45 cm (18 in.) intervals. As the shoots develop from these buds in the following spring, two are selected and trained on canes at 45° angles on either side, and a third is trained to grow vertically on a garden cane. In the autumn, the two 45° branches are lowered to a horizontal position. This process is repeated over consecutive years until the topmost wire is reached, when the leader is pruned out. Once established, summer pruning is carried out on the laterals from the framework.

Stepovers of *Malus domestica* 'Kidd's Orange Red' (apple).

Restricted Fruit Tree Forms: Stepovers

Stepovers are espaliers with just one tier of horizontal branches 30 to 45 cm (12 to 18 in.) from ground level. Not only are these a means of effectively growing apples or pears where space is restricted, they make an interesting and productive border plant for a vegetable plot or herbaceous border.

Start a stepover by planting a maiden tree—or a row of them at 1.5 metre (5 ft.) spacing—and prune out the main stem to 30 to 45 cm (12 to 18 in.) above ground level in winter when the tree is dormant. In the following summer remove the main stem, leaving two lateral branches, one on either side. These should be trained on each side and tied onto garden canes at 45° angles; in the following autumn, lower the canes with the branches attached and fix them into a horizontal position. Further pruning of the laterals and for continual pruning of established stepovers should follow the guide for summer pruning given earlier.

Hedges

A hedge is a living and often multipurpose barrier, filling many roles, from dividing the garden into various "rooms" to serving as a piece of garden architecture. A hedge can also be an opportunity to grow various species of woody plants in a different style. A fairly large selection of woody species can be used effectively in a hedge, including conifers and deciduous and evergreen species of broadleaves. These are highlighted throughout the A to Z in this book, and all require different strategies for maintaining, pruning, or clipping.

Hedges are broken down into two types, formal and informal. Formal hedges are usually planted with a single species and are much more geometric in growth and shape than informal hedges, needing regular clipping to restrict their size and growth to maintain their formal, engineered shape. Species choice can vary from box (*Buxus sempervirens*), for the small parterre-style hedges of a knot garden, to large formal garden boundary hedges of yew (*Taxus baccata*) or holly (*Ilex aquifolium*).

With deciduous species (e.g., *Fagus sylvatica*, *Carpinus betulus*) regular annual clipping keeps the trees juvenile, and they hold onto their dead leaves in the winter, creating a semi-permanent barrier. A semi-permeable barrier is often more beneficial in a garden for slowing down strong winds than the permanent barrier of a dense conifer hedge, which can speed up wind currents.

The tight face of a strong, established formal yew hedge.

A young, newly planted beech hedge before pruning to a permanent height and width.

The end of a well-grown and maintained yew hedge, showing the batter.

Using a petrol hedge cutter to maintain a yew hedge.

Using hand-hedging shears to lightly prune back a holly hedge.

Informal hedges can consist of a single or mixed species in an irregular shape and are usually planted in the informal garden to a relatively casual shape and layout. Depending on the species used, they are less maintenance than a formal hedge and are usually grown for their flower and fruit rather than for the straight geometric lines; suitable subjects may be found in such genera as *Rosa*, *Sarcococca*, *Fuchsia*, *Pyracantha*, and *Forsythia*.

Mixed species can also be used in a native hedge with local native species to help enhance biodiversity habitats. Although informal hedges are less maintenance in terms of the regularity of pruning, they can be more labour intensive, as they usually require pruning with the secateurs rather than a pair of hedging shears, as individual shoots need to be cut back to buds within the foliage canopy to hide the pruning wounds. A spur system of pruning will be required for flowering on some species.

Once the style of hedge has been chosen and the plants set approximately 45 cm (18 in.) apart, the initial training of a hedge begins immediately and discipline is needed. For evergreen species there is no need for any pruning, apart from keeping it within the bounds of the desired size and cutting back overlong shoots protruding from the proposed face. Deciduous species with vigorous upright growth that would normally make a large shade tree (e.g., *Fagus sylvatica*, *Carpinus betulus*) need to be allowed to grow approximately 20 cm (8 in.) beyond the desired final height and the sides tipped back to within the final width of the hedge.

Vigorous upright-growing plants such as privet (*Ligustrum*) and hawthorn (*Crataegus*) need pruning hard in late spring to encourage a multi-stemmed bushy plant with furnishing growth right down to the ground, or the hedge will be bare at the base in later years and hard to fill in through pruning.

As the hedge becomes established, the shape needs to be determined. For informal hedges, the shrubs need to be pruned at the relevant time of the year and to the same requirements as for the individual plant, albeit with some shaping to keep them within the allotted space. Formal hedges have a dense habit of growth from top to bottom, and the face of the hedge should have a slight batter, tapering in slightly from the bottom to the top. This makes them less vulnerable to damage from snow and high winds and increases light levels at the base of the hedge.

Once the formal hedge has reached its final dimensions and batter, it will need regular maintenance to keep it in shape and to size. This will entail regular clipping, at least twice a year, once between autumn and spring (during the dormant period) and once in midsummer. Deciduous hedges need pruning in late spring and late summer; for evergreen conifers like yew, annual clipping should be done after new growth has expanded in early summer and follow-up clipping should continue throughout the growing season. To avoid stimulating new growth late in the season, which could lead to winter injury on the soft regrowth, do not clip yews after late summer. Hand-hedging shears can be used, but for long lengths, mechanical (either petrol or electric) hedge cutters can be used to good effect by a good pruner. Ranging poles are an effective piece of kit to gain a straight line, and a level top can be achieved by a

Holly hedge renovation in progress.

Completed renovation with water and feed applied.

using a garden string line or a builder's laser line. Accuracy will be improved with the use of a purpose-made template to keep the batter and height. The hedge should be cut from the bottom to the top to prevent clippings from falling onto the area of hedge to be cut; it is often easier for the pruner to use mechanical hedge cutters this way, rather than from top to bottom.

Hedge Renovation

Despite accurate and well-executed hedge trimming each year, most formal hedges will gradually fall out of shape, losing their batter and increasing in depth from regular light clipping and growing out over pathways or onto the lawn. This is particularly true of *Ilex aquifolium*, *Lonicera nitida*, *Taxus baccata*, *Fagus sylvatica*, *Carpinus betulus*, *Griselinia littoralis*, and *Crataegus monogyna*, but all will respond to hard pruning. On a cyclic routine, possibly every ten to fifteen years, some form of renovation will be required to get the hedge back under control and to a manageable clipping size.

Deciduous hedges should be renovated between autumn and spring (during the dormant period) and evergreens in mid-spring. Heavy-duty hedging shears can be used, but there may be a need for the secateurs or a sharp handsaw if the renovation is extremely hard. On an extensive hedge, hard renovation should be phased over a period, hard pruning one side in one year and light clipping the opposite face, and vice versa the following year, as it will usually need a full growing season to recover. This is quite stressful for the hedge and a good feed with a well-balanced shrub fertiliser and plenty of water, especially during a drought period.

Care must be taken with particular random-branched conifers (e.g., *Thuja*, *Cupressus*, *Chamaecyparis*), as if they are cut back into bare wood, they will not respond by putting new foliage on, so strict discipline is important: clip these conifers regularly through the growing season and be hard with the amount of growth removed, retaining a tight hedge face. Once a conifer needs renovation, it is beyond saving and will need to be removed and replaced.

Scarlet willow, *Salix alba* var. *vitellina* 'Britzensis', grown on a short stool for winter stem effect.

Coppicing

Traditionally coppicing (or stooling) was a pruning operation carried out on willows and certain species (e.g., *Corylus avellana*, *Castanea sativa*, *Carpinus betulus*) in a coppice or woodland setting to generate vigorous young straight stems as a material to make fencing and plant supports for the vegetable garden or herbaceous border, or as a source

Pruning *Cornus alba* 'Sibirica' back to a stool.

Cornus alba 'Sibirica' after stooling.

Coppicing a mature stool of *Corylus avellana*.

of fuel for charcoal production. Today coppicing is carried out to generate vigorous coloured stems (e.g., on dogwoods or willows) or vigorous stems with exceptionally large or juvenile leaves for ornamental purposes, for example with *Ailanthus altissima*, *Catalpa bignonioides*, *Paulownia tomentosa*, and *Morus alba*. Coppicing can also be used to keep a tree relatively small and within the confines of an herbaceous border; to exaggerate the variegated or coloured leaves of certain trees (e.g., *Acer negundo* 'Flamingo'); and to highlight a tree's coloured young shoots and stems, for example those of *A. pensylvanicum* 'Erythrocladum'.

Coppicing is carried out on a rotational basis. The regularity will vary from annually to ten years, depending on the species. The coppicing of *Corylus avellana* will be on a five- to ten-year cycle, depending on the size of materials needed. For stem effect on willows and dogwoods, coppicing will be done on a one- to two-year cycle. For catalpas, paulownias, and other trees grown for their large leaves, coppicing will be done on an annual basis.

For dogwoods, willows, and other ornamental shrubs, a low framework is created and the coloured stems are pruned back to this annually.

A pollarded scarlet willow, *Salix alba* var. *vitellina* 'Britzensis'.

Tilia ×*euchlora* pruned and trained as a pleached hedge.

Tilia ×*europaea*, both pollarded and pleached.

For weaker growers (e.g., *Cornus alba* 'Kesselringii') the stooling of the growths back to the framework may need to be done biennially (every other year), or the plant may weaken and be unable to respond to the rigorous pruning.

For *Corylus avellana*, *Castanea sativa*, *Carpinus betulus*, and *Tilia* species, all the upright growths are cleanly cut back to a coppice stool with a handsaw in late winter; in the following growing season, new shoots will spring from the cut ends or the base of the stool. If too many stems are generated, they can be thinned at a later stage; however, if rabbits, deer, or other grazing mammals are present, some protection of these new shoots will be needed.

Pollarding

This is an old form of labour-intensive pruning, usually carried out as a means of managing a tree from an early age to maintain a small manageable crown, or, like coppicing, to produce small coloured stems for ornamental effect. Pollarding differs from coppicing in that trees are trained on a trunk with a framework, which can vary in height and spread to suit the species and the space. Regular pruning of the young growths with secateurs or a sharp saw is carried out on an annual basis, back to knuckles or knobs that are formed on the ends of the scaffold framework. Tree genera that respond well to this treatment include *Salix*, *Platanus*, and *Tilia*. Some trees grown for their coloured foliage (e.g., *Toona sinensis* 'Flamingo', *Catalpa bignonioides* 'Aurea') can also be pollarded to encourage vigorous shoots from a short trunk to 1 metre (3 ft.) high,

producing more young stems and leafy growth to show off the coloured leaves to their best effect.

Pruning is done in spring, before the new growth begins and can be done annually or every other year, depending on the length of new growths required and the amount of available time and resources available to carry out this work, which is—as you can imagine—very labour intensive.

Pleaching

Pleaching is the historic art of intricately weaving together the lateral branches of broadleaved deciduous trees with formal pruning to a regular shape, to produce a raised formal hedge on a freestanding row of clean trunks. Most trees that will tolerate constant clipping—*Tilia*, *Carpinus betulus*, *Acer campestre*, *Fagus sylvatica*—can be used; *Quercus ilex* is sometimes successfully pleached as a formal hedge. Despite the labour-intensive initial training and high-maintenance regular pruning it demands, pleaching has become more popular again in small formal gardens as a means of creating privacy while still being able to grow plants beneath the "screen."

It is possible to buy pre-grown pleached standards from tree nurseries; these can be planted together to form an instant formal line, saving several years' time in training. To start a pleached hedge from scratch,

Tradition! Perfectly shaped cones of *Carpinus betulus*, with box balls and a well-groomed yew hedge.

selected standard trees, with a clean trunk, are planted at regular intervals along a purpose-made metal or wooden framework, at the height and length of the desired hedge. The lateral branches are tied in horizontally along the supporting framework, and any lateral shoots that cannot be tied in are removed. Epicormic shoots will develop on the main trunk, and they too should be removed.

When the leader reaches the top of the supporting framework it should be trained horizontally and tied in, as should the extending laterals, and any other lateral shoots should be shortened. As the lateral shoots meet the laterals from the neighbouring tree, they can be woven together to form an intricate pattern. Growths extending at right angles from the hedge should be shortened back to a single bud.

Once the hedge has been created and established, it should be trimmed annually as with any ordinary hedge. As growths appear on the trunk, they can be rubbed off and not left to make woody shoots. Watch out for dead wood and any coral spot, as this is a haven for it, as when shoots are shortened back, they aren't always cut back accurately to a live bud. Feeding and mulching will be needed to keep these hedges in good condition due to the high number of leaves pruned off each year.

Trees that respond to pollarding can be trained as a high hedge, with all the laterals and the season's shoots pruned cleanly back to knuckles, creating a very interesting living garden feature.

Topiary

This artful form of pruning, a part of garden architecture for many years, creates sculptures of living plants, turning them into various geometric shapes and forms, including cubes, balls, cones, spirals, and interesting novelty shapes. Formal hedge tops are also used to add interesting archways or terminal features. Traditionally *Carpinus betulus*, *Taxus baccata*, *Laurus nobilis*, *Buxus sempervirens*, and *Ilex aquifolium* were employed, as they clip well and remain tight in growth, but more recently *I. crenata*, *Osmanthus delavayi*, *Lonicera nitida*, and *Ligustrum delavayanum* have been used for their quicker growth and interesting foliage.

Topiary turns up in both formal and informal garden designs. It requires rigorous training and precise clipping, and the more intricate the design, the more elaborate the training and clipping. A metal or wooden frame is usually formed and the plant trained into it. It may be necessary to tie in some of the branches with biodegradable jute garden twine, which eventually breaks down, meaning there are no worries about its biting into the stems and girdling the bark.

Once the shape is formed, it will need regular maintenance with hand shears or mechanical shears. The timing between clippings will be decided by the vigour of the plants, but expect to clip two or three times a year to keep them in a formal shape. The first clipping should be done after the first shoots appear and the last should not be undertaken after late summer, as any new shoots may not ripen for the winter and dieback can occur. Feed through the growing season to ensure enough vigorous growth is produced to clip; never hope for "no growth, no clipping," as the topiary will deteriorate and dead patches are likely to appear.

Climbing roses well trained against a wall.

Climbers and Walls

Many shrubs are grown against or within the shelter of walls. Not only do they provide a pleasant and interesting contrast and relief to the hard structure, but the more sheltered conditions, particularly with warm, sunny walls, increase the range of tender plants that can be grown. A wide variety of habit and form occurs among plants that are normally grown in this situation, especially where their method of climbing is concerned, and this must be taken into account when deciding upon their training and pruning needs.

Detailed information for individual species is given in the A to Z of this book, but the following examples show how pruning relates to the variable habits of growth and flowering found among climbing plants. It is only by having some knowledge of these that the best results from pruning can be obtained.

Climbing plants adopt various methods when climbing up supports, including twining stems, adventitious aerial roots, suction pads, scandent or scrambling stems, leaf or stem tendrils, and twining leaf stalks. The climbing method will often determine where a particular plant is sited, the types of supports it can be trained to grow up, and how the plant will need to be treated in terms of pruning and training to cover the supports.

True climbers are the plants that cling hard and securely, pressed tightly against the wall or support by means of small suction pads or adventitious roots (e.g., *Parthenocissus tricuspidata*, *Hedera helix*). The mature growths, which branch freely, are produced at a later stage. With these plant types, you can either clip over the whole surface once or twice a year, before and during the growing season, keeping the wall surface furnished without allowing the mature branching to develop; or

Hedera helix and *Schizophragma hydrangeoides*, trained to screen a garden wall.

Wisteria sinensis in full flower—note the stems twining anti-clockwise.

allow the mature branches to develop, partially pruning them back at a later stage if they are considered too large.

Hydrangea anomala subsp. *petiolaris* and *Schizophragma hydrangeoides* produce a creeping mat of growths, lightly held by adventitious roots against the surface. Mature branches, short and spur-like, are produced; these are the flowering shoots, and they are therefore retained, perhaps being pruned back a little at a later stage if they become too long.

Climbers are often trained and pruned hard against a wall. This is often effected by tying shrubs to a support system. They are in fact natural climbers using twining stems or tendrils and may be trained to develop over an old tree or pergola system. By using a suitable system of horizontal and vertical wires or stakes, many of these climbers can be encouraged to cover the available wall space and can be grouped for pruning purposes into four main categories.

Group 1. Climbers that are pruned back to a permanent framework and spur system. A typical example is *Wisteria sinensis*, which has a spur system of flowering. A few permanent branches are trained fanwise against the wall as a supporting framework. As the space is covered and throughout the life of the climber, the extension growths that develop (and are not required for framework purposes) are pruned back to five buds by stopping growth at 15 cm (6 in.) during the growing season, cutting these back in the winter to the lowest two or three buds. They are not cut back hard during the summer, as the secondary growths that are often produced would not ripen properly. Any that do develop from the lighter summer pruning will naturally be cut off by this shortening back during the winter. In this way, growths that are not needed for replacement extension growths are taken off, and the energies of the plant directed into the production of flower buds. This pruning also confines the plant, for the long growths would prove to be a nuisance to free passage. In addition, shoot pruning during the summer provides a check to vegetative growth while promoting good flowering.

Group 2. Climbers that are pruned annually after flowering by taking out the old wood. This is done to encourage the production of young wood that flowers the following year; *Lonicera periclymenum*, for example, responds in this way. This pruning may result in much of the older wood being cut out each year, although it is usually necessary to leave the oldest stem wood. With many climbers, it is difficult to carry out this replacement pruning cleanly, for the growths naturally twine round each other; it must be done carefully, without severing those which are to remain. Climbers treated in this way usually flower along the length of the previous year's wood.

Group 3. Climbers that are pruned back hard each year, often to near ground level. Clematis in the Jackmanii and Viticella groups are examples. They grow rapidly and flower on these growths during the same season. The pruning, carried out in the spring as the new growth buds swell, takes away the old growth, much of which has been killed during the winter, and prevents there being a bird's nest tangle between new shoots and dead stems.

Group 4. Climbers that have a scandent habit, gaining height by scrambling. Many of these climbers, if grown on a wall in a restricted space, become thick and untidy if left completely unpruned. For example, *Jasminum nudiflorum* is by nature a scandent shrub, producing large growths that scramble, but such extensive growths must be checked when grown on a restricted space such as a wall. This subject produces young growths from the old wood very freely, and these can be used for the replacement of parts of the main framework, as this becomes necessary. In the same way, a proportion of the trailing growths that furnish the surface of a mature bush can be pruned away each year on a replacement system. Normally, as this subject flowers from the previous year's wood, pruning is carried out immediately after flowering. Climbing and rambling roses would also fall into this category.

Nonclimbers and Walls

Certain shrubs can, with a permanent framework, be trained against a wall; they include shrubs that need support when grown against a wall, and strong-growing tender shrubs that are grown next to a wall for shelter.

Shrubs with a permanent framework trained fanwise hard against the wall. Shrubs that produce a crop of growths freely after pruning may be cut back annually to near the main framework, the period being adjusted with the flowering. *Vitex agnus-castus* flowers in late summer on the current season's growths; these are left for protection over winter and pruned off in the early spring. *Prunus triloba* 'Multiplex', on the other hand, flowers in spring on the previous year's wood; it is cut back after the flowers fade, and the new growths that develop bloom in the following year.

Chaenomeles speciosa, C. japonica, and their various hybrids flower on a spur system as well as on the previous year's wood. They are typical of subjects that respond to hard pruning close to the main framework; this is often most effective when it takes the form of summer pruning, which promotes spur formation. In its simplest form, the summer growths are pruned back to approximately one-third of their length as the basal portion starts to harden off. These are later, during the winter, taken back to two or three buds. A more intensive form of pruning consists of a periodic stopping, taking the young growths back to 5 to 8 cm (2 to 3 in.) or even less as they develop, repeating this with any sub-laterals that arise a few weeks later. It is often necessary to begin this system of pruning as early as late spring, but the leading growths for the main branches are left to grow freely while there is wall space to cover. The frequent stopping during the growing season results in a reduction of leaf surface, which inhibits free and rank growth in both the shoot and root systems and thus encourages spur and flower formation. Several other shrubs in the Rosaceae, such as cotoneasters and pyracanthas, respond to this treatment.

The effect of the close growth and flowering on the main branches of plants trained under this system is quite formal. The original main branches should be carefully and evenly laid out to produce a perfect design; perhaps the intent is to surround a door or window, but usually the layout is fan-shaped. Pruning and training is necessary: as the original branches grow and become more widely spaced, suitable laterals (usually two on each) must be retained to fill the gaps; and before any stopping is carried out, the required growths should be selected and secured to canes or wires laid in the right directions.

Weaker-stemmed shrubs that need support when grown against a wall. Generally, these are the more tender shrubs that need a wall for shelter. The provision of a support, while not absolutely necessary, enables these shrubs to reach a greater height than otherwise possible and thus achieve the desired coverage of the wall surface. Many of the escallonias (e.g., *Escallonia* 'Langleyensis') can be grown in this way. Pruning is often necessary in order to keep the shrub within bounds; this is carried out after flowering, when lengths of the older wood should be cut back to younger growths nearer the centre of the bush. Also, in this way the shrub is saved from using energy needlessly on a crop of fruits.

Chaenomeles japonica trained against a brick wall.

Strong-growing, self-supporting shrubs grown in the shelter of a wall. Again it is usually the tender shrubs that are planted in such a position, for shelter. Often, branches are held back nearer to the wall, but no actual support is necessary. *Garrya elliptica*, for example, can stand entirely on its own without any support. Lengths of the older wood are taken out if any pruning is required in order to restrict size.

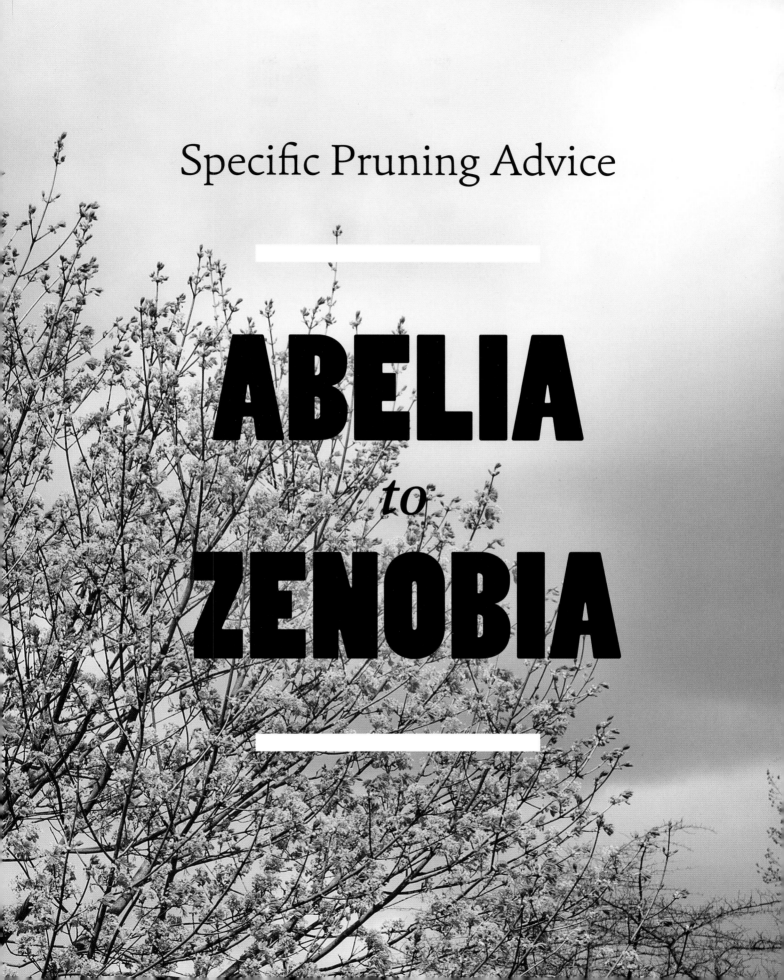

Specific Pruning Advice

ABELIA

to

ZENOBIA

ABELIA

Habit Compact, usually semi-evergreen shrubs (but can be deciduous in cooler areas) for free-draining soil in full sun. **Attributes** White and pink trumpet-shaped flowers throughout summer and autumn. **Reasons for pruning** To maintain a healthy bush with vigorous growth for flowers and remove old non-flowering wood. **Pruning time** Late winter/early spring and again following flowering to tidy up the plant.

In a sheltered, sunny position, these shrubs will produce sufficient fresh growth freely from the base, which allows some of the older stems to be pruned out to encourage the development of the younger shoots. Spring pruning consists of removing dead or damaged branches. The first flush of flowers are produced on the old wood, but the new growth can produce flowers later in the season. To renovate abelias when they become old, woody, cluttered, and untidy, cut all stems hard back to the base of the plant in early spring to produce strong new shoots from the ground.

All species are suitable for training against a wall for winter protection in the cooler areas, but the semi-evergreen species and hybrids (typified by *Abelia ×grandiflora*) usually need wall protection the most. The new growths tied up onto supporting wires allow the development of free growth, which can be encouraged by leaving the laterals unpruned. As the new growths develop, they too must be tied in; otherwise, once they have arched over, the laterals will grow upright.

Abelia chinensis is normally grown as a single bush, but even in sheltered areas, there may be some dieback after a severe winter. Pruning out the damaged growth is best left until spring.

Abelia parvifolia is tender and may be killed right back after a cold winter. If the branches survive for several years, the oldest growths may be thinned out in the spring, but do leave some small shoots at the base to encourage the natural arching habit of the shrub.

Abelia umbellata is a larger spreading shrub,

Pruning a cluttered *Abelia ×grandiflora*.

and it may be necessary to prune back some of the longer arching branches to keep it in its space. The larger branches have an interesting bark effect; it's worth growing them for several seasons to encourage and show this.

Very closely related to *Abelia* is *Zabelia triflora*, a large shrub that produces a thick mass of erect growths. Don't try to thin them out: this natural habit is best left as is.

ABELIOPHYLLUM

Habit Deciduous shrub for moist, free-draining soil in full sun. **Attributes** Fragrant white to rose-pink flowers in winter and early spring before the leaves emerge. **Reasons for pruning** To encourage new growth for training and develop flowers. **Pruning time** The flowers

are produced in late winter/early spring on growths made the previous season, so pruning should be carried out in late winter/early spring after flowering.

This is a monotypic genus, with only one species, *Abeliophyllum distichum* (Korean for-

sythia). All newly planted shrubs, including plants in the Roseum Group, should be encouraged to grow vigorously in their early years without any pruning, and so good culture and feeding will be important. This plant can be grown as a shrub with a lax, open habit in a border or trained against a sunny wall; the latter position will give its flowers the early protection occasionally needed in a hard winter. To prune a freestanding shrub, thin the older stems by removing them to just above ground level to allow space for new growth to develop. When grown against a wall, it can produce long shoots up to 2.4 to 3 metres (8 to 10 ft.) high. Tie these growths in to the framework and allow the laterals to develop; prune a proportion of these back each year to maintain vigorous growth. Remove any new plants that develop from lower branches that have rooted as soon as they are noticed.

ABIES

Habit Upright excurrent evergreen conifer, usually with a well-balanced, mirrored, conical crown, for a deep soil with plenty of moisture and full sun. **Attributes** Silver firs are grown for their conical form, blue or silver needles, and occasionally their cones. **Reasons for pruning** To maintain a leader for a uniform shape. **Pruning time** When needed.

Young plants will naturally develop a strong leading shoot; however, where two competing leaders are formed, one should be removed back to the point of attachment as early as possible to prevent a structural weakness in the future. If there is a warm autumn, some species can produce lammas growth, which should not be confused with competing leaders. The beauty of many of the silver firs is the low skirt, which grows naturally from the lower branches; when these are lost, their beauty to a large extent is spoiled. It will take two to three years for the lower branches to form a well-balanced skirt, as most of the effort of the tree is directed into developing the strong leader.

If the leader is lost in the early years, most species have the ability to grow a new one if left alone, especially *Abies concolor*, *A. pinsapo*, *A. nordmanniana*, *A. magnifica*, *A. fraseri*, and *A. grandis*. If more than one of the new leaders is successful, only one should be retained, where possible; codominant stems will potentially be a weakness later in the tree's life. General pruning is unnecessary, but any dying or dead branches should be removed back to the

Abies magnifica var. *shastensis* in its native habitat on Mount Shasta, California, showing its natural conical habit.

The perfectly balanced pyramidal habit of *Abies pinsapo*.

Abies lasiocarpa on Mount Rainier in Washington State, showing its tight, narrow form and naturally branching to the ground.

trunk. No other pruning is normally needed.

Often *Abies koreana* (Korean fir) is encouraged to lose the leading shoot to develop a low, well-branched tree that will produce many ornamental purple cones on the lateral branches. Several slow-growing selections (e.g., 'Compact Dwarf', 'Piccolo', 'Silberlocke') offer a good show of cones and foliage.

A multi-stemmed *Abies koreana* in full cone.

Abies concolor with twin leaders, a potential weakness.

ACACIA

Habit Large evergreen shrubs or trees for dry soil and full sun. **Attributes** Fine blue-grey bipinnate leaves, scented yellow flowers in late winter. **Reasons for pruning** To restrict size. **Pruning time** After flowering in late spring.

With acacias, look to plant a feathered tree; alternatively, cut the plant back hard to encourage regrowth and form a multi-stemmed bush that can be wall-trained. Wattles often produce circling roots when grown in containers; these must be cut before planting to encourage them to grow outward, reducing the potential of weak anchor root problems later in life. Plant them as young as possible after the last spring frosts. The top grows extremely fast at the expense of roots, which makes the plant unstable; it will require some support as it develops into a small tree. Most acacias (e.g., *Acacia baileyana*, *A. longifolia*, *A. melanoxylon*) will respond to hard pruning to restrict size, but this must be carried out in late spring. If done at this time of the year, living wood can easily be identified and the dead wood removed. *Acacia dealbata* can be planted against a sunny wall as a multi-stemmed shrub, and the main framework trained evenly against the wall.

Acacia dealbata in flower in a private garden.

ACER

Habit Small to large deciduous or evergreen excurrent trees for deep, free-draining, fertile soil and full sun (partial shade for some). **Attributes** Overall canopy shape, ornamental bark, leaf shape and colour, including autumn colour, and occasionally brightly coloured young samaras. **Reasons for pruning** To develop a strong framework. **Pruning time** Late summer or early autumn. Never prune in early spring as the wounds are prone to bleeding.

This complex genus is divided botanically into groups or sections, which is a convenient way to address the pruning requirements of those we commonly grow. Where the maple that you are pruning is not listed as an example, find out which of the sections it falls into before starting any pruning; otherwise, the structure of the tree may be spoiled.

The following points are standard techniques for all maple pruning:

- If the tree exhibits good, healthy growth, very little pruning should be necessary except for some early training and the retention of a leader in the strong growers.
- For training, remove crossing branches, diseased and damaged branches, and twin leaders; if a standard tree is required, remove the lower feathers to the height desired early in the tree's life.
- Carry out any pruning in late summer or early autumn as most species have a liability to bleed, especially if cut in early spring. *Acer campestre* is one of the species less likely to bleed.

It is often difficult to prune larger specimens back to a natural shape: the opposite buds make it difficult to find natural growing points, and once the terminal bud is lost, multiple branching quickly begins.

Some of the variegated cultivars (e.g., *Acer platanoides* 'Drummondii') have a tendency to revert back to green leaves. These can safely be pruned out, back to variegation, in late summer, when it is easiest to see the reversion.

SECTION PLATANOIDEA

Acer platanoides (Norway maple) has a close, rounded head with heavy branching, often with free production of dwarf shoots along the length of the framework. These should not be pruned out, nor should the branches be thinned, for this is the natural growth habit. In addition to the well-established varieties, several clones have appeared, particularly in North America (e.g., 'Crimson Sentry', 'Cleveland', 'Summer Shade', 'Columnare'); these were selected for a more compact form, which makes them suitable as street trees.

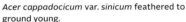

Acer cappadocicum var. *sinicum* feathered to ground young.

A young *Acer platanoides* showing rounded crown in spring.

Full tree outline of *Acer platanoides* in flower.

Acer campestre with well-spaced branching.

Acer pictum subsp. *mono* grown on a short trunk.

Acer longipes subsp. *amplum* with a straight trunk.

The lower branches of *Acer cappadocicum* (Cappadocian maple) should be encouraged to spread and sweep down to give the tree a skirt effect.

Acer campestre (field maple) can be planted as a feathered tree in a natural setting or as a standard tree in a more formal setting. When grown as a standard it will need to be trained well in the early years to retain a leader and have well-spaced branching by removing crossing branches and any strong upright growths that will interfere with the shape and form.

Acer campestre makes a good hedging plant and may be clipped in the winter. It is also now popular trained to grow over an arbour or framework, the annual shoots pruned back hard each winter.

Acer miyabei is an upright growing tree to 12 metres (40 ft.) high with tight branching.

Most of the remaining species in this group (e.g., *Acer longipes*, *A. pictum*, *A. truncatum*) are also tree size, and the best size for planting is a 2 to 2.5 metre (6 to 8 ft.) standard with a clean trunk.

SECTION ACER

Acer pseudoplatanus (sycamore) is a tough tree that hails from high, exposed positions where no other tree can grow. Often side-lined by the purists, it is nevertheless a firm favourite with many. The main reason for this is that it is a strong, quick grower, speedily reacting to any damage (particularly by harsh weather conditions) by developing growth from remaining axillary and dormant buds. As a mature tree it has the classic tree canopy shape, with billowing clouds of foliage on large lateral branches—quite a signature in any landscape.

In the nursery it should be grown as a standard with a good central leader and evenly balanced lateral branching. Very little pruning is normally required, once a well-balanced standard has been achieved, but any competing leaders should be removed to allow the main leader to develop for as long as possible into an excurrent crown.

The many available grafted cultivars offer various attributes; be sure to remove any suckers from below the graft union as soon as they appear. *Acer pseudoplatanus* 'Brilliantissimum' is slower growing and more compact than the

A mature *Acer pseudoplatanus* showing its classic canopy.

Acer pseudoplatanus 'Brilliantissimum' showing the compact, rounded outline.

The young form of *Acer macrophyllum* trained on a short clean trunk with even upright branching.

A young, well-trained *Acer saccharum*.

type. Its leader is difficult to maintain, and early in life it will form a decurrent crown. It is often sold as a small lollipop specimen—an acquired taste, but everyone to their own.

Acer monspessulanum (Montpelier maple) is very similar in form to *A. campestre* and should be treated in the same way, as should *A. sempervirens* (Cretan maple) which is slower in growth and requires a good fertile soil to encourage vigour.

Acer opalus (Italian maple) is a strong grower but quickly loses its leader and becomes decurrent, with all the effort going into the lower branches, which makes it a wide-spreading tree. The lower branching should be encouraged, and the dwarf shoots produced from these should be left.

Acer hyrcanum is very similar in appearance but is slower growing and will retain its leader for longer, making it a compact tree.

Acer saccharum (sugar maple) should be treated the same as *A. platanoides*.

SECTION LITHOCARPA

Acer macrophyllum (Oregon maple) is an excurrent form and develops into a large tree to 25 metres (82 ft.) with very large leaves. Young trees develop a framework of upright branches; as the tree matures the outer and lower branches take on a semi-pendulous habit. The low branches should be left to grow at eye level and the skirt not be lifted too high so that the beauty and scent of the yellow flow-

The very large *Acer palmatum*, growing in Japan.

A mature *Acer palmatum* 'Dissectum Atropurpureum'.

Acer palmatum 'Sango-kaku' with low, well-balanced branching.

ers and young samaras can be appreciated.

Acer sterculiaceum subsp. *franchetii* is a slow starter as a young tree, but once established in position it will begin to make new growth quickly through a central leader.

SECTION PALMATA

The trees in this group are grown for their multi-varying forms and ornamental leaves of many shapes and colours, especially autumn colour. There is considerable variation among the many varieties and cultivars of *Acer palmatum*. The straight species makes a large bush or medium-sized tree with a rounded habit, but it grows slowly, taking many years to reach full size. One mature specimen in Kyoto, Japan, witnessed by Tony Kirkham in 2013, remains the largest Japanese maple he has ever seen. Who said it was the perfect tree for a small garden?

It is important when pruning that you know the shape and form of the particular cultivar; however, the typical habit that should be encouraged on most is to leave the branches originating on the trunk as low to the ground

as possible to grow up at a sharp angle, evenly furnished with the finer lateral branches and leaves. Allow the outer branches to naturally and gracefully sweep down to the ground.

The cultivars in this section will normally be grafted in the nursery onto the species, and early training is important if the tree is to make the desired shape. None of the cultivars will produce a strong leader; if height is required, select a strong-growing shoot and train it up a strong garden bamboo cane.

These plants require shelter from cold winds and late frosts, or damage may lead to the production of dead wood and coral spot, which will need to be pruned out occasionally with a pair of sharp secateurs.

Acer japonicum and its cultivars have a similar habit and form and should be treated as for *A. palmatum*.

SECTION MACRANTHERA

This important garden group, the snake bark maples, comprises species with a smooth green bark that is striped white. *Acer davidii* (Father

David's maple) and *A. pensylvanicum* (moosewood) are examples of the typical growth habit. The branches originating at the termination of a short trunk subdivide to a very limited extent, instead producing many dwarf shoots along their lengths, creating a graceful effect. A leader should be retained for as long as possible, encouraging branching on a leg of 0.5 to 1 metre (18 in. to 3 ft.) or higher if possible and vigour allows; however, the leader will soon be lost, and multiple upright branching will start low down the trunk.

Early training consists mainly of removing any crossing branches originating at the start of the crown. Any branches that will potentially interfere and block the bark effect of the trunk should be removed at a later date but while they are still at secateurs size, as the tissue surrounding larger cuts made with a saw are prone to dieback. For the best effect, longer lateral branches should be left to form a graceful outer crown, although it will be difficult to produce a well-balanced crown shape.

Once established, trees in this section will

Acer palmatum full outline.

A young *Acer pensylvanicum* trained on a short trunk.

Acer rufinerve 'Erythrocladum' with the low branches forming the outer crown.

Acer saccharinum trained as a standard.

Acer rubrum in fall.

need minimum pruning and do not respond to hard pruning or renovation. Unfortunately all trees in this section are prone to coral spot (*Nectria cinnabarina*); any dead wood should be removed as soon as it is seen to prevent its spread.

The remainder of the species in this group (e.g., *Acer capillipes*, *A. caudatifolium*, *A. crataegifolium*, *A. grosseri*, *A. pectinatum*, *A. rufinerve*, *A. tegmentosum*, *A. tschonoskii*) are similar in habit and should be treated in the same way.

SECTION RUBRA

This group includes a hybrid, *Acer* ×*freemanii*, and two large-growing species, *A. rubrum* (red maple) and *A. saccharinum* (silver maple). The latter makes a large tree in the United Kingdom compared to *A. saccharum* (with which it is often confused) and has a more graceful, pendulous habit. It is, however, prone to scaffold and branch failure due to poor branch attachments, tends to produce cavities from old pruning wounds, and is susceptible to the bracket fungus *Ganoderma applanatum*, so pruning should be kept to a minimum and

the formal training carried out in the nursery. It should be grown as a standard with a clean trunk from 2 to 2.5 metres (6 to 8 ft.) so that the shaggy bark, one of the tree's attributes, is shown to its best effect. *Acer saccharinum* f. *laciniatum* has deeply cut foliage and should be treated the same as the type.

SECTION TRIFOLIATA

All the trees in this group are decurrent in form, and it is not possible to train a leader for long before the canopy naturally divides into a spreading tree.

Acer rubrum trained on a short trunk with multiple upright branching.

Acer griseum (paperbark maple) is the flagship of this section, making a tree to 6 metres (20 ft.). In addition to the general effect, the great attribute of this tree is the bark. This may be seen at its best when there is a definitive short trunk 1 to 1.2 metres (3 to 4 ft.) with a well-shaped head. The leader should be kept for as long as possible until the desired height of the head is formed. The branches, if allowed to grow freely without crowding or lack of light, produce an almost tiered effect.

Once the crown is formed, the upper branches will begin to shade out the lower ones, which will gradually die out. This dead wood can be removed back to the trunk, which will give an improved view of the beautiful bark. These small branches will be very hard, and the secateurs must be sharp to achieve a clean cut.

Acer maximowiczianum (Nikko maple) is a small to medium-sized tree normally trained on a 60 cm (2 ft.) trunk; the head quickly splits up into several ascending branches.

Acer mandshuricum is a small deciduous tree, sometimes a shrub, and is best trained to be multi-stemmed on a short leg.

SECTION NEGUNDO

Acer negundo (box elder) and its variegated forms grow quickly, with wide branches making a rounded tree 9 to 15 metres (30 to 50 ft.) high. Once the height of the tree has been made, the vigour is lost with the leader, and the tree becomes decurrent, all effort go-

Cleaning out the canopy of a young *Acer griseum*.

ing into the lateral branches, which become more spreading and heavy, creating an open crown. With the added light, epicormic shoots break out of the branches; and where pruning wounds have been made on the main scaffolds, strong, upright shoots develop, making a cluttered canopy. It may be necessary to thin some of these growths to reduce the weight carried by the branch framework and allow additional light to penetrate to crown. Both its variegated

selections, 'Variegatum' and 'Auratum', should be left to grow freely without pruning, for most of the buds that break out near a cut will revert to green foliage and the general effect of the tree will be lost.

Acer henryi and *A. cissifolium* should be grown on a short trunk and the crown allowed to develop and broaden naturally. Keep pruning to a minimum.

ACTINIDIA

Habit Strong deciduous climbers with twining stems for partial shade. **Attributes** Grown for their foliage and fruits, some of which are edible. **Reasons for pruning** To control size and vigour. **Pruning time** Winter for major pruning, summer to maintain size and shape.

In the wild, these vigorous climbers normally grow through trees. In cultivation they require an extensive support as they will twine around each other if there is nothing else to attach to, producing a dense, untidy thicket of growth. They are best grown against a wall and trained to cover the space allocated or on a tripod in a border. After planting, cut young plants back hard to about 30 cm (12 in.) above ground level. This encourages vigorous basal growth, from which six should be selected and trained to form a framework, tying them in as

they grow against the wall. Once the plant has established and covered the wall, any of the extension growths extending beyond their allocated space should be pruned back to keep them in check. Look over the plant several times through the growing period and take action if needed.

These shortened growths are then pruned back to two buds during the winter and any weak growth pruned out to the base of the plant. Occasionally it will be necessary to prune out some of the older wood and train and tie in younger growths as replacements.

Actinidia deliciosa (Chinese gooseberry) produces shorter growths or spurs on their older wood, and this system of pruning will encourage their development.

Another method is to use a tripod or tall

Actinidia arguta beautifully trained on a tripod.

pole for a support. The vigorous growths are left to arch downward once the desired height has been reached. Some of the older branches can be thinned each year during the winter; tie in the younger ones as replacements.

Actinidia kolomikta is a less vigorous species which if trained on a sunny wall will produce large leaves splashed with creamy pink and white. Pruning should be carried out in late winter: remove weak growth, retain five to seven strong growths, and reduce the laterals on these by two-thirds. The same pruning technique can be applied to *A. polygama*.

Actinidia arguta trained to a framework to cover a wall.

Actinidia kolomikta trained to cover a sunny wall.

AESCULUS

Habit Small to large upright deciduous trees with a rounded crown for fertile, free-draining soil and full sun. **Attributes** Large compound palmate leaves, large panicles of flowers in late spring/early summer, large chestnut-coloured fruits (conkers) in autumn. **Reasons for pruning** To develop a strong framework. **Pruning time** Between autumn and spring (when dormant).

These should be planted as a standard tree or a small feathered tree; a strong central leader should be encouraged for as long as possible so that the weight can be evenly spread over a number of well-positioned branches. It is important to know the ultimate height and spread of each species as there is so much variation across the genus and to select the right site with plenty of space before planting a tree in its permanent position.

Aesculus hippocastanum (horse-chestnut), the most common species, forms a very large tree with heavy branching. The mature scaffolds have a heavy downward sweep, some

A mature *Aesculus hippocastanum* with a well-balanced crown and a low skirt.

becoming long and pendulous. The permanent lowest scaffold should be identified as early as possible to prevent having to remove large branches later in the tree's life, leaving large wounds that never heal over and eventually decay. This early pruning will lead to a good, safe, long-lived tree.

Often when a large wound is made, a large number of growths are produced in the following spring from the cambium on the outer edge of the wound. This is one of the reasons why unnecessary pruning of established trees should be avoided, as these growths, even after selection by thinning, are not strong enough to replace any branches that have been lost. Their attachment to the tree is weak, as they have originated from surface tissues and are never directly connected to the heartwood of the parent branch or trunk. The other danger, in common with most trees, is that of the heartwood rotting before healing takes place; although the rate of healing is often rapid, the heartwood of this species quickly deteriorates.

Aesculus pavia (red buckeye) makes a small tree, but it is important to retain a short leader through the crown as the lateral branches are prone to damage in summer winds.

Aesculus ×carnea (red horse-chestnut), a hybrid between *A. hippocastanum* and *A. pavia*, is represented by the cultivars 'Briotii' and 'Plantierensis'. These are sold in the nursery as grafted specimens, probably as standards, and so any suckering growth from the base must be removed. This hybrid will produce a dense canopy, and with free unrestricted growth and full light the branching will develop closely down to ground level. There is a tendency for it to produce cavities and large burrs (corky cankerous growths) on the trunk, so a close watch must be kept on any old specimens. Where old branches have severe burrs and dead tissue, the branch should be removed to prevent failure in the future and tearing back into the trunk or parent branch.

Aesculus turbinata (Japanese horse-chestnut) tends to produce its branches from one point, and it is difficult to form a leader, with the head opening out as soon as branching occurs.

Aesculus californica (California buckeye) has the largest conker of the buckeyes, but it is a small tree, branching low and wide, with a vase-shaped crown to 5 metres (16 ft.). It is best grown on a short stem at 1 metre (3 ft.) high or as a multi-stemmed tree from ground level in a sheltered position. Pruning should be kept to a minimum, as heartwood rots very

Aesculus indica, removing damage and young feathers.

Aesculus indica after pruning.

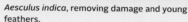

Aesculus indica young tree.

A mature *Aesculus parviflora* showing the extensive suckering clump made over several years.

quickly before callusing is complete and plenty of shoot growth is normally produced from the region of any cuts. In its natural habitat this tree can go into summer dormancy should moisture be insufficient, which makes it a suitable tree for droughty conditions.

Aesculus indica (Indian horse-chestnut) produces a well-shaped tree to 20 metres (65 ft.) high and wide, with cleanly defined branching; its selection 'Sydney Pearce' is grafted. It is best to plant a good standard tree, on a clean trunk to 1.5 metres (5 ft.), and retain the leader for as long as possible. The tree will soon become decurrent, however, and so it is important to identify the first permanent scaffold system as soon as possible and prune the trunk to that first branching. *Aesculus flava* (yellow buckeye) and *A. chinensis* (including var. *wilsonii*) should be treated in the same way.

Aesculus parviflora is more of a large shrub than a tree, as it rarely makes a single trunk and spreads by means of suckers at the base, making a wide-spreading clump 2.4 to 3 metres (8 to 10 ft.) high. There is no need for pruning unless the spread needs limiting. This should be done carefully to preserve low furnishings to the ground and flowering growth on the outer edge of the clump.

A young, well-grown *Aesculus turbinata*, standard specimen with even branching.

A large, shapely, mature *Aesculus hippocastanum* in flower.

AILANTHUS

Habit Large, very fast-growing upright deciduous excurrent trees for any soil in full sun. **Attributes** Large pinnate leaves and attractive red flowers; tolerates urban pollution but can be invasive. **Reasons for pruning** To develop a rong framework. **Pruning time** Between autumn and spring (when dormant).

In some countries *Ailanthus altissima* (tree of heaven) is considered to be an invasive species, and care must be taken to prevent it from entering into natural areas. This tree should be planted out at a young age as a standard tree but will rarely produce lateral branching until it starts to put on trunk increment. When it does produce the early lateral branches, they are naturally shaded out by the vigour of the growth and fall off on their own. It grows extremely fast in its early years and cannot be tamed by pruning, so needs space and is best planted in the open. Any pruning necessary will be to maintain shape or form and should be carried out as early as possible, preferably with secateurs so that the wounds heal quickly, as the young growth has a pith and the older wood is very soft and decay could set into large wounds. Ailanthus is also prone to developing new growth at the point of pruning; new growth can either be left to be further trained to shape or removed as soon as possible.

Ailanthus altissima can be grown for the tropical foliage effect, which it produces if annual or biennial coppicing to ground level is carried out. By planting in a group or bed at 0.6 to 1 metre (2 to 3 ft.) apart and by feeding and watering if necessary, strong growths 1 to 2 metres (3 to 6 ft.) in height are sent up annually.

Ailanthus vilmoriniana is similar, but the lateral branches are more upright and a careful watch should be kept on branch attachments, ensuring that branches with very tight crotches are removed early in the tree's life.

The upright form of a semi-mature
Ailanthus altissima.

AKEBIA

Habit Slender, semi-evergreen climbing plant with twining stems for fertile soil and full or partial shade. **Attributes** Attractive foliage, red-purple flowers, sausage-shaped fruits. **Rea**sons for pruning To control size and vigour. **Pruning time** Winter.

Both *Akebia quinata* and *A. trifoliata* are suitable for covering old stumps or trees in the wilder parts of the garden where little training is needed, but after time the whole plant will become an untidy mass of dead and living stems and will be very difficult to control in

any sort of fashion. In some countries these are considered invasive, and care must be taken to prevent their entering into natural areas.

If the plant is grown on a pergola or post, it must be tied in or it will easily slip down and form a mass of growths at the base of the supports. When grown against a wall, the stems should be trained to grow behind a system of wires, stretched approximately 10 cm (4 in.) off the face of the wall, the top wire positioned 0.3 to 0.5 metre (1 to 1.5 ft.) below the top of the wall. The growth will then arch over the top wire, forming a pendulous effect. The only pruning necessary is to cut out the weaker and dead growths during the winter. Following a cold winter, some dead tips may need to be pruned back.

Akebia quinata trained on wires against the wall of a large building between two windows.

ALBIZIA

Habit Small deciduous fast-growing but short-lived decurrent tree, vase-shaped, wide-spreading, and flat-topped, for free-draining soil and full sun. **Attributes** Delicate bipinnate foliage, pink flowers in late summer. **Reasons for pruning** To develop a strong framework. **Pruning time** Spring.

Albizia julibrissin is the only hardy species; it can be semi-deciduous in warmer areas and will need some wall protection in colder areas.

This plant needs a warm summer to ripen the new wood. If this fails to happen, the plant will succumb to frost damage and will fail to flower. It should be trained on a stem until the leader is lost, which will be quite early in the tree's life as branching begins and a crown begins to form. In the right, warm conditions it has a fast rate of growth, and some pruning to restrict it should be carried out in spring, pruning the previous year's growth back to five

or six buds. It may be necessary to encourage further branching on the trunk by restricting the top, as the stem can quickly become bare as growth is concentrated more and more at the top of the plant.

The more hardy *Albizia julibrissin* f. *rosea* will be less susceptible to frost damage and produce more flowers.

ALNUS

Habit Deciduous large shrubs or excurrent trees with a pyramidal form for full sun in wet situations. **Attributes** Riverine, tolerant of growing in any moist soil except chalk and a tough, fast-growing tree in urban situa-

tions; male flowers are in the form of catkins in late winter followed by woody cone-like fruits. **Reasons for pruning** To develop a strong framework. **Pruning time** Between autumn and spring (when dormant).

The tree alders (e.g., *Alnus cordata*, *A. glutinosa*, *A. hirsuta*, *A. nitida*, *A. orientalis*, *A. rubra*, *A. subcordata*) are strong growers that naturally produce and maintain a strong leader and so develop straight trunks with

Alnus glutinosa growing in its natural habitat, showing its pyramidal crown.

A young *Alnus glutinosa* with the lower feathers removed with secateurs.

well-spaced branches. They tend to be pyramidal and are best grown as a feathered tree in the nursery that can be crown lifted to the desired height. If a tree alder is planted as a feathered tree, remove the lower branches as early as possible following planting with secateurs to the height required. All are well-behaved trees, retaining their leader and producing a well-balanced crown with little intervention.

Alnus glutinosa 'Imperialis', a thin grower with delicate branching and finely cut foliage, needs little if any pruning; 'Pyramidalis' is narrowly upright, without any pruning.

Mature trees need very little pruning except for the occasional need to remove low branches and dead wood but will respond well to hard pruning to the ground if needed. The regrowth from the remaining stump will produce lots of vigorous regrowth, which can be thinned out to form a new multi-stemmed specimen.

Alnus glutinosa in leaf.

The smaller tree alders or shrubs will naturally want to grow with multiple leaders and bushy growth in the nursery, and this is best left rather than trying to train to a single leader. *Alnus japonica*, *A. incana*, *A. maritima*, and *A. viridis* have a tendency to branch from ground level with rival leaders, especially in exposed conditions, and are best grown naturally in this habit at the expense of height. *Alnus firma* retains a leader, develops a long graceful branch system, and casts a light shade. *Alnus maximowiczii* makes a small tree as opposed to a shrub, but as the lower branches begin to thicken, the leader slows down. *Alnus tenuifolia* is a dense grower and is difficult to retain its central leader beyond 2.5 metres (8 ft.), so should be encouraged to grow as a multi-stemmed tree. *Alnus pendula* is a broad-spreading tree with a low crown.

Alnus pendula showing low, wide crown.

AMELANCHIER

Habit Deciduous shrubs or small trees, some naturally multi-stemmed, for moist, free-draining soil in full sun or light shade. **Attributes** Racemes of small white flowers in spring, good autumn colour. **Reasons for pruning** To encourage new growth and develop flowers. **Pruning time** Between autumn and spring (when dormant).

Two distinct forms of growth are found in this genus: plants that sucker and plants that don't sucker. Generally the suckerous species (e.g., *Amelanchier canadensis*, *A. humilis*, *A. spicata*) are thicket-forming, varying in height and require no routine pruning. Thin the crowded stems in winter to renovate tired and neglected specimens.

The non-suckerous species can either be single-stemmed or multi-stemmed, depending on the initial nursery training. With a feathered tree it is possible to start the lower branching close to the ground, which looks far more natural and attractive in this group than those grown on a high trunk; the branch system will not be regularly spaced but each and every tree will have a different character, unlike those

Amelanchier canadensis in flower.

stereotyped standards. Naturally these species will develop the leader into small trees or large shrubs, but once the head has been formed, the leader will break up and the crown will become more rounded. The small tree species (e.g., *Amelanchier sanguinea, A. ×grandiflora*) will readily produce strong shoots off the main stem. If a clean stem is required, these must be rubbed off as they appear; alternatively, they can be left and trained to alter the shape of the tree. *Amelanchier laevis* and *A. lamarckii* will make small multi-stemmed trees. *Amelanchier asiatica* and *A. alnifolia* (including var. *semiintegrifolia*) are shrubby and form one or several stems.

Close-up of base, showing multi-stemmed habit from suckering.

Amelanchier intermedia grown on a single stem.

AMPELOPSIS

Habit Vigorous deciduous woody-stemmed climbers with coiling stem tendrils for full sun or light shade. **Attributes** Attractive berries in late autumn/early winter. **Reasons for pruning** To control size and vigour. **Pruning time** Early winter.

Ampelopsis brevipedunculata and *A. megalophylla* are suitable for growing over trees, garden sheds, walls, and fences. For that reason they are better planted in the wilder part of the garden where they can ramble at will and being untidy in appearance isn't a problem to the eye, as training and pruning in these conditions is difficult, unnecessary, and undesirable unless the vigorous growth goes beyond their allocated position. To grow these in a controlled fashion, two or three permanent rods can be tied into a post or trellis and pruned back annually. Allow spur growths, which are twisted and knotted in appearance, to be produced; the young growths from these points are then pruned back to the lowest bud in early winter as they will bleed if pruned too late in the winter.

Ampelopsis brevipedunculata 'Elegans' has white-variegated leaves and is not as vigorous as the species, requiring less pruning, so is better suited to the smaller garden; *A. brevipedunculata* var. *maximowiczii* has attractive deeply cut foliage.

ARALIA

Habit Spiny, suckering deciduous multi-stemmed shrubs for moist, free-draining soil in full sun or light shade. **Attributes** Large pinnate leaves, creamy white panicles of flowers in late summer followed by large clusters of black berries. **Reasons for pruning** To reduce the height of the shrub and remove tired old woody growth. **Pruning time** Between autumn and spring (when dormant).

Personal protection These shrubs are not the most pleasant to prune. You must always wear good thorn-proof, long-sleeved clothing and gloves, as all *Aralia* species are armed with sharp spines. Use long-handled loppers to remove old growths in the centre of the shrub.

Aralia bipinnata and *A. elata* are usually the largest woody growers of this genus, and if they are planted in the right conditions (light well-drained rich soil), they will extend their branch system to become a large shrub and will need plenty of space. When pruning these species it is important to preserve the old wood and create an attractive, twisted framework, keeping it as natural as possible. Occasionally it will be necessary to prune out some of the older wood as it begins to die back and produce mini-cavities in the branching unions. As they grow older, these shrubs will continue to extend their lower branches outward for light; and with the weight of the large panicles of white flowers on the tips of the branches and the large leaves, they may be prone to collapse, so it is important to carry out pruning to avoid this or some form of prop will be needed as a support. Unless a larger clump of these species is wanted, suckers should be removed.

Aralia elata 'Aureovariegata' and *A. elata* 'Variegata' are propagated onto rootstocks of the species, so any suckers will not be variegated and should be removed as soon as possible.

Aralia chinensis and *A. spinosa* are similar to *A. elata* but do not grow as large. They have more upright stems and will not branch as freely, but they do sucker freely.

ARAUCARIA

Habit Large evergreen excurrent trees with symmetrical crown for moist, free-draining soil in full sun. **Attributes** Grown for botanical interest and as an individual specimen tree. **Reasons for pruning** To maintain a leader for a uniform shape. **Pruning time** When needed.

Araucaria heterophylla shape overall.

Araucaria araucana medium-aged tree, feathered to ground.

Araucaria araucana mature tree with a clean trunk.

Personal protection Wear good thorn-proof clothing and gloves when going anywhere near a monkey puzzle.

Buy your young *Araucaria araucana* or *A. heterophylla* from the nursery grown in a container to encourage a strong root system, remove crossing branches, and encourage the lower branches to start low to the ground.

Araucaria araucana in particular must be grown as an isolated, symmetrical specimen if it is to be seen at its best. The lower skirt should be retained as long as possible and allowed to sweep down naturally and gracefully to meet the ground. The tree will naturally retain the leader until the ultimate height has been reached; however, should the central growth be damaged or removed for any reason, a number of adventitious buds will be produced on the central stem and forced to grow into several new apical dominant leaders, one of which will naturally take on the lead and extend the central trunk. The branches retain their character and will never assume the role of leading shoots, even if the adventitious buds fail to appear.

These trees will appear very ragged and untidy if dead branches and dead wood are left intact. Any tree work to remove these is rewarding, leaving an exposed, clean trunk to the lowest whorl of lateral branching. The dieback of the branches is progressive, starting at the tips; it is best to remove the whole branch back to the main trunk rather than reducing it in length. This is probably one of the most difficult and unpleasant jobs in the pruning calendar and should be avoided at all cost.

Araucaria araucana young tree.

ARBUTUS

Habit Evergreen shrubs to medium-sized trees for acid, free-draining soil and light shade to full sun. **Attributes** Shiny foliage, wonderful reddish peeling bark, white or pink ericaceous flowers followed by strawberry-like fruits. **Reasons for pruning** To develop a trunk for bark effect. **Pruning time** Spring.

Arbutus species should be given shelter and acidic conditions. They can be left to grow freely; formative pruning is not needed. In the nursery they are best grown in containers rather than in the field so the check in growth is minimised when planted into their permanent position. Provided that care is given to the soil conditions and adequate watering is available, *A. unedo* can make a very good container shrub.

After planting, *Arbutus andrachne, A. ×andrachnoides,* and *A. unedo* (including f. *rubra*) should be left to grow freely and no attempt made to develop a leader or to form a trunk. No two trees will look the same; each will have its own individual character. As the leading growth develops, the laterals are shaded out. Remove these as soon as possible to reveal the trunk, as the bark is one of the most attractive attributes of this plant.

Most species are spreading trees when mature, their low branches having a low wide-spreading angle of growth as they are weighed down by extension growth and leaf mass. They will regenerate freely if cut back hard provided that the root condition is in good health; it may be necessary to do this following a storm as they are prone to storm

Arbutus unedo grown in a container.

The champion *Arbutus menziesii* in Port Angeles, Washington, showing the ultimate size that this tree can make with space. The trunk loses the attractive bark effect with age and size.

damage or snow damage. Do not prune until after new growth starts to break.

Arbutus unedo 'Elfin King' is a bushy form and makes a medium-sized shrub to 3 metres (10 ft.).

Arbutus menziesii (Pacific madrone) is a difficult subject to transplant and grow outside of its natural range, but should, if possible, be trained with a definite trunk to show off the eucalyptus-like reddish bark. It will need an acid, free-draining soil and some shelter.

Arbutus menziesii and the beautiful bark we are showing off by removing the lower branches.

The form and habit of a young *Arbutus andrachne*.

ARCTOSTAPHYLOS

Habit Prostrate evergreen shrubs or small trees for a well-drained, acid soil. **Attributes** Reddish brown peeling bark, pink or white bell-shaped flowers, drought-tolerant. **Reasons for pruning** To restrict spread and remove dead wood. **Pruning time** Summer after flowering.

Arctostaphylos uva-ursi is a prostrate plant, forming a mass of growth and foliage that make it an ideal groundcover. It requires very little pruning except for the occasional trim along the edge of a border to restrict the spread. This should be done by pruning out individual growths with secateurs to avoid a hard-line edge.

If training is started early following planting, *Arctostaphylos* species can be trained against a wall to show off the peeling bark to best effect.

Arctostaphylos manzanita grows to a height of 1.2 to 2.4 metres (4 to 8 ft.) and needs a sunny, sheltered position. It requires no pruning and should be left to grow freely and naturally on a short leg with low branching. Good growth should be encouraged, for if this subject becomes unhealthy it will die back very quickly.

Arctostaphylos uva-ursi wall-trained.

ARGYROCYTISUS

Habit Strong-growing woody shrub for free-draining soil and full sun. **Attributes** Silver-grey leaves, yellow flowers. **Reasons for pruning** To maintain shape and encourage flowering. **Pruning time** Summer after flowering.

Argyrocytisus battandieri (pineapple broom) is usually grown in the shelter of a sunny wall but can be successfully grown as a standing shrub in the open. If it is grown against a wall, it is self-supporting, and no training or tying in is necessary. Normally it produces strong upright growths from the base, which can reach 1 to 2 metres (3 to 6 ft.) in one growing season. These can be used to replace any very old non-flowering wood or old growths that were removed as they started to lean out, making the shrub unbalanced.

Argyrocytisus battandieri grown as a freestanding shrub.

ARISTOLOCHIA

Habit Vigorous deciduous and evergreen climbers, with stems that twine strongly in an anti-clockwise direction, for free-draining soil in partial shade to full sun. **Attributes** Unusual meerschaum-pipe-like flowers with a foul smell. **Reasons for pruning** To control size and vigour. **Pruning time** Spring as the buds begin to break.

A large deciduous tree makes a good support for *Aristolochia macrophylla* or *A. manshuriensis*. When wall-trained, more regular pruning to keep the plant in control will certainly be necessary. Pruning consists of cutting out any dead, weak, or straggly growths as the buds start to break in spring, but it is not possible to retain a tidy habit; only hard pruning

back to the base will encourage new growth, which can be retrained if necessary. Leaf pruning may be needed to better display the flowers in summer.

Aristolochia sempervirens is evergreen and in a cold winter can be cut to the ground. If left, new growth will appear the following spring.

Aristolochia manshuriensis trained against a wall.

ARISTOTELIA

Habit Evergreen shrub for free-draining, acid soil in full sun with shelter in exposed gardens. **Attributes** Tough foliage on long, whippy growths, small cream flowers followed by small black edible fruits, tolerant of hard pruning. **Reasons for pruning** To restrict size. **Pruning time** Spring and late summer.

Aristotelia chilensis (macqui), native to Chile,

normally needs wall protection, but it can be grown as a freestanding shrub in the open in a relatively mild area. The main branches are strong and upright, while the laterals growing from these are more spreading. This shrub should be grown as a bush and planted 0.3 metre (1 ft.) away from the base of the wall. Pruning to restrict size should be carried out

in spring and again in late summer if further shortening back is required. The pruning cuts should be made into the bush to keep an informal surface. Occasionally, strong, long growths are produced from inside the crown of the shrub; these may become top-heavy with growth after a year or so and should be corrected at an early age.

ARONIA

Habit Small to medium-sized deciduous sun-loving shrubs, intolerant of thin chalky soil. **Attributes** White flowers in spring followed by red or black fruits and brilliant autumn colour. **Reasons for pruning** To encourage new growth and flowers. **Pruning time** Mid-winter following the displays of autumn leaf colour and fruit.

Both *Aronia arbutifolia* (red chokeberry) and *A. melanocarpa* (black chokeberry) have a spreading and arching habit that should be retained when pruning. Prune out only older, weaker branches, as close to the base of the plant as possible. They will be replaced by the good supply of strong wood that healthy plants routinely send up from the base.

ASIMINA

Habit Slow-growing upright deciduous shrub or small tree with a round crown for moist, free-draining soil and full sun. **Attributes** Large drooping leaves with a tropical look and showy, waxy black fruits. **Reasons for pruning** To remove suckers. **Pruning time** Spring.

Personal protection The leaves and fruit can cause dermatitis with sensitive skin and the seed can be poisonous, so gloves should be worn when handling the arisings and care should be taken disposing of the waste pruning material.

Asimina triloba dislikes being transplanted, as it produces a tap root, so is best planted as a young, small container-grown plant in rich, moist, free-draining soil in full sun. It can be grown with a single trunk or as a multi-stemmed specimen furnished to the ground. The edible fruits will ripen only during hot summers. Regular pruning is not required; the only pruning is to remove suckers, which are freely produced, or it will quickly regenerate.

AUCUBA

Habit Large dense dome-shaped evergreen shrub for moist soils in full sun to partial shade. **Attributes** Glossy (often variegated) foliage, shiny, pointed red fruits on female clones. **Reasons for pruning** To maintain size and remove dieback. **Pruning time** Early spring.

Aucuba japonica is often grown as a border plant to provide a background to a planting or to fill an awkward gap, usually in the shade; it is therefore desirable to have a plant as large and free-growing as possible, and seldom is pruning required. During very dry periods there may be some dieback, which needs pruning out for appearance's sake, and this can be done at any time of the year.

The minor branches extend year on year, and a vigorous plant can throw up cane-like shoots from the base annually. These reach the height of the plant before branching begins. Any form of pruning to shape should be done to leave an informal effect; this is best done using sharp secateurs rather than hedging shears, as the latter tends to cut the large, glossy leaves (which will blacken) rather than the branches, leaving an unnatural finish and unsightly damaged leaves. Prune back to main growths or just above healthy buds behind the layer of foliage. This shrub does respond to hard pruning should there be a need to maintain a compact size, although this is best done in stages over a period of two to three years.

Aucuba omeiensis is slow to establish; but should it become too large once settled, it too can be pruned back hard in early spring.

Aucuba japonica clipped to maintain a formal shape.

AZARA

Habit Evergreen shrubs or small trees. **Attributes** Fine leaves and golden yellow flowers, which smell of chocolate. **Reasons for pruning** To restrict growth and to develop and train a strong framework. **Pruning time** Late spring after flowering.

Most *Azara* species are similar in that they are bushy and will form a strong framework of branches. They will also respond to light careful pruning to restrict their growth, while retaining a pleasant evergreen surface to the plant. All can be grown against a south-facing wall and six to eight of the main branches trained fanwise. Laterals will develop, and these are used to furnish the front of the shrub; some light selective pruning can be carried out to restrict the size of the plant.

Alternatively the shrub can be planted away from the base of a wall and allowed to grow naturally as a bush. *Azara lanceolata* makes a good plant for this situation as it produces long slender branches from the base, which will furnish it from top to bottom. *Azara petiolaris*, one of the largest of the species, is another good plant to be grown in this way, developing into a very dense bush or small tree.

Azara microphylla can be grown to stand alone in the open, where with some shelter it will form a shrub or small tree 6 to 9 metres (20 to 30 ft.) in height. The lower branches should be left and allowed to grow from the base naturally.

BAMBOOS

Habit Dwarf to large evergreen grasses made up of woody canes. **Attributes** Ornamental coloured canes and green foliage that rustles appealingly in the wind. **Reasons for pruning** To thin out and remove weak, damaged stems to expose healthy canes. **Pruning time** Early spring.

TALL, OPEN, RUNNING BAMBOOS

All the bamboos in this group (e.g., *Pleioblastus linearis*, *P. simonii*, *Phyllostachys aurea*, *P. nuda*, *P. viridiglaucescens*, *Semiarundinaria fastuosa*) can be thinned out: their rigid wind-resistant canes make them less likely to fall over after being thinned. Thinning of bamboo canes in large established stands can be done to increase the diameter and height of individual canes (depending upon climate and temperatures) and to expose the attractive canes. Make sure each cane is given enough space to increase the amount of rainfall and light the new shoots and canes receive. The best time to thin the canes is in early spring, when the season for snowfall is coming to an end and sunshine is starting to warm the soil.

Remove dead and damaged canes from old stands that have become overcrowded to encourage new growth. Thin out up to 40% of the total number of canes to allow light and space for the new shoots/canes to develop.

You do not want them to become overcrowded and compete with the established canes. When completely removing canes, ensure they are cut back as near to soil level as possible, as this will help create more space for the new shoots to develop and keep the stand looking clean and tidy. It also discourages pests and diseases from living at the base of the bamboo, reducing the potential for fungal infection of the stand.

CLUMP-FORMING BAMBOOS

Thinning of this group of bamboos (e.g., *Fargesia murielae*, *F. nitida*, *Thamnocalamus spathiflorus*, *Yushania anceps*) should not be undertaken unless it is confined to removing a few

Thinning out the canes of *Phyllostachys aurea*.

canes on the edge of the clump. They have a rhizome that produces canes that are close together in a clump and can easily be distinguished from the open, running bamboos. If you were to remove too many canes from a clump-forming bamboo, the remaining canes would soon collapse and fall to the ground, as the canes are not rigid enough to stand alone. In nearly all situations, it would be unwise to thin out any canes from this group of bamboos.

HERBACEOUS BAMBOOS

Pleioblastus auriocomus, *P. chino*, and *P. variegatus* can be cut to ground level annually or biennially with a pair of shears, to encourage the healthy new coloured growths. It is not necessary to cut back *Sasa* species unless the canes and leaves become untidy and tired; they should be left for at least three years to recover following cutting back.

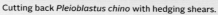
Cutting back *Pleioblastus chino* with hedging shears.

BERBERIDOPSIS

Berberidopsis corallina with congested twining stems and flowers in late summer.

Habit Evergreen climbing shrub with twining stems for an acid or neutral soil against a cool, shady wall and trained up wires or bamboo canes. **Attributes** Deep crimson flowers. **Reasons for pruning** To thin out the framework and remove weak stems. **Pruning time** Spring.

It is seldom necessary to prune or train *Berberidopsis corallina*, as it will naturally climb and twine. Occasionally there may be a need to thin out the main framework (and in this case the older weaker stems should be carefully removed), but the backdrop of fresh foliage sets off the bright red flowers in late summer.

BERBERIS

Habit Dwarf to large thorny shrubs, evergreen, semi-evergreen, or deciduous, for any free-draining soil. **Attributes** Yellow to orange flowers, showy fruits, and good autumn colour from the deciduous species. Evergreen species, with their thorny nature, are often selected for hedges or barriers. **Reasons for pruning** To maintain a healthy shrub and encourage new growth.

Personal protection Wear good thorn-proof clothing and gloves, as every species of barberry is armed with needle-like thorns. Use long-handled loppers to remove old growths in the centre of the shrub.

DECIDUOUS SPECIES

Pruning time Late spring to early summer immediately after flowering. A bonus: pruning during the growing season makes it easier to distinguish living from dead branches. Flower buds are produced the year before flowering, so it is important to give the plant as much time as possible to produce these. If the shrubs are pruned too late into the summer, there will not be enough time for the plant to do this.

With most of the deciduous species (e.g., *Berberis thunbergii*, *B. dictophylla*, *B. wilsoniae*, *B. vulgaris*, *B.* ×*ottawensis*, *B. sieboldii*), prune back the flowering stems by approximately one-third of the length into the shrub after flowering. Where there are ineffective thin stems and old stems that are starting to lose their vigour, these can be thinned out and removed to ground level, to encourage stronger, new growth from the base.

Some of the deciduous barberries (e.g., *Berberis chitria*) produce an attractive overall wide-spreading, arching effect, and this may be spoiled by any form of pruning, so it is better to position them in a place with plenty of room to avoid having to restrict their growth; however, they will begin to lose the lower growths.

Once any deciduous barberry becomes

Berberis thunbergii showing upright habit.

Berberis darwinii in flower.

unfurnished from the base and begins to lose its shape, it can be hard pruned to within 30 cm (12 in.) of ground level during the winter, allowing it to start again, but good aftercare must follow, to ensure the plant has sufficient moisture and nutrients to generate the new growth.

For the cultivars grown for their colourful foliage (e.g., *Berberis thunbergii* f. *atropurpurea* 'Aurea'), some of the older stems can be pruned out to allow light into the centre of the plant and to make room for the new stems. Occasionally a hard prune to just above ground level can be done once the colour effect begins to deteriorate; vigorous regrowth will be made, and the leaf colours will be regenerated and more vibrant on the fresh stems.

Berberis temolaica and several cultivars of *B. thunbergii* f. *atropurpurea* (e.g., 'Helmond Pillar', 'Red Pillar') have an upright habit. These require very little pruning except for the removal of any straggly stems growing out of and spoiling the upright habit.

EVERGREEN SPECIES

Pruning time Late spring to early summer following flowering.

Evergreen species include *Berberis gagnepainii*, *B.* ×*media*, *B. julianae*, *B.* ×*lologensis*, *B. candidula*, and *B. buxifolia*. Specimen plants in a border will require minimal pruning or training; however, it may be necessary to tidy up the plant from time to time or keep it to an acceptable size should it overgrow its situation.

First of all prune out any diseased, dead, or damaged wood and thin out any old or overcrowded shoots that are interfering with the growth. As with the deciduous species it is possible to completely renovate the plant by hard pruning back to 30 cm (12 in.) from the ground. Plants that have undergone this level of pruning must be followed up with an organic mulch and feeding and irrigation during dry periods.

Some evergreen species (e.g., *Berberis* ×*stenophylla*, *B. darwinii*) are often used for informal hedges with added flowering effect. Any arching growths can be pruned back after flowering to a suitable developing shoot to retain the general shape.

Berberis valdiviana should be allowed to grow to its natural shape and form and requires little or no pruning.

BETULA

Habit Small to medium-sized deciduous excurrent trees for moist, free-draining soil in full sun. **Attributes** Ornamental bark, graceful shape, autumn colour, catkins. **Reasons for pruning** To develop a strong framework. **Pruning time** Summer through winter (when dormant), especially in areas threatened by bronze birch borer (*Agrilus anxius*), to reduce the risk of infestation. Never prune in spring as the wounds are prone to bleeding.

Birches are well behaved and require little training or pruning. Any pruning is usually done to maintain the central leader and to remove the lower branches to expose the bark on the trunks. Carry this out within the first two to three years of the tree's life, and use secateurs rather than a saw, so that wounds heal as quickly as possible and leave no signs of scarring, which would obscure the lovely bark effect.

The tree birches, such as *Betula pendula* (silver birch), *B. papyrifera* (paper birch), *B. maximowicziana* (monarch birch), and *B. lu-minifera*, are normally grown in the nursery as feathered trees with a strong central leader, and it is important to retain this growing point for as long as possible until the required height is reached. They can be grown as a feathered tree with the lower branches retained or as a standard tree with the lower lateral branches removed back to the trunk to the desired height. They should be planted out as young specimens into well-prepared ground with full all-round light to develop a balanced crown and given irrigation during their early years to encourage a good start in life.

For all the tree birches, remove crossing branches; dead, diseased, and damaged branches; twin leaders; and feathers to make a standard tree, or retain the feathers if a lower skirt is preferred. If a leader is lost, the strongest growths will develop from lower down the stem into the main branch system. Once

A mature *Betula pendula* showing the graceful habit.

A mature *Betula papyrifera*.

Pruning to remove the lower feathers on a *Betula albosinensis* grown as a standard, before, during, and after.

formed, the new leader should be selected from these stronger growths, thinning out the others to leave the strongest or most desirable to take on the new role.

Some species like *Betula davurica* (Dahurian birch), *B. nigra* (river birch), and *B. albosinensis* (Chinese red-barked birch) are prone to producing small twiggy growth off the main branches, which is quickly shaded out by the canopy and dies. This dead wood can be removed easily to keep an open crown and reduce the potential of coral spot (*Nectria cinnabarina*) infecting the rest of the tree.

Birches will not tolerate a hard prune, so it is important to plant the right species in the right space so that hard pruning of a mature tree is not necessary.

They are often grown as multi-stemmed specimens to get maximum effect from the bark on the trunks, particularly the good forms with ornamental bark. In North America, where the bronze birch borer is present, growing multiple stems allows for infested dying trunks to be removed while still retaining the tree. Do not prune from May through August, as this is the flight period of the adult and fresh pruning wounds attracts the female insects, which can lead to more branch dieback and irreparable damage; pruning is best carried out during fall or winter.

Many birch cultivars and varieties are grafted onto a rootstock in the nursery and trained to a form, either on a single stem or as a multistem. The correctly trained form should be selected for planting, as it is difficult to change

A multi-stemmed *Betula albosinensis*.

the form once established without spoiling and causing serious detrimental health to the tree.

It is important to remove any suckers found growing from the rootstock as early as possible, with secateurs or by rubbing off new growth, as these will come true to the rootstock, not the cultivar, and can be more vigorous than the cultivar, eventually taking over, weakening the top and not showing the attributes of the tree.

Where weeping birches (e.g., *Betula pendula* 'Tristis', *B. ermanii* 'Pendula') are grown from

A mature *Betula utilis* var. *jacquemontii* 'Grayswood Ghost'.

a basal graft, they can be trained up a cane or small stake to the desired height. Once the soft new growth has hardened off, the trunk will support the weeping head.

BIGNONIA

Habit Evergreen climber with leaf tendrils for free-draining soil in full sun or shade. **Attributes** Orange trumpet-shaped flowers in late spring. **Reasons for pruning** To maintain vigour and encourage regular flowering. **Pruning time** Spring and summer.

In the milder parts of the country, *Bignonia capreolata* is best grown against a wall where the growths can be evenly spaced and tied onto a wire system, even though its leaf tendrils are a climbing aid. In spring, reduce the laterals produced from this main framework back to a third of their length. Completely remove weaker growths in summer as the new shoots are produced; this allows air and sunlight into the vine, which encourages ripening of the strong, young wood and hence flowering the following year. A good flowering cultivar is *B. capreolata* 'Tangerine Beauty'.

BILLARDIERA

Habit Deciduous climber with twining stems for fertile, well-drained soil in a sheltered sunny or shady position. **Attributes** Yellow bell-shaped flowers, purple fruit. **Reasons for pruning** To remove dead and weak stems. **Pruning time** Spring.

Personal protection The leaves contain saponins, which are poisonous to fish, so site this plant away from water and ensure that none of the arisings fall into the fish pond.

Billardiera longiflora (purple appleberry) is a tender plant and will need to be grown in a sheltered position in the garden or in a conservatory for protection. It climbs by means of slender twining stems, so vertical wires are needed against a wall. Little pruning is required, but dead stems and weak growths may be pruned out in the spring; the latter should be pruned back to two or three buds from the main stem.

BRACHYGLOTTIS

Habit Evergreen dome-forming shrub for well-drained soil and a sunny aspect. **Attributes** Hairy grey foliage, white and yellow daisy-like flowers, suitable for coastal planting. **Reasons for pruning** To maintain size and encourage flowering. **Pruning time** Mid-spring following the late frosts as the flowers are produced in summer in terminal clusters on the previous season's growth. Some minimal pruning may also be required in summer to tidy up the plant.

This genus is from New Zealand and Tasmania, so plants grow best in full sun and will struggle in the colder regions. They are also very happy in coastal regions, where the growth is more compact and typically little pruning is needed.

Most species (e.g., *Brachyglottis greyi*, *B. hectori*, *B. laxifolia*, *B. elaeagnifolia*, *B. monroi*) benefit from a hard pruning every four to five years, just as the new growth is about to appear. If the shrub is healthy and vigorous, new growth will break out freely. This will also occur if a hard pruning is given by cutting away wood that has been severely damaged during a cold winter. A little careful pruning carried out each spring will reduce the need for this form of periodic drastic pruning. Left unpruned, these shrubs often become heavy with extension shoot development. Heavy snow will also weigh the branches down and break them near the main plant; these must be pruned out.

Brachyglottis 'Sunshine' and the other Dunedin Hybrids should be hard pruned back to old wood to renovate old plants in spring and clipped to shape in summer to maintain a healthy free-flowering plant. When shrubs go beyond renovation, remove them and replace with young plants.

BROUSSONETIA

Habit Deciduous decurrent shrubs or small trees with low, wide-spreading crown for free-draining soil and full sun. **Attributes** Autumn colour, unusual fruits and leaves. **Reasons for pruning** To develop a strong framework. **Pruning time** Autumn through early winter (when dormant). Never prune in spring as the wounds are prone to bleeding a white latex sap.

Personal protection Paper mulberries produce a milky sap that can irritate human skin; wear latex or rubber gloves when pruning.

Paper mulberries (*Broussonetia papyrifera*, *B. kazinoki*) are fast growing when young and prone to frost damage on the soft fleshy growth, so losing the leader very early in life. The wood is very soft and liable to decay, so any necessary pruning should be carried out as early in the tree's life as possible to avoid large pruning wounds. Remove crossing branches and encourage the lower branches to start as low to the ground as possible. It is possible to coppice to ground level, especially when there has been a failure of a multi-stemmed specimen. If another tree is required from this regrowth, the resulting shoots will need to be selectively thinned in order to form a new, well-branched tree and to prevent tight crotches at the branch unions, which will be a potential weakness in later life.

Broussonetia papyrifera showing tight forks, which are very weakly attached and will ultimately break apart with snow or strong winds.

BUDDLEJA

Habit Deciduous shrubs requiring a sunny position and free-draining soil. **Attributes** Summer flowers that attract butterflies. **Reasons for pruning** To encourage flowering.

The growth and flowering habits of the plants in this genus may be classified into three types to help with pruning:

- Group 1. Plants that flower terminally on the current season's wood.
- Group 2. Plants that flower on the previous season's wood.
- Group 3. Plants that grow out in the spring, to flower from large terminal buds or growths that develop on strong wood made in the previous year.

GROUP 1

Pruning time Late winter to spring, after all danger of late frosts has passed.

If these plants (e.g., *Buddleja davidii*, *B. crispa*, *B. forrestii*, *B. nivea*, *B. salviifolia*) are left unpruned, they will develop into large spreading bushes with lots of dead wood and very little flowers of any quality; the framework will break up and eventually collapse and die. They should be hard pruned each year either to the ground or to a framework of a few of the main branches, 1 to 1.2 metres (3 to 4 ft.) high, depending on the vigour of the shrub. This framework can be made by selective pruning during the first three years after planting.

Buddleja davidii in flower.

Once the framework is made, the bush will produce vigorous shoots to 2.5 metres (8 ft.) high from the old wood. In the early years if it grows too vigorously and the regrowth grows too tall, it may be necessary to stop the growth at a selected height to form a bushier habit.

Occasionally, depending on the vigour of the shrub, the framework will have to be remade by pruning behind the old, original pruning cuts as rot will set in and the shrub will begin to break up under the weight of the top growth. This is best and easily done with a modern sharp pruning saw rather than loppers, as loppers tend to crush or tear the final cuts, which will encourage dieback.

To prevent self-seeding and save the plant's energy, the old flower heads can be removed once flowering has finished. During a long summer this can promote a second flush of flowers.

Buddleja crispa can be grown as a tree with a trunk and higher branch system in a sheltered position to show off the grey fissured bark or as a wall-trained shrub. Once a framework is produced, the young shoots should be pruned back to the frame each year as the flowers are produced on the terminal shoots of the current season's growth.

Buddleja davidii 'Harlequin' and other variegated cultivars are grown for their foliage effect; the plants must be young and vigorous to get the best show.

GROUP 2

Pruning time Midsummer after flowering.

The elegant *Buddleja alternifolia* (fountain butterfly bush), the most popular species in this group, produces long, arching growths that become pendulous under the weight of the flowers and vegetative growth. On a healthy

The elegant fountain-like habit of *Buddleja alternifolia*.

Buddleja crispa trained as a wall shrub.

specimen new growth is freely produced and if left unpruned causes the older growths to die through lack of light as new growth forms above them. To prevent this happening and to maintain the balance, prune the old flowered shoots back to new growth, which develops in midsummer as soon as the old flowers drop.

In the early years the older wood formed in previous years acts as a framework and supports the new growth; this should be left, but as the shrub becomes more mature, pruning can be hard to keep the plant in check. At all times it is important to remove dead wood and any damaged or broken stems before any attempt is made to prune.

GROUP 3

Pruning time Late winter/early spring.

The pruning of *Buddleja globosa* and others in this group is done while retaining the terminal buds of the growth produced during the previous year, which remains leafy throughout the winter. In late winter/early spring, prune the weaker and dead wood back to suitable growing points, leaving the flowering wood. If the shrub becomes too large it can be cut back hard, but flowers will be lost for at least one season.

Buddlejas in this group, particularly the more tender species (e.g., *Buddleja colvilei*, *B. fallowiana*) are often grown as wall shrubs. They are self-supporting but can be tied into a frame to keep them tight against the wall. They flower on the current season's wood, so these growths are pruned back to the lowest pair of buds early in spring to a main framework, which can be trained fanwise to the wall. Vigorous growths will be produced from the base, which should be thinned at an early stage

and the remainder trained against the wall, as renewal branches to replace the older, tired stems and to fill in any gaps.

This group also respond well to hard prun-

ing, producing vigorous, fresh growth from the old wood, which can be retrained to a new framework. This exercise must be followed up with feeding and mulching.

Renovation pruning on *Buddleja davidii*.

BUPLEURUM

Habit Small to medium-sized evergreen shrub for fertile, free-draining soil and full sun. **Attributes** Yellow flowers in summer, suitable for exposed coastal areas. **Reasons for pruning** To renovate. **Pruning time** Late spring.

Once *Bupleurum fruticosum* reaches its ma-

ture height of 1.5 metres (5 ft.), it becomes untidy with thick twiggy wood that weighs the branches down. When the shrub reaches this condition it can be renovated by cutting the main branches back to ground level in mid- to late spring. If fed and watered it will regen-

erate into a well-shaped bush by the end of summer but will not produce a show of flowers until the following year. Apart from this, there are no special pruning needs.

BUXUS

Habit Medium-sized decurrent evergreen trees or shrubs for free-draining soil in partial shade to full sun. **Attributes** Suitable for hedg-

ing and topiary. **Reasons for pruning** To create and maintain topiary features and hedges. **Pruning time** Mid- to late summer, but carry

out major renovation work in late spring.

If the plant you are growing is for topiary, then the young plant should be cut back hard to encourage vigorous dense growth. If the plant is to be grown for its natural shape, no pruning should be carried out until a desired height is achieved.

Where box is grown naturally as a bush, very little pruning is necessary, unless plants need to be kept down to a definite size. Size can be restricted by the careful pruning (with secateurs or the pruning saw) of the longer growths back into the plant to mask the pruning cuts. Very old and large specimens that have outgrown their situation can be cut back very hard to the desired height in late spring as the plant is about to grow. Regrowth will be vigorous if the plant is healthy. Overgrown and straggly specimens grown in shade can be dealt with in the same way.

Buxus sempervirens is very variable and has given rise to many named cultivars (including 'Elegantissima' and *B. sempervirens* var. *japonica* 'Morris Dwarf'); all such compact forms need no pruning or clipping.

Buxus sempervirens 'Prostrata' develops into a large spreading shrub with horizontal branching, while 'Pendula' is a large loose shrub with pendulous branchlets. It is important to recognise these particular habits before attempting any pruning in order not to spoil the shape of the bush.

Buxus balearica (Balearic box) will develop into a small tree 6 to 9 metres (20 to 30 ft.) high, especially if a leader can be maintained in the early years.

Some of the stronger-growing forms have for centuries been used for formal hedges and topiary work. Any regular clipping should be done in mid- to late summer. It is important to keep the bushes in good condition by regular feeding when necessary; otherwise, bare patches will appear.

Buxus sempervirens 'Suffruticosa', the traditional slow-growing dwarf box, is most suitable for parterres and small hedging.

Buxus sempervirens growing naturally as a tree.

Buxus sempervirens cloud-pruned as topiary.

Buxus sempervirens clipped as a parterre hedge.

CAESALPINIA

Habit Large deciduous thorny shrub for free-draining soil and full sun. **Attributes** Fine horizontal branching with acacia-like foliage. **Reasons for pruning** To restrict growth. **Pruning time** Spring.

Personal protection Wear good thorn-proof clothing and gloves, as this shrub is armed with re-curved prickles. Use long-handled loppers to remove old growths in the shrub's centre.

Caesalpinia decapetala (Mysore thorn) is best wall-trained, as it requires some form of protection through a cold winter, with branching from the base rather than on a stem or trunk. The branches will need to be tied in to the wall as they will naturally grow away toward the light. The main form of pruning will be to restrict its growth in spring. Prune the last year's growths back to the main stem, taking care, as the prickles on both branches and leaf stalks will prevent your hand and arm from retreating from the shrub.

CALCEOLARIA

Habit Small upright evergreen shrub for free-draining soil and full sun. **Attributes** Large yellow flowers in late summer. **Reasons for pruning** To remove winter damage. **Pruning time** Spring.

Calceolaria integrifolia is a tender plant and will require the shelter of a sunny wall if it is to succeed. It produces very bushy growth when happy and healthy. The only pruning necessary will be in spring, to cut back any winter damage. Where there is no winter damage, the plant will break freely from any living wood.

CALLICARPA

Callicarpa bodinieri on the edge of a path, maintained to fit the position with regular minimal fine pruning back to lateral branches.

Habit Bushy, medium to large deciduous shrubs for free-draining soil in full sun to partial shade. **Attributes** Small lilac flowers followed by tight clusters of white, violet, or purple rounded fruits. **Reasons for pruning** To restrict size or to renovate an old bush. **Pruning time** Early to mid-spring as new growth is about to break.

Callicarpa species (e.g., *C. americana*, *C. bodinieri*, *C. dichotoma*, *C. japonica*) freely send up vigorous shoots from the base. When young their growth is erect and crowded growth, but often as they mature the branching becomes spreading and eventually horizontal, with the weight of the extension growth and heavy clusters of fruits. Any branches that have grown out of shape and old woody branches that have lost their vigour can be pruned out in spring as they are about to grow. The brittle branches are easily damaged by snow, and the new growth is subject to frost damage, so it is better to wait until all threat of snow and frost is past before pruning. This pruning practice applies to all the aforementioned species and their cultivars—except *Callicarpa bodinieri* var. *giraldii* 'Profusion', which is a stronger, taller grower, so allowance must be made for this.

CALLISTEMON

Habit Sun-loving evergreen shrubs with long, arching branches for fertile, well-drained soil. **Attributes** Cylinder-like spikes of red and yellow flowers in summer. **Reasons for pruning** To restrict growth and remove winter-damaged shoots. **Pruning time** Late summer after flowering.

Formative pruning is important to form a well-branched plant with bushy growth; prune leading shoots back by about a third, early in the life of a young shrub. Further pruning is not desirable as the characteristic spikes of flowers are produced naturally along the upper lengths of the strong growths. *Callistemon citrinus*, *C. linearis*, *C. pallidus*, *C. salignus*, and *C. subulatus* can be treated in this manner. Only a limited amount of pruning is possible with *C. sieberi* (alpine bottlebrush), which forms a more compact bush with upright growths branching from ground level; adequate space should be given to allow this plant to develop naturally.

When a shrub becomes tired, with a sparse, open straggly look, it is possible to carry out renovation pruning over a period of two to three years; this will encourage vigorous new growths from the base of the plant. Once these have established, remove the older stems to ground level; this allows the new growths to develop into a fresh, healthy bush with new growth to produce flowers.

CALLUNA

Habit Low-growing evergreen shrubs for free-draining, acid soil. **Attributes** Groundcover plants with foliage of various colours, from greens through to yellows and silver, and white bell-shaped flowers in summer and autumn. **Reasons for pruning** To remove old inflorescences and keep plants tidy and furnished to the ground. **Pruning time** Mid-spring and late summer.

Following planting, young plants of *Calluna vulgaris* (heather) and its many cultivars should be pruned early to encourage a bushy plant with multiple branches from ground level. They should be clipped over, removing two-thirds of their growth.

If left unattended for several years without any intervention, heathers will become straggly and open in the centre, presenting a tired, worn-out appearance with dead patches. By annual pruning of the young growths in the spring, the branch system is kept more compact and the plants will have a longer, more useful life. Pruning, carried out annually just as the new growth is about to appear, consists of cutting back at least half of the previous year's growth to encourage a more compact bush. To retain a more natural-looking plant rather than a plant with a round dome effect, pruning should be done using a variety of tools (e.g., shears, secateurs, and a knife).

For cultivars with coloured foliage, the old flowering heads can be pruned off following flowering to expose the foliage and to encourage a further flush of growth.

Calluna vulgaris does respond to hard renovation pruning, but it may be better to dig out the old, overgrown plant and replace it with vigorous young stock.

CALOCEDRUS

Habit Upright random-branched evergreen conifer for free-draining soil and full sun. **Attributes** Distinctive, drought-tolerant specimen tree with flattened sprays of aromatic scale-like leaves. **Reasons for pruning** To control size. **Pruning time** Spring to late summer.

Calocedrus decurrens (incense cedar) is a columnar conifer best grown as a single specimen or as a group of three or more with adequate space; the foliage will be retained to almost ground level. The natural habit in the early years is for the tree to form a leader, but rival leaders will appear as the tree gets older and taller. There is no need to worry about these, as they help the tree to put on spread in proportion to height.

Old specimens in exposed areas tend to lose a considerable amount of foliage in brown patches, exposing a mass of dead stems and the main branch system. In addition to spoiling the appearance, this is a danger sign; if left unattended, the specimen can deteriorate further until recovery is not possible. The dead wood should be pruned out and a programme of

A very mature *Calocedrus decurrens* with irreparable storm damage.

A mature *Calocedrus decurrens* showing the columnar form.

aeration, mulching, and feeding implemented, to regenerate this part of the crown and improve aesthetic appearance.

Also with old specimens, the upright scaffolds heavy with end weight can begin to break apart, usually due to strong winds or weight of snow, and it may be necessary to position some form of bracing system to prevent canopy collapse in very mature specimens. Once large areas of the crown are damaged beyond the green foliage, exposing the branch framework, they will never be able to grow new vegetation.

With *Calocedrus decurrens* 'Aureovariegata', any reversion should be pruned out as soon as possible.

CALYCANTHUS

Habit Bushy, dense deciduous shrubs for well-drained soil in full or partial shade. **Attributes** Glossy green leaves, fragrant bark, and fragrant, white or burgundy-red flowers in late summer. **Reasons for pruning** To control size and vigour. **Pruning time** Spring.

The nodding flowers of *Calycanthus* (allspice) are produced terminally on the young wood during the summer, so it is important to maintain a healthy shrub. Plants produce vigorous young shoots from the base, which should be encouraged as replacement branches for the older, tired ones.

Calycanthus floridus naturally forms a neat shrub, while *C. occidentalis* spreads out more, with horizontal branching and a more open habit. *Calycanthus chinensis* is a shrub to 3 metres (10 ft.) with branches from the ground, making a dense canopy, the flowers being produced terminally on young wood during early summer. The lower branches are naturally spreading, and these should be left to furnish the base. Where old stems are removed, the branches from the base should be used as replacements. When young, this plant makes a scruffy individual; patience is needed, for in two or three years, when it settles down, it will turn into quite a wonderful elegant specimen, displaying its beautiful nodding white flowers.

Calycanthus ×raulstonii (including its selection 'Hartlage Wine') makes a multi-branched shrub to 3 metres (10 ft.) high and wide and should be treated in the same way as *C. chinensis*.

A well-shaped *Calycanthus chinensis* on its way to maturity.

A badly shaped *Calycanthus chinensis* that will self-correct—note the upright stem growing from the base of the plant.

CAMELLIA

Habit Evergreen shrubs or small trees for an acid or neutral soil in partial shade to full sun. **Attributes** Glossy green foliage, with a variety of flower forms in various colours, including white, pink, and red. **Reasons for pruning** To control size and vigour. **Pruning time** Spring, just as buds are about to break.

These popular flowering evergreens require very little pruning, but if left to their own devices and especially in a shaded situation they are likely to get a bit leggy and lose the bushy effect that is more desirable. To prevent this from happening, prune young shoots back to just above a healthy set of buds and leaves, just before the new buds begin to break. Young plants should require only a very light pruning of the previous year's growth.

Camellia japonica is grown in many varieties, which vary considerably in habit and form; the typical habit of each cultivar should be taken into account before any pruning is undertaken as the general appearance of each cultivar could be spoiled. In an exposed position it may be necessary to remove any growths that appear to be too tall or heavy or affect the stability of the plant in any way. Where plants have become too dense, some selective thinning done evenly

The wide rounded habit of *Camellia cuspidata* in flower.

A camellia trained tight against a wall.

Pruning back shoots of *Camellia japonica* to maintain a tight habit.

throughout the camellia will allow more light penetration and air circulation into its centre.

Following planting, it is advisable to disbud young plants before the flowers open in spring in order to encourage growth, as they flower so freely; if the young plant is leggy, the formative pruning back of the main stems will encourage the development of side shoots and produce a more bushy plant, with more flowering material over the entire plant. Renovation pruning can be carried out on established plants that have become weak or have become out of control; cut back hard into old wood, and with mulching and watering, dormant buds will break along the old wood and produce new growth. These resultant shoots can be thinned out a year or two later to make a balanced bush.

Camellia cuspidata, one of the hardiest camellias, has a wide, graceful habit and requires no pruning. *Camellia sasanqua* has a very loose habit and can be grown as a standalone shrub or trained against a wall. The branches should be tied into a wire support system fanwise and laterals encouraged to grow out from these. Overgrown shoots are shortened back by selective pruning after flowering. Where a branch becomes tired and worn-out, it can be removed low down near to ground level and fresh young shoots trained as a replacement. *Camellia ×williamsii* (and its many cultivars) and *C. reticulata* should be treated the same as *C. japonica*.

Camellia ×williamsii 'Donation' growing with space and flowering freely with little if any pruning.

CAMPSIS

Habit Vigorous deciduous climbing plant with twining stems (and occasionally aerial roots) for free-draining soil and full sun. **Attributes** Orange to red trumpet-shaped flowers in summer. **Reasons for pruning** To control size and vigour and encourage flower-bearing spurs. **Pruning time** Late winter/early spring as they flower on the current season's wood.

Campsis (trumpet creeper) is a genus of strong, vigorous climbing shrubs, and it should be remembered when planting one that they require plenty of room if they are to reach their maximum potential. They are best left to climb over old tree stumps or through a tree.

Campsis ×tagliabuana, *C. grandiflora*, and *C. radicans*, whose aerial roots assist it with support when climbing, can be trained against a sunny wall, but a wiring system must be used and the stems tied in to aid their support. With a young plant, early training consists of covering the available wall space with the main branches. When pruning an established plant, remember that they flower in mid- to late summer on the current season's wood. The young growths produced during the previous season should be cut back to one or two of the lowest buds, to produce spurs close to the main stem, and the new growths will flower in the summer. During the following spring they should

A well-established *Campsis ×tagliabuana* 'Madame Galen'.

be pruned back again, unless they are needed for replacement, in which case they should be pruned back by approximately one-third to the stronger wood.

Trumpet creepers respond well to hard pruning, should a branch become damaged; if pruned hard back to the ground, the vigorous regrowth can be thinned by removing the weaker shoots and the remainder retrained to a framework.

Campsis radicans pruned and trained with a wire system.

A newly planted *Campsis* ×*tagliabuana* ready for formal training against a wall.

CARAGANA

Habit Deciduous wide-spreading, sparsely branched shrubs (occasionally small trees) for free-draining soil and full sun. **Attributes** Pinnate leaves, yellow pea-like flowers in late spring. **Reasons for pruning** No pruning normally required, except for initial training. **Pruning time** Winter.

Pea shrubs (e.g., *Caragana frutex, C. microphylla, C. sinica*) are sparsely branched plants, so it is important to stop their growth in the nursery after the first season's growth to encourage a bushy plant; this will also promote suckers from the base of the plant. If left, they will develop one or two long growths, which if unchecked will produce a very leggy, unstable plant, and some form of support will be needed.

To train a tree form of *Caragana arborescens*, select a strong leading shoot and remove all the suckerous growth and remaining branches; allow the leading shoot to grow to the desired height before encouraging lateral branches to develop. Remove dead wood in the spring; otherwise, the new growth will show it up very plainly, and the shrub will look untidy. *Caragana arborescens* 'Pendula' is grafted onto a stem of the species; its trunk should be kept clear of any regrowth, or it will take over the shrub.

CARPENTERIA

Habit Bushy, medium-sized evergreen shrub for moist, well-drained soil in a sunny, sheltered position. **Attributes** Attractive foliage, fragrant white flowers with yellow stamens in summer. **Reasons for pruning** To renovate old plants to encourage new flowering material. **Pruning time** Late summer after flowering.

Ideally *Carpenteria californica* (tree anemone) should be sited so as to receive the shelter of a sunny wall; however, it cannot be wall-trained and must be grown as a freestanding shrub. It can be a vigorous grower, forming a well-furnished shrub with many growths originating from the base. The natural habit of the more vigorous branches is upright, and the laterals produced from any branch growing at an angle also take on this upright position, but the lower furnishings should be left to improve the shrub's appearance. Older branches are attractive in their own right, with flaking bark, but the older wood does thin out with exhaustion following flowering and as a result of winter damage; these branches can be periodically pruned out at the base to be replaced by the young growths produced in the spring.

CARPINUS

Habit Small to large deciduous excurrent trees for fertile, free-draining soil and full sun. **Attributes** Graceful, fine-detailed shape, smooth silver bark, autumn colour, and winged fruits. **Reasons for pruning** To form a framework when young or to maintain an established hornbeam hedge. **Pruning time** Late summer to mid-winter (when dormant). Never prune in spring as the wounds are prone to bleeding.

Carpinus betulus showing autumn color.

Plant hornbeams as a feathered tree, particularly in a natural area, or as a standard with a clean stem to show off the silver bark in a more formal setting. The only pruning necessary in the early years will be to retain the leader to produce a canopy as high as possible and to remove lower feathers to make a standard. The young growth is delicate and thin but will develop into strong lateral branches.

As the young tree begins to develop, remove crossing, diseased, and damaged branches and twin leaders; if a specimen standard tree with a central leader is wanted, remove feathers as well. The leader will often bend over, appearing to be pendulous, particularly with *Carpinus turczaninowii*, but will straighten on its own as it grows longer and needs little intervention. If twin leaders are produced, one can be removed to encourage excurrent growth; however, twin leaders do make a wide-spreading tree when full size.

Hornbeams will bleed if pruned at the wrong time of the year, so pruning must be restricted to late summer through to mid-winter.

The sweet sap can attract grey squirrels, which will strip the bark and cause irreparable harm if the damage is not pruned out immediately.

Carpinus betulus (European hornbeam) makes good topiary and has become very fashionable grown as a pyramid, cone, or clipped block. It also makes a good hedging tree: the leaves will turn brown and persist throughout the winter, forming a good visual barrier; feathered plants should be planted at 0.3 to 0.5 metre (1 to 1.5 ft.) spacing and left to grow unpruned for two to three years, or until the required height is reached. If a hornbeam grows too large for its situation, it will tolerate some hard pruning, which can later be managed by some crown renewal.

Carpinus betulus 'Fastigiata' has a close branching habit, and a young to semi-mature specimen makes a perfect, upright conical-pyramidal crown, useful for restricted spaces; very little pruning is needed to encourage this form. *Carpinus betulus* 'Columnaris' has a dense, upright growth habit; it too requires no pruning. In fact, any pruning

Carpinus betulus 'Fastigiata' as a young tree.

Carpinus coreana showing the shrubby habit of a mature tree.

is likely to spoil the overall shape and form of the tree, so it is important to give it plenty of space, despite its being fastigiate. Once mature it tends to develop a broad-spreading but upright crown.

Carpinus caroliniana (American hornbeam), often confused with *C. betulus*, should be treated in the same way. It is a small but fast-growing flat-topped tree, as wide as it is high, with a fine network of twiggy growth on its upright-spreading branches.

Carpinus coreana (Korean hornbeam), a small, very upright specimen with very close branching, needs no formal pruning. *Carpinus fangiana* is a slow-growing moody tree; it should be encouraged to produce a broad-spreading crown to show off the long pendulous fruits and long, shiny green pointed buds.

A mature *Carpinus betulus* 'Fastigiata'.

CARRIEREA

Habit Small deciduous (occasionally semi-evergreen) tree with a wide-spreading crown for free-draining soil and full sun. **Attributes** Shiny foliage, pale yellow flowers, brown horn-shaped seedpods. **Reasons for pruning** To develop a strong framework. **Pruning time** Between autumn and spring (when dormant).

Carrierea calycina (goat horn tree) is a choice plant. It should be grown with a central leader in the nursery for as long as possible in order to form a short trunk. This leading growth is difficult to maintain, even with ongoing formative pruning and training, and is naturally lost after the second year. This is when the crown

begins to form the first branching and crown framework. The horizontal lateral branches are strongly attached to the trunk and can be left to make a tree with a low skirt; however, the lower growths on the trunk can be removed if a clean trunk is required. No further pruning will be necessary, and the tree will develop and maintain a good shape and produce flowers on its own accord at a young age.

The framework of *Carrierea calycina* on a short trunk.

CARYA

Habit Large deciduous excurrent trees with a symmetrical oval crown for a deep, fertile, well-drained soil in full sun. **Attributes** Elegant shape, flaking bark, autumn colour and fruits. **Reasons for pruning** To develop a strong framework. **Pruning time** Mid- to late summer. Never prune in late winter through to spring as the wounds are prone to very heavy bleeding.

Remove crossing branches, diseased and damaged branches, twin leaders, and feathers to make a standard tree as soon as the tree begins to grow after planting. Hickories are best planted in good soil as small specimens and as young as possible, as they do not appreciate transplanting or losing their tap root and if planted later in life will produce a weak anchor root system. The ideal would be to sow the seed in the permanent planting site to avoid transplanting. They will need to be watched in the early years, and any formative pruning must be carried out in the garden as opposed to the nursery; however, they are very well behaved and naturally want to grow into fine shapely trees, retaining a good straight leader. Occasionally hickories are caught by late spring frosts and susceptible to coral spot (*Nectria cinnabarina*); affected parts must be pruned out to retain a healthy tree. *Carya illinoiensis* (pecan) grows successfully in the United Kingdom but is shy of fruiting: it needs plenty of summer heat to ripen the wood to encourage flower and fruit.

A young *Carya ovata* (shagbark hickory) with clean straight trunk.

A mature *Carya cordiformis* (bitternut).

CARYOPTERIS

Habit Upright deciduous shrub for a sunny position and well-drained soil. **Attributes** Violet-purple flower spikes in late summer. **Reasons for pruning** To control size and vigour. **Pruning time** Early spring, as the shoots are about to break.

Blue spiraeas (*Caryopteris* spp.) grown in the open are semi-woody and may be cut back to ground level following a cold winter. Even during a normal winter, much of the top growth is lost to dieback following flowering.

Cultivars of *Caryopteris* ×*clandonensis* (e.g., 'Arthur Simmonds', 'Kew Blue', 'Summer Sorbet') are the most widely grown blue spiraeas. The growths that spring from the short woody branches at the base produce a terminal inflorescence in the late summer through to autumn. These growths are pruned hard back to near the base in spring, just as the buds are breaking. Pruning is left until this period, so that the dead growth is easily distinguished from the living material; no dead growth

should remain after pruning. By pruning back hard to within approximately 2.5 cm (1 in.) of the older wood, height is only slowly built up, but the number of growths is reduced, yielding larger flower heads; at the same time, the wood is very close to the soil and is more protected.

Caryopteris incana and *C. mongholica* are very similar in their pruning requirements but are taller growers and need not be pruned back so hard; it is only necessary to cut back the dead tips as the buds break in the spring.

CASSIOPE

Habit Dwarf spreading evergreen shrubs for well-drained, acid soil in full sun. **Attributes** Scale-like leaves with white bell-shaped flowers in spring and early summer. **Reasons for prun-

ing No pruning required. **Pruning time** Spring.

There is no need to prune these shrubs (e.g., *Cassiope* 'Randle Cooke', *C. wardii*) apart from the removal of any dead pieces of foliage that

make the plants unsightly. The upright-growing *C. tetragona* may blow over and its shape spoiled if it is not planted in a sheltered, sunny position.

CASTANEA

Habit Large deciduous excurrent trees with a heavy spreading branch system for deep, fertile, free-draining soil and full sun. **Attributes** Spiralling bark, autumn colour, edible fruits, suitable specimen trees for parkland or woodland, valued for their size and characteristic shape. **Reasons for pruning** To develop a strong framework. **Pruning time** Between autumn and spring (when dormant).

Remove crossing branches, diseased and damaged branches, twin leaders, and feathers to make a well-framed standard tree. *Castanea sativa* (sweet chestnut) can be planted bareroot as a whip or larger as a standard tree, but both types of young tree will take two to three years to settle down before they start to grow and put on extension growth. Once established they are fast growing and soon develop a vigorous, straight leader, which should be encouraged for as long as possible. Light pruning can be carried out to encourage a well-branched symmetrical framework and raise the crown to the desired height; many prefer to see a skirt of branches retained as low as possible. Once the tree is more than a century old, it begins to lose its symmetrical, pyramidal shape, and some of the strong scaffolds take over the dominance. It develops into a tree full of character.

Suckerous growths are freely produced at the base and on the main trunk of a mature specimen; these should be removed annually to

Castanea sativa showing its characterful habit.

Castanea sativa in fruit.

maintain a clean trunk. This ability to sucker makes trees suitable for hard pruning later in their life—or for coppicing in early spring: large long-lived stools are produced, which can be pruned on a rotation, providing a source of stakes and fencing materials.

Several fruiting selections of *Castanea sativa* (e.g., 'Marron de Lyon', 'Belle Epine', 'Marsol') can be affected by late spring and early autumn frosts. It may be necessary to retrain the leader following a cold winter. Variegated forms (e.g., 'Albomarginata', 'Aureomarginata') are subject to reversion; keep a close eye and prune out any branches reverting to green as soon as possible.

Sweet chestnuts are under threat from chestnut blight (*Cryphonectria parasitica*), which in the early 1900s devastated *Castanea dentata* (American chestnut) trees, causing a rapid, widespread wipeout of this once-plentiful tree in the eastern United States. To prevent any possible contamination of unaffected trees in an area where this disease is present, strict sanitation will be very important, and all tools must be well sterilized between the pruning of individual trees.

CASTANOPSIS

Habit Evergreen shrubs or small trees for rich, deep, free-draining soil in partial shade to full sun. **Attributes** Large leathery dark green leaves. **Reasons for pruning** To remove frost-damaged shoots. **Pruning time** Spring.

Chinquapins (e.g., *Castanopsis cuspidata*, *C. chrysophylla*) should be left to grow naturally once planted and require no pruning; however, they can be damaged by late spring frosts and cold winds if not grown in a sheltered situa-tion. This damage can be pruned out to live, undamaged growth after the last frosts have finished. Trees regularly produce new stems from buds on the trunk.

CASUARINA

Habit Slender evergreen tree with upward-curving branches for free-draining soil and full sun. **Attributes** Makes a good (often coastal) hedging plant, as it is tolerant of strong winds and sea spray. **Reasons for pruning** To maintain size and shape. **Pruning time** Summer.

Casuarina equisetifolia (horsetail tree) is best planted when small, as small plants will need minimal support; and provided the nurs-ery stock is healthy and the roots are in good shape, establishment will be quick. It is im-portant to maintain a single leader for as long as possible to prevent weak forks in the future, and except to repair damaged branches from severe storms, very little pruning is otherwise needed. *Casuarina* does respond to hard prun-ing and will produce new growth from pruning cuts and wounds.

Casuarina equisetifolia.

CATALPA

Habit Large deciduous decurrent trees with heavy, low, very wide-spreading branches for rich, deep, free-draining soil and full sun. **Attributes** Broad shape, flaking bark, large showy leaves, and white, pink, or yellow flowers followed by long, slender bean-like fruits that persist into winter. **Reasons for pruning** To develop and maintain a strong framework and coppiced for foliage effect. **Pruning time** Late summer to mid-winter (when dormant). Never prune in spring as the wounds are prone to very heavy bleeding.

Once planted, remove crossing branches, diseased and damaged branches, twin leaders, and feathers to make a standard tree. The leader will need some encouragement in the first three years if a clean straight trunk is desired, as they are prone to losing their apical dominance following a cold winter. Some species and cultivars form a good, strong natural shape if the lower branching is started low from the ground.

The most commonly grown species is *Catalpa bignonioides* (Indian bean tree) which, when mature, makes a large wide-spreading tree with a strong branch system and an irregular crown. In the nursery it needs to be trained with a leader to form a trunk as high as is needed before losing its apical dominance, as once branching starts, it is difficult to maintain a leader. The lower branches naturally sweep down to the ground and the tips grow upward, so it will need lots of space and a clean area under the canopy; otherwise, grass cutting will be very difficult to do.

A mature *Catalpa speciosa* showing its natural upright habit compared to *C. bignonioides*.

A young *Catalpa fargesii* grown as a standard with a clean straight trunk.

A mature spreading *Catalpa bignonioides* in fruit.

Any pruning should be done as soon as needed: large wounds are slow to heal, and due to the poor nature of the wood, decay will set in quickly. Well-established trees require very little pruning with little intervention unless there is a need for lightening or shortening of heavy branches. The branches are of a brittle nature and easily broken, so repair work may be needed soon after any work is carried out under the tree or after winds.

Hard pruning to a stool annually will encourage vigorous regrowth with larger leaves, suitable for bold foliage impact in the herbaceous border. Catalpas can produce long vigorous growth during a wet summer or after hard pruning, but these can die back if the summers aren't hot enough to ripen the wood. These damaged branches will need to be pruned out during the following spring.

Catalpa speciosa (western catalpa) naturally makes a tree with a more upright habit, without the need for any formative pruning and training.

CATHAYA

Habit Medium-sized evergreen conifer with decurrent crown for shallow, free-draining, alkaline soil and full sun. **Attributes** Rarity value, fine attractive foliage. **Reasons for pruning** To develop a strong framework. **Pruning time** Between autumn and spring (when dormant).

Tony Kirkham first saw *Cathaya argyrophylla* (Chinese silver fir) in western China in 1996, before it was introduced into cultivation, growing wild on Jin Fu Shan; at 20 metres (65 ft.), it closely resembled a medium-sized pine. He has since grown one, which at six years old is a very dense, bushy tree with lots of branching from a low stem, about 30 cm (12 in.) high. It tolerates pruning, responding by producing many new shoots from the old pruning wound; however, there is no real need for pruning, even formative training. Let the tree develop naturally and be thankful that you can grow it well in the garden.

A young *Cathaya argyrophylla* with no leader and a dense multi-branching crown.

CEANOTHUS

Habit Rounded or upright and spreading evergreen and deciduous shrubs for fertile, free-draining soil and full sun. **Attributes** Bright blue (typically) flowers. **Reasons for pruning** To control size and maintain a healthy plant for new growth and flowers.

Evergreen taxa flower in spring or early summer on growths made during the previous year; many of these are not hardy and in cold areas will need the protection of a sunny wall to be successful. Deciduous taxa flower in late summer or autumn on the current season's growth.

EVERGREEN SPECIES

Pruning time Midsummer, immediately after flowering.

There are two habits of evergreen ceanothus, the tall, freestanding forms (e.g., *Ceanothus arboreus*, *C. thyrsiflorus*, *C. velutinus*) and the low mounding forms (e.g., *C. rigidus*, *C. thyrsiflorus* var. *repens*), and both should be treated differently.

In general, all are too weak to be grown next to a wall without support, as the bushes tend to grow out toward the light and become top-heavy and fail (the roots are very brittle) or are finally torn apart by strong winds or heavy snowfalls. A bushy multi-stemmed habit should be encouraged in the nursery and the young plant planted tight against the wall, its branches tied in fanwise to the main support system. This is far more effective than training a single-stemmed bush to the height of the wall, with the laterals trained horizontally off the main stem. With the fan system, the replacement of old branches is easier and more straightforward than with a single stem.

The laterals should be pruned reasonably hard to approximately one-third after flowering; do not prune back into older wood that is devoid of foliage, as ceanothus are reluctant to generate new material from this position. This pruning must be done carefully to produce an informal habit with hidden cuts.

In the early stages of training, a large quantity of growth will be produced near the base of the shrub, and these growths need to be thinned out before they develop into main branches. At the same time, replacement growths can be selected and tied in to fill in for the older growths that have been removed.

Ceanothus thyrsiflorus var. *repens* and other mound-forming taxa can be grown against a low wall, as the shoots of these low-growing form are held up by their springy nature.

Evergreen ceanothus do not respond to hard pruning. New growth does not break freely from the older wood, so when a mature plant becomes bare at the base, overgrown and reluctant to flower, it is better to remove the plant entirely and replace it with a healthy young plant.

DECIDUOUS SPECIES

Pruning time Mid-spring.

Deciduous taxa (e.g., *Ceanothus americanus*, *C. coeruleus*, *C.* ×*delileanus* 'Gloire de Versailles', *C. dentatus*, *C.* ×*pallidus*) produce growths during the spring and summer which flower in late summer or autumn. They have been hybridised extensively and are very popular garden plants. Deciduous ceanothus should be grown as freestanding plants in the open border. First pruning following planting should be light to encourage the formation of a rigid framework up to a height of 0.6 to 1.2 metres (2 to 4 ft.). The previous season's growths are then pruned back hard to two pairs of buds just as they become active in mid-spring. If pruning is done too early, the new growth will be susceptible to late spring frosts. They do recover on their own and grow out from this damage; however, flowering may be slightly delayed. Finally, unlike the evergreens, deciduous ceanothus will respond to hard pruning; when a bush becomes leggy or sprawls out of control, cut the plant hard back to the original stem in spring.

Ceanothus arboreus 'Trewithen Blue', young wall-trained plant.

Ceanothus 'Concha' showing the mound-forming habit.

CEDRUS

Habit Conical-pyramidal evergreen conifers when young, developing into large stately trees with horizontal branching, suitable for large spaces in full sun. **Attributes** Ornamental specimen parkland trees, graceful and grand, with varying shades of green/blue foliage. **Reasons for pruning** To maintain a conical shape, encourage a single leader, and remove dead wood. **Pruning time** Summer.

Cedrus libani (Lebanon cedar) is best planted as a specimen tree with adequate space all around for it to spread out and show off its grandeur to the fullest. The habit when the tree is young is conical-pyramidal; it is only at a later stage in its life (approximately 50 years)

A mature *Cedrus libani* showing the extensive, lateral branching.

that the branches spread out extensively.

A central leader should be retained for as long as possible, although at a later stage—often when the tree is 12 to 15 metres (40 to 50 ft.) high and growing vigorously—rival leaders may develop. It is almost impossible to keep a constant check on a tree at this height, and some speci-mens are likely to develop rival leaders in the upper crowns. These more upright branches are the ones that are likely to tear out during a storm when the tree is mature, especially if the crown is laden with snow, so if these can be formatively pruned out, it will pay dividends in the future.

It is important to remove dead wood as it develops for the health of the tree and to reduce the end weight of any young branches that are growing out beyond the natural lines of the canopy. All formative pruning is best carried out at an early stage in the tree's life, as an old tree will never have the ability to produce sufficient new growth to cover up the ugly effects of hard pruning.

Two kinds of growth are produced: the long extension shoot with scattered needles, and the short spur-like shoots with tufts of needles around each growing point. A specimen in full health produces a balanced proportion of extension shoots during each growing season. A lack of these, accompanied by thin and poorly coloured needle growth on the dwarf shoot system, is a sure sign that the health of the tree is declining and that the root system and the culture generally should receive more attention, such as aeration and mulching. The leading growths even on the branch systems are important, but as the tree grows into maturity and lateral branches are lost along the main scaffolds, end weight increases at the tips. This lions-tailing, as it is known, can also be caused by overzealous arborists carrying out crown-thinning exercises, and it may be necessary to reduce some end weight of the large lateral scaffolds, taking some weight off these limbs. This must be carried out by a fully skilled and qualified arborist, who will retain

A young *Cedrus deodara*, its graceful branching furnished to the ground.

the tree's shape and dignity and not overprune.

Cedrus libani var. *brevifolia* is a stunted grower with no particular pruning or training requirements. It is important to encourage a leader for as long as possible, but it will soon want to become multi-stemmed with upright branching, and the leader will be lost.

Much concerning *Cedrus libani* also applies to *C. atlantica* (Atlantic cedar) except that the latter species often produces a much thinner crown density and its growth is extremely variable in colour and form. A central leader is naturally and readily formed and retained as the crown develops.

The pruning and training of *Cedrus deodara* (Deodar cedar) is much the same as for *C. libani*, but it appreciates a sheltered position, especially when the tree is in the early stages of establishment. The leading shoot, particularly when the tree is young, has a natural arching or pendulous habit; do not attempt to straighten this (e.g., by ties to a stake), as it will naturally straighten as it grows upward. The lower branches should be left for as long as possible to show off the true form of this graceful tree.

Cedrus atlantica demonstrating the pyramidal habit of a young tree.

CELASTRUS

Habit Shade-tolerant scandent shrubs or vigorous climbers with anti-clockwise twining stems for free-draining soil. **Attributes** Butter-yellow autumn colour and orange to yellow fruits exposing red seeds. **Reasons for pruning** To control size. **Pruning time** Late winter/early spring.

Celastrus orbiculatus (oriental bittersweet) and *C. scandens* (American bittersweet) are strong climbers, producing long growths extending to 2 metres (6 ft.) in one growing season. These shoots either twine around or loop over neighbouring branches or supports with an arching habit. Laterals and a more compound branch system build on these. With such vigour, these shrubs are difficult to contain in a small area, and all that can be done is to cut back long growths that arch out too far. Carry this out in a manner that retains the natural habit; this is best accomplished by cutting out a few lengths completely rather than cutting back every growth to a given line, which leaves too formal an outline.

Celastrus orbiculatus (considered an invasive species in eastern North America) must be given space to perform. Its arching growths can spread over and surmount everything from an old stump or tree to an old building. Once it's reached the top, its long branches will hang down and produce flower and fruit freely. The tree must be sacrificial, as the twining shoots will eventually strangle its host. Little regular pruning is necessary under these conditions apart from cutting out dead wood in summer, when it can be easily distinguished from the live stems. Overpruning will encourage leafy growth at expense of flower and fruit.

CELTIS

Habit Small to medium-sized deciduous decurrent trees, often with low, wide-spreading crown, for free-draining soil and full sun. **Attributes** Interesting silver bark, dark fruits, tolerance of drought and heat stress. **Reasons for pruning** To develop a strong framework. **Pruning time** Between autumn and spring (when dormant).

Hackberries are best bought container-grown, as they produce a wide-spreading root system with little branching when field-grown and resent transplanting. Encourage a trunk by removing the lower feathers and suckers as long as the tree shows some vigour in the early years, for the leader will soon disappear and the crown will develop into an unshapely canopy. Some intervention will be needed; any potential weak branch attachments should be pruned out and other branches should be pruned back to slow the branch development down and encourage wider crotches and ultimately a stronger crown structure.

Hackberries are easily checked and stunted in the nursery by transplanting or frosts, and it may take several years for a tree to grow normally following such occurrences, which can be very frustrating. Once the leader is lost, it is difficult to regenerate and a short stunted tree may result. Sufficient shelter is essential to the successful culture of all hackberries.

The strongest and largest grower is *Celtis occidentalis* (common hackberry) from North America, which naturally retains a leader and can reach heights of 18 metres (60 ft.) with a rounded crown; the lower branches are horizontal and often become pendulous with weight. Upright growths may be produced at the ends of these lower branches, and if left untended can lead to excessive end weight. The columnar *C. occidentalis* 'Prairie Sentinel' forms a narrow tree approximately 4 metres (13 ft.) high without any form of pruning.

Celtis australis (European nettle tree), with a wide-spreading crown and less hardy than *C. occidentalis*, *C. jezoensis*, and *C. choseniana*, is better suited for milder regions and may need the removal of dead wood after a cold winter. It is slow to establish following planting, especially if field-grown. Be patient—in two or three years, it finds its roots and grows away. During this time the unripened growth will be susceptible to frost damage and it will lose its dominant leader, so some pruning and training will be needed if a taller trunk and stronger crown is required.

Celtis laevigata (sugar hackberry) is an upright-spreading tree and should be treated as with *C. occidentalis*.

The shrubby or small trees (e.g., *Celtis tournefortii*, *C. pumila*, *C. glabrata*) are best grown naturally branching from the ground as it will be difficult to maintain a single stem.

A well-established *Celtis australis*.

Celtis tournefortii grown as a multi-stemmed tree, which is how it wants to grow.

CEPHALOTAXUS

Habit Shrubby spreading evergreen conifers for partial shade to full sun. **Attributes** Drought-tolerant and semi-shade-loving, aromatic plum-like fruits. **Reasons for pruning** To control size and remove dead wood. **Pruning time** Between autumn and spring (when dormant).

The plum yews are very similar to the yews (*Taxus*) and will respond to pruning in the same way—that is, they very readily produce new growths from old wood. *Cephalotaxus*

A mature *Cephalotaxus fortunei* furnished to the ground.

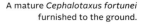

Cephalotaxus harringtonia growing as a multi-stemmed shrub in the woodlands of Japan.

Cephalotaxus harringtonia 'Fastigiata'.

harringtonia var. *drupacea* and *C. fortunei* form spreading shrubs with lateral branching that sweeps gracefully to the ground to form lower furnishing. Often these shrubs are squeezed into a densely overcrowded shady space in the garden, which will draw the plant and make it untidy, weak, and leggy. Plants in this situation should be given more light and pruned back hard to encourage a new shape.

Cephalotaxus harringtonia (Japanese plum yew) freely produces many branches from ground level compared to *C. fortunei*, which tends to produce only two or three erect stems with tiers of branches and a thinner canopy.

Cephalotaxus harringtonia 'Fastigiata' can be mistaken for *Taxus baccata* 'Fastigiata' (Irish yew), having an erect upright habit; but as the shrub matures, heavy branches pull it out of shape. This can be rectified by some tying in of branches; alternatively, cut the plant hard back to the base, from where it will regenerate despite being slow growing.

In comparison to its cousins, *Cephalotaxus wilsoniana* from Taiwan has a more open habit and makes a more graceful specimen, requiring no pruning or training.

CERATOSTIGMA

Habit Deciduous (occasionally semi-evergreen) low shrub for dry soil in full sun. **Attributes** Terminal clusters of blue flowers in late summer and autumn. **Reasons for pruning** To encourage flowering on current season's growth. **Pruning time** Late spring.

The two commonly cultivated species are *Ceratostigma willmottianum* (Chinese plumbago) and *C. griffithii*, and both, especially

the latter, should be grown in a sheltered spot, where a woody branch system will build up to a height of 30 cm (12 in.) or more. From this framework, growth breaks out in late spring, and after growing through the summer, the flowers are produced in terminal clusters in late summer and autumn. Note: in the first year following planting, flowering shoots may be few and far between. Pruning is carried out in late spring as the buds start to break; cut the old flowered growths back to their base in the living wood. If a plant becomes very old and woody at the base, remove it and replace it with a young plant.

A well-maintained *Ceratostigma willmottianum*, grown as low bushy shrub.

CERCIDIPHYLLUM

Habit Medium to large deciduous decurrent trees, often with wide-spreading branches, requiring soil moisture and full sun. **Attributes** Attractive general shape with fine branching, young pink leaves with flowers, autumn leaves with colour and a scent of burned sugar. **Reasons for pruning** To develop a strong framework. **Pruning time** Between autumn and spring (when dormant).

Cercidiphyllum japonicum (katsura) often produces several competing leaders from low down with horizontal lateral branching and is best grown in this form. It can be bought as a multi-stemmed tree from the nursery; this is probably more appropriate for a frosty area. Where a tree naturally develops a strong leader and a single trunk, this should be encouraged (and the tree grown as a standard) by removing the feathers and suckers for as long as possible while the tree is young, as the leader soon disappears and the crown develops into an decurrent canopy.

The katsura *Cercidiphyllum magnificum* is more likely to develop a single trunk than *C. japonicum*.

Trees are best grown in a sheltered position as the young shoots are susceptible to early spring frosts, strong winds, and scorch in a very hot, sunny position. A woodland situation on a moisture-retentive loam is ideal.

A well-shaped *Cercidiphyllum japonicum* f. *pendulum*.

The weeping *Cercidiphyllum japonicum* f. *pendulum* requires lots of work to develop a crown tall enough for best effect, and some cane work will be needed to keep the leader pushing upward rather than reaching a set height and going no further. This is in stark contrast to the beautiful, graceful *C. japonicum* 'Morioka Weeping', which without any intervention grows upward to a height of 20 metres (65 ft.).

Cercidiphyllum japonicum, multi-stemmed young tree in leaf.

The original 300-year-old *Cercidiphyllum japonicum* 'Morioka Weeping', just outside Morioka, Japan.

CERCIS

Habit Small deciduous decurrent trees or shrubs, often with low wide-spreading branches from ground level, for well-drained soil in a sheltered, sunny position. **Attributes** Very ungainly but characterful cauliflory trees: flowers appear directly on the trunk and branches before the leaves, in late spring. The pink flowers are followed by long flat seedpods, which hang vertically. **Reasons for pruning** To develop a strong framework. **Pruning time** Between autumn and spring (when dormant).

Encourage a strong framework for as long as possible while the tree is young and vigorous; the leader soon disappears, and the tree develops a decurrent spreading canopy.

Transplant *Cercis* species at an early age; they resent disturbance. They are sun lovers and thrive in well-drained soils, particularly those overlying chalk. They do not like heavy, badly drained clay soils. The wood often dies back badly after wet seasons and becomes prone to coral spot (*Nectria cinnabarina*). New growth is prone to frost damage, and dead or diseased branches should be removed immediately.

The most common species, *Cercis siliquastrum* (Judas tree), branches from the ground with two or more stems that grow vertically. During a cold winter these can be killed to ground level; however, they usually reshoot from the base in spring, and the dead stems can be removed back to the base.

Unlike *Cercis siliquastrum*, *C. canadensis* (redbud) and *C. racemosa* (chain-flowered redbud) can be trained on a single stem to make small trees. It is often difficult to establish *C. canadensis* 'Forest Pansy', a selection with purple foliage; it is usually sold as a grafted plant, so a careful watch for suckers and reversion is important.

Cercis chinensis (Chinese redbud) is often more shrubby and does not tolerate cold, so needs the protection of a warm, sunny wall.

The compact upright-branching *Cercis chinensis* 'Don Egolf' demonstrating cauliflory.

Cercis siliquastrum in the Mediterranean Garden at Kew.

CHAENOMELES

Habit Deciduous spreading shrubs for moist, well-drained soil in sunny positions. **Attributes** Red, orange, and white cup-shaped flowers in early spring, small sweetly scented fruits. **Reasons for pruning** To train against a wall and encourage flowering. **Pruning time** Late spring/early summer after flowering.

When these plants are young, they build up their growth at the expense of flowering, but two or three years after planting they form spurs on the older wood and regular flowering begins. Growth will slow down as the bush becomes larger and vigour is distributed across the plant, to several growing points; in later years flower buds are also produced on the young shoots at the end of their season's growth.

Chaenomeles speciosa (flowering quince), the parent of many popular cultivars, has a spreading habit and forms a tangled bush. It is best grown in a less formal part of the garden, where it can be left to develop naturally and freely down to the ground without any

Initial wall training of flowering quince using a wire system and bamboo canes.

pruning. This is one of the few plants where crossing branches may be left, as this tangled mess makes the character of the plant.

Flowering quince is also very popular for growing against a wall, where it can show off its early floral display. The first objective is to train young growths fanwise, making full use of the wall space; use a series of horizontal wires and bamboo canes for the initial training. Prune back the growths growing away from the wall at right angles to the plant, or they will extend further the following year and over time be too far away from the building. In later years, stop all growths coming away from the wall during the growing season back to five leaves unless they are required for the extension or replacement of the branch system. Stop the sub-laterals that develop from these at two leaves and repeat if further growth is put on. The original laterals, which were stopped at five leaves, may be pruned back to two or three buds in the winter.

If only thinning is carried out during the growing season, more severe pruning will need to be done in order to keep the shrub within bounds. If an established shrub requires renovation, hard prune in spring, preferably over a period of two or three years. *Chaenomeles ×superba* and its many cultivars can be treated in the same way as *C. speciosa*.

Chaenomeles cathayensis (Chinese quince), which produces strong, sparsely branched stems, is easily fan-trained against a wall. After the early vigour has been controlled by pruning and stopping the growth, flowering and regular fruit production begin. Occasionally the long growths can be replaced by young shoots growing from the base of the shrub.

Chaenomeles japonica (Japanese quince) is a small shrub approximately 1 metre (3 ft.) high, producing a framework of interlocking spiny stems with curled lateral branching; it should be left to form a natural shape.

Chaenomeles ×superba 'Rowallane' trained against a wall.

CHAMAECYPARIS

Habit Fast-growing upright random-branched evergreen conifers for moist, well-drained soil in full sun. **Attributes** Scale-like aromatic leaves in flat sprays, various foliage colours, suitable for hedging. **Reasons for pruning** To maintain size and shape. **Pruning time** Summer.

These trees are at their best when they are furnished to the ground. The ultimate effect is largely dependent upon their position in relation to the general environment and surrounding plantings. Some shelter is preferable, but it is also important to allow sufficient space and light for the development both of the laterals down to ground level and the leader itself; when planted in a group, they should be set off from each other by at least 4.5 metres (15 ft.).

Train *Chamaecyparis lawsoniana* (Lawson cypress) and its many varieties to one leader in the early years. Later, as the tree's size increases, rival leaders may form, even from along the entire length of the trunk, but this is the tree's natural habit. It is not a problem.

When used for hedging, Lawson cypress should be planted at 1 metre (3 ft.) intervals. Retain the leaders until they are 15 to 30 cm (6 to 12 in.) above the desired height. The tops are then cut to a lateral approximately 15 cm (6 in.) below this height and the upper laterals grow up to form the top surface. The best effect is obtained by using secateurs for trimming, but once a good permanent surface has been achieved, hedging shears will keep plants in good condition.

Dwarf cultivars destined for rock gardens (e.g., 'Ellwoodii', 'Ellwood's Gold', 'Grayswood Feather') can, with age, make medium-sized shrubs or small trees with a more compact habit. Pruning spoils their form, so make sure you select the right cultivar for the planting space. You don't want to have to intervene with the secateurs.

The branch systems of *Chamaecyparis pisifera* 'Squarrosa' are packed with juvenile foliage that may be weighed down and spoiled by the buildup of dead material within the tree. Removing this material is tiresome but will take weight off the branch system and improve the general appearance.

Chamaecyparis thyoides (Atlantic white cypress) is a small to medium-sized conical tree in cultivation. Its several named cultivars include 'Andelyensis' (dwarf, with dense foliage), 'Ericoides' (juvenile foliage), and 'Glauca' (blue foliage). It is not necessary to prune these except to remove dead branches.

CHIMONANTHUS

Habit Upright deciduous shrub for fertile, free-draining soil in a sunny position. **Attributes** Highly fragrant yellow flowers in late winter/early spring. **Reasons for pruning** To maintain a framework and restrict growth. **Pruning time** Early spring following flowering.

Leave *Chimonanthus praecox* (winter sweet) unpruned for at least five years following planting. It will rarely, if at all, flower during this time, but it will develop a strong mature branch system; it is not until growth slows down that the shorter flowering wood is formed. Flower buds are produced in the axils of the leaves on the current or the youngest wood and are fully formed before the leaves fall. The shorter growths can produce a flower in almost every axil. This shrub flowers most freely if a branch system is left to mature without any pruning, and when grown as a bush it can easily be left to develop naturally. Plenty of vigorous renewal shoots are thrown up from the base, and any older weak branches may be pruned out for replacement by these shoots.

Chimonanthus praecox can also be trained against a wall, but the branches will need to be tied in to a wire support system, or it will tend to grow or fall away from the wall. Free growth can be allowed provided space is sufficient, but occasionally a whole section will need to be removed and fresh young growth encouraged from the base to fill in the hole. Prune back some of the growth growing at right angles from the wall annually; do this in late winter, in order to allow a full season's growth for the new wood.

A general rule of thumb for winter sweet: the less the pruning, the more the flower—and the greater the smell of bananas!

Chimonanthus praecox trained as a freestanding shrub.

Chimonanthus praecox trained against a wall.

CHIONANTHUS

Habit Small to medium-sized deciduous excurrent trees, often with wide-spreading branches, for full sun and fertile, free-draining soil. **Attributes** Fragrant white flowers in summer, black olive-like fruits. **Reasons for pruning** To develop a strong framework. **Pruning time** Between autumn and spring (when dormant).

It is difficult to develop a central leader in both *Chionanthus retusus* and *C. virginicus*. Healthy upright growths must be encouraged

A mature *Chionanthus retusus*.

if the plants are to mature into a good shape. Plant them out in their permanent position in a good sunny spot; otherwise, their growth will be poor and stunted. The slow-growing *C. retusus* (Chinese fringetree) is the larger of the two species, forming a medium-sized tree to 7 metres (20 ft.) with a rounded crown under ideal conditions. It naturally produces multiple stems but can be trained on a single trunk. The upright branch structure should be left to develop naturally, but at maturity the branches will start to become more pendulous.

Chionanthus virginicus (American fringetree) is more often shrubby, producing multiple branches originating at the base or near soil level, so don't be disappointed if it fails to make a tree. It can be cut hard back to the base to regenerate a new plant with plenty of vigour if needed.

The shrubby *Chionanthus virginicus*.

×CHITALPA

Habit Small rounded or spreading deciduous tree for deep, well-drained soil and a very sunny position. **Attributes** Pink to white catalpa-like flowers. **Reasons for pruning** To develop a strong framework. **Pruning time** Late summer after flowering.

×Chitalpa tashkentensis is a hybrid of *Catalpa bignonioides* and *Chilopsis linearis* (desert willow). This plant needs very little pruning, apart from the removal of dead wood and some crown thinning to maintain an open centre; this last will improve air circulation—a good thing, as it is prone to mildew. Unfortunately many garden centres sell this plant top-worked onto a catalpa trunk, and the tree develops an unnatural mop head. Try to buy a plant grafted low down and grow it as a shrubby tree, which would make it more effective and bring the flowers down to eye level.

CHOISYA

Habit Dense evergreen shrub for fertile well-drained soil and full sun. **Attributes** Glossy aromatic leaves, white flowers in late spring. **Reasons for pruning** To control size and encourage a second display of flowers later in the season. **Pruning time** Late spring following flowering.

Choisya ternata (Mexican orange blossom), a shrub that loves shelter and the sun, is frequently grown against a sunny wall; however, there should be no attempt to train it hard against the surface, as a freestanding shrub

A freestanding *Choisya ternata*.

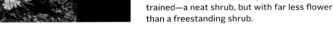

The rules broken and *Choisya ternata* wall-trained—a neat shrub, but with far less flower than a freestanding shrub.

flowers better and gives a more natural foliage effect. Plants flower in late spring, but should the old flower growths be pruned back by 25 to 30 cm (10 to 12 in.) as soon as the first blossoming is finished, a second display is almost certain. They have a very dense bushy habit and will break freely if pruned back hard to the old wood. It may be necessary to do this after damage from a very severe winter or if the shrub has become overgrown.

Choisya ternata 'Sundance', grown for its golden foliage, *C. arizonica*, and *C. ×dewitteana* should be treated in the same way.

CISTUS

Habit Small rounded or sprawling evergreen shrubs for free-draining soil and full sun. **Attributes** A succession of summer flowers, ranging from white to pinks and yellows. **Reasons for pruning** To control size and vigour. **Pruning time** Spring.

When choosing a cistus in the nursery, look for a compact bushy plant. Encourage it to get bushier by stopping it during the first and second season's growth in spring; do not prune back to the ripened branch wood. If plants grow too tall, winds will inevitably blow them over. Cistus are hard-wooded shrubs, and most (e.g., *Cistus ladanifer*, *C. pulverulentus*, *C.*

purpureus) do not respond well to cutting back, as they do not freely break from the stems and branches once the mature bark has formed. If the plant is cut back by frost, the whole plant is killed and will need to be replaced. *Cistus monspeliensis* and *C. parviflorus* are exceptions to this rule: they will regenerate from old wood if it is cut back, which allows for pruning back any sprawling branches.

Winter damage confined to the tips can be cut out, provided the cuts are not taken back into old wood; carry this out in the spring, just as growth is about to start. Remove dead twigs once the threat of frost is past.

The neat, compact habit of *Cistus populifolius*.

CLADRASTIS

Habit Medium to large deciduous decurrent trees, often with round wide-spreading crowns and low horizontal branches, for moist, well-drained soil in full sun. **Attributes** Attractive shape with architectural branching, late pea-like flowers, butter-yellow autumn colour. **Reasons for pruning** To develop a strong framework. **Pruning time** Summer. Never prune in winter or spring as the wounds are prone to bleeding.

These should be transplanted to their final planting position as young as possible, preferably from a container, as they dislike root disturbance when they get older. They must be kept growing without any check; irrigate them if they are stressed by summer drought. Any corrective pruning needed following planting must be carried out in late summer owing to the danger of bleeding at other times. If the lower scaffolds are left to grow without pruning, they will bend under the weight of the foliage and are liable to branch snap. Unpruned trees have a short life span and will fall apart.

Encourage a trunk by retaining the leader and removing feathers and suckers for as long as possible in the tree's early years, as once the leader disappears, the crown will develop into a low wide-spreading decurrent canopy and it will be very difficult to retain a central leader. Remove any laterals with narrow-angled attachment points to prevent weak crowns in the future. Where there is congestion in the branching along the trunk, evenly thin the laterals along the main stem.

Cladrastis kentukea is the largest species. Following planting, keep an eye on the branch extensions and thin out any vigorous growth to prevent heavy end weight.

Cladrastis kentukea, a young established tree growing on a short trunk with even, short branching.

Cladrastis sinensis showing low decurrent wide-spreading canopy.

CLEMATIS

Habit Evergreen and deciduous shrubs and climbers with twining leaf stalks; full sun for the flowering shoots, roots in the shade. **Attributes** Flat, cupped, and bell-shaped flowers of various colours, silky seedheads. **Reasons for pruning** To encourage flowering.

Most clematis are climbing plants, raising themselves by means of their leaf stalks, which coil around any support. The larger growers that retain a permanent and extensive branch system (e.g., *Clematis montana*) are well suited to the larger spaces on walls, fences, pergolas, or even trees. If the support is smooth, it may be necessary to add extra support by a trellis or wire system, provided that this can be strongly secured. Be prepared to tie in some of the main growths, whichever type of support is used.

The ultimate size of the clematis must be taken into account when deciding on the position and a variety. Excessive pruning to restrict size, especially with the larger growers, often spoils their effect and display.

The extent and type of pruning is directly related to the habits of growth and flowering, and clematis may be classified for this purpose into the following three groups:

- Group 1. Early flowering (species and hybrids that flower on the previous year's wood).
- Group 2. Midseason flowering (species and hybrids that grow extensively and flower from the young wood during the summer and autumn).
- Group 3. Late flowering (species and hybrids that flower on growth made in that season).

Clematis montana var. *rubens* covering a sunny wall.

A late-flowering *Clematis tangutica* flowering on growth thinned each spring rather than being hard pruned regularly.

GROUP 1

Pruning time Mid- to late spring, immediately after flowering.

These are mainly the larger growers (e.g., *Clematis alpina*, *C. ×cartmanii*, *C. chrysocoma*, *C. cirrhosa*, *C. macropetala*, *C. montana*, *C. rehderiana*, *C. terniflora*). Newly planted clematis should be pruned back hard to a strong pair of buds 30 cm (12 in.) above ground level, which will encourage many new stems from the base that can be trained to cover the full extent of the wall or support. They require very little pruning. Pruning of established plants should be kept to a minimum, except to cut out the dead wood or perhaps to attempt a reduction of size. Where long growths have come away from their support, prune them back to strong buds. If these varieties are grown in a small or restricted space they may well appear untidy and, if a cleanup is needed, hard cutting back to the base may be resorted to in the early summer as the flowers disappear, but following this operation the plant must be left to re-establish for at least three years.

The evergreen species (e.g., *Clematis aristata*, *C. armandii*) are also treated in this group and do not respond to hard pruning. If

Clematis armandii, unpruned for many years, flowering in early spring.

Pruning late-flowering clematis.

grown in a sheltered site they can reach heights of up to 25 metres (82 ft.), provided they have a support system to attach themselves to, and will produce trailing growths that flower profusely; these may be thinned out annually after flowering, which is usually done to remove scorch-damaged leaves. The cuts should be made back to suitable young shoots, which will be apparent at this stage.

GROUP 2

Pruning time Late winter/early spring and after the first flush of flowers in early summer.

These are the large-flowered hybrids (e.g., 'Barbara Jackman', 'Belle of Woking', 'Nelly Moser', 'The President') that flower midseason. If these are left to grow unattended, they can turn into a huge tangled mess with all the flowers at the top of the plant and out of view. They should be pruned annually to extend the flowering season and to create a well-balanced framework of old and new growths. In winter or early spring, prune out any dead and weak stems, and prune the remaining shoots back to healthy growth with strong buds. Avoid heavy pruning.

Following the first flush of flowers in early summer, prune off the old flowers to strong buds or side shoots immediately below the old bloom. This should encourage a second flush of flowers later in the summer. Renovate overgrown plants by pruning back hard after the first flush of flowers, but by carrying out this operation you will lose the second flush of flowers.

To save time, the plants in this group can be left unpruned and hard pruned to 50 cm (1.5 ft.) every three to four years in late winter. The new growth that appears in spring will require retraining and tying into the support. Only one flush of flowers will be had in the first year following this hard renovation.

Some of the early-flowering large-flowered

hybrids are susceptible to clematis wilt (*Phoma clematidina*), a fungal infection. The symptoms are similar to drought stress—leaves wilt and leaf stalks turn black, followed by wilting of the entire plant. To control, prune affected growth out, back into unaffected tissue. Sterilize tools following pruning, and destroy infected arisings.

GROUP 3

Pruning time Late winter/early spring, when the buds are starting to show signs of growth.

The clematis in this group—*Clematis orientalis*, *C. tangutica*, *C. tibetana*, the viticellas (e.g., 'Abundance', 'Betty Corning', 'Étoile Rose'), the Texensis Group (e.g., 'Duchess of Albany', 'Gravetye Beauty')—produce strong growth from the base every year, so they can be cut back hard to just above ground level annually to restrict the plant's growth and encourage more flowers toward the base of the plant. When establishing a new plant in this group, if it has only a single stem, it can be pruned back hard to 30 cm (12 in.) above ground level to encourage many new stems to train to cover the wall. New growths should be spaced and tied in to the support through the summer as they develop.

Annually in late winter/early spring, prune all the old stems back hard to 30 cm (12 in.) above ground level. This is to encourage new growth for flower production; otherwise, the new shoots develop from the ends of the previous year's growth and the plant will either become top-heavy over the years, collapsing in a tangled mess, or the flowers will be at the top

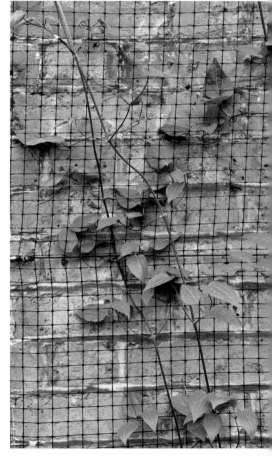

Clematis 'Ville de Lyon' with new growths being tied in.

of the wall or support and lost out of sight.

Clematis orientalis and *C. tangutica* can be trained on a pergola or arbour and the stems thinned out annually, leaving the seedheads to be viewed through winter.

CLERODENDRUM

Habit Deciduous suckering shrubs for fertile, well-drained soil. **Attributes** Fragrant late-season white flowers followed by turquoise berries surrounded by red calyces. **Reasons for pruning** To control size and encourage flowers and suckers. **Pruning time** Between autumn and spring (when dormant).

Three taxa are grown as freestanding shrubs. Two, *Clerodendrum trichotomum* (harlequin glorybower) and *C. trichotomum* var. *fargesii*, are strong growers. With training, both naturally form a head of branches on a short leg, and it will be difficult to maintain a leader for long. As the head of the bush matures, flowering will be improved by shortening the lateral branches produced in the previous year back to the last pair of strong buds in the early spring. By doing this, a number of restricted new growths are produced, which are terminated by the flowers later in the summer. This process can be repeated each year, but some

form of feeding by mulching will be needed to maintain the vigour of the plant. Other than this, very little pruning is necessary.

Avoid hoeing, digging, and other manual weeding operations that are likely to damage the roots where possible, as these will promote suckers; however, if a more bushy shrub is required these new shoots can be trained in the same way to encourage a larger, bushier plant. If not, the suckers can be removed, or lifted and used elsewhere in the garden.

Clerodendrum bungei (glory flower) is a semi-evergreen, semi-woody upright suckering shrub, and even in a sheltered position it is often killed down to ground level each year. This growth should be left on the plant over winter for protection and be pruned back to a woody framework approximately 60 cm (24 in.) above ground level in the spring after the last frost.

Clerodendrum trichotomum, close-up of suckers at ground level.

Clerodendrum trichotomum showing branching framework and suckers.

CLETHRA

Habit Deciduous shrubs or small trees for fertile, acid soil in full or dappled shade. **Attributes** Attractive bark, racemes of white flowers in summer, golden autumnal foliage. **Reasons for pruning** To control size and vigour. **Pruning time** Between autumn and spring (when dormant).

Both *Clethra alnifolia* and *C. tomentosa* develop a mass of growths from soil level; as clumps establish, they spread by means of suckerous growths. The frequent production of new wood from the base allows the older branches and the weaker suckerous growth to be thinned out at ground level in the winter. When a clump extends beyond the limits and becomes too thick and dense, the whole mass is best dug up and replaced.

Clethra acuminata, *C. barbinervis*, and *C. monostachya* form larger shrubs or even small trees and should be allowed to branch naturally from ground level. Plants will send up renewal growths, which allows for some limited pruning during winter if growth is weak. The mature branches and trunk of *C. barbinervis* have attractive flaking bark; lift the lower skirt of the shrub to expose it.

COCCULUS

Habit Deciduous climber by means of slender twining stems for any well-drained soil in full sun to partial shade. **Attributes** Small flowers in late summer, black fruits in autumn. **Reasons for pruning** To control size and vigour.

Pruning time Winter.

Cocculus orbiculatus (coral bead) is suitable for growing up pergolas, tripods, and trellises. Pruning dead wood from the mass of intertwined stems is difficult and must be carried out carefully, or there may be a loss of support. Apart from keeping it within bounds, this climber requires very little pruning.

COLLETIA

Habit Spiny deciduous shrubs for free-draining soil in full sun to partial shade. **Attributes** Architecturally interesting green stems, fragrant white flowers in late summer. **Reasons for pruning** To regenerate new growth and maintain a balanced appearance. **Pruning time** Spring.

Personal protection Wear good thorn-proof clothing and gloves: the spines on these shrubs are very sharp.

One feature of the slow-growing *Colletia hystrix* (barbed wire plant) is that it responds to pruning back at almost every stage of its growth, breaking out with one or more strong laterals beneath each cut. The main branching is sparse, and bushy plants should be encouraged in the nursery by at least one pruning in the spring. After initial pruning, and provided the shrub is growing in an open, sunny position, the shrub should make a balanced shape, and no further pruning for shape will be needed. As the plant matures, the branches bend down under the weight of the foliage; shorten them back to a suitable growing point inside the shrub. Occasionally a growth will spring straight up from the old wood at the base of the plant, extending 1 to 2 metres (3 to 6 ft.) in one growing season. These should be encouraged as replacements for the older branches. If the shrub is grown in a shaded position on one side, the plant will lean heavily out toward the light.

Colletia paradoxa (anchor plant) has flat triangular spines and needs the shelter of a wall in a warm, sunny position.

COLUTEA

Habit Spreading, upright multi-stemmed deciduous shrubs for free-draining soil and full sun to light shade. **Attributes** Pinnate leaves, pea-like flowers followed by inflated seedpods. **Reasons for pruning** To control size and vigour. **Pruning time** Late winter/early spring as new growth breaks out.

These shrubs flower freely in summer on the current season's wood. A key aim is therefore to keep them growing strongly so that a good quantity of young growth is produced each year; the more growth, the more flower. The shrub should be encouraged to branch freely from the ground and allowed to grow to a suitable height before pruning back to create a permanent framework, leaving two of the lowest buds on the young wood in late winter. The height of the framework will vary according to the species and vigour; for instance, *Colutea arborescens* is much stronger than *C. orientalis*. Hard pruning after planting will ensure a firmer hold and a more stable long-term plant.

A variation of this is to train a single stem up to a height of 0.6 to 1.2 metres (2 to 4 ft.) and to prune back to this each year, gradually forming a head of multiple spurs. Specimens treated thus will appeal to some but lack the natural beauty of a free-growing specimen. Even the hard-pruned bush lacks the natural beauty, and in a few years the response to pruning will become weak and the plant should be replaced.

If a natural free-growing shrub with a spreading habit is grown, pruning will be minimal. Cut out some of the older wood and the weaker growths or even major branches in the winter, taking care to cut back to selective growths to retain the natural shape.

CORDYLINE

Habit Evergreen palm-like branching tree for free-draining soil and full sun. **Attributes** Architectural sword-like foliage on the ends of branches, creamy white summer flowers. **Reasons for pruning** To control size and vigour. **Pruning time** Spring as new growth begins.

Cordyline australis (cabbage tree) requires very little pruning, apart from the removal of dead leaves and old flower stems. If planted on the borders of its hardiness, it may suffer from frost damage; when new growth breaks from the stem the following spring, the stem can be cut back to just above the new shoots. When cut hard back to the ground or new basal side shoots, it responds by forming a multi-stemmed specimen.

Cordyline australis with newly breaking buds produced shortly after the removal of a main branch.

CORNUS

There are two main types of growth form and habit in this genus, each requiring a different approach to pruning: the larger growers or tree-forming species, which with training form a trunk; and the shrubby species, many of which have coloured stems and respond to pruning. It's important to recognise these two habits, as there are great differences in their pruning and training.

TREE-FORMING SPECIES

Habit Evergreen and deciduous trees with strong horizontal branching for free-draining soil in full sun. **Attributes** Elegant shape and tiered form, attractive bark and flowers, striking autumn colour. **Reasons for pruning** To control size and vigour. **Pruning time** Between autumn and spring (when dormant).

Cornus mas (cornelian cherry) displays attractive yellow flowers in the spring. It will form either a large shrub or small tree; much depends on the nursery training. If a leader isn't selected, it branches from near ground level and will be very spreading, the lowest branches growing along the soil surface, forming an impenetrable canopy of foliage with crossing branches. If a leader is selected, a clean stem of 0.6 to 2 metres (2 to 6 ft.) high can be formed; this will develop into a trunk, displaying the attractive bark. Both forms, shrub and tree, should be trained to retain the lower skirt.

Cornus officinalis (Japanese cornel dogwood) is closely related to *C. mas* but the twig system is very untidy. Neither species normally needs pruning.

The North American dogwoods *Cornus nuttallii* and *C. florida* produce a round symmetrical crown and should be trained on a single leader, but low pendulous branching should be encouraged to show off the flowers and autumn colour to best effect. Normally pruning is not required or desirable, but dead wood or damaged branches, which may accumulate in the canopy, can be removed after flowering. Hard pruning is not tolerated by these species; it may result in stem dieback if carried out.

Cornus florida grown on a trunk with a symmetrical round crown.

Cornus mas showing a dense network of branchlets.

Both North American dogwoods and *Cornus kousa* are susceptible to cornus anthracnose (*Discula destructiva*), which infects and kills young shoots and leaves. Young stems die back, and small pimple-like fruiting bodies can be seen on the bark. Do not prune an infected dogwood in wet conditions, during which the infection spreads more easily, and sterilize pruning tools before working on non-infected plants to prevent the disease's spread.

Cornus kousa (kousa dogwood) forms a leader and a trunk with very little intervention. Let the lower horizontal branches develop, for the feathered, tiered effect. Very little pruning is required apart from removing dead wood. This species will not tolerate hard pruning.

Cornus kousa var. *chinensis* (Chinese dogwood) has a distinctly upright, almost fastigiate habit, and no attempt should be made to retain a leader. It flowers naturally at an early age without any pruning. Another kousa type, *C. angustata* 'Empress of China', matches any dogwood for flowering capability and length of flowering period.

Cornus capitata (Bentham's cornel) is an evergreen tree to 10 metres (33 ft.) high in nature but frequently makes a tall, multi-stemmed shrub in cultivation. Little pruning is necessary, apart from removing dead wood following a cold winter.

Cornus elliptica grows to 12 metres (40 ft.) and can be semi-evergreen, depending on the winter and planting position. It should be left to grow naturally. Very little pruning is needed, apart from keeping the tree tidy and removing any growths damaged by a cold winter.

Cornus controversa (Japanese dogwood) is a deciduous tree to 15 metres (50 ft.) high and should be trained for as long as possible with a definite leader, which forms a strong trunk in later years. The horizontal branches are tiered and tipped with deep red twigs. Give the tree plenty of room all around, so that the tiered effect can develop to its full extent—it is one of the tree's strong attributes. The timing

Cornus controversa 'Variegata' too is treasured for its tiered habit.

Cornus kousa var. *chinensis* deserves a prime place in the garden.

Cornus controversa showing the tiered effect.

A bleeding pruning wound on *Cornus controversa* colonized by a yeast fungus.

Using secateurs in spring to stool *Cornus alba* 'Sibirica' back to a framework.

Cornus alba 'Sibirica' after stooling, showing arisings.

Cornus alba 'Sibirica' and *C. alba* 'Kesselringii', winter stem effect.

of pruning is important for *C. controversa*, as wounds are prone to heavy bleeding and the sap is then colonized by a pink-coloured yeast fungus. This quickly dries up and is mainly an aesthetic problem on the tree, but it can be worrying to the pruner.

Cornus controversa 'Variegata' (wedding cake tree) is a favourite variegated tree. It is slower growing than the type but is a delightful architectural plant if the leader is retained and maintained and an upright plant is encouraged.

Cornus alternifolia (pagoda dogwood) is the Western form and very similar to *C. controversa*, but slightly smaller. If a leader is encouraged and maintained it forms a small tree to 8 metres (25 ft.) high; without intervention, it forms a large multi-stemmed shrub with numerous upright branches.

Crossing the North Americans *Cornus florida* and *C. nuttallii* with *C. kousa* from the Far East has resulted in the beautiful Rutger Hybrids, *C.* ×*rutgersensis*, which make small trees to 6 metres (20 ft.) high. They are very tough, with good drought tolerance and a high resistance to dogwood anthracnose and boring insects. Their most striking attributes are their white/pink bracts, which appear for several weeks in mid-spring.

Cornus 'Venus', one of the new Stellar dogwoods, bears huge flowers and provides spectacular autumn colour, its large, glossy green leaves taking on rich shades of yellow, orange, and purple. This hybrid has long internodes and makes a tall, open plant with an unfurnished centre and skirt. To give it a more natural-looking, balanced, compact habit, which better shows off the flowers, reduce the upright stems following establishment; this makes a bushier, stocky plant. Although it has some drought resistance, it benefits from regular watering to establish and good mulching always.

SHRUBBY SPECIES

Habit Deciduous and evergreen upright shrubs with arching branches for free-draining soil in full sun to partial shade. **Attributes** Brightly coloured stems, some with variegated or coloured leaves. **Reasons for pruning** To encourage the vigorous upright growth of coloured stems. **Pruning time** Spring, just before bud break for maximum period of stem effect.

Most of the shrubby species are pruned annually, stooled and grown mainly for their coloured stem effect. *Cornus alba* and its many cultivars (e.g., 'Sibirica', 'Kesselringii'), *C. sericea* 'Flaviramea', and *C. sanguinea* are outstanding when grown for this purpose, but a number of other species (e.g., *C. racemosa*, *C. rugosa*) respond in the same way.

Following planting from the nursery, allow at least one full growing season to let the shrub to establish with a strong root system and to begin to produce some increment on the stem.

After the second spring, just as growth is about to begin, the complete top of the plant is cut down to about 5 cm (2 in.) above ground level. In the response to this, a crop of young stems is thrown up from the remaining stem; these are brightly coloured and remain decorative during the late autumn and winter. This cutting back in the spring is repeated year after year. As the plant matures, the framework that develops low down will produce a further number of young stems following pruning (see coppicing, page 000). To maintain vigour in the plants, feeding and mulching will be necessary. If the strength of the plant begins to slow down and the new stems produced are thinner and shorter, move pruning to every other year to give the shrub some rest time.

With coppicing, there will be no flower or fruit. But these shrubby species can be left to grow naturally in bush form, which will flower and fruit. When unpruned and left to grow freely, many are spreading and suitable for the more natural areas of the garden. An overgrown specimen can be reduced to reasonable size by pruning out older growths toward the centre of the bush; prune out whole branches rather than small shoots on the outside. This practice also encourages a good number of young stems, which will lend extra winter colour to the bush.

Variegated dogwoods (e.g., *Cornus alba* 'Elegantissima', 'Spaethii') aren't as vigorous as the species. To maintain their variegation, prune out old stems biennially, always leaving a natural framework of younger material.

CORONILLA

Habit Bushy, dense, medium-sized evergreen shrub for a sunny, sheltered location in free-draining soil. **Attributes** Fragrant yellow flowers from early spring onward. **Reasons for pruning** Little pruning needed. **Pruning time** Spring as new growth begins.

For the tender *Coronilla valentina* (bastard senna), prune any dead shoot tips back to living wood in spring when new growth starts. Any old wood and tired growths can be pruned out at the same time. Little else in the way of pruning is necessary.

CORYLOPSIS

Habit Upright-spreading deciduous shrubs for moist, well-drained acid to neutral soil in partial shade to full sun. **Attributes** Lime-green new foliage, fragrant yellow flowers hanging in tassels from leafless stems. **Reasons for pruning** To maintain size and vigour. **Pruning time** Mid-spring following flowering.

Well-shaped specimens of winter hazels (e.g., *Corylopsis glabrescens*, *C. sinensis*) are among the loveliest shrubs of late winter/early spring. Give them enough space to spread out unimpeded, both in the nursery and in the final planting space. Young plants should be allowed to branch freely from ground level; any form of pruning at this stage would undoubtedly spoil their eventual naturally attractive shape. Any pruning that is absolutely necessary (e.g., the removal of tired old branches and dead wood) should be done in mid-spring, immediately after flowering.

Corylopsis glabrescens showing the upright-spreading habit.

CORYLUS

TREE-FORMING SPECIES

Habit Deciduous excurrent trees for alkaline soils in full sun. **Attributes** Shaggy grey bark and pendulous tassels of catkins in spring followed by interesting fruits. **Reasons for pruning** To develop a strong framework and remove suckers. **Pruning time** Autumn through winter (when dormant).

With *Corylus colurna* (Turkish hazel) and *C. chinensis* (Chinese hazel), the largest of the hazel trees, a leader should be selected at an early stage in the nursery. The leader will develop rapidly once the tree is planted in its permanent location. If lost due to winter cold or bird damage, a new one will naturally take over and continue to produce a strong excurrent crown. To better display the attractive bark, the canopy should be lifted by gradually removing the lower branches up to 2 metres (6 ft.), making a standard tree. The main branches are usually sparse and grow upward at a slight or distinct angle, making a symmetrical pyramidal crown in the early years; however, after about 50 years, the main scaffolds begin to grow outward and a more ungainly, unsymmetrical upper crown is formed. Little pruning is necessary, apart from some formative pruning in the early days.

A young *Corylus colurna* with a symmetrical pyramidal crown.

Corylus colurna medium-aged specimen, still showing the strong pyramidal crown before losing it, as it goes into maturity.

Corylus avellana stool, with an uncoppiced plant in the background.

Corylus tibetica (Tibetan hazel) makes a tree to 15 metres (50 ft.) high. Grow it as a multi-stemmed tree, as it will be difficult to maintain an excurrent crown.

SHRUBBY SPECIES

Habit Large deciduous suckering shrubs for rich, free-draining soil in full sun to partial shade. **Attributes** Upright straight stems, yellow lamb's-tails catkins in late winter/early spring, edible nuts in autumn. **Reasons for pruning** To maintain a vigorous shrub and remove suckers. **Pruning time** Autumn through winter (when dormant).

Corylus avellana (hazel, filbert) can be coppiced (see page 000) on a rotation to produce a crop of straight, strong branches that can be put to a variety of garden uses, such as pea and bean sticks, herbaceous border supports, and material for fence/hurdle construction. If only the suckers are removed at least annually, this and other shrubby species will reach heights of 3 to 6 metres (10 to 20 ft.) with three or more main branches from the base and a strong compound branch system, which will produce a good display of yellow catkins. To maintain a shrub in this style, it will be necessary to oc-

casionally cut a mature branch down to ground level in winter, training a young vigorous one for a replacement. This often throws the whole plant out of balance. It is more effective to coppice the bush to near ground level followed by thinning and training a fresh crop of replacement growths.

Corylus avellana 'Heterophylla' produces interesting laciniate foliage, which looks at its best when the branches are furnished to the ground. Provided the shrub has been propagated by layering or cuttings, it can be treated in the same way as the type.

Corylus avellana 'Contorta' (corkscrew hazel) is often grafted, and if the suckers from the base aren't removed, it will soon revert back to the rootstock. Plants grafted onto *C. colurna* do not sucker (or revert).

Corylus maxima (giant filbert) is stronger growing than *C. avellana*, and its selection 'Purpurea' has very dark purple leaves. Pruning to retain height; leave mature growths and thin out the weaker wood in winter.

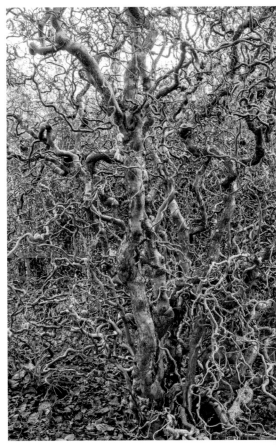

Corylus avellana 'Contorta' showing the twisted framework.

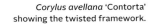

COTINUS

Habit Spreading deciduous shrubs or small trees with low-spreading branches for moist, free-draining soil in partial shade to full sun. **Attributes** Frothy pink flowers in early summer, foliage in various colours with good autumnal tints. **Reasons for pruning** Neither species requires pruning, but they can be cut back for stronger foliage effect. **Pruning time** Spring.

Personal protection Protect your skin when pruning smoketrees. Some people have an allergic reaction to the sap, which may result in a skin rash, similar to that caused by *Rhus*.

Cotinus obovatus should be left to grow naturally, furnished with lower branches to show off the wonderful autumn colour; however, for *C. coggygria*, the most commonly grown species, two methods of cultivation are possible.

Grown with no regular pruning, the plant will form a large shrub or small tree with a rounded bushy head made up of short twiggy growths on a stout trunk and branch system. Young plants should be encouraged to branch from ground level, which gives the plant stability. The stem system of a mature plant is often covered with clusters of adventitious buds; do not remove these, as this is part of the character and natural habit of the plant. Under this natural system, very little pruning is required apart from the removal of dead wood and pruning off old flower heads in spring before new growth starts.

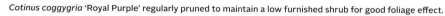
Cotinus obovatus grown on a clean trunk as a freestanding tree.

Cotinus coggygria 'Royal Purple' regularly pruned to maintain a low furnished shrub for good foliage effect.

Cotinus obovatus with the lower branches left to furnish the shrub.

Grown for foliage effect, an established *Cotinus coggygria* and especially the coloured-foliage forms involving it (e.g., *C.* 'Flame') are shown to their best effect with an annual pruning in spring that yields larger leaves. The shrub will build up a framework, which consists of one to three main stems springing from ground level. These should be allowed to branch again until a height of 0.6 to 1 metre (2 to 3 ft.) is reached with substantial wood.

Pruning is carried out annually from this point, cutting down the young wood to the two lowest buds just before growth starts in the spring. Carefully position this cut: if the cut is too low, regrowth from the adventitious buds will be later and smaller.

COTONEASTER

Habit Deciduous and evergreen prostrate shrubs to small decurrent trees for fertile soil in full sun to partial shade. **Attributes** Attractive berries through winter; some species have good autumn colour, make good groundcovers and hedges. **Reasons for pruning** To restrict size, maintain an open habit, and encourage flowering for berries. **Pruning time** Winter to encourage growth and summer to encourage flowers.

Most *Cotoneaster* species respond strongly if pruned back hard into old wood or to the base of the shrub, but normally there is little need to do this. It may be necessary to restrict the growth of the shrub, in which case a few long woody pieces of the plant should be removed, cutting carefully back into the shrub so that the wounds and the effects of the removal may be hidden by the growths that remain. Any badly placed cuts will eventually be covered by additional growth.

As always, it is best to select the right species for the position, so that the need for restrictive pruning is reduced or, better still, prevented. A bushy plant should be encouraged in the nursery; often this develops naturally without any pinching out or pruning. In order not to spoil the overall shape and effect of the plants, the pruner must take into account the four growth habits of the various species before selection and pruning. These are as follows:

- Group 1. Erect and spreading shrubs or small trees with arching branches.
- Group 2. Small to medium-sized shrubs with ascending branches.
- Group 3. Dwarf, prostrate, or creeping shrubs.
- Group 4. Informal hedging shrubs.

GROUP 1
Indiscriminate pruning very easily spoils the graceful habit of these shrubs or small trees (e.g., *Cotoneaster bullatus*, *C. franchetii*, *C. frigidus*, *C. insignis*, *C. lacteus*, *C. multiflorus*, *C. salicifolius*, *C. simonsii*, *C.* ×*watereri*), and they are best when left to grow naturally. Most have long slender branches that should be left at full

Large overextended branches on this multi-stemmed *Cotoneaster frigidus* were removed in the previous season to encourage new growth.

The base of the thinned *Cotoneaster frigidus* showing the new shoots generated.

Cotoneaster horizontalis wall-trained.

Cotoneaster ascendens showing its dwarf creeping habit.

length for best effect; cut out complete branches if necessary rather than just snipping back. Many are vigorous enough to be grown as a tree, trained on a single trunk, but this must be started early following planting.

GROUP 2

Several species in this group (e.g., *Cotoneaster conspicuus, C. divaricatus, C. horizontalis, C. lucidus*) have an almost tiered branching habit. To retain this informal effect, whole lengths of branches should be cut out rather than snipping off short lengths. One of the features of *C. horizontalis* and others in this group is the fishbone effect produced by the main growths with the regular arrangement of branchlets on either side. Retain this characteristic when pruning. When planted against a wall, these plants will push against it with a spring-like action

and gain height up the wall. Once they start to fall away from the wall it may be necessary to tie the main branches in by some means.

GROUP 3

Some form of pruning may be needed to restrict spread of these cotoneasters (e.g., *Cotoneaster adpressus, C. apiculatus, C. ascendens, C. dammeri, C. salicifolius* 'Repens', *C. ×suecicus* 'Coral Beauty'), even when young plants are spaced properly from the beginning. Rather than a quick result using hedging shears resulting in a straight rigid line, an informal effect should be maintained by carefully cutting out individual branches, taking them back into the shrub, where the cuts can be hidden by the remaining growths.

GROUP 4

Several taxa (e.g., *Cotoneaster lacteus, C. lucidus, C. simonsii*) are well suited for informal hedging, particularly the species with upright growth. To keep the hedge shapely and within its bounds, prune out whole lengths of growth, after the berry display. This is the only method of restricting size, as clipping over the entire surface will make the hedge a more formal feature. Some limited pruning can be done during the growing season with, however, the loss of growth and flowers. After flowering, be on the lookout for fireblight (*Erwinia amylovora*). Where it is found, the infected branch should be pruned at least 0.3 metre (1 ft.) beyond any sign of infection and the infected arisings burned. Before any further pruning, sterilize tools to ensure that the disease isn't spread to healthy plants.

CRATAEGUS

Habit Small deciduous decurrent trees with dense, spreading crowns for full sun. **Attributes** Thorny twigs bearing panicles of fragrant white flowers in spring followed by red or black fruits (haws). **Reasons for pruning** To develop a strong framework and clean trunk. **Pruning time** Winter or after flowering in early summer.

Personal protection Wear good thorn-proof clothing and gloves, as every species of hawthorn is armed with needle-like thorns. Use long-handled loppers to remove old growths in the centre of the tree to gain access with the pruning saw.

Crataegus monogyna showing its rounded habit and low branching.

The majority of species are small deciduous trees, often with a twisted and matted branch system. Most nursery specimens have a clean stem, branching head, and no central leader, but feathered trees are a better choice if you want to be in control of the tree's height. Do this by training and extending the central leader as the crown forms until it reaches the desired height. Remove the lower branches if you want to convert the tree to a standard. A central leader is particularly important with the larger growers, as the branching becomes very heavy for the slender trunk. An open-headed tree with branches arising from one point may become weak in later years on mature specimens.

Once a tree is established, growth is often rapid, and the leader breaks up to form a head.

In later years, the head may be so matted, you might think of thinning it, but this is the natural habit and should be left. Thinning might also encourage the production of epicormic growths, giving the specimen an unnatural appearance, and over-thinning may actually weaken a tree.

A standard tree grown in an exposed position tends to lean and may appear unsafe. Inspect it to be sure, but this is a natural habit and the tree may be perfectly sound.

Crataegus submollis grown as a multi-stemmed specimen with a round crown.

CRINODENDRON

Habit Evergreen shrubs or small trees for moist, free-draining soil and full sun to partial shade. **Attributes** Highly ornamental, with red lantern-shaped flowers on *Crinodendron hookerianum* and white bell-shaped flowers on *C. patagua*. **Reasons for pruning** To remove dead wood. **Pruning time** Spring.

Crinodendron patagua (lily of the valley tree) requires the shelter of a sunny wall. In this position, it is best left as a freestanding specimen. Little pruning is necessary apart from pruning out the dead twiggy growths following a cold winter.

The very demanding *Crinodendron hookerianum* (Chilean lantern tree) requires perfect conditions to grow well. These include shelter, a partially shaded position, free-draining acid soil, and moisture, both in the ground and in the air. A healthy specimen requires little pruning beyond cutting back any dead wood in spring.

A free-flowering
Crinodendron hookerianum.

CRYPTOMERIA

Habit Large, slow-growing evergreen excurrent conifer for moist, free-draining soil and full sun. **Attributes** Stately symmetrical tree, perfect as a lawn specimen, with elegant form and red-brown bark. **Reasons for pruning** To develop a strong framework. **Pruning time** Spring and late summer.

Cryptomeria japonica (Japanese cedar, sugi) forms a definite main leader, with a straight trunk running up through the centre of the tree. If competing leaders develop, they should be pruned out early, leaving one dominant leader. The lower branches should be left and the tree given space all around to develop a naturally low-branching canopy; however,

A young *Cryptomeria japonica*.

after a short time these lower branches will die back and need to be removed. As the tree matures, it loses its conical-pyramidal form and develops a broad, rounded crown.

If renovation is needed, an old specimen will tolerate hard pruning of the main branches or coppicing and will send up vigorous regrowth from the pruning cuts. When stooled, it makes an interesting standard tree for a Japanese garden; simply remove the lower branches back to the trunk.

Cryptomeria japonica 'Elegans', a juvenile form, produces a feathery branch system, but the main stem, although supple, is weak: a large specimen 4.5 to 6 metres (15 to 20 ft.) high is often bent down to ground level by the effects of heavy rain or snow. If this happens, cut the main trunk back hard to within 1 to 2 metres (3 to 6 ft.) of the ground, and simultaneously reduce all the main branches back close to the trunk. This cultivar also makes a good formal hedge, trimmed once a year in late summer.

Cryptomeria japonica 'Lobbii' has a more upright pyramidal form than the type and makes a better specimen for the Japanese garden.

Cryptomeria japonica in Japan, showing mature rounded crowns.

Cryptomeria japonica stooled and grown as a small standard.

CUNNINGHAMIA

Cunninghamia lanceolata, multi-stemmed due to winter cold damage.

Habit Small to medium-sized upright conifers for a sheltered spot in moist, free-draining soil and full sun. **Attributes** Specimen trees with stringy red-brown bark and architectural foliage. **Reasons for pruning** To control size and vigour. **Pruning time** Late spring.

The best way of growing *Cunninghamia lanceolata* (Chinese fir), the commonly cultivated species, is on a single, straight trunk with horizontal branching and the lower branches retained to ground level; however, in colder areas the central leader may be lost early in the life of the plant, and a multi-stemmed specimen will develop. These plants are still handsome, but weaknesses may develop where the stems originate, and as the main branches become heavy with growth, they may bend down and break out. These stems can be removed and new growth will develop into replacement stems from the pruning point.

Cunninghamia konishii from Taiwan is less hardy than *C. lanceolata*. If a tree form is required, select a leader, especially if several develop following a cold winter. This is a scruffy-looking plant, retaining all its dead branches even in the best of climates, so make sure it's well hidden and not in a prime position.

Both species tolerate coppicing and will readily reshoot from the base of the plant. Cunninghamias respond well to hard pruning; ragged old multi-stemmed specimens can be regenerated by hard pruning in late spring. This must be supported by feeding and irrigating once the growing season begins. During a cold winter, trees will shed whole branchlets, which turn brown in winter.

CUPRESSUS

Habit Upright random-branched evergreen conifers for free-draining soil and full sun. **Attributes** Fast growing in youth, with scale-like aromatic leaves of various colours on rounded shoots. **Reasons for pruning** To control size and vigour. **Pruning time** Summer.

Personal protection Regular contact between the foliage and bare skin can cause an irritating rash; wear gloves and arm protection when pruning.

Cupressus species are unable to regenerate a strong anchor root system once checked, and if the root system is poorly developed the tree will be prone to being blown over in gales. Before buying, check trees have a strong well-produced root system with no spiralling roots in the container, and plant new stock soon after taking delivery. The habit of most cypresses is to develop a definite leader from a very early stage; as this thickens and matures it becomes the central trunk and the framework upon which the mature tree is built. If the leader is damaged or lost, most species are able to form a new one from the uppermost laterals.

With strong or vigorous specimens (e.g., *C. macrocarpa*), new leaders can be formed from growths originating from much older wood, especially following extensive reduction of the crown, but this is not an approach we would advocate as it is unsightly and usually caused by planting in too small a space. If the damage is already done, several new leaders are produced; select one and remove the others.

Cupressus macrocarpa begins life upright and conical, but as it ages it becomes broader and the canopy opens up. This is when branches become vulnerable and may be lost in storms or heavy snowfalls.

Some species (e.g., *Cupressus cashmeriana*, *C. arizonica*) are not as hardy, and in a cold or exposed situation the young growth may be subject to frost damage, which will never grow back and eventually need pruning out.

Cupressus macrocarpa is often used as a formal hedging plant, but although fast growing it is not a good subject for this purpose. It does not tolerate severe clipping, often browning in patches, and too frequently whole plants in the hedge die.

Cupressus sempervirens normally has a very tight, narrow upright habit and is usually clipped in the nursery to retain this tight form. Once established, some of the main branches can fall out of shape following vigorous growth, strong winds, or snow; these may need to be pruned out or tied back in to the trunk to keep the tight, pencil habit.

Cupressus macrocarpa showing severe damage from many winter storms.

Cupressus sempervirens showing the narrow, tight upright form.

Various forms of *Cupressus sempervirens* growing in a landscape.

×CUPROCYPARIS

Habit Random-branched conical excurrent evergreen conifer for free-draining soil and full sun. **Attributes** Tough, fast-growing dense hedging plant. **Reasons for pruning** To control size and vigour. **Pruning time** Summer.

Personal protection Regular contact between the foliage and bare skin can cause an irritating rash; wear gloves and arm protection when pruning.

×*Cuprocyparis leylandii* (Leyland cypress) is made up of several clones, which vary slightly in habit yet are similar in their mode of growth to typical forms of *Xanthocyparis* and *Chamaecyparis*. A central leader is developed at an early stage, even from cuttings taken from laterals, provided they are sufficiently vigorous. From this leader a central trunk is built up, yielding a columnar tree with little spread. The lateral branching is ascending, with some variation across the clones.

As a single specimen they make a fine tree, but when used as a hedging plant in a small, domestic garden they grow too fast. They have gained a bad reputation as "the conifer from hell" and been the cause of many disputes between neighbours.

When grown as a hedging plant, the leader should be retained until the desired height is reached, leaving 15 to 30 cm (6 to 12 in.) beyond the final height. The tops are then taken off just above a lateral about 15 cm (6 in.) below this height. The best time to do this topping (and for subsequent clipping of the hedge) is summer. Avoid clipping in autumn, winter, and early spring.

Coryneum canker (*Seridium cardinale*) is a disfiguring and fatal fungal disease of Leyland cypress. Remove branches below dead bark to slow its spread, but once the infection is in a hedge, it is inevitable the trees will die and need to be removed.

×*Cuprocyparis leylandii* grown as a single specimen.

CYDONIA

Habit Dense, low-branching deciduous suckering shrub or small decurrent tree for fertile, free-draining soil in full sun. **Attributes** Self-fertile white to pink flowers and fragrant, edible yellow fruits. **Reasons for pruning** To encourage flowering shoots and maintain an open centre. **Pruning time** Winter.

Cydonia oblonga (quince) flowers on the previous year's growth and requires training following establishment. It is prone to suckering and will branch freely from low down at ground level, forming a dense thicket-like mat of growth with several upright main stems. The multi-stemmed look can be avoided and a

short standard produced by pruning these out and encouraging a main central leader.

Indeed, the standard tree or bush on a short clean stem is the best way to grow this species and its cultivars. Grown as a 2 metre (6 ft.) short standard, the main branches should be developed with an open centre. As the framework of branches is formed, the only pruning required will be to prune out crossing or crowded branches to maintain an open, tidy centre and balanced crown. As the head of the tree develops, very little formative pruning will be necessary apart from the removal of the occasional old wood, vigorous shoots, and tired branches. Never prune too hard in one season, or the plant will respond by producing vigorous shoots, which will later need thinning.

Cydonia oblonga grown as a short standard.

CYTISUS

Habit Prostrate to large deciduous and evergreen upright shrubs for free-draining soil in sunny positions. **Attributes** White or yellow pea-like flowers in late spring/early summer. **Reasons for pruning** To reduce the buildup of bare wood and remove developing seedpods. **Pruning time** Summer, immediately after flowering.

The many species and hybrids in this genus display a wide range of growth habits. Take these habits into consideration before deciding to prune or not.

Cytisus multiflorus, *C. praecox*, *C. scoparius*, and their popular forms and cultivars (e.g., 'Lady Moore', 'Lord Lambourne', 'Firefly')

A typically sprawling
Cytisus multiflorus.

should have been hard pruned in the nursery before spring growth begins. In the garden, prune them annually immediately after flowering in order to conserve vigour: the plant's energy should be spent on producing new growth, not a crop of seedpods. These shrubs flower along the length of the previous year's wood; strong-growing plants often produce growths that branch freely during one season and flower the following year. Pruning involves removing approximately two-thirds of the pre-vious year's shoots, which simultaneously removes most of the developing seedpods; new growths will spring from below these cuts. Do not cut too hard into old and hard wood, as many brooms do not break freely from this wood. This form of pruning also keeps these sprawling plants from becoming too leggy. A shapely plant is retained for longer, making it less likely the plant will fall over from being top-heavy, especially during heavy snowfalls.

The low-growing species, *Cytisus ×beanii* and *C. ×kewensis*, are seldom pruned. To prevent these compact shrubs from maturing too quickly, prune out individual fruiting stems out after flowering.

Cytisus nigricans flowers on the current season's growth in mid- to late summer and should be pruned back to developing shoots at the base in spring; the summer pruning that is carried out after flowering is then restricted to merely cutting off the flowered portion of the stems to prevent fruiting.

DAPHNE

Habit Small to large deciduous and evergreen prostrate and upright shrubs for a fertile, moist, well-drained soil in full sun to partial shade. **Attributes** Fragrant flowers followed by red or black fleshy fruits. **Reasons for pruning** To remove dieback only. **Pruning time** Autumn until mid-winter.

Personal protection All parts of daphnes are toxic if eaten. Wear gloves when pruning and wash hands immediately after pruning before eating or drinking. Dispose of arisings safely; don't leave them for pets to forage on.

Normally daphnes do not need any pruning, and often if you attempt to prune one, it dies back, so it's best not to attempt it and leave well alone, especially if the plant is healthy and growing well. They are, however, susceptible to dieback, which can be lightly pruned out to tidy the plant up. If the dieback is severe, the branch or stem should be removed back to the parent at the branch base. To prevent dieback, provide the plant with the optimum growing conditions—well-drained soil with lots of organic matter and a pH of between 6 and 7—and avoid pruning at all cost.

Daphne bholua and her cultivars can be deciduous or semi-evergreen, depending on the winter and the site. Plants are generally upright growers to 2 metres (6 ft.) and need no pruning. Other cultivars are derived from the many compact and prostrate species (e.g., *D. blagayana*, *D. cneorum*, *D. petraea*).

Daphne bholua 'Jacqueline Postill' free-flowering on a naturally well-developed framework of branches.

Daphne mezereum growing wild in Switzerland.

DAPHNIPHYLLUM

Habit Rounded evergreen shrub or small tree for moist, well-drained soil in full sun, tolerant of dappled shade. **Attributes** Stately form, long, shiny green foliage on red petioles, fragrant flowers. **Reasons for pruning** To develop a strong framework and shape. **Pruning time** Autumn until mid-winter.

Ideally, *Daphniphyllum macropodum* should be planted in full sun and in a position where it can grow unrestricted to its full potential. When grown in the shade, it becomes thin and spreading with a loose untidy habit. Very little pruning is needed for this plant, which should be encouraged to branch freely from the base, with foliage right down to the ground, forming a dense, rounded bush. Some dead wood may be generated in the centre of the bush; be careful not to damage the outer shoots when trying to remove this material, as the shoots can be quite brittle and easily snapped off. This species responds well to being cut back hard, producing new growth from the older wood. Pinch out the tips of the new shoots as they develop to encourage a well-branched specimen.

Daphniphyllum macropodum growing wild in Japan in shade, with loose habit.

DASIPHORA

Habit Dense, domed deciduous shrubs for free-draining soil in full sun. **Attributes** Silvery green leaves, white or yellow saucer-shaped flowers from late spring through late summer, easy to grow. **Reasons for pruning** To encourage a bushy plant and promote flowering. **Pruning time** Spring.

The popular *Dasiphora fruticosa* (shrubby cinquefoil) forms a dense shrub with the main branches growing upright, increasing in size to form a permanent branch system. Its many cultivars, forms, and varieties replicate this habit; however, if left unpruned they develop a mat of growth, the older and weaker branches being weighed down by the younger, with old fallen leaves building up in the fine mass of branches, making the bush look very untidy.

Each spring, cut the weaker wood and smaller growths back to stronger wood or to the base. The strong, young growths, often sent up from the base or from the older wood in the centre, should be shortened to half or two-thirds of their length. It is the laterals from these that flower the most and over the longest period; the old, small, twiggy growths do not flower extensively, nor for so long a period. Deadhead in late summer with hedging shears

Dasiphora fruticosa showing its dense, domed habit.

to give a neater appearance to the bush. The several popular low dwarf forms (e.g., 'Goldstar', 'New Dawn', 'Pink Beauty') should be pruned in the same manner.

DAVIDIA

Habit Medium to large deciduous excurrent trees for rich, moist, free-draining soil and full sun. **Attributes** Scaly bark, flowers with large white bracts in late spring. **Reasons for pruning** To develop a strong framework. **Pruning time** Autumn until mid-winter.

When buying a specimen of *Davidia involucrata* (handkerchief tree, dove tree) from the nursery, look for a feathered tree with low branching rather than a tree with a tall clean stem and a high crown. Once planted keep it as vigorous as possible, retaining the leader and lower branches until a symmetrical shape begins to form. If the leader is damaged somehow or lost to frost, select and retrain a new one. Start the forming of a clean stem after planting by pruning off the laterals to the desired height. The crown of the tree will not be evident until the tree is allowed to develop a shape. It can be grown as a multi-stemmed tree, when several of the upright laterals want to take over; however, the form is less graceful than that of a single-leader specimen.

Davidia involucrata retains a leader with-out any difficulty or need for pruning. The branches are ascending and evenly spaced along the trunk, with sparse lateral branching. Once mature the leader terminates, and the outline of the crown becomes wide and spreading. The natural graceful effect will be spoiled if the spreading branches are restricted by lack of sufficient light or pruning. If required, as the tree gains height, the lower branches may be removed back to the stem in late summer to form a 2 metre (6 ft.) clean trunk, to expose the attractive bark; however, the lower skirt should be left as low as possible so that the showy bracts produced on the previous year's growth can be easily viewed. Patience is needed to see a davidia flower following planting; the exception is 'Sonoma', a grafted selection using scion wood from an old flowering plant, which flowers relatively early in the tree's life.

Davidia involucrata does not respond to hard renovation pruning. Do not attempt it, unless the upper crown is damaged in strong winds or heavy snowfall.

A young, well-formed *Davidia involucrata*.

A mature *Davidia involucrata*.

DECAISNEA

Habit Upright deciduous shrub for fertile soil and partial shade. **Attributes** Violet-coloured young foliage, large bean-like violet-blue fruits. **Reasons for pruning** To remove weak growth and dead wood. **Pruning time** Late spring.

Decaisnea fargesii (dead man's fingers) is not freely branching. Late spring frosts sometimes kill young shoots as they break from the base, which can leave short lengths of dead wood. Prune these out later in the season, when buds below break to form new shoots. Occasionally the weaker branch systems can be cut out at ground level, provided sufficient replacement growths are growing from the base. Apart from this, no regular pruning is required.

The open, loose framework of *Decaisnea fargesii*.

The mature form of branching on *Decaisnea fargesii*.

DESFONTAINIA

Habit Small upright evergreen shrub for fertile, free-draining, acid soil and partial shade. **Attributes** Holly-like foliage, scarlet trumpet-shaped flowers. **Reasons for pruning** To remove dead wood and limit its size. **Pruning time** Autumn until mid-winter.

Desfontainia spinosa, a choice evergreen shrub from Chile, requires very little pruning apart from the removal of dead pieces that are produced on occasion. It is very difficult to please, unless conditions are perfect. If you are lucky and the shrub is happy, leave well alone; in the right conditions, it may be necessary to limit its size.

DEUTZIA

Habit Upright deciduous shrubs for fertile soil and full sun. **Attributes** Sweetly scented white/pink flowers in early summer, exfoliating bark on mature shrubs. **Reasons for pruning** To refresh the plant and encourage flowers on the previous season's growth. **Pruning time** Early summer after flowering.

Deutzias naturally have a stool habit, producing branches freely from just below ground level; a healthy bush produces many new shoots, which means you can cut several older stems right down to ground level after flowering. Deutzias flower on short laterals formed the previous year; thinning older growths to leave a framework, so that a show of flowers is still present the following year, is therefore a better practice than stooling the entire plant.

With some of the taller, more upright species (e.g., *Deutzia scabra*, *D. pulchra*), the exfoliating bark on the older wood is an attractive feature, almost as good as the flowers, and leaving a good number of mature stems as a frame and reducing the height to strong buds makes a good balance between flowering and bark

effect. Leave a few thin growths near the base to lightly furnish the lower parts of the shrub.

Strongly spreading species and cultivars (e.g., *Deutzia purpurascens*) need plenty of room to develop, for their canopy of young foliage is attractive even when flowering is finished. Pruning to confine them would spoil this effect.

Deutzia gracilis and *D. ×lemoinei* are sometimes damaged by late spring frosts, and the flower buds and young growths, particularly on the upper and exposed parts of the shrub, can be killed. Any dead stems should be cut back later in the season to strong living wood.

Deutzia coreana, *D. monbeigii*, *D. ×rosea*, and *D. setchuenensis* are less vigorous growers and need very little light pruning after flowering to side shoots.

Taller-growing deutzias can be encouraged to produce multiple strong growths from the base, which are then tied into a horizontal wire system; old stems are pruned out, and a young shoot trained to fill the gap. Tony Kirkham witnessed this formal style to good effect in a garden in Suffolk in the summer of 2015 and was inspired to try it at home.

Deutzia formally trained as an upright shrub with stems tied into a wire system.

Removing an old stem on a deutzia to encourage new shoots.

Deutzia purpurascens after pruning with old growths removed.

Deutzia purpurascens showing regrowth following pruning.

DIERVILLA

Habit Small low-growing, wide-spreading deciduous shrubs for well-drained soil and full sun. **Attributes** Small yellow flowers, good autumn colour. **Reasons for pruning** To encourage flowering. **Pruning time** Early spring.

Diervillas flower on the current season's growth; don't confuse them with their close relatives weigelas, which flower on laterals from the previous year's wood. *Diervilla lonicera* (bush honeysuckle) forms a mass of growths from a spreading and suckerous stool; *D. sessilifolia* (southern bush honeysuckle), *D.×splendens*, and *D. rivularis* have a similar stoloniferous habit. They should be pruned hard back to just above ground level in the spring as new growth is about to start at the base. Old clumps that have lost their vigour should be dug up, divided, and replanted into rich, well-cultivated soil.

DIOSPYROS

Habit Small to medium-sized deciduous trees with an unsymmetrical crown for well-drained soil and full sun. **Attributes** Deeply fissured bark, shiny dark foliage, interesting orange fruits. **Reasons for pruning** To develop a strong framework and maintain a high canopy. **Pruning time** Summer.

All species branch more sparsely in shade and are best grown in full sun. Begin formative pruning and training immediately in order to make a good, strong tree. The most commonly cultivated species is *Diospyros lotus* (date plum), but that's down to it being the easiest, not the one with the best attributes; it will reach 12 metres (40 ft.) in height with a similar spread. If trained as a standard on a clean stem of 1.5 to 2 metres (5 to 6 ft.), the branches become pendulous as the tree matures and pro-

A mature *Diospyros virginiana* showing the decurrent habit.

vide a skirt to ground level. This shows off the foliage and fruits to full effect.

Diospyros virginiana (American persimmon) is a larger, stronger-growing decurrent tree. The leader should be encouraged for as long as possible before cleaning up the trunk to get some height into the tree before the crown begins. The bark on the main trunk is a strong feature, deeply fissured and alligator-like.

Diospyros kaki (Japanese persimmon) is the most tender of the three species. Typically in the past it was trained against a sunny wall, but if the tree is grown in the open and receives enough sun to ripen the wood, it will produce edible fruits. Prune out any dead, twiggy growth created by a cold winter in summer.

Formative pruning of a young *Diospyros virginiana*.

DIPELTA

Habit Tall, upright deciduous shrubs with arching branches for fertile soil and sunny positions. **Attributes** Fragrant pink or yellow flowers, exfoliating bark on mature specimens. **Reasons for pruning** To refresh the plant and encourage flowers on the current season's growth. **Pruning time** Late spring/early summer after flowering.

Little pruning is necessary in the nursery, as bushiness is naturally produced by growths breaking from ground level, so any plant bought from the nursery will be ready to develop into a mature plant without any need for formative pruning. *Dipelta floribunda* (rosy dipelta), *D. ventricosa*, and *D. yunnanensis* share a very similar growth habit, with the main branch system growing upright, vase-shaped from the ground, and the smaller laterals arching over under the weight of their flowers. Stronger upright extension growths are often produced from the main branch framework; these too arch over in early summer as flowering begins. These growths develop vigorously, and the density of the new leaf growth will shade out the older main branches, producing early leaf drop and twig dieback. It may be necessary to prune out this dead growth to encourage healthy new growth. Plants also send up new, strong growths from the base; these can be used as replacements following the removal of any old non-flowering stems back to ground level.

Dipelta yunnanensis flowers on the current season's growth.

DIPTERONIA

Habit Upright deciduous shrub or small tree for well-drained soil and light shade or full sun. **Attributes** Elegant pinnate leaves and pink-tinged, flat-winged fruits. **Reasons for pruning** To develop a strong framework. **Pruning time** Spring.

Dipteronia sinensis (Chinese money maple) forms a large multi-stemmed shrub or small tree on a single stem, but it is important not to force formative pruning too early in the life to make a tree. Immediately after planting it produces lots of cane-like growths from ground level; with maturity, these develop into a permanent branch system. Once the framework of branches is established, any new growth from the ground can be pruned out. Any epicormic shoots produced on the main branches can also be removed, unless they are needed to form a better framework. Apart from this, no pruning is needed.

DISANTHUS

Habit Medium-sized deciduous shrub with a spreading habit and a slender branch system for a sheltered position with moist, well-drained, acid soil and some shade. **Attributes** Heart-shaped leaves, claret-red autumn colour. **Reasons for pruning** To develop a strong framework. **Pruning time** When needed.

The young growths of *Disanthus cercidifolius* (redbud hazel) are subject to frost and wind damage. There are no special pruning needs for this plant so it's best not to mess about with it.

DISCARIA

Habit Spiny, sparsely branched deciduous shrub or small tree. **Attributes** Small greenish white flowers in early summer. **Reasons for pruning** To maintain a tidy plant and remove dead wood. **Pruning time** Late spring.

Personal protection Wear good thorn-proof clothing and gloves, as these southern hemisphere shrubs are armed with pairs of needle-like thorns.

Discaria chacaye should be left to its own devices. Allow the young plant to branch low and extend annually. The laterals are semi-pendulous, and any upright shoots that develop from these will arch over and shade out the lower branches. As the lower branches die and the small tree becomes untidy, it may be necessary to prune out dead wood.

Discaria toumatou (matagouri, wild Irishman) is a tender shrub for a sunny, sheltered wall, where a permanent framework can be trained from three or four main branches. From this sparse branching, pendulous growths are produced, which should be left unpruned to hang down. When they grow too far from the wall, prune them back to the main branches, where new growths will break and start again.

DISTYLIUM

Habit Large wide-spreading evergreen shrub or small multi-stemmed tree for acid soil and full sun to partial shade. **Attributes** Glossy, leathery leaves and unusual red flowers in spring. **Reasons for pruning** To develop a strong framework and restrict size. **Pruning time** Mid-spring.

In its natural habitat in eastern Asia *Distylium racemosum* (evergreen witch hazel) makes a small tree, but in cultivation it is more often a large shrub, so don't expect too much. Many of the stiff branches have a horizontal habit with a dense, flattened twig growth, which gives an almost tiered effect. Some branches in the crown are interlacing, but it is not necessary to correct this by pruning; in fact, this shrub is effective when the branches are left to extend out into a clear foreground. When pruning to restrict size, position the cuts carefully inside the bush so that they are hidden and the natural branching habit is retained.

DRIMYS

Habit Evergreen shrub or small tree for moist, fertile soil and full sun to partial shade. **Attributes** Large leathery aromatic leaves, creamy white flowers in late spring/early summer. **Reasons for pruning** To maintain a shape and remove storm- or winter-damaged branches. **Pruning time** Late spring or early summer after flowering.

Drimys winteri (Winter's bark) usually needs some protection from cold winds, certainly in the early years. It produces several strong, main upright stems that outgrow each other, producing an erratic and untidy appearance, but this is how it grows, and pruning shouldn't be attempted to rectify this.

The only pruning necessary will be to remove old twisted branches and unwanted growth that interferes with the development of the strong growths from the base of the plant. Damaged branches should be cut back to a suitable growth as they break out in the spring.

A mature *Drimys winteri* showing its ungainly habit.

EDGEWORTHIA

Habit Low-spreading deciduous shrub for moist, well-drained soil in partial shade to full sun. **Attributes** Spherical clusters of yellow or orange flowers in late winter to early spring, papery bark on mature plants. **Reasons for pruning** To develop a strong framework. **Pruning time** Spring after flowering.

Very little pruning is needed with *Edgeworthia chrysantha* (paperbush); however, it may be necessary to prune out any old growths that have stopped flowering, to encourage new growth from the base for replacements. The inflorescences develop in the leaf axils of the newly formed wood in autumn, ready for opening—a sight not to be missed—in early spring; any pruning should be done after flowering. Some of the new cultivars are grafted onto the species, so watch to remove any suckers as soon as they appear.

The natural habit and form of
Edgeworthia chrysantha.

EHRETIA

Habit Small deciduous decurrent trees for light, well-drained soils and full sun. **Attributes** Panicles of small white flowers, attractive bark on mature specimens. **Reasons for pruning** To develop a strong framework and remove dead wood. **Pruning time** Late spring.

Ehretia acuminata (koda) needs shelter from cold winds for good growth, which will produce a strong plant. If grown in the shade of other plants, no growth is made and the shaded parts will die back. Avoid rich soils; they encourage sappy growth, which is easily damaged by frost. Lower branching should be left to develop naturally, but encourage a leader for as long as possible as once it has been lost, the tree's future height will be limited. *Ehretia dicksonii* makes an elegant textbook tree with a round crown when grown on a single trunk. All *Ehretia* species have a pithy wood and are subject to frost damage; following a cold winter, it may be necessary to prune out dead wood.

Ehretia acuminata with low branching.

Ehretia dicksonii showing low, round decurrent crown on a single trunk.

ELAEAGNUS

Habit Deciduous and evergreen shrubs suitable for formal hedges, informal barriers, and coastal planting. **Attributes** Tough (often variegated) foliage, strongly scented flowers. **Reasons for pruning** To develop a strong framework and shape and to reduce outward-growing branches. **Pruning time** Early to mid-summer after flowering.

All *Elaeagnus* species and cultivars respond well to hard pruning as they can shoot vigorously from old wood. This can be carried out as a means of renovation when plants become unruly and out of control.

DECIDUOUS SPECIES

The natural habit of deciduous taxa (e.g., *Elaeagnus angustifolia*, *E. multiflora*, *E. umbellata*) is to form a low trunk with branching from ground level. The shrub can be trained as a standard, with a narrower shape, or as a more spreading multi-stemmed specimen. For a standard, encourage the leader and train a strong trunk with a well-balanced branch system in the early stages. It may be necessary to reduce some of the stems back after flowering in summer to maintain a manageable shape. Where thinning is needed to remove crossing branches and dead wood, this is better carried out in winter, when the leaves have dropped, the stems are bare, and the framework is easier to see.

EVERGREEN SPECIES

The natural habit of evergreen taxa (e.g., *Elaeagnus glabra*, *E. macrophylla*, *E. ×reflexa*) is to branch freely from ground level to form a spreading shrub. Very little pruning is required except to maintain size and spread. To maintain a natural appearance, always prune

Elaeagnus 'Quicksilver'.

Elaeagnus multiflora.

A hedge of *Elaeagnus pungens* 'Maculata' showing reversion.

with secateurs, to a bud in front of a leaf. Do not be tempted to use hedging shears for quick results: they leave untidy cuts and half-severed leaves. The evergreen species are also often grown as a hedge; time must be taken when pruning the hedge with secateurs.

Many evergreen *Elaeagnus* cultivars grown for their variegation are prone to reversion; any green reverted shoots should be pruned off as soon as they are seen. If these are left, they will grow faster and stronger and take over the remainder of the plant, and the variegation will be lost.

The silvery *Elaeagnus ×ebbingei* is very fast growing and has an upright habit. Let it grow naturally, with plenty of space, and pruning will not be necessary. Where the shrub has grown out of its home, maintain it by carefully pruning back long growths to just above a leaf axil or lateral shoot in midsummer.

ELEUTHEROCOCCUS

Habit Deciduous shrubs for fertile, well-drained soil and full or partial shade. **Attributes** Small creamy white flowers followed by large clusters of shiny black fruits. **Reasons for pruning** To maintain a tidy plant. **Pruning time** Summer.

These shrubs require very little regular pruning. True, they are untidy growers, but this is their natural habit, and care must be taken not to spoil shrubs by attempting to prune them. They are naturally upright growers with multiple stems originating from just below ground level and an unusual manner of branching, particularly *Eleutherococcus sieboldianus*. In summer, remove any dead wood from the framework to keep it tidy and open for new growths.

Eleutherococcus lasiogyne is one of the larger species in the genus. The ends of its branches have a pendulous habit, which gives the shrub a well-furnished appearance and shows the flowers and fruits to best effect.

EMBOTHRIUM

Habit Evergreen shrub or small tree, usually multi-stemmed, for moist, acid soil in full sun to partial shade. **Attributes** Bright orange-red flowers in spring/early summer. **Reasons for pruning** Suckers may occasionally need thinning out. **Pruning time** Late summer after flowering.

More often than not it is best to allow *Embothrium coccineum* (Chilean fire bush) to grow as it wishes to reap the rewards of the beautiful flowering effect that gives it its common name. This species naturally has a multi-stemmed habit, often suckering from below ground level. It can be grown as a tree on a single trunk but will need lots of training in the first two to three years; retain the leader for as long as possible. When grown as a multi-stem, the inside of the shrub can become cluttered from the frequently produced stems, with some dieback; it may be necessary to remove this dead material, or thin the growth to make a more open, free-growing shrub after flowering.

EMMENOPTERYS

Habit Medium-sized deciduous tree with a straight, strong leader and horizontal branching. **Attributes** Unusual specimen plant, shy of flowering unless grown in an area with long, hot summers. **Reasons for pruning** To develop a strong framework. **Pruning time** Autumn and early spring.

Emmenopterys henryi (Henry's emmenopterys) is very rare, a choice plant for the connoisseur and a definite favourite with many. It should be grown as a feathered tree with a strong leader. It starts out spindly, but with time the main stem thickens and tapers naturally, making a textbook tree shape—perfectly symmetrical. Apart from maintaining the leading growth and removing dead wood following a cold winter, pruning is not needed and in any case should be kept to a minimum. If you are lucky, one day it might just flower for you.

The rarely seen flowers of *Emmenopterys henryi*.

ENKIANTHUS

Habit Small erect deciduous shrubs for well-drained, acid soil in a sheltered position, full sun to partial shade. **Attributes** Clusters of white, cream, pink, or red bell-shaped flowers in spring/early summer, brilliant autumn colour. **Reasons for pruning** To maintain shape and remove any dieback. **Pruning time** Late winter/early spring.

All species (e.g., *Enkianthus campanulatus*, *E. deflexus*, *E. perulatus*) are densely branched, the main stems springing from ground level with the laterals from these developing in whorls and in layers. In the early years form is upright, but with age a more spreading habit may develop. Very little pruning is required, except for the reduction of stems growing out of the bush to improve the overall shape and the removal of any stems that have died back. Cut overgrown plants back hard to renovate them; new growth will break quite freely.

Mature stand of *Enkianthus perulatus* growing in a Japanese garden.

ERICA

Habit Small to large evergreen shrubs for acid soil. **Attributes** White, pink, red, and purple bell-shaped flowers in winter, spring, and summer. **Reasons for pruning** To prevent old woody, leggy growth. **Pruning times (spring-flowering)** Late spring to early summer as the flowers fade; **(summer- and autumn-flowering)** early spring as new growth begins; **(winter-flowering)** mid-spring as the flowers fade and new growth begins.

As a general rule when pruning heathers (specific exceptions follow), avoid cutting into old wood as it does not freely break. Begin regular pruning early in the life of plants, and mix the types of tools used to avoid a regular/formal bush. Secateurs, a sharp knife, and hedging shears are the standard armoury; however, we are all pressed for time in the garden, and shears are the tool we all eventually turn to for quick effect. Collect all the prunings from the heathers after cutting to avoid browning and to allow for fresh new growth. Old, worn-out plants do not regenerate readily, and replacement is often the best solution.

Erica arborea (tree heath) has an upright tree form and so does not require annual pruning. Very old and leggy specimens that have outgrown their position or shrubs that have been damaged by snow or hard frosts can be cut back hard into their wood, or even down to ground

The informal overall shape of *Erica canaliculata*.

Erica carnea cultivars making a tapestry of colours.

level in spring; new growths will be produced freely from any living wood. Treat *E. ×veitchii* 'Exeter', a popular hybrid between this and *E. lusitanica*, in the same way. Likewise for *E. terminalis* (Corsican heath), with its erect, loose habit: if a more compact habit is required, the longer, taller growths can be cut back in spring.

Erica australis (Spanish heath) is a heather for milder areas, as is *E. canaliculata* (channelled heath), another of the tree heathers, making a shrub to 2 metres (6 ft.) high; both need a sheltered position and should be treated the same as *E. arborea* with no pruning except for renovation and to prune out wood damaged by cold. The tender *E. lusitanica* (Portugal heath) does not respond to hard pruning, but otherwise it too should be treated like *E. arborea*.

Although *Erica carnea* (winter heath) is nat-

urally compact, it will need annual pruning after flowering to keep it low, rounded, and free-flowering. Pruning should be light, as it does not readily break from old wood. For individual plants, selectively prune with secateurs to just below the old flowering spikes, removing a majority of the previous year's growth. For larger plantings, hedge shears are a viable option (and certainly more efficient), but be careful not to create a straight formal line along the edge of a border or path.

Erica ciliaris (Dorset heath) is an untidy grower, requiring annual pruning. The weak stems develop a prostrate habit, and upright flowering growths are produced from these. Light pruning of the previous year's growth should be done in spring, just as new growth begins, taking care not to prune into the woody stems.

Erica cinerea (bell heather) has a stiff upright habit, but if left unpruned it too becomes straggly and untidy. Prune in spring, just as new growth begins, to encourage a closer and tufted habit. The dwarf, compact forms do not need any pruning.

The cultivars of *Erica ×darleyensis* are vigorous growers, requiring annual pruning to keep them in good condition. At the beginning of the growing season, cut back any new shoots that extend beyond the flowering parts; this encourages new growths to break closer to the bush, making a more compact size.

Erica erigena also needs some annual pruning. Some cultivars are more compact than others, but count on isolated shoots to spring up and grow well above the remainder of the plants. These should be cut back after flowering in order to avoid leggy growth, which may lead to future wind damage. In spring following a severe winter it may be necessary to remove frost-damaged shoots back to new growth, which will regenerate from the base.

Annual pruning of *Erica mackayana* (Mackay's heath) is required. Shorten plants back

The broad-spreading habit of *Erica arborea*.

each spring, just as new growth is about to start. Eventually the branches build up and lie on each other, producing an untidy mat that is difficult to prune, and replacement is the only answer.

Erica scoparia (besom heath) has a loose, upright habit and once established requires no annual pruning. Hard annual pruning in spring should be done in the first few years following planting to encourage a bushy plant.

Erica tetralix (cross-leaved heath) requires some annual pruning in the spring before growth starts to keep a more compact habit. Older plants have spreading stems, which makes them untidy, but do not cut back into older wood. Replacement is the only solution.

Erica vagans (wandering heath) and its many cultivars develop a close, clump-like growth, but if left unpruned plants become overgrown and woody, and flowering will deteriorate. Prune these as new growth is just beginning; cut them back only to where the new growth breaks out, as hard pruning is not tolerated.

Erica cinerea showing the stiff upright habit of the new growths.

ERIOBOTRYA

Habit Bushy, small to large evergreen shrub for light, well-drained soil in full sun to partial shade. **Attributes** Large glossy leaves, panicles of white flowers in autumn followed by edible fruits, suitable for the frost-free woodland garden and coastal planting. **Reasons for pruning** To develop a strong framework and encourage new flowering shoots. **Pruning time** Autumn until mid-winter.

The strong-growing *Eriobotrya japonica* (loquat) can reach tree-like proportions in the right position. It can be grown on a single, short trunk, with the lateral branches encouraged to grow as low as possible on the trunk, or with wall protection, with the long laterals loosely secured to the wall. In either case, en-courage shoots to break from the base of the plant; such good strong shoots can serve as replacement branches or stems. If the plant becomes leggy and thin, prune the laterals back to a bud or shoot, which will encourage new, healthy regrowth. Flowers are produced in terminal clusters on the current season's growth.

Loquat is susceptible to fireblight (*Erwinia amylovora*). Be sure to sterilize tools before and after pruning to prevent the spread of this disease, especially if its presence is confirmed.

Eriobotrya japonica growing successfully in a walled garden.

ESCALLONIA

Habit Small to medium-sized usually evergreen shrubs for well-drained soils in full sun to partial shade. **Attributes** Shiny foliage, crimson flowers in early summer; some tolerate coastal winds. **Reasons for pruning** To conserve vigour and control growth. **Pruning time** Summer after flowering or renovation pruning in late spring.

A general characteristic of this genus is the arching habit that develops as growth hardens and goes into its second year, when it flowers; there are exceptions (e.g., *Escallonia* 'Iveyi', which has an upright habit with rigid growth), but these few are easily recognised and treated accordingly. No formative pruning is needed in the first few years unless the plant is being trained against a wall, in which case a selection of stems should be tied into the wall fanwise and the remaining growths removed. Most species and cultivars produce an abundance of new shoots each year from one-year-old growth and even old wood near the base.

Most escallonias flower in early to mid-summer from one-year-old wood. Little or no pruning is needed to make them flower. Any necessary pruning can be done just as the old blossoms fall off. Cut just above a strong side shoot or branch, leaving a natural shape and invisible pruning cuts.

To renovate old plants, cut back very hard into old wood with a good sharp saw (not loppers, which will tear and crush the stems) just as they are about to break in spring. New shoots will be produced along the length of the remaining framework, and the plant will naturally make a new shrub without any intervention.

The upright *Escallonia illinita* is unusual in that it flowers terminally on the current season's wood. Any pruning on this must be carried out in mid-spring; if pruned in late summer, the new shoots will be soft and killed over winter.

Escallonia virgata, a deciduous species with arching branches and small leaves, should be left to grow naturally, so that its shape isn't spoiled. Give it plenty of space and minimal pruning.

The dense rigid habit of *Escallonia rubra* var. *macrantha* makes it ideal for a hedge, particularly by the seaside; annual clipping produces a good, close-knit hedge face, albeit at the expense of regular flowering.

EUCALYPTUS

Habit Small to large evergreen trees, either single-trunked or multi-stemmed (mallees). **Attributes** Interesting, often shedding bark, brightly coloured smooth trunks, distinctive fluffy cream to red flowers, unusual fruits in the form of woody capsules; the leaves can be both juvenile and mature on the same plant and are heavily aromatic when crushed. **Reasons for pruning** To develop a strong framework.

Eucalyptus pauciflora grown on a single trunk.

Eucalyptus pauciflora subsp. *niphophila* trained as a multi-stemmed specimen.

Pruning time Early spring after the danger of frosts is past.

Few *Eucalyptus* species are hardy, and the selection palette will be limited by climate. In all cases, be sure to shelter them from easterly winter winds. When planting any eucalyptus, always choose as small a size as possible, less than 1 metre (3 ft.) in height, and plant in summer (not winter). Never choose a large container-grown specimen: often the top has outgrown the root system, which too often is stunted into a spiralling root ball—and before too long the top becomes too heavy for the trunk and bends over, or the root system is unable to anchor the top and it falls over. This is why gum trees get a bad name in the tree world. The smaller the plant, the less support/ staking is needed; a stout cane and tree-tying material should do the job.

The second season's growth should be very rapid, and if all is well the tree should be able to stand freely on its own with no need for further support. If not, cut it back hard to within 0.5 metre (1.5 ft.) of ground level in the spring. This may seem a drastic step, but the plant should respond to this treatment by breaking freely from the base. Once these young shoots are 0.3 metre (1 ft.) or so in length, select the strongest and cut the original stem down. This gives the root time to catch up with the stem, and the result is better anchorage. Alternatively, several stems can be retained to produce a multi-stemmed specimen.

The other method of culture, especially suited to small gardens, is to cut down growths annually (or at least quite frequently) to near ground level on a coppice system; the new growth stays juvenile, providing attractive stems for the flower arranger.

EUCOMMIA

Habit Small to large deciduous decurrent tree with upright branching and round, symmetrical crown for a sheltered spot in full sun to partial shade. **Attributes** Rarity value, interesting bark and leaves. **Reasons for pruning** To develop a strong framework and raise the crown. **Pruning time** Autumn until mid-winter.

Eucommia ulmoides (hardy rubber tree) should be raised in the nursery as a 2 metre (6 ft.) standard tree before being planted out, as the central leader can be lost fairly quickly once the branches start to develop and the crown opens up. Site this tree so that it is protected from strong winds. Once planted, keep the trunk clean to a good height. This allows the lower scaffolds to develop upright while the laterals from these branches take on a pendulous habit, heavy with twig growth and shiny foliage—one of the features of this tree. Very little other pruning is needed.

EUCRYPHIA

Habit Mostly evergreen, fast-growing densely branching shrubs or small trees for moist, well-drained soil in full sun. **Attributes** Handsome dark leaves, scented white flowers in late summer. **Reasons for pruning** To remove winter damage and dead wood. **Pruning time** Spring.

Eucryphias have a mind of their own and should be left to grow naturally without any intervention. They do not respond to hard pruning and any pruning should be kept to a minimum. *Eucryphia* species are commonly sited in a woodland setting, with the protection of surrounding trees and cooling shade for the root plate, but their rapid growth is often overlooked and the lower branches of the neighbouring trees can interfere with the development of the specimen, stunting the size and growth. Most lose their leader early and become multi-stemmed with upright growth.

Eucryphia ×*nymansensis* is a very upright, almost columnar, grower with semi-pendulous laterals; its selection 'Nymansay' is a small to medium-sized tree with a dense columnar habit, but with age the canopy becomes much broader.

EUONYMUS

Habit Evergreen or deciduous prostrate to upright shrubs or small trees for full sun to partial shade on alkaline soil. **Attributes** Variegated foliage, autumn colour, and in late autumn, showy (usually red) fruits that open to expose shiny (usually orange) seeds—a great combination. **Reasons for pruning** To develop a strong framework, keep plants neat and tidy, and maintain variegation.

DECIDUOUS SPECIES

Pruning time Late winter/early spring.

Euonymus bungeanus has an erect habit that can develop into a small tree. *Euonymus alatus*

Euonymus europaeus 'Red Cascade' showing the typical framework.

Euonymus hamiltonianus in fruit.

Euonymus fortunei 'Silver Queen' wall-trained.

and *E. europaeus* have a spreading habit and an even, well-spaced network of low, close branches with corky wings. Any congested branches can be thinned back to the main framework, opening up the centre of the shrub or small tree; remove low branches back to the trunk if a raised canopy is wanted. All deciduous euonymus have outstanding autumn colour and ornamental fruits, but *E. hamiltonianus* is especially choice, if there can be only one in this group of plants. Treat it as just described.

EVERGREEN SPECIES
Pruning time Spring and mid- to late summer.

Euonymus japonicus, one of the most popular evergreen species, forms either a dense shrub or a loosely growing tree. Little if any forma-

tive pruning is necessary, but if it is grown as a hedge plant, it should be tip-pruned to encourage bushiness. Once a hedge is established, use secateurs to cut back branches in mid- to late spring. Don't use hedging shears; they will produce an unattractive surface.

Euonymus fortunei is a creeping evergreen suitable for groundcover or wall-training. Like ivy, it has an adult flowering stage and matures as it climbs trees and the light is reached. It may need regular clipping over in the spring, as it creeps its way through the border or up the wall. Its selections 'Minimus' and 'Kewensis' are low creeping shrubs with small leaves, but even they can still climb a tree trunk, producing a larger leaf when they reach the light. As for the many variegated selections

(e.g., 'Emerald 'n' Gold', 'Silver Queen', 'Sunshine'), where reversion occurs the plain green branches will need removing back to the variegated growth. Only the green forms tolerate hard renovation pruning; variegated forms do not.

Give the semi-evergreen *Euonymus grandiflorus* subsp. *morrisonensis* plenty of room and leave it alone. Since Tony Kirkham introduced this taxon from Taiwan in 1992, he goes in with the secateurs only when it begins to outgrow its situation.

EUPHORBIA

Habit Erect evergreen subshrub for Mediterranean climates and free-draining soil. **Attributes** Drought-tolerant herbaceous perennial with greenish yellow flowers in early summer. **Reasons for pruning** To provide space for new emerging stems. **Pruning time** Midsummer after flowering.

Personal protection Wear latex or rubber gloves when working with this plant. Its milky sap is toxic. Dispose of arisings safely.

Euphorbia characias subsp. *wulfenii* (milkweed) forms a close mass of erect stems, which help keep it intact and windproof in the border. As the old growths finish flowering, the small

laterals that develop on them can spoil the overall shape and general effect of the plant. Cut these old growths down hard to strong shoots or even to ground level: the plant has great regenerative powers and quickly recovers from the removal of all top growth.

EUPTELEA

Habit Deciduous shrubs or small trees for moist, free-draining soil and partial shade. **Attributes** Copper-coloured young foliage, red flowers in spring, bright red or yellow autumn colour. **Reasons for pruning** To develop a bush or tree form. **Pruning time** Winter (when dormant).

The growth habit and appearance of *Euptelea pleiosperma* and *E. polyandra* are very similar to that of witch hazel, even to the look of the flowers. Suckers are thrown up from the base in just the same way, but they are usually not as plentiful, and the shrub as a whole is more sparsely branched. In the nursery a leader should be encouraged with the aim of making a single-trunked specimen with a head, but this is not always possible. A bushier form from the ground may be easier and more natural to produce. Little if any regular pruning is necessary. For a bush form, remove tired old stems back to ground level; for a single-stemmed specimen, remove any suckers.

EURYA

Habit Evergreen shrub or small tree for rich, moist, free-draining, acid soil and partial shade. **Attributes** Small glossy leaves, small white flowers, purplish berries. **Reasons for pruning** To control size. **Pruning time** Spring, just as the buds are about to break.

The stiffly branched *Eurya japonica* really needs to be grown unimpeded, so give it plenty of room. The branches ascend from ground level at a low angle; the lateral branches are arranged herringbone fashion along the main stems. The young plant should be grown with a bushy habit; it will respond to pruning but take great care positioning cuts, as the natural shape is easily lost.

EXOCHORDA

Habit Upright or arching, medium to large deciduous shrubs for full sun and well-drained soil. **Attributes** An abundance of white flowers in late spring on the previous season's growth. **Reasons for pruning** To develop a strong framework and remove weak and overcrowded branches. **Pruning time** Late spring, immediately after flowering.

Exochorda giraldii and *E. korolkowii* have an upright habit, the branches often being slender and covered with epicormic shoots. Numerous suckers grow up from the base of the shrub at ground level as well. These growths should be pruned off annually in winter to prevent overcrowding, unless some are required for the replacement of old growths that have stopped flowering, which can be pruned out after flowering in late spring.

Exochorda ×*macrantha* 'The Bride' and *E. racemosa* have a more spreading and arching habit, which should be taken into account when pruning. Remove entire branches back to ground level after flowering in late spring, allowing room for the development of some of the stronger suckers as replacements.

FAGUS

Habit Large deciduous shade trees with excurrent broad crowns for thin, well-drained alkaline soil and full sun. **Attributes** Specimen trees with good bark effect and autumn colour. *Fagus sylvatica* also makes a good hedge. **Reasons for pruning** To develop a strong framework and maintain size. **Pruning time** Winter (when dormant) or midsummer.

Fagus sylvatica (European beech), a true British native, is among the most iconic trees of our woodlands. When grown as an individual specimen tree in open space, the scaffold and main branch system is ascending, while the remainder are more horizontal, with the outer and lower branches pendulous. These often sweep down to the ground, forming a low skirt and if low enough may eventually root to become a thick extensive clump around the mother tree. Encourage the lower crown to grow as low as possible; the graceful effect that results is one of the many beauties of this magnificent tree. On a healthy specimen the leaf canopy can be quite dense. Often the lower laterals are shaded out and die back; remove them back to the parent branch or trunk once dieback begins.

It is better to plant a young beech as a feathered specimen and slowly lift the crown to the desired height over a period of time, rather than planting a standard specimen with a high canopy. The lower laterals act as protection from sunburn on newly planted young trees; they should be removed as early as possible, while the branches are small, leaving small pruning wounds that will heal over quickly without leaving any scars. Beeches heal large wounds well over time, but the resulting scars remain visible on the trunk for the life of the tree—a shame, because the rough, silver bark effect is another of its great beauties.

Growth on a young beech is slow in the early years; the addition of soil ameliorants, including mycorrhizae, will help young trees to establish with a higher success rate. Once

A mature *Fagus sylvatica* with a broad crown.

established, the leader will grow away very rapidly without any encouragement. The leader is easily damaged in the early years by various factors (e.g., late spring frosts, gnawing grey squirrels, roosting birds), but beech can readily produce new ones. Where several develop, only one should be retained and the rivals pruned out as soon as possible to prevent future tension forks in codominant stems. Mature beeches do not respond well to hard pruning. Any formative pruning should be carried out early in the life of a tree.

The pruning of upright and weeping forms is best kept to a minimum. *Fagus sylvatica* 'Pendula' comes in two distinct forms—a tall, upright weeping form and a low, spreading form, both grafted at ground level. Both gradually gain height and spread with no intervention. They layer naturally and more readily than the type, creating character trees.

Fagus sylvatica 'Dawyck' is a fastigiate form with twisted side branches; it retains a leader naturally, forming an upright specimen. Make no attempt to clear a length of trunk: branching from ground level is how this tree should be grown.

The slow-growing *Fagus sylvatica* 'Rotundifolia' forms a low crown with ascending main branches and foliage to the ground. It needs no pruning and should be left to grow on its own. Another cultivar with an upright, almost fastigiate form and needing no intervention is *F. sylvatica* 'Zlatia' (golden beech).

For some reason *Fagus sylvatica* Atropurpurea Group (copper beech) is longer lived than the green type, with much variation in colour across the various cultivars; these should be treated exactly the same as *F. sylvatica*.

Fagus sylvatica is often grown as a hedge plant; it retains its dead leaves throughout winter, creating the perfect visual barrier, and at Kew we consider it a length ahead of many of the conifers. When kept in a dwarf, juvenile state, it responds well to annual pruning in late summer, autumn, or winter. Let the young plants of a new hedge establish for at least two years before beginning any pruning. Once the desired height is reached, carefully remove the leaders back to growing points with secateurs, not hedge shears. Once the hedge is mature and has developed a dense face, maintain it by trimming with hedging shears.

Fagus sylvatica 'Dawyck' showing the tight upright branching habit.

A stately juvenile *Fagus sylvatica* with a short trunk.

The weeping form of *Fagus sylvatica* 'Pendula'.

Fagus grandifolia is a strong grower. Encourage and retain its leader for as long as possible, as this species tends to form a crown early in life. It is also prone to producing suckers, which can be removed when seen. *Fagus orientalis* (oriental beech) and *F. crenata*, one of the Japanese beeches, have a similar habit, making trees of great stature. They are best trained on a 2 metre (6 ft.) clean stem.

Fagus japonica (Japanese beech) forms a small, slender tree with a very light twiggy branch system. It should be allowed to branch into several stems at the base, as this is a natural habit.

A fine 250-year-old specimen of *Fagus sylvatica* Atropurpurea Group with the skirt of the crown to the ground.

A young, well-balanced *Fagus grandifolia*.

First trimming of a beech hedge with secateurs.

Maintenance trimming of a beech hedge face in winter with hedging shears.

FALLOPIA

Habit Deciduous climber with twining stems for any soil in full sun to partial shade. **Attributes** A rampant plant, useful for covering dead trees or old buildings with creamy white summer flowers. **Reasons for pruning** To control size and vigour. **Pruning time** Late winter/ early spring.

Fallopia baldschuanica (Russian vine) climbs by twining so freely that no training is needed—a good thing, since it is an impossible subject to train at all, even when young. It grows quickly, provided it has some form of support,

such as a tree or old building. Be sure it has unlimited space for development: it is difficult to restrict it to a confined space. Any necessary pruning may be carried out during the dormant season. Eventually, once it reaches its vertical limits, long trailing growths will hang down, giving a completely natural effect. Under this condition a considerable amount of dead material builds up in the centre, as more and more trailing growths are produced, depriving the older ones of light. With some care and lots of patience some of this can be cut out, but more often than not a fresh start is needed. Simply cut the entire plant back to the ground and leave it to start again.

Fallopia baldschuanica growing over a mature holly tree.

×FATSHEDERA

Habit Shade-tolerant evergreen shrub for free-draining soil in partial shade to full sun. **Attributes** Large, leathery palmate leaves with white flowers in autumn. **Reasons for pruning** To control size and vigour. **Pruning time** Late summer.

×*Fatshedera lizei*, a hybrid of *Fatsia* and *Hedera*, is a spreading, low-growing shrub that seems to develop at random rather than according to any pattern. Whatever surface it grows over, strong shoots are produced. At first upright, these are weighed down as they

extend through their second growing season, and the whole process is repeated in later years as the clump extends. Control this untidy habit by pruning these upright growths in late summer. Sub-laterals will be produced, but the shrub as a whole will be closer to the surface.

FATSIA

Habit Spreading, medium to large evergreen shrub for moist, free-draining soil in partial shade to full sun. **Attributes** An architectural specimen plant with large palmate leaves and showy white flowers in late autumn. **Reasons for pruning** To restrict size and maintain vigour. **Pruning time** Spring.

Fatsia japonica (false castor oil plant) is an outstanding autumn-flowering shrub with a wide spread, up to 3 metres (10 ft.) as it reaches

maturity. The outer branches are weighed down by leaves and flowers as they extend; very rarely do they produce laterals. Around two or three new branches or growths are produced each year, a majority of them springing from ground level, giving the shrub a stool-like appearance.

Removing an old stem with a good, sharp handsaw.

Although it is most impressive when left to grow naturally, it can become leggy, especially in a deeply shaded spot, and it is often necessary to restrict the size by pruning. Do this in spring, cutting the offending branches or stems right down to ground level. The plant responds with plenty of replacement shoots, producing fresh growths from the base of the plant and from dormant buds on the remaining main stems and even the older wood. To renovate, remove old stems throughout the plant, leaving well-spaced young vigorous shoots.

A bushy, well-maintained *Fatsia japonica*.

FICUS

Habit Deciduous or semi-evergreen shrub or small tree for moist, well-drained soil, a sunny wall, and long summers. **Attributes** Large leathery lobed leaves and edible fruits (figs) ripening in late summer. **Reasons for pruning** To control size and vigour and keep an open centre. **Pruning time** Early spring.

Personal protection Figs produce a milky sap that can irritate human skin; wear latex or rubber gloves when pruning.

In the right conditions, *Ficus carica* (common fig) can be grown as a standard but more often than not it is fan-trained against a wall, which needs to be at least 3 metres (10 ft.) high and wide to accommodate this vigorous plant through maturity. Restrict the root system of a wall-trained fig in order to slow its

Ficus carica 'Brown Turkey' fan-trained against a sunny wall.

rate of growth; otherwise, the plant produces too much vegetative growth at the expense of fruits. Fit the wall with horizontal wires so that the branch framework can be trained and tied in. It is essential to begin the formative pruning and training on a fig in the early years, immediately following planting; once this initial pruning has been done, little will be needed later in the plant's life. Remove the leader by cutting out the top of the plant, leaving five or six of the strongest lateral branches on the lower trunk; these can then be evenly spaced and tied into the wires on the wall. Remove any other smaller branches remaining on the trunk. In late spring, remove any shoots that are growing inward toward the wall or directly outward, and any that are frost-damaged. Once established, shorten all the side shoots back to five buds in late spring.

When grown as an ornamental or as a standard tree, the upright growth of the main branches should be encouraged; if left to its own devices, it will spread with an untidy habit and be difficult to control. To renovate an old plant, cut it back completely to the ground; figs have great powers of regeneration and will break freely from the base. Follow this up one or two years later with some formative pruning to create an open centre in the bush.

To restrict size, carefully prune the lateral branches into the bush, so that the cuts are hidden, at the same time leaving an informal surface. This can be carried out at any time other than spring or summer.

FIRMIANA

Habit Deciduous tree for a sheltered, sunny position on moist, free-draining soil. **Attributes** Showy green bark and trunk, large leaves, attractive flowers, oval fruits that persist in winter. **Reasons for pruning** No pruning required. **Pruning time** Mid-spring following flowering.

Firmiana simplex (Chinese parasol tree) is not common in cultivation as its hardiness is often doubtful; however, it is certainly worth trying. It has been grown successfully at Kew for several years without any form of winter protection. When siting, give the specimen plenty of space to develop freely, without being hemmed in by neighbouring trees, so that its attractions can be appreciated. It is a fast grower; retain the leader for as long as possible, so that a good trunk and strong crown are formed. Its thin bark is easily damaged; if you do prune, be careful not to tear the bark on the final cut.

FITZROYA

Habit Slow-growing random-branched evergreen conifer for a sheltered position in full sun. **Attributes** Rarity value, reddish brown trunk, fine-feathered drooping cypress-like foliage from the branch tips. **Reasons for pruning** To produce a tree form and develop a strong framework. **Pruning time** Summer.

Fitzroya cupressoides (Patagonian cypress) is the largest temperate tree in Chile, reaching a spectacular height of 60 metres (197 ft.), but in cultivation it is usually found as a large but slow-growing shrub or tree with a clear definite trunk. Given perfect conditions and grown to its best, it makes a conical tree with drooping branch ends. It is often multi-stemmed, with the main branch system consisting of several upright stems growing from ground level.

If a tree form is desired, begin initial training immediately after planting, when the plant is 15 to 30 cm (6 to 12 in.), as most young trees have a tendency to become bushy, with several competing leaders; select the strongest and train it with the help of a stout cane and soft, plastic tying tube. Many people would be happy to grow this as a large bushy specimen with multiple leaders—just to have it in the garden.

FORSYTHIA

Habit Medium-sized spreading deciduous shrubs for rich soil in full sun to partial shade. **Attributes** Yellow bell-shaped flowers on leafless stems. **Reasons for pruning** To control size and vigour and encourage flowering. **Pruning time** Mid-spring following flowering and winter or early spring for renovation pruning.

Mature plants produce flowers freely in early spring directly from growths made during the previous season; the strongest wood on vigorous young plants is occasionally devoted entirely to vegetative growth, but even it can flower profusely. Most species produce several upright branches from ground level, and it is their natural habit to grow strongly from this point; these are the growths that, in time, will replace older branches weighed down by a mass of twiggy growths, which have a poor flowering potential. We prune forsythias to encourage this habit by cutting out the oldest wood immediately after flowering, just as new growth begins. Annual pruning is not always needed or desirable, as these new growths should be given time to extend and spread, producing a natural, spreading habit that will be free-flowering in years to come.

Following planting, encourage new growth to break from as low as possible within the centre of the young plant. We are often too quick to get into the shrub with the secateurs before the new framework has formed—be patient! When the plant has established and been at full size for at least two years, a proportion of the older branches can be pruned out completely: make the cut as low as possible on the bush, just above a strong shoot or bud, immediately after flowering. Leave a grouping of smaller branches and twiggy growth near the base of the shrub; this gives a natural appearance and will still look attractive in flower and leaf.

Over the life of the shrub, this type of pruning takes a toll. To maintain vigour and a healthy shrub, mulch and feed regularly and water during dry spells following pruning.

Renovate old, weak, and neglected plants by hard pruning back to ground level in winter or early spring. If the plant is not too old, it will break strongly from the base and produce an entirely new branch system in two to three years, to which the usual pruning regimen can be applied.

Forsythias are often grown as a hedge. *Forsythia ×intermedia* 'Spectabilis' is the best cultivar for this purpose, as it has an upright rigid form and will even flower when clipped formally, often two or three times during the growing season. For the best effect, the hedge should have a natural outline. Use secateurs annually to maintain the shape and vigour of the barrier.

Forsythia suspensa (weeping forsythia) is a beautiful shrub, 3 metres (10 ft.) tall or more, with long pendulous branches and sub-branches as long as 0.6 to 1 metres (2 to 3 ft.). When grown in a border or on its own in the open, it quickly becomes untidy; it is much better grown trained against a wall. The main branch system can be grown, trained up, and supported against the wall, reaching a height of 4.5 to 6 meters (15 to 20 ft.). Let the long pendulous branches and sub-branches tail down to the ground. Remove older branches as healthy, younger branches are produced; this keeps the plant strong and vigorous. *Forsythia suspensa* var. *sieboldii*, even more slender and

Forsythia ovata (Korean forsythia) throwing up strong new shoots following the removal of old wood.

Forsythia viridissima pruned leaving the lower furnishings before the new growth begins.

pendent, requires some form of support. Both of these can be grown against a shady wall.

Forsythia suspensa f. *atrocaulis* is often grown for its black/purple stems, which are displayed

to their best as young, vigorous shoots; regular hard pruning will be necessary to maintain a good crop of young stems.

FOTHERGILLA

Habit Small, slow-growing deciduous shrubs for moist, lime-free soil and full sun. **Attributes** Creamy white flower spikes in early spring, amazing autumn colour. **Reasons for pruning** To remove dead or damaged stems. **Pruning time** Winter before flowering.

Witch alders have a stool-like growth habit, sending up woody and twiggy growths from ground level. They are renowned for their stunning floral and autumn foliage displays, with leaves in shades of yellow through to red on the same bush at the same time. All are best left to grow naturally without any intervention. Preserve the twiggy growths down to the ground; don't prune them off. Interfering with a plant often does more harm than good. Remove old or crossing branches in winter, when the framework of the shrub can be clearly seen. There is often a congestion of young shoots at the base; don't cut into this material as one of these young shoots can be trained for replacement. *Fothergilla major* is an upright grower that looks very similar to a coppiced hazel stool; *F. major* Monticola Group is also upright

The flowers of *Fothergilla major* Monticola Group.

but more spreading than the type. *Fothergilla ×intermedia* and her cultivars form compact, rounded shrubs to 1.5 metres (5 ft.) high and

tolerate lower temperatures and a more alkaline soil. *Fothergilla gardenii* is smaller, to 1 metre (3 ft.) high, and freely suckering.

FRANGULA

Habit Mainly deciduous shrubs to medium-sized trees for naturalistic and woodland plantings. **Attributes** Good habitat plants for biodiversity with red fruits turning black. **Reasons for pruning** To restrict size. **Pruning time** Between autumn and spring (when dormant).

A familiarity with the various species will help to distinguish the final form and habit of the plant to be pruned. Most develop into small trees or large shrubs that require very little pruning, apart from retaining a clean trunk as the tree develops a crown. The evergreen *Frangula californica* (California coffeeberry) can reach a height of 9 to 12 metres (30 to 40 ft.), but if allowed to develop low branching from ground level, its height will be much lower. When grown as a shrub, the ends of the branches will take on a pendulous habit and should be left to give the best natural effect. Any dead wood that accumulates under this canopy of branching should be removed carefully to avoid spoiling the overall shape and habit.

FRANKLINIA

The stewartia-like flower of *Franklinia alatamaha*.

Habit Pyramidal deciduous shrub or small tree for partial shade and well-drained soil. **Attributes** Rarity value, white flowers in autumn with orange-red fall colour. **Reasons for pruning** No pruning required. **Pruning time** Winter after flowering.

Franklinia alatamaha (Franklin tree) needs a sheltered position and a favourable climate, preferably with a little autumn sunshine to ripen the wood and show off the pretty flowers. It naturally takes on an upright habit with branching from low down on the trunk near the base. Do not restrict this plant to a single stem; leave it to do what it wants. No regular pruning is necessary apart from cutting back any growths that spoil the informal effect or become a little unruly; in fact, plan on settling for any growth this produces—it is a miffy, fussy plant.

FRAXINUS

Habit Large deciduous fast-growing shade trees with a symmetrical crown for most free-draining soils, including alkaline, in full sun. **Attributes** Grey bark, dark winter buds, cream flowers on *Fraxinus ornus*, purple fall colour on *F. americana*. **Reasons for pruning** To develop a strong crown and branch system. **Pruning time** Winter (when dormant) or midsummer.

Maintain a strong single leader in young trees for as long as possible, for once the leader is lost a low, rounded crown, which is very difficult to correct, is produced. This habit is encouraged by the strong opposite winter buds, which develop with equal vigour once the terminal bud has been lost through pest damage or a late spring frost. In the nursery, look for an ash with a good strong leading shoot. The main branches in a prematurely formed crown grow very long and heavy with foliage and are prone to break during strong gales or heavy snow.

Some of the well-shaped species, such as *Fraxinus latifolia* (Oregon ash) and *F. angustifolia* (narrow-leaved ash), produce long branches with masses of foliage and semi-weeping laterals; these are susceptible to damage in wet and windy conditions, so get the tree established quickly and do some formative pruning to develop a strong canopy. The graceful upright habit of *F. angustifolia* 'Raywood' shows off the beautiful fall colour, but its crown has a tendency to break up for no apparent reason after about 25 years of growing.

Grow the strong, well-branched *Fraxinus excelsior* (common ash) on a clean trunk with

Fraxinus excelsior with a long, low branch.

Fraxinus excelsior 'Pendula' showing habit.

the first scaffold branches at around 3 metres (10 ft.) high. When these main branches are later broken or sawn off, large upright growths are frequently produced, adding considerable weight to the canopy and spoiling the general shape; careful thinning will be needed to correct this.

Fraxinus excelsior 'Pendula' (weeping ash), a strong-growing grafted (top-worked) tree (usually at a height of about 2 metres, 6 ft.), produces a low-spreading dome with a mass of weeping growths. Watch out for suckers of the type and remove them as soon as they are seen: they are more vigorous and will eventually take over. Both *Fraxinus americana* and *F.*

pennsylvanica retain their leaders well, forming shapely trees with upright branches that eventually sweep down to form a dense canopy at ground level. This skirt should be left as low as possible to balance the canopy and to show off the excellent fall colour.

Fraxinus ornus (manna ash), with a closer, sturdy growth habit, should be left to develop naturally without any thinning and encouraged to develop a crown on a short clean trunk of 1 to 1.2 metres (3 to 4 ft.).

Occasionally following a cold winter, there ay be some dieback in the crown of species native to warmer climates; this can lead to a smaller tree overall and some difficulty forming shapely specimens, even with lots of formative pruning. Species that suffer in this way include *Fraxinus dipetala*, *F. mandshurica*, and *F. angustifolia* subsp. *syriaca*.

Most ash species in Europe are now under threat from ash dieback (*Hymenoscyphus fraxineus*). Be sure to sterilize pruning tools between individual specimens to forestall the spread of this fungal disease.

A young *Fraxinus americana* showing shape and upright branching.

Fraxinus ornus showing low crown on a short trunk.

FREMONTODENDRON

Habit Semi-evergreen shrub for free-draining soil in full sun near or against a warm, sunny wall. **Attributes** Yellow flowers throughout summer on the current season's wood. **Reasons for pruning** To maintain a framework and a well-furnished face. **Pruning time** Midsummer following first flowering.

Personal protection The small yellow hairs on the leaves are a skin irritant; wear gloves and a dust mask when pruning, particularly in dry, confined conditions.

The flowering of *Fremontodendron californicum* (California flannelbush) will not be affected or improved with pruning. It is best grown with a single leader and trained against a wall using a wire system to tie in the main branching framework. The branches tend to be brittle and are easily snapped, so be careful when training. Reduce any growths growing away from the wall back to side shoots growing parallel to the wall; remove weak shoots, leaving more vigorous side shoots. If grown as a freestanding bush, it needs the shelter of a sunny wall. Plants tend to be relatively short-lived and get tired. Hard renovation pruning is not an option; it is better to remove and replace old worn-out plants.

Fremontodendron californicum trained against a sunny wall.

FUCHSIA

Habit Small upright deciduous shrubs with arching stems for sun or partial shade and moist, well-drained soil. **Attributes** Pendent, pink or red showy flowers throughout summer, flaking bark on older woody growth. **Reasons for pruning** To encourage healthy young shoots and regular flowers, which appear on the current season's wood. **Pruning time** Spring and occasionally autumn.

Their common name notwithstanding, hardy fuchsias require a sheltered spot in a mild climate, or they will be cut to the ground regularly by cold winter weather. Leave the old stems on the plant until spring; new growth will be your general guide to living wood, to which the dead stems should be pruned back. With *Fuchsia magellanica* and its cultivars, which are some of the hardier forms, the older the wood becomes with the occasional kind winter, the less likely it is the branches will be cut back by cold weather, and the plant begins to build up a larger framework. In Chile, where this species originates, plants are up to 6 metres (20 ft.) high and wide in the wild, with trunks so huge, it would take a chainsaw to prune them.

When the main branches do survive year by year, prune the laterals back to the living, lower buds in the spring, just as they are breaking out. Take the vigour of the bush into account: cut weaker growths back harder than stronger ones and completely remove any spindly growths back to the strong framework or, if they arise from the base of the shrub, as close to the ground as possible. In exposed coastal areas, shorten any long growths or stems in autumn to prevent wind damage through the winter. To renovate plants that have experienced a hard winter, cut all stems back hard to

Fuchsia magellanica 'Pumila' showing its tight, dwarf form.

Fuchsia magellanica protected by a warm, sunny wall.

Fuchsia magellanica 'Alba' grown as an informal hedge.

5 cm (2 in.) from ground level in spring; this encourages new growths from the base.

Fuchsia magellanica is useful as a permanent border plant and makes a good informal hedge in mild areas. Prune back hard to a formal outline each year in spring, just as growth is about to begin. Its tight, dwarf forms are more suited to the rock garden and require very little pruning apart from the removal of outward-growing branches that spoil the general shape and any dead wood following a cold winter.

GARRYA

Habit Evergreen shrubs for free-draining soil in full sun to partial shade. **Attributes** Tough leathery leaves, long catkins in late winter/early spring (hence the common name). **Reasons for pruning** To restrict size and spread. **Pruning time** Spring after flowering.

All silktassels can be grown as freestanding specimens in milder areas, provided adequate shelter, but they normally grow better with the protection of a wall. As a freestanding shrub a central leader should be encouraged and then no pruning carried out, except to remove frost-damaged tips and to restrict spread. The plant will flower freely.

To train a specimen against a wall, establish an even balanced framework of branches against the wall immediately after planting, allowing the new stems to grow forward off the wall naturally. There is no need for regular pruning to encourage flowering; the only pruning necessary will be to restrict spread. To retain an informal outline, use secateurs and position the cuts to a suitable growth well within the shrub, allowing the existing foliage to hide the pruning cuts.

To renovate an old bush that has got out of hand, gradually prune back to the framework over a four- to five-year period. Alternatively, if you are prepared to miss one or two years of flowering, cut back hard to the framework in one go with a saw in the spring, and new growths from the cuts will be produced quite freely.

Garrya laurifolia subsp. *macrophylla* and *G. ×issaquahensis* can both be grown as freestanding bushes in milder areas or against a wall. In the open border, *G. ×thuretii* (a vigorous hybrid of *G. elliptica* and *G. laurifolia* subsp. *macrophylla*) will form a large freestanding bush to 5 metres (16 ft.); use the strong new growths it freely throws up in spring to replace any growth damaged by frost or cold winds.

Garrya elliptica (wavyleaf silktassel) trained as a freestanding bush in an open border rather than against a wall.

GAULTHERIA

Habit Low-growing evergreen shrubs for free-draining, acid soil in partial to full shade. **Attributes** Late-spring flowers followed by colourful fleshy fruits. **Reasons for pruning** To maintain a tidy plant and remove dead branches. **Pruning time** Mid- to late spring after flowering.

A very old straggly bush of all gaultherias can be hard pruned in the spring to encourage the production of new wood from the base. Both *Gaultheria hookeri* and *G. shallon* (salal) are very strong growers, and to prune them without creating a definite line and making them hedge-like is very difficult. Don't use hedge shears; better to get into the plant at the base with a pair of secateurs. This gives a better, much more natural effect.

Gaultheria procumbens (checkerberry), one of the creeping species, forms a mat that is only 5 to 10 cm (2 to 4 in.) high. Gaultherias with this type of growth do not need pruning apart from removal of any dead growths from winter.

Several gaultherias have a dense habit. One, *Gaultheria mucronata* (prickly heath), spreads by means of suckers and forms a dense thicket; in general, the only pruning needed will be to restrict the plant's spread into neighbouring shrubs. Any growths that are dying back should be cut off at ground level in spring.

The very bushy *Gaultheria ×wisleyensis* spreads by both arching growths and by means of suckers. By careful pruning back to upright growths within the shrub in the spring, its size can be restricted.

GENISTA

Habit Deciduous and evergreen dwarf mound-forming shrubs or small trees for full sun and free-draining soil. **Attributes** Yellow pea-like flowers in summer. **Reasons for pruning** To restrict size and shape. **Pruning time** Spring and summer after flowering.

Genistas are sun lovers, and they do their natural best when grown in sunny positions, not in the shade. *Genista aetnensis* (Mount Etna broom), up to 6 metres (20 ft.) in height, produces an ungainly shape and bushy habit that is very difficult to change through formative pruning. It usually develops with low branching, either by a natural break in the leader or by stopping it when the desired height is reached. To gain height, stake it at planting; this encourages a leader and a more open habit as the shrub matures.

Genista monspessulana (Montpelier broom) becomes straggly and overgrown, but annual pruning is not needed, as when a plant becomes unsightly it is better to replace it.

Genista cinerea and *G. tenera* 'Golden Shower' are very similar to each other in habit and appearance. In the early years, shorten growths over the whole shrub after flowering, taking them back to the young growths that develop at the base and along the length of the previous year's wood. This removes the new developing seedpods, which improves growth and vigour. Do not cut into the previous year's wood, as older parts do not break readily. Very old plants do not respond to hard renovation pruning; remove them and replace them with young, vigorous plants.

Genista hispanica (Spanish gorse) forms a low and compact hummock, but as the plant gets older and after a cold winter, dead patches often appear, ruining the overall appearance. It is possible to remove the dead portions and allow the live material to grow into the bare patches. A light clipping after flowering helps the plant stay healthy.

The distinctive habit of *Genista lydia* (Lydian broom) is easily spoiled by pruning; the same is true of *G. horrida* and *G. sagittalis*.

GINKGO

Habit Deciduous excurrent tree for most soil types and locations, including full sun. **Attributes** Maidenhair fern–like leaves with amazing butter-yellow fall colour. Females produce fruits that smell of vomit. Tolerant of urban stress and pollution. **Reasons for pruning** To restrict size and remove damaged branches and rival leaders. **Pruning time** Winter (when dormant) or midsummer.

Ginkgo biloba (maidenhair tree) is distinctive for its sparse branching, the short spur-like growths on the old portions, and the long shoots on the ends of the healthy branch system which extend from year to year. Variation in habit is considerable. Some are much more upright with semi-erect branchlets and an absence of heavy branching—almost fastigiate; *Ginkgo biloba* 'Fastigiata', 'Fairmount', 'Princeton Sentry', and 'Tremonia' are columnar selections with semi-erect branches. Others have a more natural form of branching, the main branches growing away from the trunk at right angles with the sub-branches from these being semi-pendulous. In a well-shaped specimen with a strong leader the main branches are often formed when the tree has reached a considerable height and are many years old. As trees mature, they produce chi-chis, long growths that have the ability to root once they reach the ground.

It is essential that a young tree have a good, strong leader running up through its centre. They are generally a well-behaved tree and want to form a single leader naturally, without too much intervention. Be careful: some of the lateral branches with an upright habit of growth can appear to be in competition with the main leader, but this is often not the case. Come spring, the main leader will be off the starting blocks quicker than the lateral and re-

Chi-chis on a venerable old *Ginkgo biloba*.

A grafted specimen of a weeping cultivar from the *Ginkgo biloba* Pendula Group.

A young *Ginkgo biloba* showing straight trunk.

A mature *Ginkgo biloba*.

tain its lead over the lateral. If the well-spaced lateral is removed, it could ruin the tree's overall structure and appearance in the future. Should true rival leaders develop, reduce these to the stronger one as early as possible; a weakness of this species is the tight forking habit caused by rival leaders, which will inevitably shorten the life of this otherwise long-lived tree.

Be patient with ginkgos. With adequate water and mulch, most will grow rapidly and establish in the first four to five years, but they can sit and sulk for a year or two following planting. Usually the smaller the tree, the quicker it is to grow away without a rest. And watch out for suckers with cultivars; cultivars are often grafted onto a seedling of the type, and growths from the rootstock can be more vigorous and take over the main tree.

GLEDITSIA

Habit Deciduous trees with an upright, irregular decurrent crown for a sunny spot. **Attributes** Fine foliage, tolerant of drought and pollution, and often used as a street tree, particularly in the United States. **Reasons for pruning** To improve the shape and balance of the canopy and to lift branches for access and safety. **Pruning time** Late summer or winter; sap may bleed from fresh cuts if pruned in spring.

Personal protection Wear good thorn-proof clothing and gloves, as the trunk, branch system, and young stems bear fierce spines.

If its leader is retained, *Gleditsia triacanthos* (honey locust) forms a long, fine-looking straight trunk. Clear this of growths to a height

of 3 to 4.5 metres (10 to 15 ft.). The trunk, which bears stout spines in clusters, makes this a very interesting tree, albeit not for the children's garden; however, if spines are a problem, *G. triacanthos* f. *inermis* is thornless and can be trained in exactly the same way as the type, as can the selection 'Sunburst', despite its not being as strong a grower as the type.

Gleditsia triacanthos 'Elegantissima' is shrublike with an upright habit and without a single leading shoot, so no trunk can be formed, and it seldom produces thorns. *Gleditsia triacanthos* var. *nana* can be trained with a definite leader when young, but the trunk is short and it forms a dense, narrow crown. Both need very little pruning. *Gleditsia caspica*, *G. delavayi*, *G. japonica*, and *G. sinensis* can be trained with a strong leader and should be treated in the same way as *G. triacanthos*.

Gleditsia triacanthos f. *inermis* 'Sunburst' showing the irregular decurrent canopy.

GLYPTOSTROBUS

Habit Shrub or small deciduous excurrent conifer for full sun and moist, free-draining soil. **Attributes** Rarity value, fine foliage. **Reasons for pruning** No pruning required. **Pruning time** Winter (when dormant).

Glyptostrobus pensilis (Chinese swamp cypress) is slow to grow but worth the wait. Plant it as a small single-stemmed feathered specimen; give it some shelter and winter protection. No special pruning is required, apart from removing dead branches following a cold winter. It is naturally upright with a narrow, open symmetrical crown.

GREVILLEA

Habit Evergreen shrubs for full sun and free-draining, lime-free soil. **Attributes** Red or yellow flowers. **Reasons for pruning** To maintain a compact shrub and encourage flowering. **Pruning time** Late spring after flowering and occasionally in the summer.

All *Grevillea* species are best grown at the foot of a sunny wall for maximum protection, but make no attempt to train the shrub against it. An essential aspect of cultivation is to keep the shrub as compact as possible, which will be done naturally with full sunlight. If it is overgrown or shaded in any way, the growth will draw away from the warmth of the wall and likely be damaged by winter cold. The only pruning necessary will be to prune back long straggly growths to maintain a compact habit and some flower deadheading through summer to promote a repeat flowering. Branches damaged by winter cold can be cut back to suitable growing shoots in the spring.

GRISELINIA

Habit Dense, fast-growing evergreen shrubs for well-drained soil and full sun. **Attributes** Thick leathery leaves, summer flowers, suitable for hedges and coastal planting. **Reasons for pruning** To maintain shape and size. **Pruning time** Early summer after flowering.

Griselinia littoralis hedge showing strong upright growths.

Griselinia racemosa is a small suckering upright shrub to 1 metre (3 ft.) and requires no pruning. *Griselinia littoralis* (New Zealand broadleaf) branches freely from the base and as it develops produces strong laterals, which become very thick with foliage and additional growth. This characteristic of breaking freely and strongly makes it an ideal shrub for use as a windbreak or as a formal or informal hedge plant in mild areas. As a hedge plant an even bushier habit can be encouraged in the early years, as strong shoots will grow with upright rigidity from the centre of the bush with regular pruning. Although a hedge will respond to tight cutting with hedging shears, it is best pruned to an informal surface using secateurs: cut off individual shoots in early summer to a healthy bud and leaf, to prevent leaf cut and hide the pruning cut. Tired old plants respond to hard renovation pruning in spring.

Pruning a *Griselinia littoralis* hedge with secateurs.

GYMNOCLADUS

Habit Large slow-growing deciduous tree with an unsymmetrical crown for rich, moist soil and full sun. **Attributes** Good winter twig and branch form, long pinnate leaves, late to leaf and early to drop. **Reasons for pruning** To produce a clean trunk and strong crown. **Pruning time** Midsummer. Never prune in late winter/early spring as the wounds are prone to bleeding.

Gymnocladus dioicus (Kentucky coffeetree) forms a coarsely but evenly branched tree. Even the twig growth is thick and sparse. Encourage a central leader, which naturally is usually strong, for as long as possible, retaining the lower branches. Eventually, as the head forms, the lower branches can be removed cleanly back to the trunk, encouraging a clean trunk of 2 to 2.5 metres (6 to 8 ft.). Often the outer branches on a mature tree have a pendulous habit, and the attractive foliage creates a pleasing skirt at eye level. Long after the leaflets fall in autumn, their midribs remain attached to the branches, which adds to the display. The selections 'Espresso' (a male form with no fruit) and 'Variegata' should be treated in the same way as the type with no special pruning needs.

A young *Gymnocladus dioicus* with a well-developed crown on a clean stem. Note the attached midribs.

HALESIA

Habit Deciduous shrub or small excurrent tree for full sun to partial shade and acid soil. **Attributes** Fissured bark at maturity, white bell-shaped, snowdrop-like flowers, yellow autumn colour. **Reasons for pruning** To restrict growth. **Pruning time** Late spring after flowering.

The most common species, *Halesia carolina* (Carolina snowdrop tree), can be trained on a short trunk but is best allowed to grow naturally, free-branching from the base, forming a multi-stemmed shrub or small tree, with the lower branches assuming a horizontal habit. This free spread can be allowed to develop without any need for pruning. It is natural for the branches to be thickly placed, congested and crossing throughout the crown; do not thin, as the plant will look unnatural and be likely to collapse, with holes in the canopy. Any pruning to restrict growth should be carried out after flowering.

Halesia carolina Monticola Group (mountain snowdrop tree) has more of a tree-like decurrent habit and can be trained with a definite leader. A mature specimen can have a clean stem of 1 to 1.2 metres (3 to 4 ft.). The long, trailing branches hang down to the ground, producing a low, untidy skirt, but as with the type should not be thinned.

Halesia diptera (two-winged snowdrop tree) should be trained as a shrub and will not make a tree. *Halesia macgregorii* is new to cultivation from China; young plants at Kew are promising, with strong leading shoots, and look to make tidy trees.

A mature *Halesia carolina* showing fissured bark.

×HALIMIOCISTUS

Habit Short-lived evergreen shrubs for full sun and free-draining soil. **Attributes** White or yellow flowers with a long flowering period. **Reasons for pruning** To remove dead wood and old flowers. **Pruning time** Spring.

×*Halimiocistus sahucii* and ×*H. wintonensis*, like *Cistus*, do not respond to pruning. If a plant becomes straggly and woody, dig it up and replace it rather than trying to prune it. Prune out dead wood and old flowers in spring.

HAMAMELIS

Habit Upright vase-shaped deciduous shrubs for partial shade to full sun and free-draining soil. **Attributes** Yellow, orange, and red spider-like flowers on leafless stems in winter. **Reasons for pruning** To restrict growth and remove non-flowering stems and suckers. **Pruning time** Early spring after flowering.

Normally, witch hazels require very little pruning. One of their most pleasing attributes, their winter flowers, are best displayed on free and natural growth. Some pruning may be required at the early training stage to encourage a vase-shaped shrub, and *Hamamelis virginiana* (American witch hazel) is strong enough to form a small tree with an ascending habit if the central leader is encouraged in the early years or left to grow as a bush. Most of the remaining species, cultivars, and forms have distinctive habits of growth that must be allowed for in training.

It is not appropriate to thin branches or to prune with the intention of reducing each branch to a uniform shape. To reduce shape or size (for example, if a shrub is too close to a path) or to reduce the length of vegetative shoots, prune after flowering and before growth starts. Do this annually, making the cuts just above two growth buds. Miss out the odd year if little growth has been made by the plant.

Witch hazels look far better and more natural when the lower branches are retained to keep a low skirt, and the ideal height at which to show off the flowers of this lovely plant is at eye level. When grown in even slight shade the shrubs become very straggly; their habit and flowering are best when grown in full sun. Mature specimens have a considerable low spread and in a group planting will need to be 5.5 to 6 metres (18 to 20 ft.) apart.

Most *Hamamelis* cultivars are grafted onto *H. virginiana* rootstocks, and a constant, careful watch must be kept for suckers that may grow from the base of the plant. They are best dealt with as they appear, for if left until the

A witch hazel with lower branches retained to keep a low skirt.

Pruning vegetative shoots back to two growth buds above the flowering wood on a *Hamamelis* cultivar.

Hamamelis ×intermedia 'Pallida' showing the vase-shaped habit.

end of the growing season, they can be several feet long and can spoil the inner growth of the shrub. Stressed plants, lack of light, and moisture and mechanical weeding damage to roots usually produce more suckers, whereas healthy plants over the age of four to five years rarely produce suckers. The best way of identifying suckers, besides that they are very straight, is that their leaves can remain attached long after the shrub as a whole is completely defoliated.

Shrubs that are on their own roots are usually free from suckers; however, *H. vernalis* (Ozark witch hazel) often suckers naturally.

HEBE

Habit Evergreen shrubs for free-draining soil, full sun to partial shade, and shelter from strong winds. **Attributes** Tough leathery foliage, white, purple, pink, or red flowers from spring to late summer, suitable for the rock garden or as a groundcover. **Reasons for pruning** To restrict size and maintain a tidy plant. **Pruning time** Spring or after flowering in late summer.

A key characteristic of plants in this genus is their ability to break freely from old wood when cut back, either by frost or bad weather. This is fortunate, as many are quite tender and can be damaged by a moderately cold winter. It is best to keep the dead material attached to the plant through the winter to afford some protection until spring. When the new growths start to break from living wood, it is very obvious where to prune back to. Select the strong growths and prune back into living wood. The earlier in spring this is done the better, as more light penetrating the bush ensures well-balanced growth and increases the chances the remaining material will ripen properly.

Form and growth habit vary considerably. Many species (e.g., *Hebe albicans*, *H. odora*) are naturally compact and very rarely need any pruning. Shrubs like *H. brachysiphon*, which can reach over 1.5 metres (5 ft.), will benefit from hard pruning in late spring to correct an untidy habit or repair any damage caused by snow or wind. To keep some of the forms within bounds and prevent their becoming leggy (e.g., *H. cupressoides*, *H. pinguifolia*, *H.*

salicifolia, *H. speciosa*), it's worth trimming the entire bush lightly with hedging shears in summer, removing any old flower spikes or seed capsules; this keeps their growth young and fresh, and the plants will have a more tidy appearance through winter. Some species die back for no accountable reason, often progressively one shoot after another. Little can be done to remedy this apart from pruning out any dead branches, but once a plant loses too many branches it is better to remove the shrub and replant with fresh stock.

Watch variegated cultivars (e.g., the lime-variegated *Hebe ×franciscana*, *H.* 'Silver Queen') for reversion and prune it out as soon as it is seen.

HEDERA

Habit Evergreen climbers, self-clinging by aerial stem roots, for any soil, full sun to partial shade. **Attributes** Shiny foliage, both flowers and fruits are a winter food source for animals, suitable for covering walls or trees. **Reasons for pruning** To control vigour and maintain shape. **Pruning time** Late spring/early summer.

These creeping climbers naturally produce bushy branches when mature; this growth habit allows the plant to reach the light before it starts to develop these side branches, which produce the flowers and fruits. Ivy is sometimes grown to clad the trunk of a tree, but do not let it grow along the main scaffold branches; there is little chance of strangulation, but the extra weight placed on the tree's branch system can strain a weakened framework, causing a loss of one or more its limbs. Once the ivy has developed beyond the juvenile creeping stage, keep it out of the tree's upper canopy.

Ivy is often planted to grow against the wall of a building where it will, if there is room, reach a considerable height. It does no harm to structures until the mature stage is reached; then, as the branches become heavier, they may strain and loosen the brickwork as they

Hedera helix trained as a hedge.

sway in the wind. Annual clipping overcomes this problem, as the foliage and stems are kept close to the wall and never have a chance to produce mature growths. Carry this out in late spring/early summer, as this allows new growth to develop and ripen before winter begins. If left to later in the season the new growth could be damaged by the winter frosts and leaves browned. Clip with hedging shears or hedge cutters as close to the wall as possible—and know that it will look bare for two or three weeks post-cutting. Treat ivy grown over pillars, fencing, and pergolas in the same way.

Hedera helix can be trained along a system of ropes and allowed to branch, making a dense, evergreen hedge and clipped to maintain a shape with hedging shears in early summer. Other species, including *H. colchica* (Persian ivy) and its cultivars, can be treated in much the same way.

Hedera helix showing mature growths.

Hedera colchica 'Dentata Variegata' left to grow naturally over a low wall.

HELIANTHEMUM

Habit Mat-forming evergreen subshrubs for dry, free-draining soil in full sun. **Attributes** Free-flowering from spring to midsummer. **Reasons for pruning** To maintain a tidy plant. **Pruning time** Midsummer after flowering.

All rock roses benefit from light pruning after they have finished flowering. Growths that are straggly and make the plant look untidy can be cut back, allowing the plant to break from the old wood. It may be necessary to prune back some of the older wood hidden under the carpet of foliage. This involves carefully lifting the mat of growth, carrying out the pruning, and re-covering the cut surfaces with the mat of growth.

HELICHRYSUM

Habit Low-growing spreading evergreen shrub for free-draining soil and full sun. **Attributes** Silver-grey scented leaves, yellow daisy-like flowers. **Reasons for pruning** To maintain a tidy plant. **Pruning time** Spring.

Helichrysum italicum becomes woody with age and is often damaged during an average winter. It responds well to hard pruning in spring as growth is about to start, but a very old plant in poor condition or a plant severely damaged by frost may not respond favourably. For regular annual pruning, prune back the previous year's growth lightly, removing old flower heads to form a neat plant; this will suffice until actual replacement of the plant is needed.

HELWINGIA

Habit Small deciduous (occasionally semi-evergreen) suckering shrubs for rich, moist, well-drained soil in partial shade. **Attributes** Rarity value, shiny green leaves, unusual flowers and black berries in the leaf axils. **Reasons for pruning** To remove dead or weak stems. **Pruning time** Spring.

Helwingia chinensis, *H. himalaica*, and *H. japonica* are strange plants, grown mainly for their botanical interest, not horticultural merit. They require no special pruning, apart from the occasional thinning of dead and weak stems.

HEMIPTELEA

Habit Deciduous shrub or small tree for full sun to partial shade in moist soil. **Attributes** Rarity value, dark grey fissured bark. **Reasons for pruning** To develop a strong framework. **Pruning time** Between autumn and spring (when dormant).

Hemiptelea davidii is closely related to *Zelkova*, with the same twiggy growth and branching. It is best grown on a clean trunk to 2 metres (6 ft.). Retain a leader for as long as possible before forming a branching head. No further pruning is needed beyond formative training.

HEPTACODIUM

Habit Upright deciduous shrub or small tree for rich soil in partial shade to full sun. **Attributes** Large scented white flowers in late summer; on large specimens, the bark peels off in long strips. **Reasons for pruning** To develop a strong framework and expose the trunk. **Pruning time** Early spring or late autumn.

No pruning is necessary to encourage flowering of *Heptacodium miconioides* (seven son flower of Zhejiang); however, pruning this wonderful Chinese plant at the wrong time will prevent the production of flowering buds, which are formed in spring. Ideally pruning should be carried out in early spring or autumn after flowering. Formative pruning and training will decide the plant's type, whether a large shrub with multiple branches from low down or a small tree on a single trunk. A multi-branched specimen with several large stems to show off the peeling bark is often preferred; lift the lower branches of the canopy to expose this attribute once the plant takes on a stout framework, at the same time removing any dead wood and diseased or dying stems.

A large multi-branching specimen of *Heptacodium miconioides*.

HETEROMELES

Habit Multi-stemmed evergreen shrub or small tree for full sun and well-drained soil. **Attributes** White summer flowers, large quantities of bright red berries. **Reasons for pruning** To restrict size and encourage a bushy plant.

Pruning time Late winter/early spring.

Heteromeles arbutifolia (Christmas berry) is naturally multi-stemmed but can be trained as a small tree on a single trunk. It also makes an interesting hedge: pinch out the growing tips before hardening to encourage bushy growth and a dense barrier. Apart from restricting size, very little pruning should be necessary. When it outgrows its space or requires renovation, hard prune to a framework.

HIBISCUS

Habit Upright vase-shaped deciduous shrub for free-draining soil and full sun. **Attributes** Large trumpet-shaped flowers in late summer. **Reasons for pruning** To maintain a compact shape and renovate an old specimen. **Pruning time** Spring or summer.

Hibiscus syriacus (rose of Sharon) has many cultivars, all of which vary in habit and form, but generally they are upright, often branching low from near ground level. Flowering is on the current season's wood. Plant a small, vigorous low bush, or prune a larger plant quite hard directly after planting as the anchor roots are not very strong and any wind rock in an exposed situation leads to air space developing around the root collar—which in turn leads to the bark rotting and eventual failure of the plant. To prune, first cut out dead or diseased wood and crossing branches. When there is large-scale dieback it is often better to replace the plant completely rather than attempting to prune it out. Little other pruning is required apart from light tip-pruning to maintain a compact shape, although overgrown speci-mens may be thinned and cut back quite hard in late spring, exposing the older wood from which new growth will freely regenerate.

HIPPOPHAE

Habit Spiny shrubs to medium-sized decidu-ous decurrent trees for free-draining soil and full sun. **Attributes** Deeply furrowed bark, sil-very willow-like foliage, orange berries. Toler-ant of salt-laden winds and therefore good for coastal planting. **Reasons for pruning** To train a standard tree or maintain vigour. **Pruning time** Summer.

Personal protection Sea buckthorns are armed with needle-like thorns. Always wear good thorn-proof clothing and gloves when pruning. Use long-handled loppers to remove old growths in the centre of the shrub.

Hippophae rhamnoides (sea buckthorn) is often found in coastal areas, where it may be partly buried by drifting sand yet continue to survive. When it grows inland under the right conditions it is suckerous, often forming large clumps or thickets, and very little pruning is required, but it can be trained as a small to medium-sized tree on a short trunk clear to 1.2 to 2 metres (4 to 6 ft.). It is difficult to retain a leader and to form a shapely head; in fact, it wants to produce a twisted, muddled head with semi-pendulous growths. Unfortunately when grown as a tree it is susceptible to strong winds, and weak root plates are often blown out of the ground. It can soon regenerate into a new plant from suckers developing from any old roots left in the ground.

Hippophae salicifolia (willow-leaved sea buckthorn) should be grown with a clean trunk to expose the attractive bark; its branch system too is often twisted, which can lead to weak-nesses in the future; the outer branches have a semi-pendulous habit. When either species is grown as an informal hedge, prune in late summer if needed.

Hippophae rhamnoides grown on a single trunk.

HOHERIA

Habit Evergreen, deciduous, and semi-decidu-ous shrubs or small trees for fertile, free-drain-ing soil. **Attributes** Dense clusters of sweetly scented white flowers in mid- to late summer. **Reasons for pruning** To thin out the centre of the shrub, removing weak and old stems, and to restrict size. **Pruning time** Spring.

Hoheria glabrata and *H. lyallii* are not com-pletely hardy and can be cut right down to the ground during a severe winter; however, if there is still living tissue at the base, strong regeneration will take place. Both species have an upright habit, branching from ground level, and vigorous growths are occasionally thrown up from these low branches or from the base. Some of these branches can be pruned out; the remainder should be left to add to the branch system or be used to replace older branches when these are pruned out. Remove any old wood or weaker branches in the spring as this genus is susceptible to coral spot (*Nectria* *cinnabarina*), especially if the shrub is grown in a damp, shady woodland spot.

The very tender evergreen species *Hoheria populnea* (New Zealand lacebark) and *H. sexstylosa* should be grown in the shelter of a sunny wall for protection. Both should be left to branch freely from the base. If necessary they can be carefully pruned in spring to restrict their size, making the cuts at suitable points inside the bush in order to retain an informal surface.

Hoheria sexstylosa has a shiny sap and lace-like fibre immediately under the bark, which leads to the bark stripping and tearing, leaving an untidy cut when secateurs are used. To overcome this, finish off the cut with a razor-sharp knife and extra care.

HOLBOELLIA

Habit Evergreen climbers with twining stems for fertile soil and full sun or shade. **Attributes** Shiny green foliage and purple, fleshy sausage-shaped fruits. **Reasons for pruning** To control vigour and remove dead wood. **Pruning time** Spring.

These climbers freely produce a large number of slender but extremely vigorous stems. The tender *Holboellia latifolia* needs to be trained against a sunny wall in a sheltered position. The main support should be a horizontal wiring system. Allow some of the growths to grow between the wires and the wall; other growths can be laid along the wires and tied in position. Vertical wires are useful for the young plant as it grows to cover the available space. When the full height is reached, the pendulous growths provide an attractive curtain of greenery. At this stage the climber has a considerable spread outward from the wall; to keep it within bounds, thin some of the weaker growths in spring. Dead wood can also be cut out at this stage or later during the summer, when another thinning of the longer growths may be necessary.

Holboellia coriacea (sausage vine) is hardier and may be used to climb trees or a system of tripod stakes in the border. An old specimen can be full of dead wood in the centre, which can be cleaned out by pulling away the brittle growths by hand.

Holboellia coriacea wall-trained.

HOLODISCUS

Habit Arching, multi-stemmed deciduous shrub for well-drained soil in full sun to partial shade. **Attributes** An elegant spreading shrub with creamy white panicles of flowers in late spring/early summer. **Reasons for pruning** To regenerate young canes and encourage more flowers. **Pruning time** Early summer after flowering.

Holodiscus discolor (oceanspray) produces its heavy panicles of flowers on leafy shoots that spring from the previous year's wood. Young canes are produced from the base of the shrub, and so older woody stems can be pruned out annually after flowering, which has the effect of maintaining the flowering display year by year and allows the strong growths to arch over freely to produce the best effect. Leave enough older wood on the shrub to maintain furnishing and a good framework; allow the best of the young canes to develop freely to replace the framework.

HOVENIA

Habit Small to medium-sized deciduous tree with a rounded crown for free-draining soil and full sun. **Attributes** Shiny green foliage, white flowers, small round fruits with edible pedicles (hence the common name). **Reasons for pruning** To develop a strong framework and remove dead wood. **Pruning time** Spring.

For the best display of its flowers, grow *Hovenia dulcis* (Japanese raisin tree) as a standard with a leader on a 1 to 1.2 metre (3 to 4 ft.) clean trunk; with open space all around, it will develop a perfect symmetrical crown outline.

When this tree is grown in a harsh climate, any unripened wood will be killed back in winter, and even healthy wood is very susceptible to coral spot (*Nectria cinnabarina*). There is therefore a considerable amount of dead wood to cut out each spring.

HYDRANGEA

Habit Deciduous domed to spreading shrubs or deciduous and evergreen climbers for free-draining soil and full sun to light shade. **Attributes** Large, attractive flowers and seedheads of various colours in summer. **Reasons for pruning** To encourage regular flowering, maintain the shape of shrubs, and control some of the climbers.

One characteristic common to all hydrangeas is that they grow freely from the base, which allows old and tired branches to be removed, even on those subjects that are not normally pruned regularly. The extent and type of pruning is directly related to their habits of growth and flowering, and hydrangeas may be classified for this purpose into the following four groups:

- Group 1. Hydrangeas that flower terminally on the current season's wood.
- Group 2. Low-growing hydrangeas that produce a clump-like growth freely with young growths from the base.
- Group 3. Hydrangeas that form large shrubs, retaining a more permanent framework.
- Group 4. Hydrangeas that climb by aerial rootlets.

GROUP 1

Pruning time Early spring.

The growth of hydrangeas in this group (e.g., *Hydrangea arborescens*, *H. paniculata*, and their cultivars) develops during the season from the dormant buds, producing large heads of flowers in late summer. If these growths are left to develop year after year without any pruning, they will produce small heads of flower. Hard pruning should be carried out each spring before the new growth starts. Make the cuts just above the lowest pair or two of buds, allowing only two or four buds to grow from each position. Over a period of several years, this pruning (a form of disbudding) will result in the buildup of a short, stout branch system a few centimetres in height. In exposed situations,

A well-tended *Hydrangea paniculata* 'Unique'.

lower branching should be encouraged to give protection to the shrub; taller shrubs could be snapped in strong winds. It is important to reward plants with mulch, fertiliser, and water annually to maintain the vigour of the shrub following pruning.

GROUP 2

Pruning time Spring.

Hydrangea macrophylla (Hortensia Group), *H. serrata* (Lace-cap Group), and others in this second group flower from the strong, overwintered buds, which were produced terminally on growths generated from the base during the previous season and on growths that flowered then. Know when pruning that the large fat buds are those likely to produce an inflorescence the next year, the small ones only vegetative growth. Remember too that a flowering stem might also form flower buds for the following season. If this group of shrubs were not pruned, they would still flower well, especially given well-drained soil and full sun; however, pruning will assist and improve flowering.

Leave the old flower heads on the plant through winter; they offer some protection against very severe weather. In spring before growths from the buds have advanced, thin the upright branch system: remove weaker and older branches right back to ground level and cut the old flower heads back to strong outward-facing buds, which may mean cutting back 15 to 30 cm (6 to 12 in.) of stem. The flowers of the lace-caps should be removed as they fade to prevent wasted vigour in seed production. By carrying out these pruning operations, strong flower buds are retained, crowded growth is avoided, and the wood in the stems ripens better—all of which boosts flowering capacity in both the hortensias and the lace-caps.

Should any Group 2 hydrangea be cut back to the ground in the spring by adverse weather, the regenerated growths will be strong but will not flower until the following year, and the subsequent dense cluster of vegetative growth will need thinning as they develop.

GROUP 3

Pruning time Spring or after flowering.

Hydrangea aspera and the other plants in this group require very little pruning. The only pruning necessary for the untidy *H. quercifolia* (oak-leaved hydrangea), for example, will be to maintain its size and shape. *Hydrangea*

Hydrangea macrophylla in late winter before any pruning.

Hydrangea macrophylla being pruned.

Hydrangea macrophylla after pruning with a nicely balanced branch system and space for new growths to come from the base.

Hydrangea macrophylla 'Red Rock' following regular annual pruning.

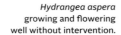

Hydrangea aspera growing and flowering well without intervention.

heteromalla is a variable, vigorous shrub and if grown on a trunk, even makes a small tree. These hydrangeas can suffer from late spring frosts and some adjustments to the timing of pruning may have to be made when new growths break out. Weaker growths may be thinned or pruned out in spring, or after flowering in late summer. A weak or poor bush may be pruned hard, allowing strong renewal growths to be thrown up from the base of the plant. Some encouragement to the new growths may have to be made by watering, mulching, and feeding.

GROUP 4

Pruning time Spring and summer.

The aerial rootlets produced by *Hydrangea anomala* subsp. *petiolaris*, *H. serratifolia*, and other species in this group, generated from the young extension growths, allow them to cling naturally to walls and other surfaces without any support. Their hold can be retained for

Hydrangea anomala subsp. *petiolaris*, cutting spurs back to a suitable bud in spring.

Hydrangea anomala subsp. *petiolaris* growing naturally on a wall.

Hydrangea heteromalla grown as a small tree in a border.

many years as they thicken, and the flowering shoots develop laterally from them. Even greater stability is gained if the plant is allowed to develop its extensive branch system on top of the wall. This it will do on its own.

Prune back extension growths that are not required through the summer. In time the flowering branch system has a considerable spread from the wall; these branches can be pruned back closer to the wall, carefully cutting back a proportion of the spurs to a suitable bud in the spring. In order not to disrupt flowering, stagger this pruning over three to four years.

The evergreen climbing hydrangeas, particularly *Hydrangea seemannii*, can also be left to grow naturally up a tree or scramble over a rock; no attention is needed apart from removing any extension growths that are not required.

Hydrangea seemannii
growing naturally up a
mature oak.

HYPERICUM

Habit Deciduous and evergreen upright to spreading shrubs for well-drained soil and full sun or dappled shade. **Attributes** Yellow saucer-shaped flowers from late spring to autumn. **Reasons for pruning** To control size and remove dead wood. **Pruning time** Early spring.

There is a considerable variation among the St. John's worts: some are hardy and retain their wood from year to year, others are semi-woody, almost herbaceous in nature. In the nursery, all woody members should be cut hard back as they break into growth in the second season, in order to encourage a bushy habit. The common *Hypericum calycinum* is seldom more than 0.3 metre (1 ft.) in height; it is stoloniferous and spreads extensively,

which makes it a good groundcover plant. Cut it hard back with hedging shears every year in early spring, just before new growth begins, to within a few centimetres of the ground to tidy it up. A few weeks later, once new growth begins, it will look quite attractive and fresh.

Hypericum androsaemum need not be pruned regularly or cut back as hard, but it will throw up shoots strongly if it is reduced to ground level occasionally in early spring in order to clean up the surrounding area.

Distinctly shrubby species and cultivars (e.g., *Hypericum beanii*, *H. forrestii*, *H. ×hidcoteense* 'Hidcote', *H. hookerianum*) should be pruned in spring when it is easy to identify the difference between living and dead wood.

Remove dead, thin, and weak stems back to ground level and shorten the remainder of the stems to suitable buds or shoots. Often this entails removing only the old seedheads. This form of pruning is basically to regulate the size of the plant.

The semi-evergreen *Hypericum* 'Rowallane' is quite tender and often killed to ground level in all but the mildest areas. It is best planted against a sunny wall or some such sheltered position. In its case, pruning takes the form of removing any dead stems back to ground level in the spring, allowing any living wood to build up in height.

IDESIA

Habit Medium-sized deciduous tree for fertile, well-drained soil in full sun to light shade. **Attributes** Heart-shaped leaves, fragrant yellow-green flowers, orange to red berries. **Reasons for pruning** No pruning required. **Pruning time** Late winter/early spring.

From a young age, the distinctive *Idesia polycarpa* (igiri tree) develops a strong single leader, with sparse branches growing horizontally from the trunk in tiers. If grown with plenty of space, with no interference from neighbouring plants, it will form a shapely tree naturally, and pruning is not necessary. Any shading of branches causes dieback, which leads to its decline. We have not had luck with this tree at Kew, but when glimpsed in the wild and in other gardens, it looks impressively symmetrical, architectural, and quite spectacular, especially when in fruit.

Idesia polycarpa is dioecious; both male and female plants are needed to produce the wonderful fruit.

ILEX

Habit Mainly evergreen shrubs to medium-sized trees for free-draining soil, tolerant of shade or full sun. **Attributes** Attractive foliage, many with variegation, and clusters of bright red, black, and yellow berries in winter. **Reasons for pruning** To restrict size and maintain a neat specimen. **Pruning time** Mid- to late summer.

Personal protection Wear good thorn-proof clothing and gloves—some hollies bear prickly leaves.

Ilex aquifolium (English holly) reacts well to close annual clipping in late summer with hedge cutters or hedging shears, which makes it a good subject for a formal hedge (although the berry show may be diminished). If a more natural appearance is desired, it is possible to cut back any growths that extend beyond the general shape with secateurs or a sharp handsaw. This pruning should be carried out in mid- to late summer, making each cut well back to a suitable growth, preferably hidden by the retained leaves. Despite efforts to achieve this, some cuts may appear unsightly if hard pruning is needed, but if hollies are healthy they will respond vigorously, and the pruning points will be hidden after a few months. This ability allows us to prune individual specimens

Several hollies with skirts down to the ground.

very hard, removing all the leaves and cutting back into old wood if renovation is needed. Most hollies respond quickly, provided pruning is followed up with feeding and mulching. The aim for normal pruning should be to retain a low skirt and have a coverage of foliage

The variegated *Ilex aquifolium* 'Golden Queen'.

down to the ground, which is more attractive than a lollipop specimen.

Encourage a leader from a young plant for as long as possible after planting. If a plant with a bushy, stunted top is planted or formed after a cold winter, it is easy to select a shoot from the strong natural regrowth and train this on to be the main leader. With variegated varieties,

keep an eye out for any reversion and prune it out as soon you spot it.

If overgrown, a hedge of *Ilex aquifolium* will respond well to very hard cutting back, provided this is spread over two or three years; first one side should be cut back, then the other, and finally the top. You may need to use a combination of shears, secateurs, and a handsaw, as you will be cutting back into old wood.

The many varieties and cultivars of hollies all behave differently; some if left unpruned will lose the character for which they are known and grow vigorously into tree forms. It is your choice, and if the tree effect is undesirable, it will be best to begin formative pruning and training from an early age.

The vigorous *Ilex ×altaclerensis* forms a strong leader and impressive pyramidal shape, but its habit is more open than that of *I. aquifolium*, making it difficult to create a dense canopy even with regular pruning.

Ilex cornuta (horned holly) forms a dense rounded bush, up to 2.5 metres (8 ft.) high. *Ilex pernyi* has a very wide and stiff branching habit.

Many of the better selections of *Ilex opaca* (American holly) have a dense, pyramidal

shape without the need for pruning. Where any pruning is needed, they should be treated the same as *I. aquifolium*.

The variable *Ilex crenata* (Japanese holly) and its many forms can make anything from a dwarf, compact shrub to a tree 6 metres (20 ft.) tall, but they are united in their small leaves. This makes it a good plant for close-clipping and topiary. It also transplants and grows well, particularly in free-draining soils. It has met with success as a close replacement plant for *Buxus sempervirens* in parterre gardens where box blight has been a problem.

The deciduous *Ilex verticillata* (winterberry), grown for its abundance of berries on naked branches, may require annual thinning in late winter/early spring to encourage better fruiting; at the same time prune out any crossing, spindly, or dead branches and remove any branches that extend beyond the shrub's uniform shape.

Ilex ×koehneana (particularly in its selection 'Chestnut Leaf') makes an attractive small tree with a pyramidal crown when grown on a single clean trunk.

ILLICIUM

Habit Slow-growing evergreen shrubs or small trees for moist, well-drained, neutral to acid soil in light shade. **Attributes** Leathery leaves, fragrant foliage and flowers; some have poisonous fruits. **Reasons for pruning** To restrict size. **Pruning time** Summer after flowering.

Little pruning is required apart from the occasional tipping back of growing shoots to restrict and maintain the size of the plant in certain positions in the shrub border. The growths for this type of pruning should be carefully selected, making the cuts at suitable points behind others so that an informal surface is maintained. *Illicium anisatum* (Japanese star anise), the most commonly cultivated illicium, makes a large shrub or a small tree. *Illicium simonsii* naturally forms a narrow conical shrub and requires very little pruning, usually flowering at an early age all over the plant, looking like a lit Christmas tree. With the very dense *I. floridanum*, whole branches that are weak and old can be cut out at ground level; if the shrub is healthy with some vigour, new growths are freely produced from ground level.

A young conical
Illicium simonsii.

INDIGOFERA

Habit Arching deciduous shrubs for full sun and fertile, well-drained soil. **Attributes** Fine foliage, late-season pink flowers. **Reasons for pruning** To remove dead stems to encourage new growths for flowering. **Pruning time** Spring.

Many *Indigofera* species (e.g., *I. heterantha, I. kirilowii, I. pendula, I. potaninii*) are killed back to the ground by an average winter, losing all the new wood they made during the previous spring and summer months, but *I. amblyantha* will retain a low woody branch system and build up in height from year to year. The attractive flowers are produced during late summer and early autumn on the current season's wood. Prune in spring, cutting away the previous year's growth down to near ground level. Any species that have retained wood above ground level may be pruned hard back to this frame, leaving just the basal portion of the younger wood to increase the size of the woody framework. If wood is left in this way, it should be checked over later, as the buds become more prominent; remove any dead wood by pruning further back into the framework.

Indigofera hebepetala three months after being pruned down to ground level.

ITEA

Habit Medium to large evergreen and deciduous shrubs for a south-facing aspect in fertile soil. **Attributes** Young bronze foliage and good autumn colour; flowers are long white catkins. **Reasons for pruning** To encourage new growths for flowers and colour, wall training. **Pruning time** Midsummer.

The evergreen *Itea ilicifolia* (holly-leaved sweetspire) is best grown as a shrub against a south-facing wall, as it requires some shelter from a harsh winter. Where space is unrestricted both in front of the wall and along the length, very little pruning is required. Alternatively, growths from the previous year can be pruned back by one-third to half to keep the shrub tidy and stop its falling away from the wall or being damaged by heavy snowfalls. The best displays of catkins are produced on the strong, young growths made during the previous year, which will be produced annually from an established framework. Once a framework has been formed against the wall, the older, weaker branches should be cut out, allowing the best of the new growths to be tied in as replacement training.

The deciduous *Itea virginica* (Virginia sweetspire) will naturally produce a bushy plant from the base as it suckers freely. This allows some of the oldest and weakest wood to be cut out altogether back to the ground, although this is only occasionally necessary. Some of the oldest wood on the ends of the branches may also be cut out annually after flowering to maintain a young framework. This is best done in midsummer after flowering. Cut back to promising young growths, the majority of which will originate from just below the flowering shoots. The young growth produces the best bronze foliage and autumn colour.

JAMESIA

Habit Upright deciduous shrub for full sun to partial shade and well-drained, acid soil. **Attributes** Grey foliage, white flowers in spring. **Reasons for pruning** No pruning required. **Pruning time** Late spring after flowering.

When grown in the open the rather stiff *Jamesia americana* (cliff bush) has a close, upright-branching habit. It produces growths freely from the base, and these may be used as replacements for any older wood that is cut out. Saying that, this plant requires very little pruning. Keep the crown as intact as possible, with foliage down to the ground.

JASMINUM

Habit Deciduous and evergreen climbers. **Attributes** Yellow flowers hanging in tassels from leafless stems. **Reasons for pruning** To control size and vigour. **Pruning time** Early to mid-spring following flowering.

The hardy jasmine species are vigorous, freely developing young growths from all parts of the plant. They fall into two groups: some cling to a support by twining anticlockwise (Group 1); others have a loose scrambling or arching scandent habit (Group 2).

GROUP 1

Jasminum officinale (common white jasmine) must be grown on a strong support, especially if left to grow to heights of 6 metres (20 ft.) or more. It is difficult to train and prevent its becoming a tangled mass; it is best left to grow naturally. This climber flowers on laterals produced from the previous year's growth but also terminally, on growths produced during the summer. It is possible to thin out cluttered growths and remove weak shoots after they have flowered back to strong buds or to the main stem. It does tolerate hard pruning should it become out of control, but flowering will be poor for a few years after, until a new framework has developed. *Jasminum beesianum*, with beautiful pink trumpet-shaped flowers, is not as strong a grower but can be treated in the same way.

GROUP 2

Jasminum nudiflorum (winter jasmine) is best grown as a wall shrub or against a fence. In the early years after planting it should be trained fanwise and tied into bamboo canes attached to a horizontal wire system. Later as the growth increases, the leading shoots may be loosely tied to the wires. The laterals from these, which hang down, should be hard pruned immediately after flowering in the early spring, taking the growths back to strong newly formed shoots from the main framework, which will have broken by this time. Carry this out an-

Jasminum nudiflorum showing an untidy habit without any pruning for several years.

nually; otherwise, the subject quickly gets out of hand with the new growths falling over the old growths, depriving them of light and killing them; the result will be a buildup of untidy masses of dead wood. At pruning time, check the ties. If a plant is left to become untidy and out of hand, it can be hard pruned back to form a new framework.

Jasminum mesnyi (Japanese jasmine) has similar pruning requirements but is tender and should be grown against a sheltered, sunny wall. *Jasminum fruticans* and *J. humile* have a stiffer habit, frequently appearing in bush form as border plants, but they too can be wall-trained. As they flower on the previous year's growth, this may be cut out after flowering, tying in the new growths as they develop on the framework.

JUGLANS

Habit Deciduous shade trees of various forms, all with broad crowns, for full sun and fertile soil. **Attributes** Architectural shape, pinnate leaves, edible fruits. **Reasons for pruning** To develop a strong framework and maintain a leader. **Pruning time** Summer when actively growing, to avoid bleeding.

Walnuts need to be sited away from frost hollows, as they are very susceptible to late spring frosts; in the first three to five years after planting, their leading shoot is often lost to these, and a stunted tree results. Keep the leader growing strong for as long as possible to gain height and a straight trunk. If the leader is lost to transplanting shock or frost, several new leaders will be formed; select a strong one and prune the rejects out after all threat of frost is past. Walnuts do not respond well to hard

A mature *Juglans nigra* showing the elegant branch system.

A bleeding pruning cut on a walnut.

Juglans mandshurica grown as a multi-stemmed tree on a short trunk.

Juglans nigra showing a clean trunk and sweeping lower branches.

pruning, and all bleed badly if pruned in the spring. That said, we have yet to see a walnut bleed to death, and it probably hurts you the pruner psychologically more than the tree.

Juglans nigra (black walnut) forms a graceful and shapely tree, retaining the leader better than many other species. This allows the lower branches to be removed as the tree develops, forming a clean trunk to 4.5 to 6 metres (15 to 20 ft.). Even with a crown this high, the lower branches will naturally sweep down to the ground to produce an elegant effect.

Juglans regia (English walnut) often forms rival leaders after frost damage; correct this by selection and pruning out the rivals. Remove frost-damaged wood well back into live wood. This species naturally develops into a feathered tree with laterals from the ground. As with *J. nigra*, the lower laterals should be removed to produce a clean trunk. Do this soon after planting, with secateurs rather than a saw, to keep pruning wounds small. Treat cultivars of *J. regia* in the same way. This species quickly loses the leader and forms a broad, round crown.

Juglans mandshurica (Manchurian walnut) and *J. ailantifolia* (Japanese walnut) are small trees that lose their leader early in life. They do not respond well to any form of pruning and

A mature *Juglans regia* showing the broad, round crown.

Early formative pruning of *Juglans regia*, before, during, and after.

should be left alone to grow naturally into multi-stemmed trees on a short trunk. Their broad crowns will shade out lower branches, and these dead branches will need to be removed as they develop to keep the specimen tidy.

Juglans californica (California walnut) and *J. microcarpa* (Texas walnut) are both small graceful trees, even large shrubs, and they too should be left to develop naturally without any pruning, apart from the removal of crossing and weak branches.

With this wide variation in growth rate and final form across the genus, it is important that the characteristics of the species are taken into account before and during formative pruning.

JUNIPERUS

Habit Evergreen conifers, trees or shrubs, with upright conical-pyramidal or low-spreading bushy forms, for full sun and free-draining (and sometimes alkaline) soil. **Attributes** Black berries on conical-pyramidal specimens, low bushy forms suitable for groundcover. **Reasons for pruning** To maintain a neat shape or restrict size. **Pruning time** Early spring.

One common feature of all junipers, regardless of their form and size, is that they produce a dead area in the centre of the plant due to shading caused by the foliage on the outside. If junipers are pruned back to this dead area, they will not respond and produce new growth: there are no live buds. It is therefore important not to expose the dead area, or it will forever remain unsightly. No regular pruning is normally needed, but if it is, the best way to prune a juniper and retain a natural appearance is to thin out branches within the canopy, removing them back to the parent branch or a strong lateral with a natural growth pattern. At the same time, remove dead or broken branches, taking care not to leave holes in the outer shape. Do not over-thin, which will result in a weak canopy that is more prone to collapse in snow or adverse weather.

With the spreading junipers (e.g., *Juniperus ×pfitzeriana*), maintain the layered effect by

Juniperus ×pfitzeriana showing the natural layered effect.

selectively reducing the length of the branches back to strong laterals evenly across the plant from the top down, or remove entire branches to keep a natural layered effect. Do not prune beyond the foliage into the dead area, or it will

not be able to flush and cover the wounds.

The tree species (e.g., *Juniperus chinensis, J. communis, J. osteosperma, J. virginiana*) may be thinned to reduce dominant branches to maintain a uniform shape. These junipers have a

Juniperus occidentalis (Sierra juniper) growing wild in California, pruned only by wind and snow.

tendency to produce multiple leaders, which can break out or fall apart later in life during bad weather. Remove these when the plant is as young as possible to prevent this.

Junipers can be clipped to a formal shape with hedging shears but it's not recommended. Plants pruned to create a formal hedge or topiary will look unnatural, produce excessive regrowth from the pruning points, and need regular pruning in spring to maintain their shape and size.

Juniperus chinensis growing upright as a tree form, making a uniform shape with no intervention.

Juniperus osteosperma growing wild in Utah.

Juniperus communis producing multiple leaders with a low form.

KALMIA

Habit Dense, rounded evergreen shrubs for free-draining, acid soil and full sun to partial shade. **Attributes** Late spring/early summer flowering, resistant to rabbits. **Reasons for pruning** To encourage a bushy, vigorous plant and remove spent flowers. **Pruning time** Between autumn and spring (when dormant) or after flowering in summer.

Personal protection The leaves of these plants are poisonous. Always wear gloves and wash your hands following pruning. Dispose of arisings safely; don't leave them for pets to forage on.

These plants must have the right growing conditions and pruning will not in any way compensate for a failure to provide them. Some regeneration will occur following the hard pruning of a neglected specimen, but the response will be maintained only if the conditions and culture are suitable.

Kalmia angustifolia (sheep laurel) normally requires very little pruning but may become old and woody with some of the older growths bending over to the ground, exposing the centre of the bush. These stems can be cut right down to the ground, leaving some of the small, thin woody growths to form a new bush. The strong growths that are needed as replacements will not develop from these but from completely new shoots that will form at their bases or on the old wood. Sometimes after planting, young plants can send a strong shoot up that grows well beyond the normal level of growth; these should be left, as they are a sign of a happy plant and a new shape will form from further growths.

Kalmia latifolia (mountain laurel) forms a rather dense bush with a stout branch system, and no pruning is needed with a healthy specimen. Unsuitable growing conditions result in a straggly plant, with poor growth and a weak branch system. Usually a plant in this state will not respond to corrective pruning or hard renovation pruning; however, a plant in this state can be effectively renovated with a light pruning programme that is carried out over a three- to five-year period, choosing a few growths at a time and pruning back to a suitable growing point.

Both species benefit from deadheading immediately after flowering, and flowering will be improved the following year.

The typical dense, bushy form of *Kalmia latifolia*.

KALOPANAX

Habit Prickly deciduous tree with upright branching habit and rounded crown when mature, for fertile, free-draining soil and full sun or light shade. **Attributes** Maple-like leaves give a tropical appearance, white flowers in autumn. **Reasons for pruning** To develop a strong framework. **Pruning time** Spring.

Personal protection Tony Kirkham climbed a medium-sized tree on an expedition to South Korea several years ago, not realising the trunk and branches were covered in stout prickles, and paid the price. Wear thick gloves and take care, especially when pruning the smaller branches: they are well armed.

The beautiful maple-like *Kalopanax septemlobus* (prickly castor oil tree) is slow to establish after planting. It has a stiff habit when young and should be trained on a single trunk. Encourage a strong leader for as long as possible, as the bark is attractive on a large trunk and the main framework will be much stronger. The main scaffolds have an upright habit and any rival leaders will form very tight angles off the main stem, which will be a potential weakness in the future. The tree as a whole is sparsely branched with a very short spur system, even on the main branches and trunk. Keep the trunk clear of these and branches, up to a height of 2 to 2.5 metres (6 to 8 ft.).

Kalopanax septemlobus f. *maximowiczii*, with deeper lobed leaves, has a similar habit and should be treated in the same way. With both taxa, dieback can occur on young shoots with the first frosts if these young growths are not fully ripened, and the removal of some dead wood may be needed to maintain a tidy appearance.

KERRIA

Habit Vigorous, suckering upright deciduous shrub with arching stems for free-draining soil and full sun. **Attributes** Green canes bearing yellow flowers in spring. **Reasons for pruning** To encourage new canes for flowering. **Pruning time** Late spring after flowering.

Kerria japonica (Japanese rose) forms a close, bushy shrub, throwing up new canes from the base at ground level; these reach the height of the shrub in one season and will flower in the next. The shrub also spreads by means of suckerous growths, and very soon the whole area around it becomes a dense mass of intertwining stems and foliage. Often the old flowering stems die back to strong, young growths that appear on the stem. This habit of growth and flowering allows the old stems to be thinned and cut out to ground level after flowering in late spring.

Kerria japonica 'Pleniflora' (bachelor's buttons) is similar in habit, but more extensive pruning is needed, as once the flowers have finished and die back, the plant looks very unsightly. *Kerria japonica* 'Picta' is variegated with an attractive spread of branches, but it does not sucker readily—which is a good thing, as the suckers have a tendency to revert back to green leaves. If this happens, prune them out.

The green canes of *Kerria japonica* in full flower.

KOELREUTERIA

Habit Deciduous trees with a broad irregular decurrent crown for free-draining soil and full sun. **Attributes** Large panicles of yellow lantern-shaped flowers in late spring/early summer followed by dry lantern-shaped fruits. **Reasons for pruning** To develop a strong framework and remove dead wood. **Pruning time** Spring.

Koelreuteria paniculata (pride of India), the species most commonly grown, will make a tree with a single trunk and a sound branch system. Plant a healthy, vigorous tree from a nursery in spring so that it gets off to a good start, as if their growth is checked they seem to want to die back and need a boost to get going again. The leader needs to be encouraged for as long as possible for a tall trunk, and formative pruning should be carried out to encourage an even and strong branch system, which will prolong its life span. As the tree develops, the lower branches will die through lack of light, and these can be removed to expose the trunk. At a later stage the lower branches will sweep down to meet the ground if unrestricted by shade or growth; this gives the tree a very elegant effect. This tree needs full sun and will not flower if grown in the shade; it also needs the summer sun to ripen the wood, which pre-pares it for winter and prevents frost damage. It will not respond to hard pruning of the main scaffold branches.

Koelreuteria paniculata 'Fastigiata' has a growth habit similar to the Lombardy poplar; it grows extremely slowly but is worth the wait, as the columnar effect is very architectural without any pruning. We have yet to see one flower, however.

Koelreuteria bipinnata has a more upright branching form and an irregular untidy crown and should be treated the same as *K. paniculata*.

Koelreuteria paniculata in its natural habitat in western China.

A young *Koelreuteria bipinnata* showing the upright branching form.

KOLKWITZIA

Habit Large deciduous upright-arching shrub for free-draining soil and full sun. **Attributes** Small leaves with pink flowers in late spring/early summer on old wood. **Reasons for pruning** To remove old wood and encourage new growth from inside the shrub. **Pruning time** Midsummer after flowering.

Encourage a healthy, bushy habit in *Kolkwitzia amabilis* (beautybush) from the start, and it will send out strong arching growths as it becomes established. These should be left to grow freely and unpruned, and the arching habit will continue at maturity. From these main branches, cut out whole lengths of old and weak wood after flowering in midsummer to make way for suckers to take over. Many of these will be found on the underside of the branch system; prune them back to a suitable growing point. Leave the lower branches to add a natural effect to the shrub and hide the lower stems.

Kolkwitzia amabilis flowers on new wood.

+LABURNOCYTISUS

Habit Small, bushy, upright deciduous tree for rich, well-drained soil and full sun. **Attributes** Flowers in late spring/early summer; some branches have yellow laburnum flowers, while others produce dense clusters of purple broom flowers. Most branches will also produce coppery pink flowers, which are midway between the two parents. **Reasons for pruning** To develop a strong framework and remove suckers. **Pruning time** Late summer to midwinter.

Personal protection All plant parts are highly poisonous if ingested by humans and pets and may cause a skin irritation. Wear gloves when pruning and dispose of arisings carefully.

+*Laburnocytisus* 'Adamii' (Adam's laburnum) has a habit similar to laburnum and should be grown as a standard. No pruning is required other than the removal of suckers to maintain a standard specimen with a clean trunk. Occasionally a specimen will grow out of its chimera form; no pruning operation will prevent this from happening, and once the entire tree has reverted to laburnum, a new tree should be planted.

The graft hybrid +*Laburnocytisus* 'Adamii'.

LABURNUM

Habit Small, bushy, spreading, upright deciduous decurrent trees for free-draining soil and full sun. **Attributes** Small, downy, matte leaves, drooping racemes of yellow flowers in late spring/early summer. **Reasons for pruning** To develop a strong framework and maintain a standard tree. **Pruning time** Late summer to midwinter.

Personal protection All plant parts are highly poisonous if ingested by humans and pets and may cause a skin irritation. Wear gloves when pruning and dispose of arisings carefully.

An established laburnum tunnel in full flower.

Laburnum anagyroides grown on a single trunk.

Laburnum anagyroides trained to the shape of a tunnel frame.

Laburnum anagyroides trained to a two-bud spur system.

Laburnums are small, spreading but neat trees, quite fast growing, but frequently remain in good condition for only a short period. Cultivars and hybrids are often produced in the nursery by grafting and so are prone to producing suckers from the rootstock; these should be removed as soon as they are seen by rubbing the soft shoots off with your thumb. They can be grown as multi-stemmed bushes, but they look much better grown as a short standard. Once the head and the main framework of the tree has been developed on the trunk, they need very little pruning. Where there is a need to remove a large branch, it should be done in late summer to midwinter to prevent bleeding from the pruning wound. Large wounds tend not to heal quickly, particularly with old, mature specimens, and a careful watch should be kept on these, as they have a tendency to decay quickly and weaken the main trunk.

Laburnum anagyroides (golden chain tree), *L. alpinum*, and *L. ×watereri* 'Vossii' respond to spur pruning, the young growths being pruned back to the older wood, leaving only one or two buds; do this in early winter. The young growth is also very flexible, which makes them ideal candidates to cover pergolas, archways, and tunnels. Low-branching fan-shaped specimens are best suited for this purpose. In the early years, the positioning of the main stems should be looked at carefully; remove crossing branches or branches badly situated as early as possible.

LAGERSTROEMIA

Habit Upright vase-shaped deciduous shrubs or small trees for free-draining soil, frost-free climate, and full sun. **Attributes** Showy, smooth coloured bark, large terminal panicles of deep pink or red flowers. **Reasons for pruning** To remove dead wood and encourage young growth, which will bear flowers in mid-to late summer. **Pruning time** Between autumn and spring (when dormant).

Crape myrtles require the shelter of a sunny wall to grow well and need a hot summer to ripen the wood, which will encourage the terminal panicles of late-season flowers. They can be trained on a short stem or as a multi-stemmed specimen. Once a framework is produced, prune them annually when dormant to encourage vigorous new growth for flowers, which are produced on the current year's growth. If they should be damaged by a cold winter, they can be pruned hard to renovate and encourage a new framework. If you are very lucky, dead-heading can encourage a second flush of flowers and discourage fruit production.

Mature plants, particularly *Lagerstroemia fauriei*, should be grown with a strong framework, or multi-stemmed and pruned to open up the interior of the plant, allowing their mottled bark to be shown to its best.

Lagerstroemia indica trained to a framework and regularly pruned as a shrub.

Lagerstroemia fauriei in its natural habitat on Yakushima, showing the wonderful mottled bark.

LAPAGERIA

Lapageria rosea effectively trained against a shady wall with little regular pruning.

Habit Evergreen climber with strong twining stems for shade and partial shade in cool, moist, free-draining, lime-free soil. **Attributes** Waxy red bell-shaped flowers. **Reasons for pruning** To maintain a tidy plant and remove weak stems. **Pruning time** Early spring.

Lapageria rosea (Chilean bellflower) is a strong twining evergreen climber from Chile suitable for growing against a sheltered wall in a shady, frost-free part of the garden. There should be vertical wires stretched between horizontal wires; this helps with initial training and gets the plant to cover the wall more easily. Cut out the weaker stems in spring before new growth begins, to tidy the plant up; naturally the best of the new growths break from the thicker and healthier stems. Following pruning, carefully tie back any stems that have become loose on their support. *Lapageria rosea* var. *albiflora* has white flowers.

LARDIZABALA

Habit Evergreen climber with twining stems for a sheltered, shady wall in a frost-free area. **Attributes** Glossy leathery leaves, small purple flowers in late autumn through to winter followed by interesting, knobbly, sausage-shaped fruits. **Reasons for pruning** To remove dead wood and old and weak growths. **Pruning time** Spring.

The Chilean *Lardizabala funaria* (zabala fruit, aquiboquil) is best trained against a sheltered, shady wall with vertical wires tied between horizontal wires to facilitate climbing in the early years. Carefully prune out old and weak stems and dead wood in spring, so as not to disturb and damage the remainder of the shrub. Any young growths that spring from the lower parts of this vigorous plant should be encouraged as replacement shoots; any that develop beyond its bounds should be pruned off or tied into the wiring system to fill gaps.

LARIX

Habit Small to medium-sized upright fast-growing deciduous excurrent conifers with open crown and pendulous branching for full sun. **Attributes** Distinctive, graceful form, fresh spring foliage, golden yellow autumn colour. **Reasons for pruning** To develop a strong framework, maintain a leader, and lift the crown. **Pruning time** Autumn through winter (when dormant).

Tony Kirkham planted his very first tree at Kew in 1981; it was a *Larix decidua* (European larch), and it never ceases to amaze him just how quickly it has grown in the years since. When grown in the right conditions, larches form a straight trunk through their centre, with the branches radiating laterally from this, often with pendulous tips. The outline shape and habit of a young larch is conical and very different to that of a mature specimen, which will grow out of its symmetry with age. A good leader should be encouraged, but with a vigorously growing tree, a broken leader will quickly be replaced by growths from adventitious buds or by the upper branches, which will develop an upright habit.

Larches demand light, and if planted too close to other trees, the lower branches will be lost one by one due to shading as they grow in height. A single specimen grown in a sheltered position can be quite heavily branched, provided there is no shading. If the lower branches are retained on *Larix decidua*, they will sweep gracefully down almost to ground level. *Larix kaempferi* (Japanese larch) can also be grown for this purpose, but the branches will take on a more horizontal habit.

All larches should be pruned when dormant. Retain the natural habit of the species, and if any of the lower branches become too long and interfere with access beneath the tree, it is always better to remove them back to the trunk rather than reducing them in length.

The *Larix decidua* planted at Kew in 1981, showing its beautiful, naturally graceful habit.

Larix kaempferi showing the horizontal branching habit.

Larix decidua in its natural habitat, the Swiss Alps, showing the canopy outline.

LAURELIA

Habit Broad upright evergreen shrub or small tree for a sheltered position with moist, free-draining, acid soil in dappled shade or full sun. **Attributes** Clean, leathery, aromatic leaves. **Reasons for pruning** To encourage a strong leader and restrict spread. **Pruning time** Summer.

If sited in the shelter of a wall or woodland garden, away from wind, the very elegant *Laurelia sempervirens* (Chilean laurel) will be large and self-supporting, with a habit similar to that of *Ilex aquifolium*. Encourage a leader for as long as possible to get height in the plant. To restrict the plant's spread, selectively prune back the branches to a natural shape, hiding the cut ends within the retained foliage.

LAURUS

Habit Dense, bushy evergreen shrubs or small trees for any free-draining soil. **Attributes** Tough, aromatic foliage, suitable for exposed coastal areas and topiary. **Reasons for pruning** To maintain size, remove scorched foliage, and create topiary. **Pruning time** Spring and summer.

Bay laurels (*Laurus nobilis*) are thickly branched, producing a plentiful supply of young growth annually if pruned. To produce a tree form, encourage the leader to develop and grow for as long as possible without any pruning, retaining the lower branches to the ground; if a smaller plant is desired, remove the leader in spring once the desired height is reached.

These plants regenerate freely and can break into growth even if killed to the ground by a cold winter, which makes them suitable for topiary. *Laurus nobilis* is often grown in containers and clipped regularly to a formal design; maintain the shape by carefully cutting back the new growths several times during the summer, using a pair of secateurs rather than hedging shears. Pruning positions should be made in front of a bud or leaf, hiding them in the canopy of leaves left. Occasionally they suffer from summer scorch (browning of the leaves); these can be removed in spring back to living wood or strong leaves. Don't throw the leaves away: these are bay leaves and can be dried and used for culinary purposes.

Laurus azorica is less hardy than *L. nobilis* and needs the shelter of a sunny wall for protection from cold winds and frosts.

An old specimen of *Laurus nobilis*.

Laurus nobilis grown as a lollipop standard.

LAVANDULA

Habit Evergreen shrubs, several with rounded habits, for warm, free-draining soil and full sun. **Attributes** Aromatic silvery foliage, scented purple flowers. **Reasons for pruning** To create a compact plant and encourage flowering. **Pruning time** Early to mid-spring and autumn.

Lavandula angustifolia (English lavender) is the most common species, but the many cultivars vary in height and vigour, and these factors must be taken into account when pruning. Left to grow without any pruning, lavenders eventually become leggy, with many bare stems; regular pruning will keep plants more compact and decorative. Do this in early to mid-spring, just as new growth begins. This way, the young growths are protected by the mature growth that was retained over winter, particularly in a cold part of the garden; they will then grow away unchecked with the improving weather conditions. Prune the branch system back to a point where there are several new shoots, and leave these to develop and furnish the shrub. Use hand shears, not secateurs.

Do not cut back hard into the old wood, as this does not break freely; it is better to keep the plant in a healthy condition and prune it annually than to allow it to grow unpruned for several years. If plants have become straggly, start again and replace them with fresh young stock.

Immediately after planting a healthy new lavender, prune it hard to encourage a bushy habit. To keep the plants looking tidy over winter, the old flower stems can be cut back to the foliage in the autumn. Lavender is often used a formal hedging plant and should be pruned in exactly the same way.

Lavandula stoechas (French lavender) and some of the other species can be a little tender, needing a sheltered, warm, sunny position; growth is improved with some light pruning.

Lavandula angustifolia 'Hidcote' flowering well after hard clipping in mid-spring.

A single plant of lavender after flowering with the old flower heads.

Clipping a lavender with hedging shears to remove the old flower heads.

The same plant after a clipping with the hedging shears.

LAVATERA

Habit Medium to large subshrubs for a sunny, sheltered position and free-draining soil. **Attributes** Showy pink to white flowers with a red centre. **Reasons for pruning** To maintain a tidy shrub on a woody framework. **Pruning time** Late spring.

Tree mallows (*Lavatera ×clementii*) are vigorous but not fully hardy. Usually a woody framework of older branches survives a winter, and new growths break freely from this in spring. Cut these young growths back late each spring, after all threat of frosts is past, to near their bases. Flowers are produced along the terminal lengths of the current season's wood, and this flowering portion dies back naturally as the fruits ripen. Unpruned, these subshrubs develop a loose, untidy habit.

LEPTOSPERMUM

Habit Evergreen shrubs for a sheltered sunny position and fertile, free-draining soil. **Attributes** Fine aromatic foliage, showy flowers. **Reasons for pruning** To encourage a bushy plant. **Pruning time** Late spring.

Leptospermum myrtifolium (myrtle teatree)

and *L. scoparium* (New Zealand teatree) are real sun lovers for a mild climate, and even then, some protection from a sunny wall is often necessary; however, they should be grown as freestanding shrubs rather than being trained against the wall. To encourage bushiness, prune young growths in late spring, before they start to ripen and harden. Plants do not break from old wood if pruning cuts are made into it.

LESPEDEZA

Habit Arching deciduous shrubs or subshrubs for free-draining light soil and full sun. **Attributes** Fine trifoliate foliage, pea-like flowers in late summer. **Reasons for pruning** To encourage new growth for flowering. **Pruning time** Spring.

In most years, the woody members of this genus (e.g., *Lespedeza bicolor*, *L. kiusiana*, *L. thunbergii*) are killed down to the ground following a cold winter. If not grown in full sun, bush clovers will need the shelter of a warm, sunny wall. In spring, prune the old growths from the previous year down to ground level; vigorous new growth will develop from these, and the flowers will be produced on the current season's growth in late summer.

LEUCOTHOE

Habit Bushy evergreen groundcover shrub with arching stems for shade and acid soil. **Attributes** Leathery leaves, white flowers along the stems in late spring. **Reasons for pruning** To thin out old and weak stems. **Pruning time** Late spring after flowering.

Leucothoe fontanesiana (dog hobble) should be planted well back from the edge of a border, allowing the plant to grow naturally to its full extent without having to intervene with the secateurs, as pruning to restrict the shrub can spoil the plant's appearance. If necessary a few of the oldest and weakest stems can be thinned out by cutting them out at ground level after flowering, retaining a natural, branching habit.

LEYCESTERIA

Habit Clump-forming deciduous shrub for well-drained, fertile soil in a sheltered position with shade or full sun. **Attributes** Upright, bright green canes, terminal white flowers with red bracts in late summer followed by purple berries. **Reasons for pruning** To encourage flowering growth and to renovate. **Pruning time** Spring.

Leycesteria formosa (Himalayan honeysuckle) breaks freely from the base with strong green hollow-stemmed shoots that reach the full height of the shrub and flower in one season. If left unpruned, the shrub becomes thick and congested with many weak growths, and the flowering capacity will be weaker. Thin out the weaker shoots annually in the spring before any growth starts, taking the canes right down to the ground. To renovate a plant that is congested with old, woody canes, cut all the top growth down hard to within 5 to 8 cm (2 to 3 in.) of ground level. Follow this operation up with mulching, feeding, and watering. Once the plant has responded and produced a new clump, revert to annual thinning the following year.

Leycesteria formosa fruiting on the upright canes.

LIBOCEDRUS

Habit Small, columnar evergreen conifers for free-draining soil and full sun. **Attributes** Rarity value. **Reasons for pruning** No pruning required. **Pruning time** Spring to late summer.

Both *Libocedrus bidwillii* and *L. plumosa* are from New Zealand and need a sheltered position. Should any pruning be needed, they should be treated the same as *Calocedrus*.

LIGUSTRUM

Habit Fast-growing deciduous and evergreen upright and spreading shrubs to large trees for any soil type in full sun or shade. **Attributes** Tight, bright green and variegated foliage, cream flowers, black fruits. **Reasons for pruning** To restrict size and develop a strong framework. **Pruning time** Spring and summer.

The most common representative of this genus in cultivation is *Ligustrum ovalifolium* (California privet), which makes a good hedging plant, but several species will—if allowed to grow freely and pruned correctly—form

A mature *Ligustrum lucidum* showing perfectly symmetrical habit.

shapely bushes as decorative as many other shrubs. All respond well to clipping, forming a tight face; most species regenerate very strongly if hard pruned, and many throw new shoots freely from the base.

Ligustrum lucidum (Chinese privet), the strongest grower, makes a fine, round-headed large tree to 25 metres (82 ft.) high; the laterals from its erect main branches are spreading and are gradually weighed down by extending growths. It is best grown when allowed to branch low as a single specimen. Leave

any young shoots that develop from the main branches, as they will thicken up the centre.

Other species, if allowed to grow as freestanding shrubs, should be pruned only as necessary so that the natural habit is retained. The growth habit varies considerably within the species. *Ligustrum vulgare* (common privet) and its selections 'Densiflorum', 'Fastigiatum', and 'Glaucum' are upright growers, and their habit makes them suitable for close planting to form an informal screen in coastal areas.

Ligustrum japonicum 'Rotundifolium' has a compact, stiff habit and needs shelter, especially in exposed areas.

Ligustrum ovalifolium and its selection 'Aureum' are commonly used as hedging plants. After planting they should be pruned back to within 30 cm (12 in.) of ground level and pruned back hard annually for two or three years afterward, in order to fill in the bottom half of the plant before too much height is put on. This hedge will need clipping frequently during the growing season, but if it is overgrown it will respond to hard pruning on both the top and the sides in mid-spring.

Ligustrum delavayanum (Delavay privet) can be cut very hard and made into a tight plant by regular clipping. With its small evergreen leaves and spreading habit, it frequently replaces *Buxus sempervirens* as a plant for topiary in the nursery industry.

Ligustrum quihoui (waxyleaf privet) is a popular, elegant medium-sized shrub that should be left to grow naturally with little pruning. If it becomes too large for its situation, thin it by selectively removing the more vigorous stems in early spring.

LINDERA

Habit Evergreen or deciduous shrubs or small trees for moist, free-draining, lime-free soil in full sun to partial shade. **Attributes** Aromatic foliage, good autumn colour from the deciduous species. **Reasons for pruning** To develop a strong framework. **Pruning time** Between autumn and early spring (when dormant).

These plants require very little pruning if any at all, apart from the removal of dead wood or the reduction of dead tips following a cold winter. They are able to break into growth freely from old wood at the base of the plant even after the entire top has been killed off by a severe winter.

Lindera praecox is a deciduous, bushy shrub to 5 metres (16 ft.), producing lots of dense, upright growth from its base. If one to three stems are encouraged to form clean trunks, it can be trained into a small tree to 8 metres (25 ft.) high. Alternatively, prune it back hard after planting to encourage several stems that can be trained fanwise against a sunny wall; the eventual framework will require little pruning apart from shortening back shoots that extend too far from the wall. When laterals are hard pruned back to the framework, lots of young growths result; thin these out to prevent a cluttered wall plant. Remove any suckers that break from the base of wall-trained plants as they appear.

Lindera benzoin (northern spicebush) and *L. obtusiloba* (Japanese spicebush) need very little pruning, and if left to grow naturally will develop into neat rounded bushes with branching from low down on the plant. The latter has spectacular butter-yellow autumn colour.

Lindera megaphylla (feverbush) naturally forms a perfectly symmetrical evergreen shrub or small tree to 10 metres (33 ft.). Any attempt at pruning will spoil its shape, so give it plenty of space at the start.

Lindera megaphylla grown as a tree with branching to the ground.

LIQUIDAMBAR

Habit Deciduous shrubs to large trees with a symmetrical crown for most soils, including moist acidic clay, except shallow alkaline soil. **Attributes** Aromatic maple-like leaves with amazing autumn colour, interesting corky winter twigs. **Reasons for pruning** To develop and maintain a strong framework. **Pruning time** Late summer through winter (when dormant). Never prune in spring as the wounds are prone to bleeding.

The most widely planted and hardiest species is the North American *Liquidambar styraciflua* (sweetgum), which forms a large, handsome excurrent shade tree.

It should be planted as a young feathered tree with a strong central leader, as the younger the better for successful establishment. Larger semi-mature specimens are readily available in the nursery world, and these can be successfully transplanted if the lower lateral branches are reduced or removed; however, they will need several years of good aftercare before they become independent in the garden. A good mature tree forms a long straight trunk with beautiful alligator-like bark, the effect of which can be enhanced by removing the lower branches back to the trunk up to 4.5 to 6 metres (15 to 20 ft.) as the tree's overall height increases with age. Even from this height the lateral branches, which are pendulous, will with some encouragement spread and drop down to eye level, allowing the full beauty of the leaves, especially when tinted in autumn, to be seen to best effect. On a single feathered specimen, retain the lower branches for as long as possible. As the tree reaches maturity, some of the branches will take on dominance and the crown will grow out of the symmetrical shape; these competing branches should be removed as early as possible if the symmetrical form is to be retained.

Most sweetgum cultivars are selected for their autumn colour, others more for their form. *Liquidambar styraciflua* 'Gum Ball' is a dwarf, shrubby specimen, and 'Palo Alto' has a more pyramidal habit. 'Stella' is often grown as an upright, multi-stemmed specimen, but the branching is weak and easily damaged in strong winds. 'Worplesdon' remains a favourite "all-rounder."

Liquidambar orientalis (Oriental sweetgum) is a slow-growing decurrent large shrub or tree similar in appearance and habit to that of *Acer campestre*. When young, it is often full of twiggy growth. Encourage a leader as soon as possible to get at least 6 metres (20 ft.) height

A semi-mature *Liquidambar styraciflua* trained on a single clean trunk with leader.

A mature *Liquidambar styraciflua.*

to the plant, and then allow the branch system to follow; otherwise, the branching will become very heavy, leading to structural weakness later in life. Once mature, the branches form a skirt to ground level. In a warmer climate it can make a large excurrent tree.

Liquidambar formosana and plants in the Monticola Group are susceptible to damage from late spring frosts, just as new growth is breaking; if they lose their main leader, train another, to grow a larger specimen. They are better behaved than their American cousin, *L. styraciflua*, and form a symmetrical shape on their own without too much intervention.

Liquidambar acalycina from China quickly loses its leader at an early age and is not very well behaved when it comes to training. If a tall specimen is required, you will have to be very strict and work very hard with the secateurs from day one until the desired height is achieved.

Liquidambar orientalis showing the shrubby growth and branching down to the ground.

A young *Liquidambar styraciflua* feathered to the ground and retaining its leader.

A young *Liquidambar formosana* showing the straight form.

LIRIODENDRON

Habit Medium to large deciduous excurrent shade trees for rich, free-draining soil and full sun. **Attributes** Interesting leaf shape and flowers, autumn colour. **Reasons for pruning** To develop and maintain a strong framework. **Pruning time** Late summer through winter (when dormant).

Both *Liriodendron chinense* (Chinese tulip tree) and *L. tulipifera* (tulip tree, yellow poplar) are intolerant of shade. The latter, more common in gardens and tree collections, is best grown as an excurrent tree on a single trunk with a strong central leader. The branches are then well spaced and able to carry a considerable amount of growth when the tree reaches maturity. The extreme ends of the branches are often semi-pendulous and will reach ground level with encouragement; if the low skirt is left, it allows the flowers to be seen at close quarters. For best establishment, choose a

young feathered nursery specimen and plant in spring, before the leaves appear; do not use the heel to firm in the soil backfill as its fleshy roots are easily broken with rough handling. If a standard form is required, the trunk can be cleaned of growths with secateurs up to a height of 2 to 3 metres (6 to 10 ft.) as the crown develops; however, young, container-grown trees are available in nurseries as standards and with care they too can be successfully established. These should never be without a leader. The attachments of the branch system to the main trunk vary tremendously from tree to tree, and specimens that are left to branch low without a central leader reach a stage when each limb carries considerable weight. Weakness may develop in a crotch with disastrous results. Any branch should be removed as early as possible in the age of the tree, preferably with secateurs or a small handsaw, as

the larger wounds are susceptible to decay before they have occluded. Some form of branch bracing is often necessary with a mature specimen in this condition.

Apart from the training, there is little need for pruning; however, some trees show a tendency to throw strong, upright shoots, even from mature horizontal branches. Prune these out if they appear to be congesting the inner crown; otherwise, the crown will be thrown completely out of balance. Epicormic growths need not be removed unless they are thick and unsightly. Provided the tree is healthy with a naturally thick canopy, these are not troublesome. With *Liriodendron tulipifera* 'Aureomarginatum', it may be necessary to remove any branches that revert from the golden variegation to green. With 'Fastigiatum', selected for it narrow and upright habit, branching is best left to develop from ground level.

Liriodendron chinense is very well-behaved, always forming a good straight leader with little intervention, and has a delicate, slender branch system. If there is a need for pruning, it will be to raise the canopy for access. This should be done as early as possible with secateurs or a small pruning saw.

Liriodendron 'Chapel Hill', a hybrid of the two species, should be treated the same as *L. tulipifera* as this is the dominant character in the tree's form.

A mature *Liriodendron tulipifera* with low branching.

A medium-aged *Liriodendron tulipifera* showing symmetrical outline and shape.

Liriodendron tulipifera 'Fastigiatum' with the trunk cleaned up to fit into the existing landscape.

LOMATIA

Habit Small to medium-sized evergreen shrubs or trees for a sheltered, sunny or shady spot. **Attributes** Rarity value, attractive fern-like foliage, late-summer flowers. **Reasons for pruning** No pruning required, apart from some early formative pruning. **Pruning time** Summer after flowering

Lomatia ferruginea (fern tree), *L. hirsuta*, and *L. tinctoria* are southern hemisphere trees—very fussy and difficult to grow in gardens with harsh winters and so planted more for rarity than ornamental value. In the early years, decide whether you want a multi-stemmed tree or a tree on a single trunk. Either form should be left feathered, as the lower growths will furnish the lower half of the tree well. New shoots regularly develop from the base of the plant; use these as replacement stems for branches and stems, which may need pruning out following winter damage.

LONICERA

Habit Vigorous deciduous, semi-evergreen, and evergreen woody shrubs and climbers with twining stems, for moist, free-draining soil in full sun to partial shade. **Attributes** Fragrant flowers. **Reasons for pruning** To produce the correct growth to encourage flowers.

Honeysuckles have a wide variety of growth and flowering habits. The genus can be classified into three groups to help with pruning:

- Group 1. Shrubs with branches and growths springing from the base.
- Group 2. Climbers that flower on the current season's wood.
- Group 3. Climbers that flower on the previous year's wood.

Lonicera maackii showing established framework and bark effect.

GROUP 1

Pruning time Deciduous species after flowering; evergreen species in spring and summer.

The habit of the honeysuckles in this group is considerably varied and often untidy, typical of shrubs that regenerate well by sending up young growths after being cut back, both from the base and from the mature branch systems. Remove old wood when it is weak or partly dead, taking the cut back to a suitable point just above a promising growth. Branches that arch over often produce upright growths from their lower portions, and these may be in an ideal position to be used as replacements. Take care to retain the natural habit, however; otherwise, by cutting all the arching branches to an upright growth, bare sections of the old wood will be visible, especially during the winter months.

Lonicera quinquelocularis and *L. maackii* (Amur honeysuckle) produce only a few branches at the base that later become quite large and often twisted and gnarled but full of character, which should be encouraged to show off their wonderful bark; they will need full sun and rich soil to get the best of their fruiting. Many more species, such as *L. korolkowii* (honey rose honeysuckle), branch freely from ground level as well as produce a mass of new growths from the base. The shrubs with this habit can be pruned by removing the oldest wood com-

Lonicera fragrantissima wall-trained.

pletely back to ground level after flowering.

Some shrubs with weaker stems and longer, congested main stems sometimes arch over and even spread on the ground during wet weather or heavy snowfall. *Lonicera fragrantissima* (winter honeysuckle), *L. standishii* (Standish's honeysuckle), and the hybrid of the two, *L. ×purpusii*, should be pruned following flowering in late spring: remove older, weaker

growths at the base of the shrub to encourage new growths from the base.

Lonicera fragrantissima can also be wall-trained, using the older wood of the main branches tied into the wall as a framework; these can later be replaced with new growths from the base. Leave the flowering laterals to develop from the wall; this allows for easy annual pruning of the younger shoots in the

spring and is a great way to display and enjoy the fragrant winter flowers. Any strong growths that spring from the base and are not needed for replacement can be cut out as they

Close trimming a formal hedge of *Lonicera nitida* with electric hedging shears.

Lonicera nitida used informally as a tight hedging plant.

Lonicera fragrantissima grown as a freestanding shrub.

Lonicera periclymenum growing informally over a fence.

Lonicera sempervirens growing informally over a small trellis.

develop through the growing season.

The naturally dense *Lonicera nitida* (Wilson's honeysuckle), one of the evergreen shrubby honeysuckles, is very easily propagated and makes a good informal hedge. It also responds well to frequent clipping on a rigid line, but as a formal hedge it is prone to being blown over and out of line. When it becomes bare at the base, cut it down to within 15 cm (6 in.) of ground level in early summer and allow it to regrow to the desired height, which it usually achieves quickly. It is a rapid grower and requires frequent clipping during the summer to keep it in line.

Lonicera pileata (box-leaved honeysuckle), a low-growing semi-evergreen shrub often used as groundcover, requires very little pruning.

GROUP 2

Pruning time Spring.

The few evergreen twining species with their flowers in pairs comprise this group. The most common is *Lonicera japonica* (Japanese honeysuckle), a vigorous climber that is best rambling over stumps or small trees. It can be grown on a pergola or archway, but it is not an easy character to prune successfully and orderly. Keep it within bounds by hard clipping over the entire surface in early spring with a pair of hedging shears. Following hard clipping, new growths will soon break out and flower. To renovate, cut the whole plant back to about 60 cm (2 ft.) in late winter/early spring. Treat *L. henryi*, *L. acuminata*, and *L. hildebrandiana* in the same way.

GROUP 3

Pruning time Late spring/early summer after flowering.

These are the deciduous species, including *Lonicera ×americana*, *L. ×brownii*, *L. caprifolium*, *L. etrusca*, and *L. periclymenum* (woodbine), whose flowers form on short laterals from a vine made during the previous year.

Less hardy species like *L. sempervirens* (trumpet honeysuckle) will grow much better if afforded the protection of a sunny wall or other support. All should be pruned by carefully cutting out a portion of the vines that produced the flowers as soon as they fade. Avoid damaging the young, developing vines, which are often intertwined with the older ones. When these climbers are grown in a natural setting, some of the smaller growths may be left to hang down from the supporting vines. This shows off the flowers to best effect.

LOROPETALUM

Habit Medium-sized upright vase-shaped evergreen shrub for full sun to partial shade and fertile, free-draining, acid soil. **Attributes** Attractive foliage, witch hazel–like flowers in spring, tolerant of drought. **Reasons for pruning** To develop a strong framework and remove dead wood. **Pruning time** Spring after flowering.

Loropetalum chinense (Chinese fringe flower) and its selections should be planted in the right place with plenty of space to avoid any pruning. They do respond to light pruning but can be easily over-pruned and shaped to look unnatural and balled! Taller varieties (e.g., *L. chinense* var. *rubrum*) can be crown lifted to form small multi-stemmed trees, but they look much better furnished to the ground and free-flowing, in their natural shape. Just remove dead wood and crossing branches as needed.

Loropetalum chinense var. *rubrum* 'Burgundy'.

LUMA

Habit Bushy, upright evergreen shrub or small tree for free-draining soil in full sun to partial shade. **Attributes** Smooth cinnamon-coloured bark, aromatic foliage, small white flowers in late summer, blue/black fruits in autumn. **Reasons for pruning** To reveal the bark and remove dead wood. **Pruning time** Spring.

In milder climates, *Luma apiculata* (Chilean myrtle) can be grown with a leader, but in cooler climates it should be grown with three to five stems, as with a multi-stemmed specimen, there are multiple trunks to show off the incredible bark. Remove the lower laterals as early as possible with secateurs and gradually lift the crown as the tree develops to better display the bark on the main stems. Once the crown is at the required height, the only necessary pruning will be to remove dead wood and open up the centre of the crown by light thinning.

A well-developed *Luma apiculata* grown as a multi-stemmed tree.

LYCIUM

Habit Arching deciduous suckering shrubs for moist, well-drained soil in full sun. **Attributes** Purple flowers in summer followed by orange-red berries. **Reasons for pruning** To maintain a tidy plant. **Pruning time** Winter.

Lycium barbarum (Duke of Argyll's tea tree) and *L. chinense* (Chinese box thorn) are untidy woody shrubs, but corrective pruning, carried out annually in winter, delays the need for a

more drastic pruning operation: cut away any dead growths, which tend to collect beneath the layers of live branches, and reduce heavy horizontal branches back to young upright shoots near the centre of the bush. Any young growths that are too long can also be shortened back. To restrict the spread of these suckering shrubs, dig a root barrier into the ground around the plant. Both respond well to hard pruning, which is the way they should be treated when they become out of hand. Plan on doing this every three to five years to keep plants in check and tidy. These shrubs are often grown near the sea, with lots of space, so they do not need pruning. They are also used as informal hedging plants, being cut back hard in the spring, with at least one additional trim in the summer if the feature is to be kept close and formal.

A root barrier restricts the spread of *Lycium barbarum* in a border.

LYONIA

Habit Dense deciduous suckering shrub for lime-free, fertile soil in full sun to partial shade. **Attributes** Panicles of white flowers in summer, red autumn colour. **Reasons for pruning** To thin out the older wood and maintain a vigorous shrub. **Pruning time** Early spring.

Lyonia ligustrina (maleberry) branches freely from ground level, and strong, young growths are sent up from the base if the shrub is growing well. This gives an opportunity for a limited amount of pruning, as the oldest growths can be cut out completely at ground level. The extent to which this is done will depend upon the age and vitality of the shrub. The natural habit is dense and close, and the shrub should be left with branches furnished to the ground.

MAACKIA

Habit Medium-sized deciduous decurrent trees with rounded, vase-shaped crown for well-drained soils in full sun. **Attributes** Newly emerged pinnate leaves have a silvery effect, upright cream flowers. **Reasons for pruning** To develop a strong framework. **Pruning time** Between autumn and spring (when dormant).

Maackia amurensis (Chinese yellow wood) is often shrubby but may develop into a small tree. Retain the leader for as long as possible, difficult as this is. Branching is naturally sparse, and vigour and health will determine the ultimate height of a specimen before the head opens completely. The branching has a flattened appearance, with the ends of the branches having a trailing effect. *Maackia hupehensis* has an upright branch system and can easily be trained to a definite tree form with a short trunk of 0.6 to 1.2 metres (2 to 4 ft.); the branching is also sparse, but the ends are twiggier than *M. amurensis*. Maackias are slow to occlude over old pruning wounds, so carry out any formative pruning as early as possible in the tree's life with secateurs. The large wounds that would be left by a saw may start to decay back into the older wood.

MACLURA

A female *Maclura pomifera* grown on a single trunk and showing the congested crown.

Habit Spiny, small to medium-sized deciduous decurrent trees and shrubs for deep, fertile soil and full sun. **Attributes** Large green fruits resembling a brain. **Reasons for pruning** To develop a strong framework and restrict growth. **Pruning time** Between autumn and early spring (when dormant).

Personal protection Plants exude a milky white sap, which is harmful to some people. Wear latex or rubber gloves when pruning and good thorn-proof clothing.

Maclura pomifera (Osage orange) is dioecious, so both male and female plants are needed to produce the odd fruit. It is best grown as a feathered tree with a strong central leader, which soon slows down to form a broad, congested upper crown. Very little pruning is necessary apart from keeping the plant within bounds. With its spiny branches, it makes an impenetrable hedge; once trained to form a barrier, clip it to shape with hedging shears.

Maclura tricuspidata forms a dense thorny shrub or small tree and is best trained to a clean stem 2 to 2.5 metres (6 to 8 ft.) in height. Prune out dead wood in summer, when it is easily distinguished from living material.

MAGNOLIA

Habit Medium to large deciduous and evergreen trees and shrubs for fertile, free-draining soil in partial shade to full sun. **Attributes** Graceful form, aromatic waxy flowers, knobbly fruits exposing an orange seed. **Reasons for pruning** To develop a strong framework and encourage flowering. **Pruning time** Evergreen species in spring. Deciduous species in summer while in leaf; avoid pruning in winter or early spring, as pruning wounds are subject to bleeding.

Magnolias grow and perform to their best in a well-sheltered position, as the wood is brittle and the branches are susceptible to damage in high winds. They are very fussy plants and must be planted with as little damage to the root system as possible. Do not firm in the soil backfill with the heel of the boot, and water them in after planting. Selection of nursery stock is also very important. The root systems of many magnolias are killed in the containers by overheating in summer or freezing in winter, and potbound plants never get off the starting blocks and decline in vigour before establishment. Always buy plants from a reputable nursery, or you may end up planting dead trees.

Magnolias must be kept growing well in order to produce a good shape and show great powers of regeneration by throwing up strong shoots from very old wood. Take advantage of this attribute by carefully cutting damaged specimens back hard into the old wood; the final cut can be re-positioned a few years later, back to a suitable, selected shoot that will develop into a natural overall shape. This attribute can also be a disadvantage: when a branch is reduced, it generates lots of new shoots, creating a shaving brush effect that will need to be thinned out to produce a new framework.

Large-scale pruning, if it becomes necessary, should be carried out in late summer to avoid the risk of bleeding; this also leaves enough time for the healing process to get under way before winter sets in. The heartwood is soft, and rot quickly sets in, so the smaller the pruning wounds and the least damage from large

A well-grown *Magnolia* 'Star Wars' without any formative pruning.

branches tearing out, the less chance of cavities forming.

There is much variation across this genus—so consider the form of the tree or shrub carefully before planting. With the right plant in the right place, the chances of having to prune to restrict size are minimal. At Kew we like to plant a small feathered specimen and then, besides encouraging a strong leader, leave it to establish. Remove any competing leaders as early as possible with the secateurs.

With *Magnolia ×soulangeana* (saucer magnolia) and other bush forms, the vigour of the leader weakens as the branches increase in girth and length. As specimens reach maturity, encourage the lower branch systems to grow and develop even down to ground level, which will show off the flowers to their full glory.

Many of the vigorous growers produce strong suckers and sometimes epicormic growths, which grow up through the centre of the shrub. These should be encouraged, perhaps with some thinning, if the older branches are weak or in need of replacement. If they are not needed, remove them before they get too large or spoil the shape and character of the

Magnolia ×soulangeana showing low branching habit.

plant; also they may, if left, reduce the vigour of the older branches. If grafted plants send up suckers from the rootstock, remove them as soon as possible, as they are usually more vigorous than the scion and will soon take over.

Magnolia campbellii (Campbell's magnolia)

and other large tree species are strong growers and can be trained very easily to form a strong central leader. Trees grown from seed naturally have a tendency to form a really strong leader, whereas grafted trees will need an element of training in the initial years. One of the

A mature *Magnolia campbellii*.

The nodding flower of *Magnolia sieboldii*.

Magnolia grandiflora wall-trained.

more untidy growers is *M.* ×*thompsoniana*; its branches are very wide-spreading and rest on each other as they become heavy. It is difficult to correct this habit if it develops.

Magnolia macrophylla and *M. rostrata* require summer heat to ripen the wood; otherwise, it will be damaged beyond repair with winter cold. Plants checked by winter cold suffer from dieback and coral spot (*Nectria cinnabarina*), never making a strong healthy plant.

Magnolia sieboldii and *M. wilsonii* require minimal pruning, such as the removal of crossing branches and dead wood, and should be encouraged to make as tall a plant as possible in the early years in order that their nodding flowers may be viewed from underneath.

Magnolia stellata (star magnolia) grows slowly, eventually making a small rounded, multi-stemmed shrub to a maximum height of 3 metres (10 ft.). It requires little if any pruning and will flower very young.

The evergreen magnolias are usually grown in the shelter of a sunny wall and, if trained against the wall from an early age, make a good wall shrub. *Magnolia grandiflora* (bullbay)

A large specimen of *Magnolia doltsopa* in a warm, sheltered position.

should be trained up for at least two-thirds of its height with a central leader and the lateral branches tied into the wall horizontally or fan-shaped; prune off any branches growing away from the wall. Sub-laterals growing away from the wall should be pruned back to two or three leaves/buds unless they bear flower buds; if they must be shortened, prune them back after they have flowered. In warmer climates it can be grown as a freestanding tree with a conical crown if a central leader is encouraged, or as an informal hedge, which makes a great change from laurel or aucuba.

Magnolia delavayi usually needs wall protection, especially if it is to flower. It produces very strong, heavy wood and so requires a large, high wall, where a strong leader can be encouraged.

Under favourable conditions *Magnolia compressa* will develop a leader, and every effort should be made to retain this for at least 1 metre (3 ft.) or so, until a head of branches is formed. Depending upon the environment, *M. doltsopa* may form a tree or shrub, although in a very favourable situation with shelter, it is possible to retain a leader for some time and make a substantial tree.

Magnolia figo (port wine magnolia) forms a very leafy medium to large shrub and occasionally the lateral branches have a spreading horizontal habit, the young growths toward the centre of the bush being very upright. It is possible to restrict its size by careful pruning in spring, concealing the cuts and leaving an informal surface. In the mildest of localities it needs wall protection, but even so it is better grown as a freestanding shrub rather than hard trained against the surface.

Magnolia 'Jack Fogg', a small tree with an excurrent conical form, will produce flowers from an early age.

The semi-evergreen *Magnolia virginiana* (sweet bay) is one of the most ungainly growers. A straight, upright textbook tree will never be achieved, even with plenty of training, but it's well worth growing for its blue-green leaves and small white flowers in late summer.

Magnolia grandiflora grown as an informal hedge.

×MAHOBERBERIS

Habit Upright evergreen shrub for moist, well-drained soil in full sun to partial shade. **Attributes** Leathery foliage, yellow flowers in late winter followed by black fruits. **Reasons for pruning** To correct untidy growth. **Pruning time** Spring after flowering.

Personal protection Wear good thorn-proof clothing and gloves when pruning hybrid mahonia, as the leaves are spiny with sharp edges.

This genus, a bigeneric hybrid between *Mahonia* and *Berberis*, produces an untidy growth habit that can be corrected by pruning back loose straggly growths to suitable buds in spring after flowering.

MAHONIA

Habit Groundcovering or specimen evergreen shrubs for free-draining soil and some shelter in partial to full shade. **Attributes** Leathery pinnate leaves, yellow flowers in winter or early spring. **Reasons for pruning** To encourage fresh growth for flowering the following year. **Pruning time** Spring after flowering.

The spring-flowering *Mahonia aquifolium* (Oregon grape) is the most commonly planted species. It is a strong grower and spreads easily by suckers, so should be planted where it has the space to colonize and spread naturally without the need to restrict it by pruning; however, it can be controlled by pruning in late spring after flowering and digging out suckers. A group planting in the shade can become untidy over several years producing extended growths without flower, and the stems can become cluttered with fallen leaves and dead twigs from neighbouring trees. Where this occurs, clip upright growths down to 10 to 20 cm (4 to 8 in.) every two to three years, or annually if required, using hedging shears. In the open with some sun, this plant can reach a height of 1 to 2 metres (3 to 6 ft.). To renovate, remove old, woody stems to ground level, leaving the younger growths to develop.

The stiff erect habit and beautiful form of the larger-leafed, winter-flowering species (e.g., *Mahonia bealei*, *M. japonica*, *M. lomariifolia*, *M. ×media*) and their cultivars can be spoiled by pruning. Where possible, new stems that break from the base should be encouraged and used as replacements as the older, woody stems become too tall and bare of foliage and flower up the stems. If necessary, shorten tall

The extended flowering growths of this *Mahonia aquifolium* will need shortening after flowering has finished.

Mahonia ×media 'Charity' showing the whorls of leaves and side shoots to which the shrub can be pruned back.

stems back to a side shoot or strong buds in the leaf whorls lower down the stems. Do this over a period of time: a shortening exercise in one go would ruin the shrub's natural shape.

Several species (e.g., *Mahonia fortunei*, *M. napaulensis*) need a mild climate or some protection. They require very little pruning and are best left alone; however, if they become untidy, they can be treated in the same way as the larger-leafed species and carefully and thoughtfully cut back to strong buds.

Mahonia japonica showing a neat compact habit that can be maintained by staggered regular pruning.

MALLOTUS

Habit Spreading, rounded deciduous shrub or small tree for moist, free-draining soil in partial shade to full sun. **Attributes** Large rounded leaves with a pink tinge when newly formed, upright yellow female flowers. **Reasons for pruning** To develop a strong framework and remove dead wood. **Pruning time** Between autumn and spring (when dormant).

Mallotus japonicus (Japanese mallotus) may need the shelter of a sunny wall, as the twigs and young growth are pithy and susceptible to frost damage. Carry out some formative pruning and training in the early years to develop a strong framework. The leader is impossible to retain and will be lost after the first year. The plant dictates the position of the branches, which start low, near to the ground, and become wide-spreading. No regular pruning is necessary apart from the removal of dead wood.

An established *Mallotus japonicus* showing the wide-spreading branches.

MALUS

Habit Spreading, rounded small to medium-sized deciduous decurrent trees for moist, free-draining soil in full sun. **Attributes** Clusters of white or pink late-spring flowers followed by small orange, yellow, or red crab apples. **Reasons for pruning** To develop a strong framework and remove suckers. **Pruning time** Between autumn and spring (when dormant).

Crab apples (certain *Malus* species and many cultivars) are strong and reliable. The main branches on an old specimen, even when full of cavities, are able to withstand considerable strain without failure. But don't try your luck and leave them unmanaged: a well-balanced and well-maintained crown, kept in good condition from an early age, is a much better long-term proposition.

The form of the tree is important. Most are sold in nurseries as standard trees on a clean trunk with an open branching head, but many gardeners prefer a feathered tree with a strong central leader, which is the natural mode of growth. The branches will be evenly spaced around this leader, which eventually opens out to form the topmost system of the crown, thus the weight is spread more evenly along the length of the central leader. As well, by using a feathered tree for *Malus baccata* (Siberian crab), *M.* 'John Downie', and *M.* ×*zumi* 'Golden Hornet', you can encourage a much lower branch system, which is often more desirable for these taxa. A crab apple with a central leader on a short trunk of 0.8 metre (2.5 ft.) is very attractive and more natural in the garden, but where access under the canopy is desirable, a 2 to 2.5 metre (6 to 8 ft.) clean trunk is effective and will support the wide-spreading branch system once it is allowed to develop.

A young *Malus yunnanensis* with a well-balanced crown.

Malus hupehensis grown as a standard.

As trees mature, some of the lower branches will be shaded out and eventually die; prune these out, back to the parent lateral or the main trunk. Epicormic growths may also develop on the lateral branches, especially following any pruning; these can be unsightly and spoil the overall effect of a mature crab apple. They are more likely to be found on trees that have been heavily thinned out in the centre to allow more air and light into the crown. There seems to be little point in doing this type of heavy thinning, as a twisted, crowded head of branches in *Malus floribunda*, *M. ×moerlandsii* 'Liset', *M. ×moerlandsii* 'Profusion', and many other

Malus ×moerlandsii 'Liset' left to grow without intervention.

Malus trilobata showing its natural pyramidal form.

Malus baccata trained with a low, wide-spreading crown and short trunk.

Malus toringo with lower branches furnished to the ground.

cultivars is typical and makes for a more natural and interesting garden specimen.

Once the main framework of branches has been established, a natural head of growth should follow without too much intervention, allowing the outer and lower branches to become pendulous and furnish the lower skirt of the tree. This is typical of *Malus toringo*, which is naturally weeping.

Malus tschonoskii and *M. trilobata* are distinct from many other crab apples in having upright growth with a pyramidal habit. Both develop a crown naturally with very little pruning.

Malus toringoides (cut-leaved crab apple) produces vigorous growths in the early years that twist and bend the main central leader, eventually making an ungainly specimen with lots of twisting and crossing branches, even when planted as feathered nursery stock. As a grafted plant it is often unstable, and after several years will begin to fall over with the top weight. Retrospective staking will not overcome this problem. It may be necessary to carry out some harsh pruning, shortening some of the overly long lateral branches. This allows the tree time to establish a stronger root system until it can support the developing crown.

Many *Malus* cultivars are budded or grafted at ground level. Remove all the suckers growing from below the graft union as soon as possible with secateurs, as they will soon dominate the trunk and begin to take over the tree, reverting back to the rootstock.

Malus tschonoskii showing a well-balanced, upright branch system on a short trunk.

MANDEVILLA

Habit Vigorous deciduous climber with twining stems for free-draining soil in full sun. **Attributes** Clean foliage, aromatic white flowers. **Reasons for pruning** To remove dead wood. **Pruning time** Spring.

Mandevilla laxa (Chilean jasmine), with slender stems up to 3 metres (10 ft.) in length, is suitable only for a very sunny corner or wall. When trained on a wall, vertical strands of wire should be stretched between the horizontal wires to help the climber gain height. Pruning consists of cutting out the dead wood and weaker growths in the spring, as the shrub becomes active. There should be no hesitation in cutting out some of the older wood, provided that no damage is done to the growths that remain, for they are often wound very tightly together. Renovate if the plant becomes too congested to carry out regular maintenance and begins to fall away from the wall, as this shrub breaks out readily from the older wood.

Mandevilla laxa trained against a warm, sunny wall.

MELALEUCA

Habit Small to medium-sized upright evergreen shrubs for a sheltered position with full sun to partial shade and moist soil. **Attributes** Fine dense foliage, spikes of aromatic creamy white flowers in summer. **Reasons for pruning** No pruning required. **Pruning time** Late spring, midsummer after flowering.

Melaleuca gibbosa and *M. squarrosa* (scented paperbark) are tender and need a sheltered spot, preferably against a wall. Leave them to grow freely; they will always do what they want, despite any intervention with the secateurs. The younger wood may break into new growth following winter damage, but any old wood is more reluctant to break.

MELIA

Habit Fast-growing medium-sized deciduous decurrent tree with a rounded crown for moist, free-draining soil and full sun. **Attributes** Fragrant pale lilac-purple flowers in late spring followed by small yellow fruits. **Reasons for pruning** To develop a strong framework. **Pruning time** Between late autumn and early spring (when dormant).

Melia azedarach (bead tree) needs full sun and a hot summer to ripen the wood before winter. If the climate is too cold, it will struggle and be susceptible to winter damage. Grow this elegant tree as a standard on a clean trunk up to 2 metres (6 ft.), retaining the leader for as long as possible before permanent lateral branching begins. Any formative pruning should be done while the tree is dormant.

Melia azedarach in full flower with old fruits still intact.

MELIOSMA

Habit Slow-growing deciduous trees and shrubs for fertile, well-drained soil and full sun to partial shade. **Attributes** Architectural plants with simple or large pinnate leaves, panicles of creamy white flowers, and good autumn colour. **Reasons for pruning** To develop a strong framework and remove dead wood. **Pruning time** Spring as new growth begins.

The genus is broken down into two groups for pruning: species with pinnate leaves should be grown as trees (Group 1); and species with simple leaves should be grown as large multi-stemmed shrubs (Group 2).

GROUP 1

Both the rare *Meliosma beaniana* and the architecturally interesting *M. veitchiorum* produce a perfectly shaped, symmetrical crown and a strong central leader, which should be encouraged for as long as possible. The latter produces a stout framework of lateral branches that radiate evenly from the central trunk with a sparse, almost spur-like habit; give this tree ample all-round space to develop to its full potential, as its response to pruning is not strong.

Meliosma pinnata var. *oldhamii* has a more ascending branch system and again ample space is needed for it to develop without any form of formative pruning. All the species in this group are prone to frost damage in the spring, as growth begins; make sure that only one leader is left to grow should the terminal bud be lost.

GROUP 2

All the species in this group (e.g., *Meliosma dilleniifolia*, *M. myriantha*) should be allowed to branch naturally from the base. Never attempt to train them on a single trunk as a small tree, as they will turn up their toes and die. All freely produce young growths from ground level; use these as replacements for old stems, which are generally short-lived. *Meliosma parviflora* has an upright habit, from which almost horizontal branches extend; the twig system is often tangled, but this is the natural habit and should be left to grow naturally. This species often regenerates well from around pruning cuts, and if branches are shortened back, the regrowth will spoil the natural habit.

Close-up of the spur-like habit of *Meliosma veitchiorum*.

The naturally architectural *Meliosma veitchiorum*.

MENISPERMUM

Habit Suckering semi-woody deciduous twining shrub for moist, shady spots. **Attributes** Yellow flowers followed by small black fruits, which are poisonous. **Reasons for pruning** To maintain a tidy plant. **Pruning time** Winter.

Menispermum canadense (moonseed) will quickly cover a wall, trellis, or a similar structure to 3.5 metres (12 ft.). Vertical wires may be necessary to assist climbing. This subject is so vigorous once established that it can be cut down to nearly ground level each winter, in which case short woody stems will start to build up below the pruning position. Alternatively, cut it down to the ground every two or three years.

MESPILUS

Habit Small deciduous decurrent tree with an open, spreading crown for deep, rich, free-draining soil in a sheltered position with full sun to light shade. **Attributes** White flowers in late spring/early summer followed by large brown edible fruits. **Reasons for pruning** To remove dead and diseased wood and overcrowded branches. **Pruning time** Late summer.

Mespilus germanica (medlar) is best planted as a standard or half-standard with an open head and no central leader on a clean, well-developed trunk. Strong branches spread out laterally from the trunk in an interesting twisting way, giving this tree great character; leave them to sweep down to the ground or as low as possible in the space allocated. Don't try to shorten them; often when pruned, they produce strong epicormic growths, which will, if left, grow up through the crown and spoil the character of the tree completely. Prune out dead and diseased wood and overcrowded branches in late summer. Apart from that, regular pruning is not necessary for fruit production. The selection 'Nottingham' is more upright in habit.

Mespilus germanica showing twisting, decurrent growth habit.

METASEQUOIA

Habit Large columnar deciduous excurrent conifer for deep, moist, free-draining acid to neutral soil in full sun. **Attributes** Outstandingly quick and evenly balanced grower, fine needle-like foliage with good autumn colour, showy red/brown bark on a deeply fluted trunk. **Reasons for pruning** To develop a strong framework and remove dead wood. **Pruning time** Between autumn and spring (when dormant).

Metasequoia glyptostroboides (dawn redwood) should be grown with a single leader and feathered to the ground without the removal of any laterals; this will increase the basal butt flare of the tree. The habit is columnar with a definite leader, which is readily and naturally maintained for the whole height of the tree. One outstanding feature of this tree is its ability, provided the tree is young and vigorous, to form a new leader naturally should the original be lost. It should be encouraged to retain its furnishing to the ground for a natural, aesthetically pleasing look. This tree

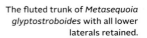

The fluted trunk of *Metasequoia glyptostroboides* with all lower laterals retained.

needs little pruning, apart from removing the occasional dead branch.

Metasequoia glyptostroboides 'Gold Rush' is one of the best golden conifers and a real favourite of mine, retaining its colour throughout the year; 'Spring Cream' begins the season with cream foliage, which gradually turns a pale green through the year; and the more narrowly pyramidal 'National' is more suited for planting in an avenue or restricted space.

Metasequoia glyptostroboides showing its columnar habit.

A group of closely planted dawn redwoods showing the central, straight tapered trunks that are naturally produced.

METROSIDEROS

Habit Slow-growing evergreen trees and shrubs for well-drained, warm soil in a sunny location. **Attributes** Shiny foliage, showy red flowers, resistant to honey fungus, suitable for coastal planting. **Reasons for pruning** No pruning required. **Pruning time** Winter (when dormant).

A genus of tender species (e.g., *Metrosideros diffusa*, *M. excelsa*, *M. robusta*), all sensitive to frost. Even *M. umbellata* (southern rata), one of the hardiest, requires a very sheltered position in a very mild climate. No pruning is necessary; rather, it's a fight to retain the shoots and foliage intact through the winter.

MICROBIOTA

Habit Dwarf prostrate evergreen conifer with wide-spreading branches for well-drained soil in partial shade to full sun. **Attributes** Green foliage turning bronze in winter, suitable for the rock garden. **Reasons for pruning** To remove occasional dieback. **Pruning time** Early spring.

Microbiota decussata (Siberian cypress) is an amazing, tough plant, worthy of a place in any garden for its bronze winter colour. Give it space to develop and spread naturally into a fine specimen without the need for intervention; it does have a habit of dying back in winter for no apparent reason, and this dead growth may need pruning out in spring.

Microbiota decussata showing its wide-spreading prostrate habit.

MIMULUS

Habit Evergreen shrub for a sheltered sunny position against a wall with free-draining soil. **Attributes** Orange flowers in summer and autumn. **Reasons for pruning** To correct an untidy shrub. **Pruning time** Spring.

Mimulus aurantiacus (shrubby musk), a tender woody shrub from California, can be grown freestanding but is most successful when grown on a sheltered sunny wall. Train it to grow up a support system, and prune it back hard to the old woody framework each spring. Young growths are generated from the old wood very readily, and the shrub will respond to hard pruning in late spring if this is necessary to correct an untidy appearance. When young, the tips should be stopped early to encourage a dense bushy habit.

MORELLA

Habit Dense, upright evergreen or deciduous shrub or tree for moist, acid soil in full sun. **Attributes** Aromatic foliage, brown-purple berries in autumn. **Reasons for pruning** To maintain a tidy plant and remove dead branches. **Pruning time** Summer.

In a severe winter *Morella californica* (California wax myrtle) may be killed back to ground level, but usually new growth will break freely from any remaining living tissue in the spring. Once the new growths have broken from this live tissue, prune out the old dead stems, back to living growth.

MORUS

Habit Slow-growing deciduous trees with a decurrent crown for fertile soil and full sun. **Attributes** Heavily spreading, gnarled branches with clean, shiny foliage and delicious edible fruits. **Reasons for pruning** To develop a strong framework with occasional thinning to reduce excessive weight on the lateral branches. **Pruning time** Late autumn to early winter (once fully dormant), as the cuts are prone to bleeding if pruned in spring.

Personal protection Wear gloves; the milky sap that exudes from pruning wounds is very sticky and difficult to wash off bare skin.

Morus nigra (black mulberry) is often encountered as an ancient tree of historical value, usually leaning under the weight of its branches. There is a danger of these branches breaking during summer gales, when the branch system is heavy with leaves and fruit. To reduce this possibility, thin the laterals on these major branches in early winter. Take great care when doing this—the natural shape and character of the tree is easily spoiled by over-thinning. Propping will help to support the weight of a leaning tree and increase longevity without heavy thinning.

The best type of nursery stock specimen is a feathered standard. Retain the leader for as long as possible and either retain the lower branches or remove them to create the desired height of the skirt. In any case, the lower branches will grow down and close to the ground, which helps with fruit harvesting.

A mature *Morus alba* showing the nicely rounded crown.

A mature *Morus nigra* with lower branches left furnished to a low level.

Morus alba 'Pendula' showing the dense skirt of weeping branches.

Morus alba (white mulberry) is also heavily branched with a rounded crown and should be treated the same as *M. nigra*; however, it has a tendency to produce epicormic shoots, often in great quantity, from the horizontal branches post-thinning. Prune these back annually; otherwise, they can spoil the character of the tree. *Morus alba* can be pruned back quite hard and can even be stooled on a regular basis to produce vigorous growths with large leaves for foliage effect in the border.

Morus alba 'Pendula' has tightly grouped weeping branches that will need to be cane-trained by tying up the leading shoot until the desired height has been reached. It will then produce a dense skirt of branching around the main trunk.

Morus cathayana (Chinese mulberry) is a small tree, very distinct in growth and more adaptable to training to a central leader than the other species.

MUEHLENBECKIA

Habit Semi-deciduous climbing or creeping shrub for full sun to partial shade. **Attributes** A fine dense groundcover with variably sized and shaped leaves. **Reasons for pruning** To restrict size. **Pruning time** Spring and summer.

Muehlenbeckia complexa (creeping wire vine) produces a mass of thin, wiry stems, which intertwine to form a dense mat over the ground. Once established, it invades nearby shrubs, covering them quickly and thickly with a tangle of slender growths. To restrict size, prune it back to an informal edge by cutting away individual growths; a clipped effect, which involves masses of growth being cut off at one level or line, should be avoided. It may be necessary to do this two or three times during the growing season. If a hard winter cuts it down to ground level, it will regenerate freely.

MUTISIA

Habit Decumbent evergreen shrublets or climbers, requiring some protection in cold climates and fertile, well-drained soil in full sun. **Attributes** Dark green foliage, brightly coloured daisy-like flowers. **Reasons for pruning** To restrict growth and remove dead wood and weak growths. **Pruning time** Summer.

All *Mutisia* species (e.g., *M. decurrens, M. ilicifolia, M. oligodon, M. spinosa*) climb with the help of leaf tendrils that are modifications of the midrib. They need the shelter and protection of a warm, sunny wall and should be encouraged to grow up the wall, either through a shrub or by means of short pea sticks. Once against the wall, tie them into a wire system. If plants are vigorous and healthy, they may leave the wall and climb further up nearby shrubs and trees, but this will not be excessive or harmful and is often the better way of showing these plants off. Cut out dead or weak growths in the summer, but be careful: it is very easy to cut through vital living growths that supply the rest of the plant. One to two weeks after pruning, check the plant again for any growths that were inadvertently severed during that pruning and remove them.

MYRICA

Habit Dense, upright deciduous shrub for moist, acid soil in full sun. **Attributes** Aromatic foliage, red berries in autumn. **Reasons for pruning** To maintain a tidy plant and remove dead branches. **Pruning time** Summer.

Myrica gale (bog myrtle) needs to be grown in a clump of several plants together, as the male and female flowers are produced on separate plants. Plants are suckerous and possibly invasive. Mature plants can become untidy, producing long straggly branches. Cut these branches down to ground level; they will produce plenty of suckers. Some can be trained as replacement growths, and any remaining suckers can be left intact to act as groundcover within the clump. This plant is a joy to prune as all its parts are aromatic.

MYRTUS

Habit Dense evergreen shrubs for fertile, well-drained soil in full sun. **Attributes** Aromatic shiny green foliage, scented white flowers in late summer. **Reasons for pruning** To restrict size and remove growth damaged by cold weather. **Pruning time** Late spring after the last frost.

Myrtus communis (myrtle) is the most commonly grown and hardiest of the species, most of which are quite tender and best grown in the shelter of a wall for some protection. Normally it is not trained against a wall but planted as a freestanding bush, with branching from the ground, about 0.5 metre (1.5 ft.) from the wall's base. The main branches are upright, and it is completely self-supporting. The longer branches may be cut back to a suitable growth inside the bush, so that the wounds are hidden. If a severe winter kills it down to ground level, it will often break freely from the old wood at the base, so the main framework can be cut back to live growth. A wall-trained plant reaches a considerable height with a minimum of support; clip its surface over annually, in spring or early summer.

Myrtus communis subsp. *tarentina* is compact and very rarely needs pruning, even to prevent encroachment, but can be clipped to be a more formal shape.

NANDINA

Habit Upright, suckering evergreen shrub for moist, free-draining soil and full sun in a sheltered position. **Attributes** Pinnate leaves, small white flowers in summer followed by clusters of red berries. **Reasons for pruning** To renovate after a severe winter and maintain a tidy plant. **Pruning time** Spring after berry drop.

Nandina domestica (sacred bamboo) is a bamboo-like shrub, grown for its large clusters of red berries in winter. It requires some shelter and can have a very ragged appearance after a severe winter. With a strong-growing specimen, vigorous growths are freely produced from the base. Use them as replacements for the ragged growths, which can be cut out at ground level in the spring. Newly planted shrubs branch freely, and this bushiness should be encouraged. Long, unbranched stems are also thrown up through the plant, and pruning at any point down such stems is not effective as they will not break from the pruning point; they should be cut right down to ground level, if pruned at all.

Nandina domestica 'Fire Power' has excellent fiery red autumn foliage, makes a maximum size of 50 cm (20 in.) high and wide, and requires no pruning, apart from the removal of dead foliage to tidy the plant up.

The neat, low-maintenance, compact habit of *Nandina domestica* 'Fire Power'.

NEILLIA

Habit Deciduous suckering shrubs for fertile soil and full sun to partial shade. **Attributes** Brown winter stems with racemes of pink flowers in late spring. **Reasons for pruning** To generate young canes for winter stem effect and flowering. **Pruning time** Early summer after flowering.

A key part of pruning these shrubs, including *Neillia thibetica* (Tibetan neillia), is to leave them well furnished with young growths that spring freely from the base and from older wood. Suckers are also produced, quite a distance from the parent plant, originating from adventitious buds on the roots. Pruning consists of thinning the plant, cutting back some of the oldest wood to ground level. At the same time, shorten mature branches back to suitable growths, thus removing the old flowered parts and allowing light and air into the centre of the bush. Carry this out immediately after flowering. The extent of the pruning will depend upon the amount of young wood being produced; *N. ribesioides*, for example, does not always have sufficient young wood for all the old wood to be cut away annually.

NEOLITSEA

Habit Fast-growing medium-sized broadleaved evergreen tree with a round crown for a rich, moist, free-draining soil and full to partial shade in a sheltered position. **Attributes** Aromatic foliage, flowers in autumn followed by bright red berries. **Reasons for pruning** To produce a tree with a single trunk or a bushy plant. **Pruning time** Late autumn to winter after flowering.

Neolitsea sericea (Japanese silver tree), a common tree in Japan, makes a perfectly shaped specimen without any intervention and should be left to grow naturally. If a specimen tree is required, retain a single stem following planting. It also makes a good evergreen screen or informal hedge plant; regular tip-pruning in spring thickens up the branching and produces a denser habit. Little maintenance is necessary. If you haven't seen this plant before, it can be quite alarming as the new leaves unfold: it looks like the plant is suffering from a severe wilt, but the silver, suede-like leaves, resembling a young rabbit's ears, soon open out to the mature, glossy dark leaves, which set off the bright red fruits.

NEOSHIRAKIA

Habit Small deciduous tree or large shrub for fertile, well-drained soil in full sun. **Attributes** One of the best small trees for autumn colour—a spectacular red. **Reasons for pruning** To maintain shape. **Pruning time** Late summer through winter (when dormant). Never prune in early spring as the wounds are prone to bleeding.

Personal protection Wear rubber or latex gloves when pruning this plant; its milky sap is very toxic.

Neoshirakia japonica (Japanese tallow tree) is very fussy and difficult in cultivation. It can be grown with a single leader, requiring very little pruning, apart from keeping the plant in shape, should it outgrow its planting space. The wood is very brittle; if the plant is left to grow naturally, without any formative pruning, it can be prone to branch break. Its roots are very shallow, which can be a problem if grown in a lawn.

NERIUM

Habit Large sun-loving upright evergreen shrub for free-draining soil. **Attributes** Pink or white summer flowers, suitable for coastal planting. **Reasons for pruning** To maintain shape. **Pruning time** Late summer to autumn.

Personal protection: All parts of this plant are toxic if eaten, and contact with the foliage, especially the sap, can irritate skin. Wear rubber or latex gloves when pruning and carefully dispose of the arisings to protect animals and small children.

Nerium oleander can be grown in a variety of ways, including as a standard or free-growing specimen, in hedges, or against a sunny wall. It is often a container subject, grown outdoors for the summer heat and overwintering indoors under glass, as it does not tolerate below-freezing temperatures. Very little pruning is required, unless some form of shaping is needed.

NOTHOFAGUS

Habit Fast-growing upright deciduous and evergreen shade trees, with broad-spreading crowns at maturity, for moist, free-draining soil and full sun. **Attributes** Magnificent botanical specimens with fine-textured foliage. **Reasons for pruning** To develop a strong framework. **Pruning time** Deciduous species autumn to spring (when dormant); evergreen species late spring.

Of the deciduous southern beeches, take care with *Nothofagus obliqua* (roble beech) to encourage a single central leader with well-spaced lateral branches around the trunk, with the ends of the branches sweeping down to the ground. As the tree grows in stature, the lower laterals can be removed to expose the trunk (and the attractive bark) for up to 4.5 to 6 metres (15 to 20 ft.). In exposed situations, growth is more stunted. As the tree matures, the branching becomes heavier, with pendulous sub-laterals.

Nothofagus alpina (rauli beech) can suffer frost and wind damage and is more successful in a sheltered position; the stunted tree form that otherwise develops is difficult to correct with pruning.

Nothofagus antarctica (antarctic beech) is best planted as a feathered tree and then trained for the garden setting, although it is readily available as a more mature specimen and can be successfully transplanted. It is not a free-growing species; the main leader is often quickly lost and the branches grow with a twisted habit, becoming decurrent.

Of the evergreen species, *Nothofagus dombeyi* (coigue) is unruly and needs a firm hand with the secateurs in the early years to remove rival leaders and retain a single leader. Where rival leaders are left, tight, often weak forks develop, and these are likely to split out during strong winds, ruining what was a beautiful tree, skirted with low lateral branches. It does not respond to hard pruning. *Nothofagus betuloides* can be treated in the same way.

Nothofagus menziesii (silver beech) from New Zealand and *N. cunninghamii* (myrtle beech) from Australia both make small graceful trees or large shrubs; they are not the easiest subjects in cultivation and are best left to grow naturally without any pruning.

Nothofagus obliqua with a tall straight trunk.

NOTHOLITHOCARPUS

Habit Small evergreen tree or large shrub with broad, rounded crown for well-drained soil and full sun in a sheltered position. **Attributes** Shiny, leathery leaves. **Reasons for pruning** To develop a strong framework. **Pruning time** Mid- to late summer.

Notholithocarpus densiflorus (tanoak), the only species in its genus, is common in cultivation. In its early years, it forms a pyramidal, evergreen tree with a slender branch system. Retain the leader for as long as possible to develop a strong framework, as the foliage is very heavy and if rival leaders are formed, they are easily weighed down and broken, especially under snow or strong winds with rain.

NYSSA

Habit Medium to large deciduous trees for a deep, rich, lime-free loam in full sun. **Attributes** One of the best trees for autumn colour. **Reasons for pruning** To develop a strong framework. **Pruning time** Between autumn and early spring (when dormant).

Nyssa sylvatica (tupelo) forms a large decurrent tree to 15 metres (50 ft.) or more in height at maturity. A small, young, strong plant with some vigour should be planted and a strong leader encouraged, as they dislike transplanting and sulk for a while. A stunted specimen is likely to break out with a strong shoot, from low down or near to ground level, which will run up through the centre of the crown and spoil the overall shape. If this happens and there is sufficient vigour in this new shoot to develop beyond the lower branch system, leave it to provide the tree's future framework.

Height is variable. Where the crown forms at an earlier stage in development, a more compact tree with shorter growth is produced. This variation may be due to soil conditions; a good, deep, rich loam is more likely to yield the strong growth essential to the production of a leader, which will run right up through the crown as the height increases. As the tree becomes established in its permanent planting site, the lower branches can be gradually removed, to an eventual height of 2 to 3 metres (6 to 10 ft.). This allows the remaining branches to develop their typical semi-pendulous habit and display the fine autumn colour at eye level.

Nyssa sinensis is far easier to transplant and less moody than *N. sylvatica*, getting off to a better start, retaining the central leader, and making a more excurrent form. Otherwise, it should be treated in the same way.

A mature *Nyssa sylvatica* trained on a clean trunk with a well-balanced decurrent crown.

OEMLERIA

Habit Medium-sized suckering deciduous shrub for fertile soil in partial shade to full sun. **Attributes** Bright green young foliage, pendulous white flowers in spring, plum-like fruits in winter, suitable for the natural part of the garden. **Reasons for pruning** To restrict spread and correct overarching growths. **Pruning time** Late spring after flowering.

Oemleria cerasiformis (osoberry) has male and female flowers on different plants, but both are similar in form and habit, with erect stems forming a thicket of growth. It suckers freely, and a single specimen can soon develop into a clump, which also layers freely. As the clump begins to enlarge in size, pruning is difficult to carry out effectively. To restrict spread, regularly spade around the plant to sever any suckers or layers; alternatively, include a root barrier at planting. Where the plant is grown as a specimen in the border, some pruning of the older wood can be carried out after flowering; remove the stems right down to ground level and some of the suckers. With age some of the older growths begin to arch over into neighbouring plants; these can be pruned back to selected young upright shoots, which relieves weight and thus corrects the position.

OLEA

Habit Upright evergreen shrub or small tree for free-draining, droughty soils in full sun. **Attributes** Silver foliage, edible fruits. **Reasons for pruning** To produce and maintain a strong main framework with an open centre easily accessible for pruning and to encourage young growths that will flower the following year. **Pruning time** Early summer.

The wood of the olive tree, *Olea europaea*, is very hard and tough to cut; even young branches will require good-quality, sharp secateurs and a rigid or folding handsaw. You can carry out most pruning operations on a mature olive tree with a Silky, apart from the thinning cuts, where secateurs come into their own.

The olive normally requires wall protection, particularly when grown in cooler climates, but more and more it is grown as a freestanding tree in a sheltered position. When grown as a wall-trained shrub, six to eight of the main branches of a young feathered shrub planted against the wall should be trained fanwise, with additional laterals tied in as growth extends over the wall. The growths that develop from this system must be restricted and thinned by careful pruning; this will encourage fresh young growth and flowers. Strong promising shoots from any part of the plant can be used and trained as replacements for any older branch that show signs of declining.

In the nursery, most freestanding olive trees are grown on a single clean trunk 1 to 1.2 metres (3 to 4 ft.) high with a framework of strong upright branches growing from the top, to form a vase-shaped form.

On a young feathered tree, retain the leader until a straight trunk is formed, which should then be hard pruned, removing the crown at 1.2 metres (4 ft.). Strong new shoots will be produced naturally from the pruning cut, and three or four strong, evenly spaced and balanced shoots can be selected after the first year and encouraged to form a strong framework

A young olive tree on a short trunk with three main branches forming the framework.

Reducing the overall height of mature olive trees with the thinning cut, before and after.

Pruning the laterals on the main frame to encourage flowering.

A mature olive tree in Italy with a dense crown.

The same olive tree after the elimination cut.

from which young, pendulous laterals will develop. Restrict the tree to a height of 4 to 5 metres (12 to 16 ft.) by using the thinning cut, which entails stopping the main leaders on each of the main framework branches, back to healthy side shoots, roughly every two years, or when needed. This allows future pruning and fruit collection to be carried out without the need of ladders; rather, the pruner can stand safely and comfortably in the main crotch of the tree. The laterals on the main frame should also be pruned to encourage young vigorous growth that will bear flowers the following year.

Over time the centre of the tree will become overcrowded with straggly branches or strong epicormic shoots. Prune these back to the main branches regularly to produce an open centre: allowing air and light to penetrate the crown helps fruit to ripen and reduces pest and disease outbreaks. This "elimination cut" also prevents increased competition from new shoots and helps to develop branches that will flower the following year.

Olives are tough trees and will endure poor soil, drought, and other harsh conditions, living to a ripe old age, often well over 100 years. To renovate, prune back into the main branching; the tree will respond by producing fresh material, which can be trained back into a desired shape. If damaged by cold winds or low temperatures, trees can be pruned back to live wood; they will respond and recover.

OLEARIA

Habit Compact, sun-loving evergreen shrubs for well-drained soil, including chalk. **Attributes** White or cream daisy-like flowers in summer, wind-resistant, suitable for coastal planting. **Reasons for pruning** To renovate old plants, repair frost damage, and restrict size. **Pruning time** Spring, once new growth begins.

In areas where there is a threat of harsh weather, olearias are best planted with the protection of a sunny wall, but they need to be freestanding rather than formally trained against the wall. One general characteristic of the daisy bushes is that they all break freely from pruning cuts, a response that can be made use of in various circumstances; for example, tired and untidy bushes may be pruned very hard in spring, and growth will break out very freely from the old wood. In the same way, severe injury from frost or cold winds may be followed by hard pruning. This pruning should be done after the new growth appears, which will indicate the severity of the damage.

Specimens that have grown too large for the position may also be carefully pruned in the spring, making the cuts inside the bush at suitable points so that an informal surface is retained. This restrictive pruning may be needed for large growers (e.g., *Olearia avicenniifolia*) when grown in a fairly confined space. The gradual process of shortening may need to be carried out over a period of two or three seasons, rather than a more drastic hard pruning over the whole of the bush. If needed, *O. phlogopappa* may be cut back after flowering by several inches once the shrub is two or three years old and has reached full size.

Olearia ×haastii is often grown as an informal hedge and will need regular pruning in summer to maintain an informal surface.

OPLOPANAX

Habit Spiny medium-sized deciduous shrub for free-draining soil in partial shade to full sun. **Attributes** Wide, maple-like leaves, upright cream conical flowers. **Reasons for pruning** No pruning required. **Pruning time** Spring.

Personal protection All parts of this plant are covered in tiny needle-like spines that can be irritating to the skin, so wear thorn-proof clothing and gloves when pruning.

Very little pruning is required for *Oplopanax horridus* (devil's club), apart from keeping it tidy, which should be carried out in spring; however, the tall stems can become decumbent and begin to layer, and it may be necessary to remove these layers to keep the plant in check.

ORIXA

Habit Small suckering deciduous shrub for most free-draining, fertile soils in partial shade. **Attributes** Large, glossy green leaves, aromatic when rubbed. **Reasons for pruning** To restrict spread. **Pruning time** Between autumn and spring (when dormant).

The dense and shapely *Orixa japonica* (Japanese orixa) sends out spreading growths. These are horizontal at first; but the extended branch ends become pendulous, and as they touch the soil they root and form strong shoots, extending the shrub in size all around. If necessary this spread can be checked by careful pruning; hide the cuts, so that the natural habit is retained. The rooted layers can be severed from the main plant, uprooted, and planted elsewhere in the dormant season. It is often used for hedging in the Far East, so why not give it a go in your garden as one of those unusual hedging plants?

OSMANTHUS

Habit Evergreen shrubs or small trees for well-drained soil in full sun to partial shade. **Attributes** Tough holly-like leaves with various colours and variegation, small, sweet-scented white flowers. **Reasons for pruning** To restrict size. **Pruning time** Late spring after flowering.

All species flower on old wood and will produce more flowers if left unpruned. They tolerate severe pruning and regenerate freely from old wood; if they become overgrown for their location, they can be hard pruned and allowed to grow into a new framework.

The slow-growing *Osmanthus heterophyllus* (holly osmanthus) is best left to branch freely from ground level, the lower branches being almost horizontal. Small growths are produced freely on the old wood, even inside the bush, so it can be restricted in size by cutting any long growths back to suitable laterals inside the general branch system, preserving the natural, informal effect. Do this in late spring; hard cutting back of the whole bush is better done in mid-spring.

Osmanthus heterophyllus also makes a good hedging plant, although it is slow to fill in the gaps, and any trimming should be carried out before midsummer. If grown as a formal hedge, it will not flower as freely as a naturally grown specimen, as the flowers are produced in the axils of the previous season's wood and are followed a few weeks later with more flowers from the base of the young growths.

Osmanthus heterophyllus 'Purpureus' is often grafted onto a rootstock of *Ligustrum*. Keep an eye out for suckers, which will be very easy to identify, and remove them as soon as they are seen.

Other species also respond to pruning if it is necessary to restrict their size, using the same method as with *Osmanthus heterophyllus*. Where the growth is stiff and upright and the leaves are larger, more care is necessary to find the correct pruning cut, or the overall shape and character will be spoiled.

Osmanthus delavayi can be wall-trained or (in mild areas) grown as a freestanding specimen. It will also behave when close pruned, which makes it a suitable subject for a formal hedge in milder areas. When freestanding, prune immediately after flowering in late spring. Cut out any overgrown branches, which may be weighed down, spoiling the lower growths. Make the cuts to strong lateral shoots, and use the new growths as replacement shoots, if needed. If wall-trained, the main branches are trained fanwise, and the laterals produced from these provide the furnishings as they extend and branch. Any further pruning is as for the freestanding shrub.

Osmanthus ×burkwoodii is a compact and slow-growing shrub, particularly in the first few years after planting. Once planted it produces strong upright growths that will protrude through the close branch system. To restrict size, prune after flowering in mid- to late spring, cutting back the longer branches inside the shrub, taking care to leave a natural, informal surface. It also regenerates well if pruned hard and will form a close-knit hedge face if clipped regularly in midsummer. If pruning is done too late, the soft growth produced in early autumn can be damaged by frost.

Osmanthus decorus (sweet olive) has large leaves and a spreading, rounded habit; its branching is very rigid, even to the outer edge of the plant. To restrict size, prune in late spring after flowering, cutting back the longer growths to suitable growing points well inside the bush. With a badly overgrown specimen, stagger the pruning over several years, selecting the growths carefully so that the plant retains a well-furnished shape and surface.

Osmanthus delavayi grown as freestanding shrub.

OSTRYA

Habit Slow-growing medium-sized deciduous trees with a decurrent, broad crown for most free-draining soils in partial shade to full sun. **Attributes** Interesting bark, autumn colour, showy hop-like fruits. **Reasons for pruning** To develop a strong framework. **Pruning time** Late summer to mid-winter (when dormant).

These trees should be planted more frequently as interesting shade trees in our gardens. They can be trained up with a central leader and become very shapely if grown on a 2 to 2.5 metre (6 to 8 ft.) length of clean trunk, requiring very little pruning once the desired trunk is formed. *Ostrya carpinifolia* (hop hornbeam) has a particularly shapely round head, with fine branching evenly spaced around the central leader. Its lower scaffolds sweep down to eye level, where the persistent fruits and catkins can be appreciated after the leaves have fallen. It does not like competition from neighbouring trees and needs space to develop into a fine, spreading tree.

Ostrya virginiana (ironwood) is similarly upright in habit, but its branching tends to be heavier and its form wider. Where a major scaffold is lost or removed, it has the ability to produce replacement branches that will naturally fill the gap.

Ostrya japonica (Japanese hop hornbeam) retains a strong leader and has slender branches. It should be grown with a strong clean trunk to show off its very attractive, almost hickory-like bark.

A young *Ostrya carpinifolia* grown on a short trunk, showing the fine, even branching.

A mature *Ostrya virginiana* showing its broad wide-spreading shape and form, on a short trunk.

OXYDENDRUM

Habit Dense, conical deciduous shrub or small tree for acid soil only, in shade. **Attributes** Long, pendulous white flowers in late summer, amazing autumn colour. **Reasons for pruning** No pruning required. **Pruning time** Late autumn to winter (when dormant).

Oxydendrum arboreum (sourwood, sorrel tree) is very miffy, especially if conditions are not right. The key to growing it is lots of good aftercare after planting to promote free, feathered growth with a single leader; often the leader is lost following transplanting. Encourage branching to ground level for a well-furnished skirt. Mature trees will not tolerate any form of pruning; if soil conditions are perfect and a good specimen is established, it is better to prune neighbouring sheltering trees and shrubs to prevent a specimen from becoming overgrown and the shape spoiled.

OZOTHAMNUS

Habit Heath-like evergreen shrubs for well-drained, rich, organic soil in full sun and a sheltered position. **Attributes** Golden, sticky foliage with a sweet honey scent, white flowers in late summer. **Reasons for pruning** To encourage a bushy plant. **Pruning time** Spring.

All species will withstand hard pruning. Young, newly planted specimens should be stopped early to encourage a bushy habit, which will help the plant to grow unsupported later in its life. To maintain an untidy or weak-stemmed plant, cut back to 30 cm (12 in.) from soil level in spring, retaining a low branch system, from which the new growth will appear.

PAEONIA

Habit Sparsely branched upright deciduous shrubs for deep, rich, moist, free-draining soil in a sunny, sheltered position. **Attributes** Flamboyant, blowsy, white to red flowers in late summer. **Reasons for pruning** To maintain a tidy plant and remove dead wood. **Pruning time** Summer after flowering and autumn after leaf fall.

The shrubby species of *Paeonia* (e.g., *P. delavayi*, *P. ludlowii*, *P. suffruticosa*), known collectively as tree peonies, normally require very little pruning. After the fruits have ripened, the old flower stalks die back to the terminal bud on the new shoot. If fruits are not required, deadhead during the summer to encourage further stronger growth. If these old stalks are cut off in autumn after the leaves have fallen, the shrub will have a tidier appearance. At the same time, any old and worn-out growths that have stopped producing flower buds can be removed at ground level. Summer is also a good time to look for and prune out any dead wood as it is sometimes difficult to pick out during the winter.

PALIURUS

Habit Spiny, spreading deciduous shrub or small tree for well-drained soil and full sun. **Attributes** Small yellow flowers and round, winged fruits. **Reasons for pruning** To restrict size and develop a strong framework. **Pruning time** Between autumn and spring (when dormant).

Personal protection Wear good thorn-proof clothing and gloves, as Christ's thorn is armed with needle-like spines along the branches. Use long-handled loppers to remove old growths in the centre of the shrub.

When grown as a shrub *Paliurus spina-christi* (Christ's thorn) has a spreading habit with the main branches growing from ground level, the lower branches being weighed down to a horizontal position, lying on the ground as more and more growth is generated laterally. It is a very untidy grower with many crossing branches that intertwine through the interior of the shrub; small dead lateral branches make it impenetrable. It is not worth trying to correct this habit by removing these crossing branches or dead wood, as the shrub will become very open and lax and the general appearance will be spoiled.

It can also be trained as a small tree with a 1 to 1.5 metre (3 to 5 ft.) clean stem, by retaining the leader for as long as possible and pruning out any rival leaders. Whether grown as a shrub or a tree, the size can be restricted by carefully pruning back lateral branches to suitable, strong shoots and hiding the cuts, retaining an informal effect. If very overgrown, it can be cut hard back, almost to ground level, and it will respond by breaking out strongly.

PALMS

Habit Clump-forming or upright evergreen shrubs or trees for moist free-draining soil in a sunny position. **Attributes** Tropical-looking, architectural fan-like foliage. **Reasons for pruning** To maintain a clean, healthy-looking plant. **Pruning time** Summer after flowering and autumn after leaf fall.

Personal protection: Wear good thorn-proof clothing and gloves when pruning. Several palms have spines along the leaf stalk and sharp leaf edges that can cut bare skin.

Pruning palms differs greatly from the general pruning of branching woody plants. If carried out incorrectly, it can result in permanent damage to the plant. Palms are made up of a pithy fibrous trunk without annual rings and lack the ability to branch or create a new leading shoot; however, some species (e.g., *Chamaerops humilis*) can generate multiple stems from the base. Once this growing point is damaged or removed, the palm is unable to regrow from lower down the trunk and will probably die and need replacing. Generally no training is needed.

Trachycarpus fortunei (Chusan palm) is often planted as an individual specimen or en

Pruning old palm leaves that have dropped below the horizontal.

Trachycarpus fortunei, before and after grooming.

masse, with several of varying heights clumped together for a random multi-stemmed appearance. Every two or three years, it will be necessary to groom plants by removing old leaves that remain attached to the trunk. Do not pull the leaves off, as this can damage the tissue on the main trunk leaf stalk. Use a pair of loppers or secateurs, close to the trunk, leaving about 3 cm (1 in.) of leaf stalk attached, protruding from the trunk with the petiole fibres. Never prune the leaf off flush with the trunk! A good guide as to which leaves should be left and which should be removed is to prune out only leaves that have dropped below the horizontal position. Anything above this line should be left.

Following a good flowering season, if fruits are not wanted, the flowering stalks can be removed back to where they are attached, to prevent fruit production and to retain a vegetative palm.

PARROTIA

Habit Upright or spreading deciduous shrubs or small trees for fertile soil and full sun. **Attributes** Smooth, flaking bark, bright red late-winter flowers on naked stems, superb yellow to red autumn colour, leaves retained well into winter. **Reasons for pruning** To develop a strong framework. **Pruning time** Between autumn and spring (when dormant).

Once *Parrotia persica* (Persian ironwood) begins branching, the head quickly opens up and the leader is lost, even on upright forms like 'Vanessa'. The best form for planting is a young, well-developed specimen on a short trunk to 1 metre (3 ft.) high. Allow the crown to grow naturally from this height; the result at

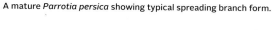

A mature *Parrotia persica* showing typical spreading branch form.

maturity is a strong, evenly branched specimen, rather than a multi-stemmed form with tight forks, which are more likely to break apart. The branches have a spreading habit, and many are horizontal, even pendulous, growing along the ground as they reach it. In order to retain the grandeur of this plant, these growths should be left to grow unrestricted. The branch-ing is quite dense and crowded but no attempt should be made to thin them out, as this cross-ing and overlapping of branches is the natural habit of this tree and one of its beauties. When wall-trained, its lateral branches evenly spaced and trained horizontally to three storeys high, it looks as good as a Boston ivy in full autumn splendour.

Parrotia subaequalis, introduced from China in 2000, makes a small tree to 10 metres (33 ft.). Leave this species to grow naturally as a shrubby specimen. If pruned with a clean trunk, its vigour is dampened. Most nursery specimens are grafted onto *P. persica*, so keep a close watch for any suckers below the graft union.

A multi-stemmed *Parrotia persica*.

PARROTIOPSIS

Habit Dense, upright deciduous shrub, rarely a small tree, for acid or neutral soil or soil over chalk in partial shade to full sun. **Attributes** Yellow flowers surrounded by white bracts in late spring, golden autumn colour. **Reasons for pruning** To develop a strong framework. **Pruning time** Between autumn and spring (when dormant).

Parrotiopsis jacquemontiana should be grown on a short leg, 0.3 to 0.6 metre (1 to 2 ft.) high, from which the dense twiggy head forms very quickly. One of the beauties of this shrub is its extensive branching, and this should be encouraged to develop right down to the ground. Once the head is formed, any suckers that appear from the trunk should be removed unless a multi-stemmed shrub is wanted.

PARTHENOCISSUS

Habit Deciduous climbers, self-clinging by leaf tendrils that twine or stick, for fertile, free-draining soil in full sun or shade. **Attributes** Strong, fast-growing wall covering, with crimson-red autumn foliage, clusters of blue-black fruits. **Reasons for pruning** To restrict size and remove from roof gutters, windows, etc. **Pruning time** Early winter when there is no danger of sap bleeding and summer to tidy up the surface of the plant.

A major characteristic of this genus of climbing plants is that the leaf tendrils usually flatten upon contact with solid objects and form discs or pads that cling very tightly to the surface. *Parthenocissus quinquefolia* (Virginia creeper), one of the strongest species, is typical of the majority, which are suitable for growing over trees, sheds, walls, or fences. Pruning is unnecessary when these are grown in the wilder parts of the garden, although a careful watch should be kept to see that nearby shrubs or trees are not smothered unintentionally.

These self-clinging vines are often planted against buildings, *Parthenocissus tricuspidata* (Boston ivy) being the most frequently grown, but this can lead to damage if they are allowed to grow beyond the eaves and among the roof

Parthenocissus quinquefolia grown to the top of a garden wall and allowed to hang down.

Parthenocissus henryana showing the silver veining on the leaves.

Parthenocissus tricuspidata using adhesive pads to cling to a house wall.

tiles. As the plant grows, so does the thickness of the stems, which in turn can dislodge loose objects such as roof tiles, while at the same time the annual leaf fall can block gutters. It is certainly worth pruning the outer bounds of the plant annually in the autumn to prevent this type of damage from occurring.

Pergolas too can be used to support these vines, but pruning will need to be carried out annually. A permanent framework of rods are trained and tied in to the uprights and along the beams of the pergola and the young growths pruned back to these rods in early winter, the pruning point being just above the

lowest bud. Under this system, spurs build up on the vine, and the new growths hang down, forming a curtain of attractive foliage.

Parthenocissus henryana is best grown against a wall and produces bright silver veins on the leaves when grown in the shade.

All *Parthenocissus* species can be clipped with hedging shears during the summer months to maintain a flat, tidy surface and to prevent a buildup of weight from pulling the plant off the wall or support. To renovate an out-of-control vine, cut the entire plant back to 1 metre (3 ft.) from ground level in winter.

PASSIFLORA

Habit Evergreen climber by means of stem tendrils for a sunny, sheltered wall and free-draining soil. **Attributes** Extremely showy flowers, which can develop into edible fruits. **Reasons**

for pruning To develop a strong framework, restrict size, and encourage flowering. **Pruning time** Spring.

Passiflora caerulea (passion flower) should

be trained against a wall and grown to a height of 2.4 to 3 metres (8 to 10 ft.), where it can be easily managed. It will need the aid of a trellis, to which it can be tied in, or a wire system, to

The showy flowers of *Passiflora caerulea* held on the new lateral growths produced on the permanent framework.

which it can naturally cling for support with its tendrils. The available space of the wall should be covered by a framework of main branches that are trained hard up against the structure, evenly spaced approximately 15 to 25 cm (5 to 8 in.) apart, but it may become necessary to thin these out later. Remember to snip the tendrils attached to the support system to make it easier to remove the prunings. Once a framework is established, shorten vigorous stems annually to keep the plant manageable, but don't prune too hard as this will result in excessive leafy growth devoid of flowers. Allow the laterals to hang down at full length and prune them back annually in spring, to a good bud at the base—a type of spur pruning. Flowering occurs on the long lateral growths that are produced during the summer. Plants do not respond to very hard pruning, so if one becomes neglected and overgrown, it is better to replace it with a young plant.

PAULOWNIA

Habit Fast-growing deciduous decurrent trees with a rounded crown for deep, fertile soil in a sunny, sheltered position. **Attributes** Large leaves, terminal panicles of sweetly scented blue to purple foxglove-like flowers in late spring. **Reasons for pruning** To develop a strong framework and remove dead wood. **Pruning time** Spring or early summer.

All paulownias, not just *Paulownia tomentosa* (foxglove tree, princess tree), can be pruned in the same way. If conditions are right and they have plenty of irrigation, they can reach a height of 2 to 2.5 metres (6 to 8 ft.) after two years from seed. They prefer a rich soil; however, they grow well at Kew on thin sandy soils, provided they get water during dry summers. They are especially tender when young. Often when grown on a rich soil they produce sappy growth that is unripe at the tips when winter sets in and is damaged or killed. This does not matter too much, for the damaged or dead growth may be pruned back to a strong developing shoot; in fact, seldom is a terminal bud produced on the tip of the shoot, and an axillary bud beneath invariably takes over in the spring. Build up a single leader for as long as possible. The first main branch should be formed with a clean stem of at least 2 metres (6 ft.).

Occasionally after a wet year, several shoots can be thrown up through the centre of the tree which may eventually rival the leader. These can be removed at an early stage, but they can be left on a weak specimen as a means of taking over the lead and forming a stronger crown.

Paulownia tomentosa coppiced in the herbaceous border to produce large leaves for foliage effect.

It is difficult to grow shapely trees on wet, cold soils, as cavities form quickly in the soft pithy wood and whole branches tend to die back for no apparent reason. Often lower branches are shaded out by the large leaves, which produce a dense canopy, and they will naturally crown lift themselves.

Paulownias can also be grown in the herbaceous border for their tropical foliage effect. Cut the stems down to within 5 to 8 cm (2 to 3 in.) of ground level each spring before growth begins. The resultant shoots can then be thinned out to one, and with feeding and watering, fast, vigorous, luxuriant growth will be produced.

Training a two-year-old specimen of *Paulownia kawakamii* to a single main trunk following winter cold damage.

PEROVSKIA

Habit Semi-woody upright deciduous shrub for deep, rich soil and full sun. **Attributes** Aromatic silver foliage, terminal panicles of violet-blue flowers in late summer. **Reasons for pruning** To encourage flowering. **Pruning time** Spring.

Perovskia atriplicifolia (Russian sage) and its cultivars flower on the fast-growing growths that develop each spring and early summer from the woody rootstock. During the winter these growths are killed back, often to within 5 to 8 cm (2 to 3 in.) of their bases, but in the spring, buds break freely from the living part near to the ground. Every spring, just as the buds break, cut plants hard back to the base of each shoot, leaving only one or two developing buds on each stem. The severity of the pruning can be adjusted annually, depending on the winter and the number of newly breaking buds, which are easily seen in spring. This is a form of thinning and results in few shoots and better flowering spikes in summer. If a taller framework begins to form over the years, it can be hard pruned to create a lower plant as a means of renovation and will respond well.

PERSEA

Habit Small decurrent evergreen trees with dense, spreading, rounded crown for full sun to partial shade and free-draining soil. **Attributes** Foliage aromatic when crushed, small white flowers in late spring/early summer followed by showy, sometimes edible fruits. **Reasons for pruning** To maintain a strong framework and remove damaged branches. **Pruning time** Summer after flowering.

Persea borbonia (red bay) and *P. ichangensis* do well in cultivation, provided they get some protection from any cold weather. Very little pruning is needed apart from the removal of crossing and damaged branches, as their wood is brittle and susceptible to wind damage. Prune in summer after flowering, unless the blue fruits are wanted for show; if left, however, they attract birds, which can cause problems with their dirty droppings on pavements or patios. *Persea palustris* (swamp bay) looks better in the border furnished to the ground and allowed to grow naturally.

Persea americana (avocado) is not frost hardy and requires a warm climate to grow successfully; however, it can be grown in the glasshouse, which will help it to fruit. Many cultivars are grafted and grown for their fruits, flowering early in their life after planting. Fruits are often borne on the terminal parts of the plant. Prune after fruiting, removing dead

Persea palustris furnished to the ground showing the spreading habit.

and crossing branches and shortening the laterals and any upright branches back by a half to strong buds, which will encourage more spreading, lateral branches and ultimately more flowers. When a tree becomes too large or too leggy, it can be renovated by hard pruning. It will respond with lots of vigorous new shoots from the pruning cut and below.

PHELLODENDRON

Habit Small to medium-sized deciduous decurrent trees with wide-spreading, vase-shaped crown for any free-draining soil and full sun. **Attributes** Corky bark, pinnate leaves, white flowers in summer followed by clusters of black fruits. **Reasons for pruning** To develop a strong framework and prune out frost damage. **Pruning time** Between autumn and spring (when dormant).

These trees are fast growing in their early stages, growing well on any soil but thriving on fertile soil. They have a rather stiff upright branch system but provided they are watered and good growth is encouraged, they can be easily trained. Encourage a strong leader until the crown has been formed; the vigour of the tree is then lost along with the leader and a wide-spreading crown develops. Late spring frosts can be particularly damaging to young growths, with the loss of terminal buds, particularly on *Phellodendron amurense* (Amur cork tree) and *P. chinense*, and as a result the branching will not be clean and definite, but twiggier. Where the falling fruits of the Amur cork tree could be a problem (on paving or in the formal garden, for example), choose *P. amurense* 'Macho', an upright male clone with no fruits.

Phellodendron sachalinense is the most outstanding species of this genus, usually forming and retaining a strong leader, making it easy to train a clean trunk of 2 to 2.5 metres (6 to 8 ft.).

PHILADELPHUS

Habit Upright deciduous shrubs with arching branches. **Attributes** Exfoliating bark, fragrant white flowers in summer. **Reasons for pruning** To remove old wood and encourage flowering growths. **Pruning time** Early summer, immediately after flowering.

Most mock oranges grow freely from ground level and form a stool. They flower on laterals produced on growths made in the previous year. A good soil and plenty of water during the summer months, with feeding and mulching, provide the conditions necessary if these plants are to remain healthy and free-flowering year after year. Their general condition can be judged by the amount of new growth, which should develop rapidly during and after flowering. After planting, the strong shoots of young plants should be pruned back by half

A well-structured *Philadelphus purpurascens* in the shrub border, showing plentiful amounts of new growth.

their length to encourage a bushy plant from the start, with as many strong, vigorous shoots emerging from soil level as possible.

Take into account the natural habit and vigour of the species or variety as there is considerable variation across this group of plants, although the general principles of pruning apply across the range. In most cases some annual pruning immediately after flowering is necessary to regulate growth and flowering. The wood that has flowered should be cut back to a suitable growth a few centimetres from the old wood. Thin dense shrubs by removing entire branches back to ground level, where there should be new growths for replacements:

annual pruning keeps a good supply of young wood growing up from the base. As a general rule, most wood above ground level should be no older than five years. Tip-prune young, healthy flowering shoots, removing the old flowers back to a healthy bud. Really old overgrown bushes that have been neglected over the years can be hard pruned. Cut all the old top growth back to ground level during the winter or early spring, or after flowering; however, it is often better to replace such plants with young ones.

Philadelphus coronarius is a strong grower reaching up to 3.5 metres (12 ft.); its selections 'Aureus' and 'Variegatus', grown mainly

for their foliage effect, are much smaller, producing thin, wiry stems. The best colour is found on the younger growths; it is therefore important to maintain a good proportion of these on the shrubs. *Philadelphus microphyllus* is a low-growing shrub with fine growths and small leaves; carefully prune back any branches that trail and overhang other plants but generally an informal shape should be retained.

Aphids can be a serious pest of mock oranges especially after pruning, and the young fleshy growths that are so important often suffer badly. Apply a control in good time following pruning.

PHILLYREA

Habit Evergreen shrubs or small trees for most free-draining soils in full sun to partial shade. **Attributes** Shiny, dense foliage, clusters of fragrant white flowers in the leaf axils of the previous year's growth in late spring/early summer followed by small black berries. **Reasons for pruning** To restrict size and renovate. **Pruning time** Summer.

The overarching characteristic of this genus is that all taxa regenerate freely, producing a plentiful supply of new growths from the general region of any pruning cut, even those made into old wood. They also produce substantial branches from ground level.

Phillyrea angustifolia (narrow-leaved mock privet) has a close habit, but with *P. angustifolia* f. *rosmarinifolia* the density of individual branches is such that there is considerable buildup of dead twig growth inside the bush. This in turn increases the weight to such an extent that the upper branches are bent down onto the lower ones; the inner branches are deprived of light, and living growths inside the bush become fewer. It is difficult to prune this subject with the aim of restricting size; better to give it space where it can grow naturally without any restriction and the need to prune. If the plant is damaged from heavy snow or very strong winds, prune the plant hard to near

Light tip-pruning of *Phillyrea latifolia* with secateurs to restrict size without damaging the leaves.

The final cut will be hidden inside the foliage.

ground level and allow it to break and form a new bush.

By contrast, the elegant *Phillyrea latifolia* (broadleaved mock privet) can easily be lightly tip-pruned to maintain a regular size, without spoiling its shape or natural habit. Cuts should be made to strong shoots and, where possible, hidden by the remaining foliage. By using secateurs (not hedging shears) and tar-

geting pruning cuts, the individual leaves are left intact, not severed in half, which spoils the character of any evergreen.

Both *Phillyrea* species are used very successfully for topiary and hedges and even trained as cloud trees, as they will tolerate regular tight clipping and shaping.

PHLOMIS

Habit Low-growing evergreen subshrubs for very free-draining soil and full sun. **Attributes** Drought-tolerant, grey-green leaves with hairy stems, whorls of white, yellow, or pale pink

flowers around the stems in summer. **Reasons for pruning** To encourage new growth in spring for flowering. **Pruning time** Spring.

Phlomis fruticosa (Jerusalem sage) has a

woody branch system, but the leafy shoot tips are soft and prone to injury in a severe winter. Fortunately, in common with all species in the genus, new growths break freely from old wood, provided that this is in a healthy condition. After a severe winter, cut back the damaged parts of the plant as the new shoots break out in the spring. Very old and tired woody specimens may not have the vigour to break freely and should be replaced rather than renovated. Overgrown specimens also respond to hard cutting back in spring. It is possible to maintain a healthy plant, in good condition, by pruning back a selected number of stems each year in spring, removing any that have become weak and woody or that have overgrown into neighbouring plants.

Phlomis longifolia can become leggy with time, and it pays to prune out the tips after flowering to prevent this.

Phlomis chrysophylla (golden-leaved Jerusalem sage) can become very heavy, with growths eventually weighed down to the ground. These will root and form new plants well away from the parent bush.

The dwarf *Phlomis italica* (Balearic Jerusalem sage) is suitable for the rock garden and has a woody habit that will develop a very ragged appearance unless controlled by regular pruning.

A mature *Phlomis fruticosa* showing benefits of regular pruning.

PHOTINIA

Habit Deciduous and evergreen trees and shrubs for fertile, free-draining soil in full sun to partial shade. **Attributes** Corymbs of white flowers in spring. The deciduous species usually produce fruit (unlike the evergreens) and have good autumn colour; the evergreens have attractively coloured young foliage and make good container plants. **Reasons for pruning** To develop a strong framework and restrict size.

DECIDUOUS SPECIES

Pruning time Between autumn and spring (when dormant).

Photinia beauverdiana and *P. villosa* make large shrubs or small trees and normally

The natural shape and form of *Photinia beauverdiana* grown as a tree on a low trunk.

need little if any regular pruning. They can be trained as a multi-stemmed specimen or on a low, single trunk up to 1 metre (3 ft.) high and allowed to form a crown from low down. Strong, young growths are often thrown up from ground level; these can be thinned or trained to replace old, tired branches if necessary, as when the plants age, the top growth often does not produce much young wood, and the shrub begins to lose its strength. Renovate tired old plants by pruning hard back to a new framework and allowing it to break; follow this by thinning out the new growth to create a strong framework.

EVERGREEN SPECIES

Pruning time Spring and summer.

Most of the evergreens (e.g., *Photinia davidiana, P. glabra, P. serratifolia*) have a stiff, erect branching habit and can appear to be ungainly growers when compared to many other shrubs; however, this is the plant's natural habit and there should be no attempt to correct this by pruning—leave well alone. In fact, apart from the removal of dead wood, the less pruning the better, as these species are very susceptible to fireblight (*Erwinia amylovora*).

Photinia davidsoniae should be trained with a central leader and with branching from ground level. It will occasionally get cut back by cold weather but will break freely from living wood, even old wood in the spring.

Photinia ×fraseri and its various forms are usually grown for their attractive, brightly coloured young leaves in the spring; to keep the shrub tidy and compact, shorten out-growing branches by tip-pruning to an outward-facing bud in that season. When grown as a hedge, tip-pruning two to three times from late spring to early summer, allowing time for the new growth to harden off before the winter.

All the evergreens can be renovated by cutting back hard into old wood. They usually respond by generating plenty of new growth, albeit at the loss of flowers for at least one season.

Photinia ×fraseri trained as a hedge.

Photinia ×fraseri 'Red Robin' with its red, young foliage, ready for tip-pruning.

Tip-pruning a hedge of *Photinia ×fraseri* back to healthy leaves or buds for a natural finish.

PHYGELIUS

Habit Small, suckering, evergreen or semi-evergreen subshrubs (occasionally perennials) for moist, free-draining soil in a sunny, sheltered position. **Attributes** Trumpet-shaped red and yellow flowers in summer and autumn. **Reasons for pruning** To remove winter damage. **Pruning time** Late spring.

All the Cape figworts (e.g., *Phygelius aequalis*, *P. capensis*, *P. ×rectus*) shoot freely from the base and are often damaged by winter cold. Prune lightly by removing all winter-damaged growth to strong buds on living growth. Following a hard winter or to renovate old plants, all the stems can be cut back to the

ground. With a feed, light mulch, and plenty of moisture, plants will respond with vigorous regrowth. If trained against a wall, prune the side shoots back to the framework of branches and thin out any old woody stems, allowing new shoots from ground level to be tied in.

PHYLLODOCE

Habit Bushy, compact, mound-forming evergreen shrubs for acid soil in full sun to partial shade. **Attributes** Pink bell-shaped flowers in late spring/early summer, suitable for the rock garden. **Reasons for pruning** Little pruning

needed. **Pruning time** Spring.

These small shrubs (e.g., *Phyllodoce breweri*, *P. caerulea*, *P. empetriformis*, *P. ×intermedia*) are rather exacting in their cultural requirements. Encourage a bushy habit; plenty of strong

growths will be thrown up from the base of the plant each year. Any dead growths that do occur should be cut out, but more often than not there is wholesale browning over the whole of the plant, which is a sign that it is dying.

PHYSOCARPUS

Habit Dense, deciduous suckering shrubs for fertile, well-drained, acid soil in partial shade to full sun. **Attributes** Exfoliating bark, palmate leaves in various colours, white flowers in early summer. **Reasons for pruning** To remove old wood and encourage fresh vegetative or flowering growths. **Pruning time** Summer after flowering.

Physocarpus opulifolius (Atlantic ninebark) and its cultivars throw up many young growths among the older branches from ground level. Pruning consists of cutting out a proportion of the older wood after flowering. The extent of this pruning must depend on the amount of growth made and the plant's condition, but

the shrub should be left well furnished to the ground. The older, mature branches are attractive in their own right, with bark that peels in papery strips through the winter. When pruning, the objective is to remove some of the oldest woody stems back to ground level, taking away whole branches or cutting out some of the old wood on the remaining growths to a suitable point and thinning out some of the young canes, which originate at ground level. When shortening part of a branch system, cut back to an outward-growing young shoot.

Physocarpus capitatus (Pacific ninebark) is a medium-sized shrub and stronger growing than *P. opulifolius*, producing a larger number

of canes from ground level, which will need thinning annually. It also suckers extensively and is more suitable for the less formal border, where it has the space to develop freely.

Physocarpus monogynus (mountain ninebark) has a short, stool head with a spreading but stiff branch system. Give it enough space for a 2 to 2.5 metre (6 to 8 ft.) spread, as a greater proportion of the older wood will need to be left on the plant.

Physocarpus malvaceus (mallow ninebark) is a medium-sized shrub to 1.5 metres (5 ft.) high and throws up plenty of new growths, allowing the old ones to be pruned out severely after flowering.

PICEA

Habit Pyramidal excurrent evergreen conifers with a strong leader for moist, free-draining soil and full sun. **Attributes** Stately trees with pendent cones and needle-like foliage in various shades of green and blue. **Reasons for pruning** To develop a strong framework and maintain the lower skirt. **Pruning time** Mid- to late spring.

As with many conifers, all spruces develop a strong central leader from the seedling stage. Encourage this for as long as possible following planting. If they are given the right conditions and grown well, they will naturally retain their leading shoot. Occasionally though they can develop competing twin leaders and one should be removed as soon as seen, to main-

tain a single growing point. The goal is a strong single-trunked tree upon maturity.

Although most are naturally pyramidal, spruces vary greatly in size and shape; for example, *Picea omorika* (Serbian spruce) has a very narrow habit compared to *P. abies* (Norway spruce), which is more broadly pyramidal. All are best grown with a low and free branch spread down to ground level. Most species will thrive only on sufficiently moist soils with some form of shelter, and adequate light must reach the whole of the tree, so give them ample space in which to develop into maturity.

As the lower branches develop with age, they will shade out the first whorls of branching or lower skirt, and as these die they will

need to be removed back to the parent trunk to maintain a clean-looking plant and allow access to the base of the trunk. When carrying out this exercise, it is best to remove the entire whorl of branches to maintain an even, lower canopy.

Picea smithiana retaining its leader and a skirt to the ground without any intervention.

Picea abies showing its broadly pyramidal habit.

Removing a competing twin leader from a young *Picea jezoensis* with the secateurs.

A young *Picea orientalis* with a strong central leader.

Picea omorika showing its narrow pyramidal habit, which prevents damage from heavy snow.

PICRASMA

Habit Small vase-shaped deciduous decurrent tree for moist, free-draining soil in full sun. **Attributes** Smooth grey bark, pinnate leaves with good autumn colour, and green-white flowers followed by metallic blue fruits. **Reasons for pruning** To develop a strong framework. **Pruning time** Autumn through winter (when dormant).

Picrasma quassioides (bitterwood) is grown for its foliage effect. The branches are ascending, forming a vase shape in the early years. It should be trained on a short leg 60 cm (2 ft.) high. Even the lower and outer branches on a mature tree are horizontal and seldom droop. Pruning cuts heal very well, but in a mature tree, the long branches—with little furnishing apart from on the ends—sometimes split at the narrow crotches, so over-thinning is not advisable.

Picrasma quassioides showing the even, vase-shaped symmetrical branching.

PIERIS

Habit Dense evergreen shrubs for acid soil in a sheltered position in full sun to partial shade. **Attributes** Shiny leaves, attractive when fresh, and white ericaceous flowers in spring. **Reasons for pruning** To retain a balanced shape and remove winter damage. **Pruning time** Spring after flowering.

There is quite a variety of growth across members of this genus, but all have one or two requirements and characteristics in common. Growth is more likely to be healthy and typical when grown in a sheltered spot. Provided the plants are healthy and strong, they will respond well to hard pruning, but this should not be resorted to unless it is absolutely necessary. It is best to grow these shrubs naturally with an informal shape and form and give them the space needed to do this without interference from other plants. When planted in positions where there is light from only one side, *Pieris floribunda* and *P. japonica* become unsymmetrical and unbalanced, with the heavy unbalanced growth pulling the shrub out of shape. This can be corrected by pruning these branches back to an upright branch, or if there are none to cut back to, by pruning back to a suitable point.

All the species and cultivars should be well furnished to ground level, and the aim should be to retain this surface by good culture. All are susceptible to damage from severe winters or late spring frosts; remove the these damaged shoots or branches, and they will respond with new growth from the pruning points. They will even respond to hard renovation pruning, provided they are fed and watered adequately following the operation. *Pieris formosa* and its forms respond better than the others.

A well-furnished *Pieris japonica*.

PILEOSTEGIA

Habit Evergreen climber, self-clinging by aerial roots, for fertile, free-draining soil in full sun or shade. **Attributes** Panicles of creamy white flowers in summer. **Reasons for pruning** To restrict size. **Pruning time** Spring and summer.

Pileostegia viburnoides (climbing hydrangea) is suitable for growing against a wall or over an old tree stump, attaching to any support thanks to the masses of adventitious roots along its stems. When grown against a garden wall, the long extension growths should be allowed to develop on the top as this gives additional support to the mature flowering wood that is built up. A wire system is also necessary for supporting ties as the heavier branch system develops. Cut back any surplus extension growths that develop once the allotted space has been covered in spring; shorten the flowering branches if they become heavy, are in danger of breaking, or grow too far out from the wall. Further pruning can be done in summer, should the extension growths need stopping early.

Pileostegia viburnoides fan-trained against a wall.

PINUS

Habit Shrubby to large evergreen excurrent conifers for any free-draining soils, including poor, infertile soils in full sun. **Attributes** Long needle-like leaves, coloured bark and cones. **Reasons for pruning** To develop a strong framework and maintain the lower skirt. **Pruning time** Mid- to late spring.

Personal protection All pines produce very sticky resin from pruning wounds. It is impossible to remove from clothing, so wear old clothes and gloves when carrying out any pruning operations.

As with most conifers, the retention of the leader is very important to the form and well-being of the vast majority of the plants in this large genus, but their habits vary considerably. It is important to have some knowledge of the growth habit of each species, especially when selecting a pine for planting, as they can be completely ruined if an attempt is made to change the form to fit the setting. The retention of a healthy leader is only possible if the tree is growing vigorously. The radial branches produced around the main central stem must also be healthy and vigorous to give support and shelter to the main extension shoot.

Should the main leader be lost for any reason, a vigorous tree will often produce several growths that will grow up in its place. These should be thinned down to one in the following spring, retaining the strongest and bearing in mind the desirability of selecting a growth that is in direct line with the main axis. Don't confuse competing leaders with lammas growth, common on pines, which is the late summer growth of the lateral buds; the terminal bud stays dormant rather than risk loss or damage from early autumn frosts. In spring, the terminal bud will break and grow beyond the growth made by the lateral buds in the previous year.

The best time for pruning is in the spring when the new growths (or candles) are 5 to 8 cm (2 to 3 in.) long. Once a flat-topped effect has developed and the tree has reached its ultimate height; it will no longer produce a new leader to grow any taller. If a compact, uniform specimen is wanted or to restrict size in general, pinch one-third to one-half of each candle when it expands in the spring. Do not prune back into woody stems or inactive areas where there are no needles, as new growth will not develop from these areas.

Lammas growth on *Pinus thunbergii*; the white bud in the centre is dormant and the lateral buds have grown a short length around the central bud.

A young *Pinus pinea* with a dense crown ready for crown lifting.

After crown lifting, an entire whorl of lower branches removed back to the trunk.

A mature *Pinus nigra* showing the flat-top stage that signals ultimate height.

A mature *Pinus pinea* showing the definite upper crown, formed where space and light is available all around.

A young *Pinus wallichiana* evenly branched to the ground.

A mature *Pinus wallichiana* with random branching.

Some pines—mostly the larger and more vigorous growers, including *Pinus nigra* (Austrian pine), *P. pinea* (stone pine), and *P. sylvestris* (Scots pine)—have two distinct phases of growth, but the transition from one to the other is very gradual. The first is an extension in height within the limits set by the environment and exposure generally. It is during this period, which lasts until the ultimate height for the tree is reached, that the preservation of the leading shoot is important. In the second phase many or all of the lower branches die, partly through lack of light and also because the vigour is taken into the upper system. Often in the higher canopy, a definite crown forms as a number of the branches thicken, as a result of which the smaller ones usually die out completely. The extent to which the thickening occurs and the crown develops varies, even within a species, but a crowded specimen is less likely to form an extensive head. The amount of all-round light is the most important deciding factor. This may appear confusing, for there is no definite advice to give on the different species that develop this habit, but the general rule is to keep the specimen growing healthily and to cut any dying branches back hard to the trunk. The thickening and extension into main branches will soon become evident when it occurs.

Pinus wallichiana (Bhutan pine) retains and builds on the lower branch system if it is in an open situation receiving sufficient light. These branches often spread horizontally with pendulous tips and will even lie on the ground. Like many of the other larger pines, once the tree reaches maturity, the form of the tree changes from the juvenile stage. With all the five-needled pines, care needs to be taken during periods of extreme drought, as the topmost branches and the leader die back, which spoils the general shape of the tree, often generating multiple leaders.

Pinus bungeana (lacebark pine) grows very slowly to 15 to 20 metres (50 to 65 ft.), its attractive bark shown to full effect on its many upright trunks.

The upright, multi-trunked habit of *Pinus bungeana*.

PIPTANTHUS

Habit Short-lived evergreen (occasionally semi-evergreen) shrub for a sheltered position in full sun and free-draining soil, including chalk. **Attributes** Bright green foliage and stems, yellow pea-like flowers in late spring/ early summer. **Reasons for pruning** To encourage flowering growth and to renovate. **Pruning time** Spring.

Piptanthus nepalensis (evergreen laburnum) produces strong growths from the base, a habit that in time results in overcrowding, which, along with the damage caused by harsh winters, can spoil its effect. It is often grown as a freestanding shrub in a sheltered border, or it can be trained against a wall, which will protect it from cold winds. In spring, once the danger of severe frosts is past, prune out the old wood and tired growths completely, down to ground level, leaving sufficient mature shoots for furnishing. Any laterals on the main upright, healthy branches should be tip-pruned only if they have been injured.

PISTACIA

Habit Deciduous shrubs or small trees with a broad, round, symmetrical, open crown for well-drained soil in partial shade to full sun. **Attributes** Pinnate leaves, clusters of cream flowers on the ends of branches followed by small peppercorn-sized fruits, wonderful crimson autumn colour. **Reasons for pruning** To develop a strong framework. **Pruning time** Midsummer.

Pistacia chinensis (Chinese pistache) is the most common and reliable species for growing as a freestanding tree. The main stem should, if possible, be trained up to form a trunk 1.5 to 2 metres (5 to 6 ft.) in height before the branch system is formed. Maintain the leader until a vase-shaped, open crown is formed. In the early years, clusters of branches will develop at a point below the terminal bud; these should be encouraged to begin the start of the lower crown. As the leader continues to develop, so too will the lateral branches. Younger specimens take on an unshapely, asymmetrical appearance and generate a considerable amount of dead wood, due to the twiggy nature of growth; prune out dead wood in midsummer. As epicormic shoots develop, they can be left and encouraged to balance up the loss of smaller branches in the crown.

Pistacia terebinthus (turpentine tree) grows more slowly, to an eventual height of 5 to 10 metres (16 to 33 ft.). It needs the protection of a sunny wall to be successful. It should be trained up with a central leader and is capable of growing as a freestanding small tree or large shrub. The laterals are pendulous and can begin to take on an untidy look as it matures.

A young *Pistacia chinensis* showing twiggy growth.

PITTOSPORUM

Habit Bushy, upright evergreen shrubs or small trees for free-draining soil in full sun to partial shade. **Attributes** Small leathery leaves with crinkled edges, fragrant flowers in late spring. **Reasons for pruning** To restrict size. **Pruning time** Spring.

Normally, even the hardiest species require the protection of a sunny wall or a very sheltered position. They are not trained hard against the surface of the wall but are grown as freestanding bushes 0.6 to 1 metre (2 to 3 ft.) from the base. Growth habit varies not only with the species but also with the microclimate. A well-drained, open, sunny position tends to produce a more compact habit with well-ripened growth, and such plants have a better chance of overwintering successfully.

Those species, such as *Pittosporum ralphii* (Ralph's desert willow), that produce a bush with a spreading habit may be pruned in the spring, in order to develop a more compact bush. The cuts when pruning all pittosporums should be made to a suitable growing point inside the bush in order to maintain a more natural, informal surface. Pittosporums regenerate freely from the old wood and will respond to hard pruning in the spring; however, a severe winter will usually kill the more tender species outright.

Pittosporum patulum has ascending branches and is more upright in growth. The tender *P. tenuifolium* (New Zealand pittosporum) reaches the proportions of a small tree and should be left to form a single trunk. It will branch very quickly from the trunk and on growths that

are sent up from ground level, which is why it is used for hedging in mild climates. The slow-growing 'Tom Thumb', a popular selection with reddish purple foliage, naturally makes a dense dome.

Pittosporum tenuifolium 'Tom Thumb' showing its dense, domed habit.

PLATANUS

Habit Large deciduous shade trees with a broad, round crown for free-draining soil and full sun. **Attributes** Majestic specimen trees, large leaves and trunk, flaking bark when young, fissured bark when mature, globular fruits, very tolerant of urban pollution and stress. **Reasons for pruning** To develop a strong framework. **Pruning time** Autumn through winter (when dormant).

Personal protection The young leaves produce fine, stiff hairs until early summer. These hairs can cause breathing difficulties when disturbed and inhaled by the pruner.

The planes are strong-growing trees that respond well to good, early training and make shapely, stately specimen shade trees, even in urban situations. *Platanus ×hispanica* (London plane) is shapely even when young and retains a leader readily; however, rival leaders often develop and must be dealt with as soon as they are seen. Keep the trunk clear to 2 to 2.5 metres (6 to 8 ft.) in the nursery; when planted, as the crown extends, the trunk can be lifted and cleaned up higher to allow pedestrian and vehicular access under the canopy and show off the flaking bark of the trunk and main scaffolds. At maturity, the lower branches can be 6 metres (20 ft.) or more in length; their ends are pendulous, producing a pleasing effect and eventually reaching the ground; a low skirt should be encouraged.

Platanus orientalis (oriental plane) develops a more rounded crown with heavier branches and a shorter trunk. It is a strong tree, but the older wood on specimens beyond their prime produces cavities, which have the potential to fail; thinning and end weight removal is recommended to prevent this from occurring.

Platanus occidentalis (American sycamore) does not grow well in the United Kingdom, as the young growths suffer severe damage from late spring frosts; at home in the United States, however, it makes an impressive tree to 40 metres (130 ft.) high with a rounded crown.

Canker stain of plane (*Ceratocystis fimbriata* f. *platani*), a disease affecting all *Platanus* species in Europe, is not yet present in the United Kingdom. It is associated with bark and pruning wounds. Prevent its spread by reducing pruning operations altogether and sterilizing all tools and equipment between any necessary pruning operation.

A mature *Platanus ×hispanica* with a low pendulous skirt.

PLATYCARYA

Habit Small to medium-sized deciduous decurrent tree, slender with a rounded crown, for most free-draining soils in partial shade to full sun. **Attributes** Shiny pinnate leaves (often retained into a mild winter), small green cone-like fruits, drying to a dark brown. **Reasons for pruning** To develop a strong framework and remove dead wood. **Pruning time** Summer when actively growing to avoid bleeding.

Platycarya strobilacea needs shelter and protection in the early years: if its branch tips are damaged by late frosts, a young tree becomes unruly and difficult to train. Once established, though, and a strong crown formed, it is a tough, robust tree, particularly if the right provenance has been chosen: trees from South Korea are naturally hardier and stronger growing than those from Taiwan. If trained well, it retains its leader until a clean trunk of 1.5 to 2 metres (5 to 6 ft.) can be formed; the slender branches are naturally well spaced around the leading shoot, while the upper crown is fairly dense. Occasionally there may be a need to remove dead wood, depending on the provenance and the harshness of the winter.

Platycarya strobilacea showing slender branching.

PLATYCLADUS

Habit Slow-growing, random-branched columnar evergreen shrub or small tree for free-draining soil. **Attributes** Flattened sprays of cypress-like foliage. **Reasons for pruning** No pruning required. **Pruning time** Summer.

Platycladus orientalis (Chinese arborvitae) has a strong leader and erect, open branching when young. No attempt should be made to retain this leader, as the trunk naturally wants to divide near ground level. When mature it and its popular selections 'Aurea Nana' and 'Elegantissima' form conical domes, retaining a skirt of foliage right down to the ground, making ideal individual specimens.

PODOCARPUS

Habit Low-growing to upright evergreen conifers for well-drained soil in full sun to partial shade. **Attributes** Needle-like foliage, attractive fruits. **Reasons for pruning** To restrict size. **Pruning time** Summer or autumn.

Many *Podocarpus* species can be grown successfully only in a mild climate. As with so many conifers, the general rule of thumb applies: don't prune unless you must keep them under control beside a path or in a border. *Podocarpus salignus* (willow-leaved podocarp) forms a very attractive large shrub or tree with lush, long-needled foliage and sometimes breaks freely from the ground. The lower-growing species (e.g., *P. lawrencei*, *P. nivalis*) require no special training and need only space and light for development; should they need containing within a set space, they are best pruned with hedging shears, and it doesn't really matter when in the year this takes place. If pruning is carried out in summer, a flush of secondary growth bearing the same colours as on the spring new growth is encouraged. If pruning is done in autumn, a better flush of new growth in the spring can be expected, but there will be a loss of the attractive fruits.

POLIOTHYRSIS

Habit Small, slender, upright deciduous decurrent tree for free-draining soil and full sun. **Attributes** Shiny green leaves on red petioles, fragrant creamy yellow flowers in late summer. **Reasons for pruning** To develop a strong framework. **Pruning time** Between autumn and spring (when dormant).

The unusual *Poliothyrsis sinensis* (Chinese pearl-bloom tree) is well worth a place in any garden. It needs full sun to ripen the wood to produce a good show of flowers, which open when almost every other tree has finished blooming. It is best to plant a feathered tree, trained with a single leader for as long as possible, to gain height in its early years. The trunk can then be cleaned up to a height of 1.2 to 2 metres (4 to 6 ft.). Once the lower branches are established, it will naturally, quickly lose its leader and develop a wide, rounded, bushy crown. The flowers that make this tree so special are produced terminally on the short twiggy growths of the current season. Once the tree is established and a crown is formed, no regular pruning is necessary.

A young feathered
Poliothyrsis sinensis.

POLYLEPIS

Polylepis australis grown as a short standard.

Habit Small deciduous (occasionally semi-evergreen) tree for a sheltered position in rich, free-draining soil and full sun. **Attributes** Exfoliating cinnamon-coloured bark, grey pinnate foliage, yellow autumn colour. **Reasons for pruning** To develop a strong framework and remove dead wood. **Pruning time** Autumn through winter (when dormant).

Most gardeners don't plant *Polylepis australis* (queñoa), thinking that it is very tender, but it is tougher than you think, especially when trained against a sunny wall and grown as a multi-stemmed shrub. After planting the stems or branches should be evenly spaced and fan-trained against the wall, removing some of the lower laterals to better showcase the amazing bark, which rivals that of *Acer griseum* (paperbark maple). It also makes a perfect, freestanding, small standard tree when trained with a single trunk; begin the crown once the trunk has attained the desired height. It requires very little pruning, apart from the occasional thinning of the crown and the removal of dead wood.

PONCIRUS

Habit Very dense, spiny deciduous tree or large shrub for fertile, well-drained soil in full sun. **Attributes** Architectural plant, fragrant white flowers in late spring followed by round orange-like fruits on green stems. **Reasons for pruning** To develop a strong framework and remove dead wood. **Pruning time** Spring.

Personal protection Wear good thorn-proof clothing and gloves, as this is among the fiercest garden plants, armed with viciously long, stout thorns. Use long-handled loppers to remove growths in the centre of the shrub.

The large flowers of *Poncirus trifoliata* (Japanese bitter orange) are indeed incredibly fragrant of orange blossom. They are produced on growths produced the previous year, so care must be taken when pruning not to remove the flowering wood. The shrub forms a very thick, fierce-looking bush when it is growing freely, and in the early stages strong shoots are thrown up from near the base. A bushy habit should be encouraged in the early years by at least one pruning to prevent a leggy plant. As the bush matures it will thicken up considerably with lots of crossing branches, and no attempt should be made to thin this or cut out the offending branches, as this dense growth is one of its attractions. The lower outer growths will bend down and almost reach the ground; these should be left to furnish the lower part of the plant.

This plant is a true sun lover and will not tolerate shade. Any branches that are shaded out will inevitably dieback, especially in a severe winter; cut out any dead wood each spring, as this will spoil the overall effect of the shrub if left. It is sometimes grown as a formal or informal hedge and will certainly stop the access of any animal or person better than any mesh fence or barbed wire. With close clipping carried out in early summer, a very dense surface is produced. Often growths are produced later in the season, particularly on the sunny side, and a second light pruning may be necessary.

Poncirus trifoliata and the framework of congested twigs.

POPULUS

Habit Large, fast-growing deciduous shade trees with broad-spreading crowns for moist, fertile soil and full sun. **Attributes** Stately trees, with interesting, occasionally colourful and scented foliage and cotton-like seedheads. **Reasons for pruning** To develop a strong framework. **Pruning time** Late summer through late autumn.

Many poplars, both species and hybrids, develop quickly into large shade trees and respond well to training, rapidly forming a strong leader and trunk. For ornamental purposes they are often grown with a clear length of trunk, but the branches should not be pruned back for a greater height than 6 to 9 metres (20 to 30 ft.) unless it becomes absolutely necessary due to dieback of this lower skirt. Epicormic growths develop freely even on mature trunks once they have been crown lifted; remove these annually to prevent their developing into new branches. If left too long, removing them becomes a major operation and creates wounds on the trunk, as they are quick to develop in size. This and any other pruning should be carried out in late summer through to late autumn and completed by mid-winter at the latest, as poplars are prone to bleeding from new pruning cuts. The wood of poplars is soft but tough and does not saw easily unless a Silky or other good, sharp pruning saw is used.

Poplars generally have strong branch attachment, holding their branches remarkably well, and are seldom damaged by winter storms due to the flexible nature of the wood. They do suffer minor twig damage, but this doesn't seem to be a problem and the tree will quickly heal small, natural wounds. Although many poplars do respond to hard pruning by producing lots of regrowth from the cut ends, the new framework that develops from the sucker growth is weakly attached to the ends and can fall apart, especially following strong winds and snow. Due to the soft nature of the wood, large wounds do not occlude well and often decay sets in before wounds heal, producing weaknesses in the crown.

Most poplars produce their main root system close to the surface, and as they thicken, they may be on or above the ground. This often leads to difficulty when mowing grass and the only remedy is to raise the soil level slightly to cover the surface roots or mulch around the tree out to the dripline. With really large trees a mound often builds up around the base of the trunk as the buttress roots thicken and push the surface soil up.

Among the most serious diseases is poplar canker (*Xanthomonas populi*), which causes large branches or scaffolds to be killed or weakened. These are a hazard in high winds, and branches with cankers should be pruned out to reduce the risk of failure.

Poplars are grouped into four sections botanically, and it is convenient to deal with the pruning requirements accordingly.

WHITE POPLARS AND QUAKING ASPENS

All the species in this section (e.g., *Populus ×canescens, P. grandidentata, P. tomentosa*) are medium-sized trees to 20 metres (65 ft.) high with a multi-branched, broad-rounded crown, often

Populus tremuloides showing the white trunks generated from suckers.

Populus lasiocarpa showing an ascending tiered framework.

with the lower scaffolds starting low down on the trunk. A central leader should be encouraged for as long as possible before allowing the natural form of the tree to develop. All are more effective when the foliage moves in a light breeze (hence, quaking aspens), and the crown should be left feathered as low down as possible. They will all sucker freely and form large clumps, so the suckers must be regularly removed unless a clump effect is desired—for example, *P. alba*, *P. tremuloides*, and *P. tremula*, whose white trunks have distinctive lenticel markings, are best shown when grown as a group.

LARGE-LEAVED POPLARS

One of the most ornamental of the poplars in this section is *Populus lasiocarpa* (Chinese necklace poplar). It forms a pyramidal-headed tree to 20 metres (65 ft.) high and has a stiff branching habit, with the individual branches either ascending or horizontal. A tiered effect is often produced by the strong development of the terminal bud and those immediately below it. Both *P. lasiocarpa* and *P. wilsonii* should be trained on a clean trunk 1.2 to 1.5 metres (4 to 5 ft.) high and neither respond to hard pruning. *Populus wilsonii* is particularly susceptible to canker.

BALSAM POPLARS

Both *Populus balsamifera* and *P. ×jackii* sucker freely, which can be obtrusive when these trees are grown as specimens, so regular de-suckering may be a requirement. Love it or hate it, *P. ×jackii* 'Aurora' is a good foliage plant and produces an attractive cream-mottled leaf when coppiced or pollarded on a regular rotation. *Populus trichocarpa* and *P. ×generosa* are strong, large growers. Maintain a leader for as long as possible; very little pruning apart from removing suckers is needed.

BLACK POPLARS

All the taxa in this section (e.g., *Populus ×berolinensis*, *P. deltoides*) are strong growers and can make trees to over 30 metres (100 ft.) high with broad-spreading crowns and dark, almost black trunks, often with large burrs. Retain a leader, as failure to do so will result in very heavy and unnatural branching. The ability to retain a leader varies considerably with the species and variety: *P. ×canadensis* 'Eugenei', for example, forms a long straight trunk quite easily with light lateral branching and a columnar crown, whereas *P. ×canadensis* 'Marilandica' will often produce very heavy

This young, well-developed *Populus nigra* 'Italica' will need no pruning.

branching and a wide-round head. Familiarise yourself with the various branching habits of these trees before attempting to carry out formative pruning.

Populus nigra 'Italica' (Lombardy poplar) is a very popular fastigiate form. It is extremely well behaved, requiring very little pruning, and is most effective with the branches left down to the ground. Any pruning should be carried out during summer, when the healing of wounds is rapid, to prevent infection from poplar dieback (*Discosporium populeum*), which is often found around pruning wounds of Lombardy poplars.

PRINSEPIA

Habit Spiny, rounded, arching deciduous shrubs for fertile, free-draining soil and full sun. **Attributes** White or yellow flowers in late winter. **Reasons for pruning** Very little needed apart from removing dead wood. **Pruning time** Summer.

Personal protection Wear good thorn-proof clothing and gloves when going anywhere near these shrubs.

Prinsepia sinensis (cherry prinsepia) forms a lax, dense, thorny, disorderly bush with a large number of young growths originating from the older wood, particularly from the more upright portions of branches, which as a result become weighed down to and below horizontal. Its natural habit can be ruined by restrictive pruning or overzealous thinning, so give this and all prinsepias plenty of space for free and full development. *Prinsepia uniflora* is an even more disorderly spreading shrub reaching up to 2 metres (6 ft.) high. *Prinsepia utilis* is a more rampant grower to 3 metres (10 ft.) high with a graceful arching habit and needs some wall protection from cold winters; however, it should be grown as a bush and no attempt to wall train should be made.

PRUMNOPITYS

Habit Slow-growing evergreen conifer with a broad, spreading pyramidal crown for any moist, free-draining soil in partial shade to full sun with some shelter. **Attributes** Rarity value, yew-like foliage and fruits. **Reasons for pruning** No pruning required except when grown as a hedge. **Pruning time** Late spring or early summer.

Typically *Prumnopitys andina* (plum-fruited yew) forms a very low but broad-spreading crown and produces a very short trunk before splitting into a number of upright stems, but often these will break directly from ground level. The branches then grow out of these horizontally, but the lowest ones will sweep to the ground, which adds greatly to the attraction of this beautiful tree. It will tolerate light pruning and can be grown to make a low formal hedge, about 1 metre (3 ft.) high. Space plants 30 cm (12 in.) apart and encourage low branching near the base by hard pruning. The young growths, especially on the very top surface, are susceptible to frost damage; to avoid this, no pruning should be carried out later than midsummer, which allows sufficient time for subsequent growths to harden. It may be necessary to clip this type of hedge twice during one season, in late spring and early summer.

PRUNUS

Habit Deciduous and evergreen trees and shrubs for deep, fertile, well-drained soils in full sun to partial shade. **Attributes** White or pink flowers, edible or ornamental fruits, shiny bark in some. **Reasons for pruning** To develop a strong framework. **Pruning time** Summer.

Very few *Prunus* species need annual pruning; the majority seldom need attention after nursery training, apart from the removal of dead or diseased wood. It is difficult to overstress the importance of good-quality propagation techniques and good formative pruning, especially in the early years, as a bad start through the choice of incompatible stock cannot be corrected by culture and pruning in later years. It is very important to buy grafted cherries from a reputable nursery or garden centre. Look for clean, low graft unions rather than those trees grafted high up the rootstock, as these will be likely to bulge up the trunk. Do not attempt to plant the tree over the nursery mark on the trunk to hide unsightly grafts as this will lead to a rapid decline in the tree's vigour and induce rot around the base of the trunk.

Even an occasional pruning when needed can be harmful to the plant. Fungal diseases like silver leaf (*Chondrostereum purpureum*) and bacterial canker of cherry (*Pseudomonas syringae* pv. *morsprunorum*) can both enter into the tree through pruning cuts, especially during winter when trees are dormant, so the best time to be pruning large branches is during summer, preferably before midsummer. When pruning back infected branches, cut well beyond the brown staining that can be seen in the exposed wood. Don't just prune off the silvered parts, as they are merely the symptom, and the fungus is present in the wood below.

Blossom wilt of flowering cherries (*Monilinia laxa*) is usually associated with fruits, but can pass into the spurs and supporting wood. Dead branches, twigs, or spurs should be pruned out during the summer months, when they are easily seen among the foliage, and not left until winter or the following spring, when the infection can spread into the healthy buds.

Prunus is subdivided into various subgenera based on well-known groups; the five sections that follow describe their different pruning techniques. To reduce the need for pruning trees to a definitive size and shape, select the right species or cultivar most carefully before planting. The genus boasts a huge variety of size, shape, form, and attributes. With the ideal selection, trees can be left to develop naturally with unrestricted growth.

PLUMS AND APRICOTS

The habits of the many species in this section vary, but all have wood that is very hard and

Fan-trained *Prunus persica* 'Duke of York'.

difficult to cut, even with a sharp pair of by-pass secateurs. Have some knowledge of their natural growth before planting: some become tree-like on a single trunk (e.g., *Prunus domestica*), and others form thickets (e.g., *P. spinosa*). Even though *P. domestica* (garden plum) makes a large tree, to 6 metres (20 ft.) high, it can also be fan-trained against a sunny wall.

The spiny *Prunus spinosa* (blackthorn) is usually found in thickets or in hedgerows. It spreads rapidly by means of suckers, eventually clumping and colonizing extensive areas. It can be grown on a single stem and providing any suckers are removed annually or as they grow, it will make a small, slow-growing tree to 5 metres (16 ft.) high. The thorn-like spurs that are produced along its branches are very sharp and dirty, and when they pierce or scratch the skin, the wounds can quickly go septic. Wear thorn-proof gloves when pruning this plant.

Prunus cerasifera (cherry plum) and *P. cerasifera* 'Pissardii' (purple cherry plum) form small trees to 10 metres (33 ft.) high with a dense, of-ten cluttered crown: they tend to throw strong vertical branches directly up through the crown's centre. This is the natural habit, and it is difficult to maintain a neat and tidy crown, so leave them. If you pruned these out back to the parent branch, the resultant proliferation of growths would require an annual thin.

Prunus armeniaca (apricot) will make a tree to 12 metres (40 ft.) high with a rounded crown but needs to be fan-trained on a short leg against a sunny wall to ripen the fruit. Formative pruning should be done in spring as the buds break, but once the apricot is established, pruning should change to summer. Never prune in winter.

Prunus mume (Japanese apricot) and its cultivars are often grown as small or half-standard trees to 3 metres (10 ft.) high and need shelter. They are usually grafted onto *P. cerasifera* so keep an eye out for any suckers growing from the root-stock and remove them as soon as they appear.

ALMONDS AND PEACHES

Prunus dulcis (common almond) and several of the cultivars make shapely trees with upright branching; *P. persica* (peach) and its flowering cultivars are usually sold as half-standards. Most peaches and almonds are grafted onto a suitable rootstock to help control tree size, to increase disease resistance, and to produce fruit within three years after planting. Trees that are grown on their own roots often die back by whole branches at a time, especially on heavy soils or after a very wet winter; the shape of the overall tree is spoiled and regenerating growths tend to grow from the main trunk, which are out of character with a strong, upright tree. It is better to replace such trees with new stock. With peaches some of the oldest, twiggy branches can be cut back to suitable growths after flowering, letting light and air into the centre of the tree to improve flowering display the following spring. Peaches can also be fan-trained against a sunny wall or inside a cool glasshouse.

Prunus triloba 'Multiplex' fan-trained against a sunny wall.

Tying stems of *Prunus persica* 'Duke of York' to wires on a glasshouse wall.

Prunus triloba 'Multiplex' makes a shrub or small tree to 3.5 metres (12 ft.) and can be planted as a half-standard or grown as a bush with multi-branching from the base. Its branches are relatively thin and whippy, allowing it to be easily fan-trained against a sunny wall. Spread the branches out evenly and train them fanwise to cover the space provided, tying them onto horizontal wires on the wall; in the early stages of formative pruning, the light branches can also be attached to bamboo canes fixed at 45° to the wires. Any branches that grow out at right angles from the established framework can be used as replacements in the framework or cut back hard to one or two buds immediately after flowering. Growths that are not required in the framework can also be cut back hard to one or two buds. Branches shouldn't overlap as this will restrict light and affect flowering. This tree flowers on the previous season's wood, and a good annual display will be given provided that growth and vigour are maintained.

Prunus tenella (dwarf Russian almond), a low shrub to 1.5 metres (5 ft.) high, does not require any pruning.

Most peaches and almonds are very susceptible to peach leaf curl (*Taphrina deformans*), a fungal disease that seriously damages the leaves and impairs growth, especially in a bad spring. This can be controlled by removing and burning fallen leaves or using copper fungicides between autumn and early spring.

CHERRIES

The species and cultivars in this section also display great variation in growth and size. This is clearly seen even among the Japanese flowering cherries (Sato Zakura Group), most of which are forms or hybrids derived from *Prunus speciosa* and *P. jamasakura*. One of the beauties of these trees is their spread, which is shown to full effect with *P. serrulata* or *P.* 'Taihaku'. These can look untidy with low pendent branches reaching the ground as the tree matures, but do not be tempted to alter this natural shape.

As a contrast to these varieties, the well-known *Prunus* 'Kanzan' and *P.* 'Asano' have ascending branches that form a vase-shaped crown, while *P.* 'Amanogawa' has an erect, almost fastigiate form. The latter has a weak, loose habit when young; some of the lax upright growths have a slight twist in them and may need tying in to encourage a tighter upright habit. A neater appearance can also be maintained by pruning off any offending growths that grow out of the overall canopy outline back to the parent branch in summer. The overall height of 'Amanogawa' will depend on the length of the trunk and the height at which the crown is formed.

All flowering cherry cultivars are grafted onto a stronger-growing cherry to aid their vigour. This is usually *Prunus avium* (wild cherry), and occasionally this rootstock will produce suckers from below the graft union. If left, they will grow stronger and faster than the scion and eventually take over, so remove them at once.

With the species, it is a matter of allowing free growth after formative pruning. The main objective is to get young trees off the starting blocks quickly without checking and to encourage healthy growth immediately after planting, as if good healthy growth is produced, most cherries will flower well.

Cherries are normally trained as decurrent trees with an open-headed crown, but with *Prunus avium* and other large tree-like species, they can be trained as a standard tree with a central leader running up to 10 metres (33 ft.) high with a clean trunk. Well-spaced horizontal lateral branching develops at first; however, the symmetrical look is lost as the tree

Prunus serrulata showing low, wide-spreading branching.

Prunus 'Asano' showing ascending branching and vase-shaped crown.

The columnar *Prunus* 'Amanogawa'.

Prunus avium 'Vega' fan-trained against a sunny wall.

matures, especially in an open situation, and the branching becomes wider spreading. Pruning can be carried out during summer, but as always with this genus, minimal pruning is advised. For fruit production in a small garden where space is precious, fruiting cherries can be fan-trained against a sunny wall or fence.

Prunus sargentii is a hard-working cherry with several horticultural attributes: single pink flowers, copper-coloured young foliage, orange-red autumn colour, and lenticelled bark. It can be grown as a standard with a vase-shaped rounded crown on a clean trunk to 1.5 to 2 metres (5 to 6 ft.) high or multi-stemmed, on a short, 30 cm (12 in.) leg. Allowing for this short leg yields a tree with stronger attachment points than from ground level. To make a wider-stemmed specimen, children's footballs can be gradually forced into the crotches to push the branching out.

Although it can be grown as a multi-stemmed tree, *Prunus serrula* (Tibetan

A mature *Prunus avium* has low branching and has lost its symmetry.

cherry) is best trained as a standard, with the lower part of the branches and trunk kept clean and free of suckers to reveal the beautiful shiny, mahogany-like bark. The feathers and any unwanted branchlets should be removed as soon as possible during training and as they arise after planting, preferably in midsummer, so that the pruning wounds are kept small and heal quickly, preventing scarring of the bark.

Prunus incisa (Fuji cherry) is almost alone among the cherries in that it does not produce gum in the region of wounds and thus

Prunus incisa 'Kojo-no-mai' making a small shrub.

Prunus sargentii grown as a multi-stemmed tree on a short leg.

Prunus sargentii grown as a standard with a perfectly balanced crown.

reacts better to pruning. This allows it to be wall-trained. Its selections 'Kojo-no-mai' and 'Mikinori' make small, slow-growing shrubs to 1 metre (3 ft.) high, with twisted, wiry stems; they need no pruning, apart from an occasional tipping back after their early-spring flowering to restrict overall size.

BIRD CHERRIES

Train *Prunus padus* (bird cherry) and *P. serotina* (rum cherry) as standards with a central leader, allowing the leader to develop through the main part of the tree until the desired overall height is reached. As the trunk develops, it should be cleaned up to 2 to 2.5 metres (6 to 8 ft.); in this way, a fairly large tree, about 18 metres (60 ft.), is attained. If rival leaders are developed too early, the branch systems produced will have very narrow angles and will be weak later in life. One habit of mature specimens of *P. padus* is that strong branches are thrown up through the centre of the tree from horizontal branches. Do not thin these: it will check the tree and eventually kill it.

Prunus maackii (Manchurian cherry), particularly as represented by its selection 'Amber Beauty', has a beautifully coloured golden brown bark and stem. Remove the feathers and twiggy growths from the main trunk and branches with secateurs before they become too large, their removal leaving unsightly pruning wounds in the bark.

EVERGREEN CHERRY LAURELS

The perfect screen plant, *Prunus laurocerasus* (cherry laurel) makes a large shrub or medium-sized tree to 6 metres (20 ft.) high and at least twice as wide when left to grow naturally. When grown as a screen, any attempt to restrict the size should be carried out with the aim of retaining an informal effect. Do this with secateurs, pruning back branches to a strong bud or shoot inside the bush so that any pruning

Prunus lusitanica 'Myrtifolia' trained into a cone.

Removing unwanted feathers on the trunk of *Prunus serrula* with secateurs.

Prunus serrula with a clean trunk, suckers removed and bark preserved.

A branch of cherry laurel needing to be shortened back to restrict size.

Position of pruning cut to a strong side shoot.

The branch end after the removal of material showing final pruning cut.

cuts are hidden by the vegetation. Cherry laurel regenerates and grows very strongly and, if cut back hard and coppiced periodically, will make a good cover shrub. Carry out this form of hard pruning in spring to early summer to avoid infection from cytospora dieback of cherry laurel (*Cytospora laurocerasi*), a disfiguring disease that can sometimes kill outright. Trimming hedges by clipping one-year-old shoots with hedging shears or secateurs will reduce the chance of infection.

Prunus lusitanica (Portuguese laurel) is similar in many respects and is at its best when left to grow freely, when it will develop into a small tree. It does respond to pruning and formal clipping, though. In particular its selection 'Myrtifolia', which has smaller leaves, is an ideal candidate for fine topiary.

PSEUDOLARIX

Habit Deciduous, larch-like excurrent conifer for free-draining soil and full sun. **Attributes** Rarity value, foliage turns gold in autumn before fall. **Reasons for pruning** To develop a strong framework. **Pruning time** Autumn through winter (when dormant).

The beautiful *Pseudolarix amabilis* (golden larch) will respond to training provided the growing conditions and environment are suitable. Encourage a good central leader. The strong horizontal branch system that develops naturally from the main trunk should be allowed a full spread in open surroundings. In this way the beauty of this deciduous conifer can be fully appreciated, as the lower branches, perhaps laden with cones, sweep down almost to ground level. Often after planting, a young tree is checked and remains stunted for a few years, losing vigour in its central leader. A careful watch should be kept for any rival leaders, which usually spring from below the weaker, main leader at this stage; should one be spotted, remove the weaker to retain an excurrent form for as long as possible.

A pair of *Pseudolarix amabilis* grown as specimen trees with space to develop.

PSEUDOPANAX

Habit Architectural evergreen trees or shrubs for free-draining soil and full sun to partial shade. **Attributes** Very unusual in having two distinct stages of growth, with bronze foliage in the juvenile stage. **Reasons for pruning** No pruning required. **Pruning time** Summer.

Pseudopanax crassifolius (lancewood), *P. ferox* (toothed lancewood), and *P. lessonii* (houmapara) should be attempted only in the mildest climates, and even then will most likely need a sunny wall for protection. *Pseudopanax ferox* grows to a height of 1 to 2 metres (3 to 6 ft.) and is usually a slender plant, completely unbranched. The temptation to prune out the top to encourage branching is ever-present; however, regular pruning is out of the question and should be avoided. If anything is needed, it will be a good stake, as it becomes top-heavy with increased height and prone to falling over.

Mature bushes of *Pseudopanax lessonii* throw strong, young growths from the base and branch system. This can be pruned to restrict the size or spread by carefully pruning to the most promising of these growths.

Pseudopanax ferox showing both juvenile and mature stage.

PSEUDOTSUGA

Habit Fast-growing evergreen conifers with excurrent conical form for all fertile soils and full sun. **Attributes** Stately specimen trees with thick, corky bark, aromatic foliage, and pendulous cones with attractive bracts. **Reasons for pruning** To develop a strong framework. **Pruning time** When needed.

Pseudotsuga menziesii (Douglas fir) is the tallest tree in the British Isles and will reach a good height anywhere conditions are right.

A healthy young tree will develop a leader and produce tiers of branches that should be encouraged to spread to their full extent. Although the general habit of this tree is conical, it is naturally irregular in growth and outline, and no attempt should be made to prune it into shape by cutting back individual branches. If any cutting back is needed, the branch should generally be removed entirely, and the pruning cut be made right back to the main trunk,

apart from the removal of small, dead twiggy growth. This tree is prone to producing twin leaders early in its life; any rival leader should be removed as early as possible to prevent future weakness in the branching structure. Treat *P. macrocarpa* similarly.

PTELEA

Habit Deciduous shrubs or small trees with a broad irregular, spreading canopy and slender trunk for free-draining soil in partial shade to full sun. **Attributes** Scented greenish white flowers in summer followed by winged green fruits. **Reasons for pruning** To develop a strong framework. **Pruning time** Between autumn and spring (when dormant).

Apart from formative pruning, very little further pruning is necessary. *Ptelea trifoliata* (hop tree) has a spreading habit and upright branching in the early years of crown formation, which later may be lost to a more slender branch system. It should be trained on a short leg 0.6 to 1 metre (2 to 3 ft.). Even with this short trunk, the species is prone to leaning fol-

lowing planting, due to its weak root system, and may need some form of support for one or two years after planting. Regeneration is good, and good growth can be expected to break freely from low down to form a new crown following hard pruning to near ground level. Treat all other *Ptelea* species similarly.

PTEROCARYA

Habit Large, fast-growing deciduous trees with wide-spreading crowns for fertile soil and a sheltered position in full sun. **Attributes** Large pinnate leaves, necklaces of green fruits turning brown in autumn. **Reasons for pruning** To develop a strong framework and clean trunk and remove root suckers. **Pruning time** Late summer. Never prune in autumn or early spring as the wounds are prone to bleeding.

Pterocarya fraxinifolia, *P. hupehensis*, *P. macroptera*, *P. rhoifolia*, *P. ×rehderiana*—all these trees are strong growers but should be planted in a sheltered position with full sun as young shoots in particular suffer in a cold winter or late spring frost. Cut damaged growths back to living tissue as the buds break. A sunny position will ensure that the growths are ripened and will overwinter better. Be the boss and

firm with young trees and retain the leader, as young trees, especially *P. stenoptera* (Chinese wingnut), will naturally be multi-branched, branching low, and develop a crown without a leader. All the taxa will produce a feathered effect down to ground level, even with a 1.5 to 2 metre (5 to 6 ft.) trunk; feathers can be removed as they develop, depending on how low or high a crown skirt is wanted.

Pterocarya fraxinifolia with low branching and a broad round crown; the root suckers have been removed out to the dripline.

The hybrid *Pterocarya ×rehderiana* suckers from the roots, as does *P. fraxinifolia* (Caucasian wingnut), one of the parents, and unless a thicket is desired, suckers should be cut down annually. *Pterocarya rhoifolia* (Japanese wingnut) naturally has a narrow crown, but when grown with space to develop, the crown becomes more pyramidal and symmetrical. Grown as a specimen tree with a low skirt on a short trunk, it makes a superb shade tree.

All wingnuts have a shallow root system, with many surface roots; when grown in a lawn, they are best mulched out to the dripline to prevent their causing damage to grass cutting equipment—and vice versa. Epicormic shoots are sometimes produced on the more horizontal branches, but these should be left unless they are very thick. Removing them only results in a heavier crop the following year.

Pterocarya rhoifolia retaining its leader and a low skirt.

A young *Pterocarya macroptera* trained as a standard on a clean trunk.

PTEROSTYRAX

Habit Medium-sized deciduous excurrent trees with a strong central trunk, for deep, rich soil in full sun. **Attributes** Hanging panicles of fragrant white or cream bell-shaped flowers in summer. **Reasons for pruning** To develop a strong framework. **Pruning time** Between autumn and spring (when dormant).

The overall shape and form of *Pterostyrax hispida* (epaulette tree) will be determined by formative pruning in the early years. It is readily trained as a tree on a single stem, but the more common approach is to let it form a large, slower-growing shrub, by allowing the natural development of the few main stems, which grow up from ground level. Where it is to be grown determines which form is best adopted: as a lawn specimen, train as a tree; grown in the border, best to let it grow as a large shrub. Both forms will reach up to 6 metres (20 ft.) in height. The choice is yours.

A healthy specimen will freely produce young growths from the main branches and from ground level; these can be thinned and the strongest trained as replacements or additions to the branch system. No regular pruning of the main framework of branches is needed.

Pterostyrax corymbosa makes more of a spreading tree or large shrub and is more difficult to train as a tree with a single central leader.

PUNICA

Habit Spiny deciduous shrub or small tree for fertile, free-draining soil and full sun. **Attributes** Red trumpet-shaped flowers in late summer, large round edible fruits. **Reasons for pruning** To develop a strong framework and remove dead wood. **Pruning time** Spring and summer.

Personal protection Wear good thorn-proof clothing and gloves when pruning pomegranates.

Punica granatum (pomegranate) will start to produce fruit three or four years after planting. Flowers are produced on spurs on the new shoots, so overpruning will reduce the number of flowers and fruit production. They need a long, hot summer to ripen the fruits or a sunny glasshouse. Outdoors they are best grown trained against a warm, sunny wall or as a freestanding multi-stemmed bush within the shelter of the wall. In the latter case, plants will be low branching and have a considerable spread, up to 2 to 2.5 metres (6 to 8 ft.) from the wall. Following a severe winter plants can be cut back into the old, living wood, which will break freely and after two or three years can be trained back to a strong framework. Routinely prune some of the older and weaker wood during the late spring or summer, when it is easy to distinguish between living and dead wood.

When grown close against a wall, the main branches should be trained fanwise and tied to horizontal wire supports. Shorten growths coming away from the wall as the buds break in spring. The free production of strong growths along the branch systems allows for some replacement of the older wood in the framework.

A young *Punica granatum* trained on an arbor in a wall garden.

PYRACANTHA

Habit Dense, thorny, upright evergreen shrubs for free-draining soil in partial shade to full sun. **Attributes** Shiny foliage, clusters of white flowers in late spring/early summer, yellow, orange, or red berries in autumn. **Reasons for pruning** To develop and train a strong framework. **Pruning time** Spring and summer.

Personal protection Wear good thorn-proof clothing and gloves, as every species of firethorn is armed with long, sharp thorns, from which the genus gets its common name.

The natural habit of the species is to form a system of closely knit branches, and they are very effective when grown naturally as speci-

men shrubs in the informal part of the garden. When grown in these condition they require very little pruning; if any is carried out for any reason, the cuts should be made right back into the centre of the bush so that the wounds are hidden. The stiff, abrupt ends of cut look very unsightly and spoil the effect of free growth and form. Use long-handled loppers for this exercise to preserve your hands and arms, even when wearing thorn-proof gloves and clothing.

All pyracanthas conform well to extensive wall training as flowers and fruit are freely produced from spurs on the old wood. The main

branches can be trained fanwise or espalier style to cover the support. A free form of shrub can be grown with very little pruning at all; the main branches are loosely tied into a wiring system, and if necessary invasive branches are cut back in the spring after flowering to points hidden within the bush.

A closer system of training consists of cutting back all the growths that are not tied in for furnishing or replacement, which is done after flowering. Any branches growing out from the framework that are hiding the berries can be pruned off to reveal the main attribute of the firethorn. Another system of rigid control is

Pyracantha 'Golden Charmer' wall-trained in an espalier style.

to clip over the whole surface annually in the spring or even two or three times during the growing season. Under this system the surface is given a very close covering, but the actual flowering may suffer.

Freestanding plants make an impenetrable hedge. They can be clipped in spring and summer to make a more formal feature; however, this may be at the expense of berries if the previous year's wood is removed, so a light pruning is better to encourage flowers, fruit, and wildlife.

All pyracanthas are susceptible to fireblight (*Erwinia amylovora*), and any brown infected branches should be pruned back beyond the staining in the wood. Hard pruning as a form of renovation often makes them more susceptible to fireblight; replacement with disease-resistant hybrids (e.g., *Pyracantha* 'Teton') may be the better option.

PYRUS

Habit Small to medium-sized upright deciduous trees for any moist, well-drained soil in full sun. **Attributes** Early shiny leaves, some grey (e.g., *Pyrus nivalis*, *P. salicifolia*), very showy white flowers, and fruits, some edible (e.g., *P. communis*, *P. ussuriensis*). **Reasons for pruning** To develop a strong framework and encourage flowering. **Pruning time** Between autumn and spring (when dormant).

Personal protection Wear thorn-proof gloves and clothing. Some pears have seriously sharp spurs along the branches.

Most species are propagated from seed, but all the cultivars are grafted onto seedling stocks, which are normally *Pyrus communis* (common pear), one of the largest of the ornamental pears. Carefully train these in the early years; the best form is a 2.4 to 3 metre (8 to 10 ft.) standard with a central leader. Often they grow so strongly that rival leaders are formed; deal with these quickly to prevent weak unions from forming. Following planting, when the growth is free, it is difficult to avoid crossing branches as the natural growth of many of the species is thick; when the head finally matures, the outer and lower branches have a pendulous habit. *Pyrus ussuriensis* (Chinese pear) is typical of the larger upright growers with a dense crown and pendulous outer branches. As always, some knowledge of the final form is necessary. *Pyrus nivalis* (snow pear), one the best silvery-leaved pears, makes a sturdy upright tree to 12 metres (40 ft.) high. *Pyrus amygdaliformis* (almond-leaved pear) has a rounded, spreading shrub-like habit, making a small tree to 6 metres (20 ft.) high, while *P. salicifolia*

Pyrus salicifolia 'Pendula' with a low furnished skirt.

'Pendula' (weeping-willow-leaved pear) forms a small tree that is distinctly pendulous. For this tree to be appreciated and to get the maximum benefit of the grey foliage, the stem should be grown as tall as possible, preferably to 1.5 metres (5 ft.) high, before being allowed to weep. Over time the canopy gets dense and congested, and the inner crown should be cleaned out of dead wood and thinned to prevent spoiling the overall curtain effect.

Pyrus calleryana (Callery pear) makes a small tree 5 to 8 metres (16 to 26 ft.) high, beginning with a symmetrical conical crown, but with maturity it often develops a low wide-spreading rounded crown, with thorny branches and superb flower and autumn colour. Its selections 'Bradford' and 'Chanticleer' have an upright pyramidal form and are thornless, but 'Bradford' has tight crotches, which sometimes fail. 'Chanticleer', with stronger crotches, is planted more often.

Keep a careful lookout for fireblight (*Erwinia amylovora*), especially after flowering, as many of the species are susceptible. Prune it out, beyond the internal branch staining, with clean secateurs.

Pyrus nivalis showing upright habit.

Pyrus amygdaliformis showing rounded habit.

QUERCUS

Habit Deciduous and evergreen shrubs or trees for deep, fertile, free-draining soil in full sun to partial shade. **Attributes** Variety of shapes and sizes, from small and shrubby to large and stately, many with large shade-providing crowns, a diverse range of acorns and leaves with autumn colour, suitable for specimen, avenue, or woodland plantings with high biodiversity values. **Reasons for pruning** To produce and maintain a strong framework.

This great genus of trees contains over 500 different species that vary enormously in size and shape and, while a few of the hardier species are evergreen or semi-evergreen, the majority are deciduous. On good soils the hardy species grow well and, provided that a good leader and shape is formed in the nursery and the situation is not too exposed, fine trees are quite easily produced. It is more difficult to grow shapely trees in exposed sites, but a few (e.g., *Quercus petraea*, *Q. ilex*) will succeed even in coastal situations. Oaks are generally good and satisfying trees to work on, holding their framework well, even during severe gales, and it is more likely to be the odd small branch that is twisted off than a large one, provided the tree has been well trained. Even dead branches are retained for a long period, as the heartwood does not rot quickly. Most oaks heal well following pruning, but even large wounds made on very old specimens, which may never callus over completely, remain healthy, provided that the surface of the exposed wood is firm and intact.

Many oaks produce epicormic growths, often on an extensive scale, especially if they are stressed. These commonly occur on the branch systems and provided they do not become too large and out of proportion, they can be left. Usually their removal is quickly followed by a more vigorous outcrop. If, however, they occur on the trunk, remove them with a saw, unless the specimen has been cut hard back to the extent that there is little growth left other than in this region.

The oaks are classified botanically in a number of sections, all requiring varying approaches to pruning. The following sections are those most commonly cultivated.

SECTION QUERCUS
Pruning time Between autumn and spring (when dormant).

These are the white oaks, deciduous or evergreen trees or shrubs from North and Central America, North Africa, Europe, and Asia. Most species in this section are strong growers and will develop into large shade trees. *Quercus frainetto* (Hungarian oak), *Q. canariensis* (Algerian oak), *Q. macranthera*, *Q. pyrenaica*, *Q. petraea* (sessile oak), and *Q. robur* (English oak) all form good leaders and with training branch well to form a good height of clean trunk, with a large head that becomes broader with age. *Quercus pubescens* is a smaller tree, but it is usually possible to retain a leader of 4.5 metres (15 ft.) or more through the tree before it is left to open out. *Quercus pontica* (Armenian oak) branches low on a short trunk and is often shrubby. It should therefore be left to form a head even though the leg may be only 0.6 to 1 metre (2 to 3 ft.) in height. *Quercus robur* in particular suffers from dieback on the topmost and outer branches. A tree that is stag-headed in this way does not necessarily show a general decline in health, for much depends upon the causes of this condition. Often the primary cause is a lowering of the water table or soil compaction, and the fact that the living part of

A mature *Quercus robur* showing a wide crown with low scaffolds.

the tree may remain in reasonably good condition is an indication that, with encouragement, the effect can be delayed or even offset for many years. Eventually, of course, rot and decay gain a foothold on the cut ends formed by the removal of the dead wood, but a number of years usually elapse before such trees die completely, and this gives time for new plantings to mature. Impoverishment, physical damage to the root system, and acute oak decline (AOD) may be another cause of dieback.

Quercus robur takes many forms. Those in the Cristata Group, for example, form a small crowded head, and it is usually difficult to retain the leader for long. 'Atropurpurea' is found in several forms, but in one it produces a dwarf, stunted tree whose branches are covered with epicormic growths. These should be left, as it is a characteristic of this variety and an attraction. 'Filicifolia', which tends to produce a branch system in layers, has most beautiful foliage and should be allowed to branch low in an open space for this to be seen to best effect. The columnar forms of *Q. robur* Fastigiata Group (cypress oak) must be allowed to grow freely unpruned; purchased nursery stock usually has been clipped to exaggerate the narrowness of the crown and should be left to grow out naturally. They can be trained with the lower crown starting at ground level or trained on a short trunk as a standard. They will grow to 18 metres (60 ft.) high with a crown up to 6 metres (20 ft.) wide. *Quercus robur* 'Koster' and 'Attention' have a narrower and more compact crown and will reach 20 metres (65 ft.) high. An alternative fastigiate oak is *Q.* ×*rosacea* 'Columna', a hybrid of the two British native oaks, *Q. robur* and *Q. petraea*; it is a densely branched medium-sized tree with branch tips that curl inward to make a perfect symmetrical form.

Quercus bicolor (swamp white oak) is worthy of consideration for planting, for it produces a good leader, and the trunk, if it is kept clear of branches, will display a lovely shaggy bark to full effect. *Quercus montana* (chestnut oak) produces thin, wiry branchlets, and the general effect of the foliage is seen to best advantage if there is full light on at least one side, for the branching to come down to eye level. *Quercus dentata* (Daimio oak) produces an abundance of dead twigs with the slightest cold weather. A hot summer ripens the wood for the winter, but as we rarely see enough summer heat to prepare it, it is usually a stunted, short-lived specimen in the United Kingdom. Good provenance is important when selecting the right stock to plant, and material from South Korea

A young *Quercus robur* recently planted as a standard.

The fastigiate *Quercus robur* 'Koster'.

The fastigiate *Quercus* ×*rosacea* 'Columna'.

grows better than its Japanese cousin. On *Q. dentata* 'Carl Ferris Miller', dieback often occurs on the younger wood during the winter, causing bushy growths on the tips of the branches as a result of regeneration. Both it and the type retain their large leaves through the winter.

SECTION CERRIS

Pruning time Between autumn and spring (when dormant).

The oaks in this section are deciduous or evergreen trees and shrubs from Europe, North Africa, and Asia. Two species that will often

A young standard *Quercus ilex*, which can be retained clipped or allowed to grow out to make a natural crown.

Quercus dentata, stunted and showing lots of dead wood in the crown.

grow into very large shade trees if given the correct space and position are *Quercus castaneifolia* (chestnut-leaved oak) and *Q. cerris* (Turkey oak), the former being the largest broadleaved tree at Kew with a magnificent height of 33 metres (110 ft.) and a spread of 30 metres (100 ft.). Both should be trained with a strong single trunk and single leader maintained for as long as possible. The latter species produces outer and lower branches that are almost pendulous. The result of this is that the inside branches are likely to die off through lack of sufficient light and will then need to be removed, revealing an open centre to show off

the dark, deeply fissured bark. *Quercus castaneifolia* 'Green Spire' has a more columnar habit and is less vigorous than the type.

Quercus variabilis (Chinese cork oak) is slender with light branching, but the main attraction is the corky, diamond-patterned bark of the main trunk. To show this to full effect the trunk should be trained up as straight as possible and kept clear of lower branches up to 3 metres (10 ft.); remove the branches before they get too large, so that no pruning scar is left.

Some of the evergreen species will suffer during a hard winter; however, provided the

growing conditions are suitable, new growth will occur. Prune damaged branches back to the parent branch, strong healthy growths, or a strong bud. *Quercus alnifolia* (golden oak) of Cypress and *Q. coccifera* (kermes oak) are usually dense shrubby trees, and unless the specimen shows a definite tendency to form a leader they should be left to grow freely and bushy.

The one distinctive tree in this section is the hybrid *Quercus ×hispanica* 'Lucombeana' (Lucombe oak), which is semi-deciduous, losing all its leaves in early spring as the new ones are about to break. It should be trained to form a large shade tree. *Quercus cerris* is one of the parents, and the form that this tree takes on is similar in appearance, albeit the branches are very heavy and wide.

Quercus ilex (holm oak) is one of the most important evergreen trees in this section. In earlier days it was much used in formal designs, and very large specimens were often clipped annually in the late summer to maintain a dense, rigid outline. Even as a hedge, the holm oak will maintain a good surface. However, the beauty of this tree is shown to perfection in free growth and heavy branching. Provided there is ample space, the outer growths and branches can be left to grow down to ground level; they look particularly fine

A young *Quercus castaneifolia* retaining a strong, dominant leader.

A magnificent, broad-crowned 250-year-old *Quercus ×hispanica* 'Lucombeana' with scaffolds retained from low down on the trunk.

A mature *Quercus ilex* with the lower skirt raised to the first scaffolds to reveal the trunk and improve access below the canopy.

A young *Quercus suber*, clipped to a cube and trained as a standard on a single trunk in the nursery but since allowed to grow out naturally.

with the light green growths set against the dark foliage. A trunk of 2 to 2.5 metres (6 to 8 ft.) is preferable, but the shade that is cast is very dense, and there should be no attempt to have a border beneath or near a large specimen. It is better to use grass as a foreground, running this up to the base of the tree or, if the growths are already touching the ground, up to the outer perimeter of foliage. It will also take many years for this subject to reach the ground again once the lower branches have been removed, and therefore this should not be done lightly. Where there is insufficient labour to attend to their very necessary annual trimming,

large formally clipped specimens will quickly develop a free, natural growth with very little attention. As free growth develops after two or three years the trunk can, if necessary, be cleared and formed, while at a later stage some of the smaller growths may be thinned out in the centre as the stronger branches become more evident.

Quercus suber (cork oak) can be trained as a standard with a single trunk or as a multistemmed tree to increase the potential to show off the amazing bark; either way, remove any feathers or lateral branches early in their life to prevent scarring the bark on the main trunks and scaffolds. Plant relatively small, container-grown trees to increase the success rate of establishment, as they are not easy trees to move and will often turn their nose up. Many nurseries sell them with a heavily clipped crown, which can be left to grow out over a period of three to four years to form a natural shape; this clipped crown also helps reduce transplant shock and increase the establishment success rate. *Quercus phillyreoides* (Ubame oak) is more often shrub-like, with wide, low branching; it should be left to grow freely and furnished to

A mature *Quercus ×turneri* 'Pseudoturneri' grown as a standard on a vista.

the ground.

There are always exceptions to the rules of taxonomy. *Quercus ×turneri* 'Pseudoturneri' (Turner's oak) is an intersectional hybrid between *Q. robur* in section *Quercus* and *Q. ilex* in section *Cerris*. As a young tree it is columnar but soon grows out to make a wide-spreading tree with a rounded crown. It can either be grown as a standard with a clean trunk or with the lower branches retained to form a low-spreading crown, often with character at maturity.

SECTION LOBATAE

Pruning time Between autumn and spring (when dormant). Never prune during the warm season between spring and late summer.

Here are the red oaks, deciduous and evergreen trees or shrubs from North and Central America. In the United States, the red oaks (particularly *Quercus rubra*, *Q. coccinea*, *Q.*

palustris, and *Q. velutina*) are extremely susceptible to oak wilt (*Ceratocystis fagacearum*), a lethal fungal disease that is potentially as serious as Dutch elm disease. Insects, attracted to fresh injury, transmit the spores of the disease to recently pruned healthy trees during the warm months of late spring and early summer, and within one to two months of coming into contact with the infection, the tree inevitably dies. By not pruning during this period, you will greatly reduce the chance of infection in areas where the disease is present. Should a storm-damaged branch have to be removed during the closed pruning time, use a tree paint or sealer to cover and seal the wound. Although this is now considered bad practice, it is the lesser of two evils.

The oaks in this section vary considerably, *Quercus rubra* (red oak) is one of the strong growers, making a typical shade tree to 30 metres (100 ft.) high with a broad crown. The

leader is retained well into maturity, although the tendency is for the ascending lateral branches to rival this at a later stage—clearly demonstrating the importance of good training in the early years. Other rapid growers in this section include *Q. palustris* (pin oak), which transplants very comfortably, even as a semi-mature specimen, and is readily available in nurseries for that reason. The crown is dense, with pendulous branches often developing on the ends of the main scaffolds on mature specimens. 'Green Pillar' has a more slender, upright habit and is an excellent selection for more confined urban spaces.

Quercus phellos (willow oak) will grow to a large size, often 30 metres (100 ft.) high, with very heavy branching and a wide crown. Develop a strong trunk and keep the leader running up through the head in a young tree.

The well-behaved *Quercus marilandica* (blackjack oak) forms a small tree with a straight, tapered trunk and wide canopy. Retain its even lateral branching, allowing it to form a low skirt, to show off the unusual leaf shape and fall colour.

Quercus georgiana (Georgia oak) is a rare deciduous oak with spreading branches. It generally makes a large shrub, but with some early training a trunk can be formed and a small tree developed.

The evergreen oaks in this section need a good summer to ripen the new wood, in preparation for a hard winter. For example, a mature tree of Quercus agrifolia (coast live oak), which hails from sunny California, will often lose a considerable amount of small growth after a severe winter; an annual check in the spring is advisable. The bark on the trunk often lifts in blocks and large patches, and this too needs attention before cavities form. In the early years, it must be trained to form a leader, from which a trunk will finally develop. The crown will be low and broad, but with some light pruning it will make strong specimen. The healing powers of this species are usually very strong, and it should grace more English gardens.

The related Quercus wislizeni (interior live oak) is also found in California. It produces dense, twiggy growth, and there is often considerable dieback to attend to after a severe winter.

A young *Quercus agrifolia* trained on a short trunk with a low crown beginning to form.

The Mexican oaks, particularly Quercus crassifolia and Q. rysophylla (loquat oak), are increasingly popular trees in collections and hardier than we first imagined. Provided the planting stock is strong and the conditions are suitable (with shelter), they will grow and establish very quickly. Train them with a firm hand, even if it means bringing out the handsaw: it will be necessary to remove competing leaders and clean up the trunk within the first two or three years, or a bushy tree with no height and weak leaders will be produced.

A young *Quercus palustris* with an uneven lower crown.

The same tree with the branch removed and lower crown balanced.

Quercus georgiana before pruning, with several unruly branches.

Using a pruning saw on the same *Quercus georgiana*, to identify the lower permanent scaffold, thin the lower crown, and remove crossing branches.

A very old *Quercus agrifolia* at home in California; root protection to prevent compaction from foot traffic has prolonged its life.

SECTION PROTOBALANUS

Pruning time Late spring as they come into growth.

This section comprises six evergreen species from the U.S. Southwest and northwestern Mexico. *Quercus chrysolepis* (canyon live oak) can reach up to 15 metres (50 ft.) high, but more often than not it will be a shrubby tree with low, wide-spreading branches; at Kew, we leave it to grow naturally. *Quercus vacciniifolia* (huckleberry oak) is a prostrate shrub making a height of 1.2 metres (4 ft.); it needs no pruning but does require well-drained soil and full sun as its natural habitat is rocky hillsides.

SUBGENUS CYCLOBALANOPSIS

Pruning time Late spring as they come into growth.

Here are the ring cup oaks, which are evergreen and restricted to Asia. The slow-growing *Quercus glauca* (Japanese blue oak) forms a dense, roundly symmetrical canopy. Without formative pruning it produces many upright trunks and branches, which generally grow

Quercus vacciniifolia growing above Lake Tahoe in California.

from one point on the trunk, which could lead to a weak tree. Even with formative pruning to develop a strong central leader with well-spaced branches, the tree remains susceptible to breaking apart following severe gales or heavy snow. The remainder of the species in this subgenus (e.g., *Q. morii*, *Q. myrsinifolia*, *Q. sessilifolia*) should be trained in the same way.

REHDERODENDRON

Habit Wide-spreading deciduous shrub or small tree for fertile, free-draining, neutral to acid soil in full sun to partial shade with some shelter. **Attributes** Small white cup-shaped flowers in early summer followed by pod-like red fruits. **Reasons for pruning** To establish a strong framework. **Pruning time** Between autumn and spring (when dormant).

Often with a rarity like *Rehderodendron macrocarpum* we are grateful to be able to grow it successfully to any shape and size and not worry about formative pruning; however, if possible it should be grown with a single leader and the lower, spreading branches retained closely furnished to ground level. Once established, little if any pruning should be needed. This species is best grown in a woodland situation within the shelter of surrounding trees; it is better to prune to restrict the size of neighbouring trees, once more space is needed, than the long lateral branches of the subject.

RHAMNUS

Habit Deciduous or evergreen shrubs or small trees for woodland plantings. **Attributes** Not fussy about their soil needs, red fruits turning to black at maturity. **Reasons for pruning** To restrict size. **Pruning time** Between autumn and spring (when dormant).

There is considerable variation across the genus: *Rhamnus davurica* (Dahurian buckthorn) makes a large deciduous shrub or small tree, while *R. pumila* (dwarf buckthorn) makes a low-growing, almost prostrate shrub suitable for the rock garden or the front of a border. Many of the larger buckthorns will develop into small trees on a single trunk, which should be kept clear of growth as the crown begins to develop. *Rhamnus alaternus*, a freely branching evergreen, should be grown with branching down to ground level; by careful pruning in spring, an informal surface can be maintained. The tender *R. alaternus* 'Argenteovariegata', among the very best variegated garden plants, will need shelter and some protection in cold areas.

RHAPHIOLEPIS

Habit Small, dense, slow- and low-growing rounded evergreen shrubs for moist, free-draining soil in full sun and a sheltered position. **Attributes** Terminal white/pink-tinged fragrant flowers in early summer followed by small black fruits. **Reasons for pruning** To restrict size and shape. **Pruning time** Mid-spring.

Rhaphiolepis umbellata (Yeddo hawthorn), the most commonly grown species, makes an untidy spreading shrub when grown in any amount of shade, sending out long growths at random, which unbalance the plant and send it out of shape. Formative pruning to maintain a rounded, compact shape can be carried out in mid-spring; prune any long growths back to a suitable growing point inside the outer surface of the shrub. Dead branches will suddenly appear for no apparent reason; these can be cut out at the same time. Otherwise no regular pruning is necessary.

Rhaphiolepis ×*delacourii* and *R. indica* need the protection of a warm, sunny wall. They should still be grown as freestanding rounded shrubs about 0.5 metre (1.5 ft.) from the base of the wall rather than being formally wall-trained.

RHODODENDRON

Habit Evergreen and deciduous trees and shrubs for moist, well-drained, acid soil in dappled shade. **Attributes** Some with attractive bark, some with large leaves and/or interesting indumentum, clusters of large, sometimes scented flowers. **Reasons for pruning** To develop a bushy growth habit and encourage flowering. **Pruning time** Immediately after flowering.

Rhododendron is a large genus, with more than 1,000 species and many cultivars. Normally this large group of plants requires very little pruning, the main essential being to maintain healthy growth by the provision of correct growing conditions. Not only is it necessary to provide for their soil and moisture requirements, but some will tolerate quite exposed and sunny positions, while others require shade and shelter. Failure to provide the ideal environment will result in an unhappy and unhealthy plant with dieback that will necessitate pruning. This cutting out of dead branches is usually the start of deterioration, and it is only a matter of time before the poor specimen is cut away completely. The rule should be to follow the use of the secateurs or saw with improved culture.

From time to time it will be necessary to carry out maintenance pruning and to prune out dead branches that have developed inside the bush as a result of a lack of light; this is most likely to occur on crowded or large-leaved specimens (e.g., *Rhododendron rex*, *R. sinogrande*) with a buildup of dense foliage. Wood damaged by storms or a harsh winter should be pruned from the plant. Diseased stems, often identified by their wilted, curled yellow-green leaves, should also be removed, making the pruning cut below the damaged portion of the plant, taking care to cut into

A mature *Rhododendron sinogrande*.

healthy wood immediately above a dormant bud.

Annual deadheading is another form of maintenance pruning. As the old spent flowers or trusses die and brown, they become unsightly and will eventually form seed, which uses energy that would otherwise be available to the plant for fresh vegetative growth. To remove old flower trusses on rhododendrons, use secateurs to snip the truss at its base, about 1 cm (0.5 in.) above the emerging flush of new growth. Most people grasp the stem with their thumb and forefinger and snap the truss from the plant. This works well most of the time, but occasionally the truss takes some of the new growth with it as it breaks off. By using secateurs, these accidents are avoided.

Many species and cultivars regenerate with young shoots after being cut back hard; however, it may be a matter of trial and error, and some preparatory work will be needed to ascertain if a plant will respond to this level of pruning. *Rhododendron augustinii*, *R. davidsonianum*, and *R. yunnanense* are very responsive and will break out freely after being cut back to the old wood or even near to the ground. In fact, most species in series *Triflorum* respond well to a hard prune. As a general guide, the species and cultivars with a rough bark respond to hard pruning, whereas the ones with smooth bark do not.

Some of the evergreen and deciduous azaleas like the Kurume and Exbury azaleas also benefit from some annual maintenance pruning. Prune out dead and diseased stems and branches in the shrub during early spring as it is about to grow. Use secateurs for the smaller branches or stems, and don't be tempted to use loppers on the larger branches; use a good sharp saw and remove the branch back to the parent branch or trunk, whichever is the healthy wood, making the cut as clean as possible. An annual shearing or clipping over of the Kurume azaleas maintains a short compact growth with lots of flowers rather than leggy

Rhododendron 'Dawn's Delight' showing the typical round shape on a short trunk system with a clean centre free of dead wood.

growths with all the flower on the top of the shrubs. The Kurume azaleas also make an effective hedge if the cultivars are mixed and provided the hedge is regularly clipped to create a dense habit and to prevent leggy growths.

Deadheading a rhododendron using thumb and forefinger, leaving a clean break and newly exposed shoots, which can make fresh vegetative growth.

Kurume azaleas grown as a formal hedge.

Kurume azaleas clipped annually and still flowering.

RHODOTYPOS

Habit Deciduous shrub with long, arching stems for moist, well-drained soil in partial shade to full sun. **Attributes** Rarity value, white flowers in late spring followed by persistent black fruits. **Reasons for pruning** To encourage flowering. **Pruning time** Late spring to early summer after flowering.

Rhodotypos scandens (jet bead) is very closely related to *Kerria japonica* with a similar growth habit. Stems are thrown up from the base of the shrub freely, allowing a portion of the older wood to be cut down to ground level. The shrub flowers on short laterals from the previous year's growth, which means that young canes produced in one season will flower during the next. The intensity of the pruning will depend upon condition, growth, and flowering. Sometimes the cuts are made to suitable growths on the old wood, at other times at ground level. Pruning is best carried out after flowering but may also be done during the winter dormant season.

Rhodotypos scandens flowers on short laterals from the previous year's growth.

RHUS

Habit Erect, open deciduous shrubs to medium-sized trees for fertile, free-draining soil in full sun. **Attributes** Pinnate leaves with good red/orange autumn colour, suitable for specimen plantings. **Reasons for pruning** To develop a strong framework and remove suckers. **Pruning time** Autumn.

Personal protection Wear latex or rubber gloves when pruning as the milky sap of sumachs is extremely toxic and can cause irritation or a rash when in contact with bare skin. Take extra care when disposing of the arisings: if they are burned they can give off toxic fumes,

and when composted the toxic sap persists and the reaction is delayed, affecting the user of the compost. Best to bury the arisings on a spare piece of ground, although this may not be the easiest or most practical solution.

The various species in this genus vary considerably in their growth habit, but for all, very little pruning is necessary. They are all susceptible to coral spot (*Nectria cinnabarina*), which should be pruned out as it appears. Train the tree species on a single leader to avoid multi-stemmed trunks, which can be weak at the unions when mature, and encour-

age a well-balanced crown. *Rhus verniciflua* (varnish tree) makes a wide-branching tree to 18 metres (60 ft.) high with a round crown and open branching, similar to *R. chinensis*, which is smaller by half. Both species respond well to pruning if needed, and the cuts quickly callus and heal well, provided this is done in autumn just before leaf fall to avoid the risk of bleeding.

Rhus typhina (stag's horn sumach) can be grown as a large shrub with a flat top when grown with low branching from ground level or as a small tree to 8 metres (26 ft.) high if

A mature *Rhus verniciflua* showing the stout branching framework.

trained on a short single trunk. The branchlets are thick and pithy, exuding a milky yellow sap when pruned that quickly turns hard and black when exposed. Hard pruning encourages vigorous suckering, which can be a problem in a lawn or border.

Rhus glabra (smooth sumach) is similar to *R. typhina* but smaller, making 2 metres (6 ft.) high, and for the best effect the lower branches should be left furnished to the ground. *Rhus trichocarpa* is beautiful in its red autumn garb, with stiff upright branches requiring nothing beyond some formative pruning.

Rhus typhina 'Dissecta' and *R. glabra* 'Laciniata', both grown for their foliage effect, should be pruned to gradually form a framework, by cutting back the young growths to within 10 cm (4 in.) of the old wood. The pruned shrubs will need to be mulched, irrigated, and fed each year to retain vigour, and any new crowded growths should be thinned as they shoot up in the spring.

Rhus trilobata (skunkbush), *R. aromatica* (fragrant sumach), and other shrubby species should be allowed to branch freely from ground level; young growths thrown up from the base can be used as replacement branches to retain an evenly balanced shrub.

Rhus typhina grown as a small tree on a short leg.

RIBES

Habit Deciduous and occasionally evergreen shrubs for fertile, free-draining soil in full sun. **Attributes** Aromatic foliage, dangling clusters of flowers, some with edible fruits. **Reasons for pruning** To encourage flowering. **Pruning time** Mid- to late spring, immediately after flowering.

The two main groups within *Ribes* are easily separated: plants with spiny stems and plants with spineless stems. All have a similar growth habit, freely producing shoots and branches from just below the soil surface, and most require a sunny position, which is needed to ripen the wood to encourage flowering. The most ornamental forms flower freely along nearly the entire length of shoots made during the previous growing season; *R. rubrum* (red currant) and several other less decorative forms flower near the base of the previous season's wood and also from spurs on older branches.

These minor differences do not affect pruning: the general habit of currants allows whole branches to be pruned out to ground level, thus giving light and air to the new growths springing from the base. By this means a balance is maintained between old and young wood.

Ribes sanguineum (flowering currant) and many of the other currants are best pruned immediately after flowering, cutting out the older branches, pruning them down to a bud

Ribes speciosum trained fanwise against a wall.

A free-flowering bush of *Ribes sanguineum*.

will be broken, so expect to pay a few visits with the secateurs.

The natural habit must also be taken into account and the pruning method varied accordingly. Most *Ribes sanguineum* cultivars produce a strong and fairly rigid framework—a complete contrast to *R. odoratum* (buffalo currant), which has a loose habit and supple branches that lean over into surrounding shrubs. *Ribes alpinum* is a dwarf, compact shrub with erect, twiggy branches; the only pruning necessary for it (or its selection 'Pumilum') will be to remove dead branches should they arise. *Ribes sanguineum* 'Brocklebankii' is a slow-growing shrub, grown for its golden yellow foliage; unlike the rest of the currants, it needs some light shade to prevent the leaves from scorching and very little pruning.

Ribes speciosum is nearly always treated as a wall shrub and should be given a sunny wall where, with good training, it will reach a height of 3 metres (10 ft.). This is an unusual habit for *Ribes* and must be taken into account before attempting any pruning. Young shoots produced at the base of the shrub can be used as replacements for older wood, which will weaken as it ages. Replacement pruning should be done during late summer, after the new growths have been produced, and the new growths tied in hard against the surface of the wall fanwise.

Ribes sanguineum cultivars make good hedging plants. By pruning after flowering, using secateurs to cut the older wood, the dimensions are restricted but the whole effect is informal. If the outline is cut rigidly to a definite height and width, a buildup of old wood reduces the amount of new growth, which in turn affects flowering. By using secateurs the pruner can be more selective and the strongest growths preserved, saving the stronger buds. This species has good wind resistance and thrives even by the coast, despite periodic scorching from sea gales.

The dwarf *Ribes laurifolium* (laurel-leaved currant), with pendulous greenish white flowers in early spring, makes an interesting evergreen groundcover. It needs no pruning apart from the occasional removal of very old stems.

Many *Ribes* species suffer badly from attacks by aphids in spring and early summer, especially after a hard prune. The tips of young growths are badly distorted, affecting the overall health of the bush. To control, apply a selective insecticide in the early stages of an attack.

or healthy growth, as close to the ground as possible. A good guide is to remove a quarter to a third of the mature bush each year, aiming to leave wood above ground that is no more than five years old.

Most members of the genus respond well to hard pruning when they are neglected and overgrown. This can be carried out during the summer or the winter, removing all but the youngest growths. If all the top growth is to be removed, prune in the dormant season only, to give plants the best chance of recovery. Often the new growths are many and soft and lush for the first season, and they will need to be thinned once they have hardened up. They will also be susceptible to strong winds, and some

ROBINIA

Habit Thorny, fast-growing, suckering deciduous trees with an upright irregular canopy for free-draining soil in partial shade to full sun. **Attributes** Deeply fissured bark, fine pinnate leaves, fragrant white/pink pea-like flowers in late spring, resists drought. **Reasons for pruning** To develop a strong framework. **Pruning time** Mid- to late summer after flowering to avoid bleeding from pruning wounds.

Personal protection Wear good thorn-proof clothing and gloves, as the branch system and young stems bear sharp thorns.

A 250-year-old *Robinia pseudoacacia* showing the beautiful branch system.

A young *Robinia pseudoacacia* before crown lifting.

Clearing the trunk of branches up to the required height.

The same specimen after crown lifting.

These leguminous trees are distinctive for their very light, thin foliage canopy. The wood is brittle, and older specimens are prone to shedding large branches during storms at the branch union, leaving nasty tears, so formative pruning to develop a strong framework is key to their longevity. They grow quickly, producing long heavy growths that can snap out if they are not reduced or trained in the early years. They are also prone to bleeding from pruning wounds, so all pruning should be carried out in mid- to late summer. Remove dead wood at the same time: young growths can be damaged by later spring frosts, causing a buildup of dead, weak branches. Trees are generally healthier after a hot summer has ripened the young wood, preparing it for winter cold.

All species should be planted as young as possible and grown as standard trees, with a strong single leader growing up through the centre of the crown and a clean trunk of 2 to 2.5 metres (6 to 8 ft.). Remove any rival leaders as they develop, and where there is a congestion of multiple branches from a single point on the trunk, these too should be thinned out to prevent narrow angles of attachment.

Robinia pseudoacacia (false acacia) is the most commonly planted species. It produces suckers freely from the root system, which is one of the ways it regenerates. Once established, trees need very little pruning except for the removal of sucker growth on the branch system and, where needed, end weight removal on the lower, spreading scaffold branches.

Robinia pseudoacacia 'Umbraculifera' (parasol acacia) naturally forms a tree to 6 metres (20 ft.) high with a very close and compact habit, normally maintained without pruning.

Keep a close watch for strong growths that sometimes break from the rootstock at the graft union, which is usually just below the head of the tree. If left, the mop-headed effect of this selection will be spoiled.

Robinia pseudoacacia 'Pyramidalis' has a habit very similar to that of the Lombardy poplar and should be left with the branching down to the ground.

Robinia pseudoacacia 'Frisia' is a commonly grown golden-leaved tree to 10 metres (33 ft.) high with a narrow trunk and a delicate branch system and foliage. It needs full sun and is relatively short-lived; once it has reached maturity, it will start to show signs of thinning and dieback in the upper canopy.

Robinia ×*ambigua* 'Bellarosea' forms a small tree with upright branching and a twiggy shoot system.

ROSA

Habit Prickly, freestanding (often suckering) and climbing shrubs, mostly deciduous, for fertile, free-draining soil and full sun. **Attributes** Extraordinarily ornamental and well-armed flowering plants with showy fruits (hips) and autumn colour. **Reasons for pruning** To restrict size and encourage free-flowering. **Pruning time** Late winter/early spring.

Personal protection Nearly all roses are armed with prickles. Whether hooked or straight, they are sharp and designed to hold firm, especially those of the climbers. Wear thorn-resistant clothing and gloves whenever pruning roses.

This vast genus displays three distinct habits of growth and flowering, which must be understood before any form of pruning is attempted:

- Group 1. Roses that flower best on growths made during the previous year.
- Group 2. Roses that flower from laterals, which are produced from growths made during the previous year.
- Group 3. Roses that flower from laterals but also directly from growths made during the current season.

Rosa wichuraiana and the Rambler Hybrids are good examples of Group 1, in which long growths are thrown up, often from the base of the plant, each year. Many species and allied hybrids fall into Group 2—for example, *R.* *moyesii*, with its beautiful blood-red flowers and hips. In Group 2, all growths are part of a framework that is retained in a vigorous condition for many years. The framework is invigorated by strong growths from ground level, and new growths are also sent up from the base. There is usually a definite period for flowering, followed by fruiting; however, summer pruning, or an extended period of mild weather in the autumn, sometimes results in flower production on the new growths soon after their development is completed.

Group 3 roses offer continuous flowering from early summer until the first frosts in the autumn, starting with the growths produced on the last season's wood and continuing with the young shoots that are produced, often from near the base; those in section *Chinenses*, which includes *Rosa* ×*odorata*, have this habit.

It will be seen at a glance that Group 2 roses, those that flower best on laterals, may have much of the old wood cut out after flowering, provided there is sufficient of the new. With the two remaining habits, on the other hand, to cut this older wood out would be wrong when it supports a good flower display, and when there is not sufficient replacement wood. This is perhaps an oversimplification, and it may be dangerous to apply these rules generally. Take it in the spirit in which it is offered: a simple attempt to give an overall understanding of a complicated subject.

Most roses grow naturally by a system of replacement of the older flowering branches by young ones. The nature of the pruning depends in many cases upon the vigour of the plant and the extent of this ability to replace old wood. With this understanding, intelligent pruners, using their powers of observation to the full, will adjust the pruning according to the vigour and type of wood of each bush in turn, in order to obtain the maximum display the following season.

All rose species are divided botanically into subgenera and sections, each with a typical growth habit and therefore its own pruning requirements. Only the most popular of these are covered here.

SPECIES ROSES

SECTION PIMPINELLIFOLIAE
The roses in this section are mainly of the Old World, flowering white or yellow. They have a diverse habit with needles and bristles on the stems. Some of the stronger growers—*Rosa xanthina* f. *hugonis* (Father Hugo's rose), for example—have graceful, arching branches, but they may become untidy as they grow older, for as extension growths are produced on the older wood these too arch over and thus the shape is spoiled and bare stem exposed. By looking over the bushes after flowering, this habit may be checked: cut out the oldest wood low down and near ground level. Leave the remainder of the branches and the laterals

Rosa moyesii flowers best on laterals.

intact; many have a definite horizontal habit, and with the foliage being almost fern-like, an attractive effect is produced. The following taxa may be treated in a similar manner: *R. primula* (incense rose), *R. ecae*, *R. elegantula*, *R. sericea* (winged rose), *R. sericea* subsp. *omeiensis* (Mount Omei rose), and *R. sericea* subsp. *omeiensis* f. *pteracantha*. The latter bears broad, flat, red translucent thorns that are better on new growth so, again, thin out the old wood to encourage young shoots from the base.

Rosa foetida (Austrian briar) produces strong, arching growths that readily extend over neighbouring shrubs and become a nuisance; to correct, thin out older wood that weighs the new growth down.

Rosa spinosissima (burnet rose) normally suckers, especially in a light, sandy soil where it is very much at home, reaching heights of 1 to 1.5 metres (3 to 5 ft.). The suckers need constant attention during the summer months; even so, it is difficult to restrict it and many of its varieties to a given area. Occasionally, some older wood can be pruned out of the larger growers, for example *R. spinosissima* 'Grandiflora', which can make a height of 2 metres (6 ft.).

SECTION GALLICANAE

Many old-fashioned garden hybrids, including the Moss Roses, belong to this group. They have a suckering habit with a mixture of needles and bristles on the stems. *Rosa gallica* (French rose) and its varieties vary in growth and habit. Most need fertile soil and good growing conditions, but the branches often become thick and crowded, especially as the new growth is put on during and after flowering. Some thinning will be necessary; after flowering, take the older shoots down to good healthy growths or buds, even to ground level. Final adjustment may be made in early spring before new growth commences, taking out more of the thinner and older wood and even shortening a number of the young growths. Hard renovation pruning will not improve the performance of these roses if the growing conditions are not suitable.

Rosa ×*centifolia* (cabbage rose) is also related to many of the old hybrids, including *R.* ×*centifolia* 'Muscosa' (common moss rose). If necessary, some of the weaker and older wood may be thinned after flowering and a final look over the shrubs made before growth starts in the spring. Vigour must be taken into account; for example, *R.* 'William Lobb' reaches up to 3 metres (10 ft.) and needs the support of a pillar

Rosa 'William Lobb' tied down and formally trained.

or wall or strict formal training by arching and tying down the stems. *Rosa damascena* (damask rose) has similar pruning requirements, but again the importance of taking vigour into account cannot be overemphasised.

Rosa ×*alba* (white rose of York) is a strong, tall-growing shrub with arching stems, flowering in midsummer, and the branches can be

so heavy with fruit that they spoil the shape of the bush. Prune these back to suitable upright growths after the fruiting display is over, in winter.

SECTION CANINAE

All the roses in this section are European species. They vary considerably in growth, some

Rosa glauca showing young growths in a mixed border.

starts. *Rosa tomentosa* (harsh downy rose) has an arching habit and will rest on neighbouring shrubs; it is better suited to the more natural parts of the garden. *Rosa glauca* is suitable for the border or as a coloured-foliage feature; little pruning is needed, except to thin out the oldest wood after the fruits have vanished.

Rosa corymbifera, *R. micrantha*, *R. stylosa*, and *R. canina* (dog rose) have arching growths, and if growing strongly they are a nuisance in the border unless a stake or support is given. They are better in the wilder parts of the garden, for it is difficult to prune them on a restrictive policy and yet do them justice. Growths can be looped over and around stakes, but unless some pruning is carried out before the season's growth starts each year, the bushes develop into an impossible tangle of shoots, which will prove difficult to control. Early spring is the time for this, as many of these species have an attractive fruiting display. *Rosa rubiginosa* (sweet briar) has an erect habit with arching branches, but it is easier to keep under control. It is also grown as a hedge plant, being tied down to the fence or supporting wire system. Prune in late winter/early spring, when the fruit display is over; cut out some of the older wood and tie in the new growths.

SECTION CAROLINAE

This group of roses naturally occurs in the eastern and southeastern United States. *Rosa carolina* and *R. virginiana* are similar in habit as they both form dense clumps of erect stems, the former spreading by means of suckers. Both species are better suited to the more natural parts of the garden, for the branches arch over as they become laden with fruit. In the border, unless they are surrounded by shrubs that are of equal size, they need staking, as otherwise this habit spoils their effect. Pruning consists of cutting out the oldest branches after the fruits have disappeared, but the stems tend to support each other and they should not be over-thinned. *Rosa foliolosa* (prairie white rose) has the same habit although it is only 1 metre (3 ft.) in height; its branches are thin, it spreads by means of suckers and in the border needs quite a large and sheltered area. *Rosa nitida*, a dwarf suckering rose, has similar requirements, although it is not as invasive or untidy in its habit. With both species, just the oldest wood should be cut out after the fruiting display is over.

being sturdy, others producing long, arching branches, all armed with hooked or straight prickles. Those with a sturdy habit are suitable for border culture, but the scrambling species are difficult to control and satisfy in such a situation and need a small tree or artificial structure for support.

Rosa pulverulenta spreads by means of suckers. Being dwarf and compact, it should be planted in a group in the front of the border. There is little pruning with this beyond the removal of dead wood. *Rosa villosa* (apple rose) and *R. mollis* (soft downy rose) have a fairly erect and sturdy habit and are also suitable for border culture. After the fruiting display is over, thin the older wood before the new

SECTION CASSIORHODON

The roses in this section occur across the northern hemisphere and generally freely sucker. They show considerable variation in habit and size, but the general rule is again to cut and thin out the older wood after the fruiting display has finished, remembering as always that the natural growth habit must be taken into account. The habit of *Rosa rugosa* (Japanese rose) need only be compared with that of *R. davidii* (Father David's rose) for one to realize how wide this variation is—wider in fact than in any other section; however, pruning to confine these strong growers spoils their free and vigorous habit. This is also true of other strong growers (e.g., *R. moyesii*, *R. willmottiae*). Some species (e.g., *R. arkansana*) sucker so freely that the only way to prevent their roaming across the bed through other plants is to provide them with their own bed and allow the mower to keep them in line. Another alternative is to insert a form of root barrier material around the clump.

SECTION SYNSTYLAE

The roses in this section are the climbing, creeping, or prostrate shrubs. These are strong growers and many of the species and hybrids in this group may reach considerable heights, provided that a suitable support is available.

They will even climb 9 to 12 metres (30 to 40 ft.) over large trees. *Rosa multiflora* (many-flowered rose) and *R. moschata* (musk rose) are good examples. Both, with others, have been used for hybridisation purposes, the rambler roses (of which more later) having been derived partly from the former species. Little pruning is necessary if these are growing unrestrictedly unless its purpose is to invigorate, in which case old wood may be cut out after flowering back to suitable young wood. Normally, if the plant is strong the old wood should be left for the fruit display. *Rosa wichuraiana* (memorial rose) and *R. maximowicziana* have long, prostrate or trailing growths that are ideal for groundcover and covering banks. Again, pruning is unnecessary provided growth is strong, apart from restricting size and spread.

Many, even the most vigorous in this group, will also trail well over banks when no support is available. As an example, *Rosa multiflora* will, under these conditions, form a large, dense clump that would defy all efforts to produce a tidy bush by pruning; indeed, under natural or semi-wild conditions it would be wrong to try. It is only when they are grown in a confined space, perhaps tied to a single stake or tripod in a border or a pergola in a formal setting, that annual pruning becomes necessary. By cutting out lengths of the old wood after flowering the development of young wood is encouraged, that which originates from near the base being especially valuable. The amount of old wood to be cut out depends entirely upon the condition of the young, developing growths. The long, arching growths that are left may also be looped over and tied in, a good method of containing large climbers in a small space. It is an advantage to hard prune a young plant intended for this restricted training and habit for the first season or two after planting, for this ensures the production of sufficient young growth from the base. Flowering does not matter at this early stage and pruning can therefore be carried out in the spring back to growths or buds near the base of the plant.

Rosa soulieana produces long, arching stems and can be left to form a natural freestanding bush without any support, cutting out old woody stems to the ground, allowing new growths to grow through and fill in the gaps.

SECTION CHINENSES

The species and hybrids in this section flower over a long period during the early summer on growths from the old wood, and later in

Rosa rugosa 'Alba' requires only occasional thinning of the main stems, following the fruiting display.

the year from shoots produced during the current season, often from near the base of the plant. *Rosa* ×*odorata* (tea rose) and *R. chinensis* (China rose) both have this habit. Pruning in late winter/early spring consists of cutting out some of the oldest and weakest growths and branch systems, often close to ground level. In this way the bushes are thinned out, allowing less crowded conditions for the growth and flowers that are produced later. Leave some of the previous year's growths on the more promising branch systems, and shorten these laterals back by a third or more, removing the old heads and the unripened portions. *Rosa* ×*odorata* 'Mutabilis' makes a slender shrub to 1.5 metres (5 ft.) high and flowers all summer, the blooms changing color as they age (hence

Rosa ×*odorata* 'Mutabilis' following light annual pruning.

the cultivar name). In winter, when the plant is dormant, prune the laterals back by one-third; keep its centre open by pruning to an outward-facing bud. To renovate, remove any old woody branches.

SECTION BANKSIANAE

Of the roses in this section, all tall climbing plants with white or yellow flowers, the most important is *Rosa banksiae* (Banksian rose). This strong climber, which may reach a height of 12 metres (40 ft.), is not likely to be successful in the open garden, even with a suitable support, for it is not sufficiently hardy. A warm, sunny wall is often necessary, using a fixed horizontal or vertical wire support system in order that the plant may be tied in

as close to the wall as possible. As maturity is reached some annual pruning is advisable; the plant otherwise becomes very untidy with trailing growths that extend 1 to 2 metres (3 to 6 ft.) from the protective surface of the wall. It is also necessary to keep the young growths close to the wall for protection during the winter, as otherwise they may suffer considerable cold damage.

The main pruning period is after flowering when some of the very old wood may be cut out and the young growths tied in as replacements, thereby preventing overcrowding. Much of the main framework, however, remains for the life of the plant, although sometimes strong growths several feet in length are produced from the base in one season. There need be no hesitation in cutting out even the main branch systems if they are considered to be old and weak. In late autumn, before winter sets in, any growths that have developed away from the wall should be tied in. Pruning in mid-spring consists of cutting out any wood or shoot tips that were frosted during the winter. The method of pruning by spurring back all the young growth after the petals fall results in a loss of flowering potential in the following season. *Rosa banksiae* 'Lutea' should be treated in the same way.

SECTION LAEVIGATAE

Rosa laevigata (Cherokee rose), a tender, semi-evergreen rambler, is more suited to growing against a sunny wall, except in the mildest climates, where it can be grown in the open with a tree or strong tripod for support. Trained on a wall, the young growths should be tied in to replace some of the older wood after flowering. The same method of pruning may be applied to hybrids derived from this species (e.g., 'Anemone', 'Silver Moon').

At a later stage the laterals produced from the framework grow out from the wall and flower. Prune annually in the spring, the aim being to keep the plant tidy and as close to the wall as possible for maximum protection. Also, the extent of the winter's damage is then evident, and any dead pieces may be cut back to living tissue. The laterals that have flowered during the previous season may be shortened to strong, healthy growths, which should be developing near their bases. Some of the older branch systems may be cut out entirely, provided there are young growths that have wintered and are suitable as replacements. These young growths are more certain to winter well if tied in against the wall as they develop during the summer and autumn. The old branches that they will replace are not cut out until the spring, as they will protect the young growths, which are more likely to be killed by severe weather.

The evergreen hybrid 'Mermaid' is hardier and may be grown in colder areas, provided a sunny wall is selected. In milder climates a tripod or pergola will be suitable. This hybrid is often budded onto one of the rose stocks, but it may be grown successfully on its own roots and has even been known to sucker strongly from these. Pruning is similar to that just described. A low branching should be encouraged in the nursery. By having the lower part of the shrub shaded, perhaps by suitable shrubs, the wood is prevented from hardening and is thus more likely to throw strong, young, basal shoots that can be used for replacement purposes.

SUBGENUS PLATYRHODON

The lone species in this subgenus, *Rosa roxburghii* (burr rose), originates in eastern Asia. It is distinct for its prickly orange-yellow hips and peeling bark. If left to grow naturally, this rose will make 3 metres (10 ft.) in height and spread. No pruning is needed, apart from the removal of dead wood or to open up the plant to view the attractive flaking stems. *Rosa roxburghii* f. *normalis* can be treated in the same way.

The unusual orange-yellow hips of *Rosa roxburghii*, which should be retained.

SUBGENUS HESPERHODOS

Rosa stellata (desert rose) is a small plant with thin stems forming dense thickets, difficult to grow, liking a well-drained, sunny position. *Rosa minutifolia* (Baja rose) has similar requirements and is even more difficult. Both species, the only two in the subgenus, are from southwestern North America and are best suited to warm, sunny climates.

Rosa stellata subsp. *mirifica* (Sacramento rose) is a stronger grower but also prefers a sunny, well-drained position. It has a suckerous habit and flowers better on this younger and stronger wood from laterals produced in the second season. Pruning consists of cutting out the old and dead wood in the spring and looking over the plants again after flowering, when the new season's growth may be taken into account in deciding just how much of the old should finally be removed. The suckers often appear among neighbouring plants as the clump becomes established and, if these are valued, must be removed at an early stage, tracing the root back to the parent plant if possible. A shrub with this habit is better in an isolated bed surrounded by grass or among taller shrubs that will not suffer in any way. This rose should be sited at least 0.6 to 1 metre (2 to 3 ft.) from a path, as the thorny branches will be weighed down over the edge as they age and extend, becoming a real nuisance.

MODERN HYBRID BUSH ROSES

LARGE-FLOWERED BUSH ROSES (HYBRID TEAS)

Examples *Rosa* 'Just Joey', 'Lovely Lady', 'Peace', 'Remember Me', 'Royal William', 'Silver Jubilee'.

This is a very large group of mixed origin, having absorbed many of the older hybrids, such as the Tea, Hybrid Tea, Hybrid Perpetual, and Pernetiana groups. Hybridisation for colour, scent, disease resistance, vigour, and repeat flowering has taken place to such an extent that it is impossible to define or to classify many of the modern roses. At first sight this seems very confusing, but there is one safe guide: continuity of flowering during the growing season, possibly even extending into late autumn or early winter. This characteristic has been handed down from at least one parent that is common to most: *Rosa ×odorata*. Refer to the earlier discussion on section *Chinenses* and the pruning advised for this species and for *R. chinensis*. The early crop of flowers is produced on laterals from the old wood, while a later display is provided by the young growths during their first season, these often being long and originating from low down near the base.

Normally these are pruned when dormant, between late autumn and early spring, just before growth starts. If left till later, when growth is under way, much of this is wasted, as the shoots most forward and active are those on the topmost portions, which are cut away. Damage may also be done to the plant by knocking off swollen buds or shoots that would otherwise have been retained. Many rose growers prune in the autumn after the leaves fall or during the winter, but at Kew we wait until the first week after Christmas if the weather is kind.

If left to grow on from year to year the bushes will become large and congested, with a mass of growths that often form an impenetrable thicket. By contrast, a well-managed plant is healthier and more balanced, and the flowers, although fewer, are better shaped and more typical. The annual pruning, which is advised for most (if not all) the large-flowered (Hybrid Tea) types old and new, is designed to control growth and bush formation, and is based upon the cutting out of the old, weak, and dead shoots and the preservation of the new wood. It is helpful to carry out the annual pruning of this type of rose in stages, which are well defined.

Stage 1. The cutting out of dead, diseased, and frosted wood. Sometimes dead or dying snags from previous prunings are found. These should be removed together with any other dead material. Frosted wood is likely to be found on the tips of the unripened, young wood produced late in the season. These should be cut back hard into sound wood.

Stage 2. The removal of the older branch systems. This is an important, if not the most important, stage of the pruning. A healthy bush produces a crop of new growths annually, often from the lower portions of the bush or even from the base. By cutting out the branch systems that are made up partly of old wood (perhaps three or more years old), the young growths are encouraged. Use long-handled loppers; this helps to protect you from the armaments on the retained stems and allows for easier access to the point of removal.

Living branches will, of course, be made up of some young wood, but, when this is compared with the younger shoots coming from the base, it will be found to be much weaker. In some cases only a portion of such an old system can be cut out; but often it is possible to make a complete removal at or near ground level. As the pruner you must decide just what proportion of the older systems should be removed, taking the cuts back either to good dormant buds or to younger and more promising growths. A balance must be maintained which can be adjusted from year to year, taking response and the previous season's growth into consideration at the time of pruning. No hard and fast rule can be laid down, for behaviour varies both with the soil and with different varieties. The weaker the bush, the greater the care needed in cutting back the old branch systems to a suitable point, for some of the older and weaker wood may need to be retained in order to keep an adequate furnishing.

Stage 3. The shortening of the previous year's wood which is to remain on the bush. The growths of the previous season that are to remain should be shortened, as a general rule, to half their length. Thus the number of buds which remain and possibly develop is reduced, as the cuts are made into stouter wood. It must be clearly understood that this shortening takes place after the weakest wood has been cut back to a suitable bud, or to the base.

The height of the bush is to some extent controlled by the measure of the pruning, but no attempt should be made to keep a large and strong grower down by severely cutting

The positioning cut when deadheading roses with secateurs, taking off two or three leaf nodes.

back. In fact, the strongest growers need only light pruning, taking the young growths back by a quarter or less. The weaker growers are pruned harder, leaving only a third or less of the young wood. If the plant is too large, then it's the wrong plant for the space and a smaller cultivar should be planted.

Choice of bud or growth above which the cut is made. Select the position of the cut very carefully. The bud or growth left just beneath the cut is, by virtue of its position, the leading growing point. It must be healthy and strong enough to take the lead. In addition, in order to keep the centre of the bush open as a means of countering congestion, it is advisable to prune to an outward-pointing bud. Ideally, the cuts should be sloping and made just above the buds or eyes, in order to avoid dead snags, which are not only unsightly but may encourage diseases to gain a foothold and spread later into healthy wood. No plant will grow to order but if necessary the annual pruning may be corrective. A bud that grows in toward the centre of the bush, for example, may result in crossing branches. This position may be corrected during the winter's pruning that follows for, if left, other branches may eventually be weighed down and broken, spoiling the shape and general effect.

Summer pruning and deadheading. This operation, which entails looking over the bushes at regular, perhaps weekly, intervals during the growing and flowering season (summer to early autumn) improves the appearance and

Using long-handled loppers to prune out a dead snag.

Using secateurs to accurately position a cut to just above a live bud.

display and, if carried out carefully, it is also a partial growth regulator. Deadheading (the removal of withered blossoms) prevents seed production and thus conserves energy in addition to giving the plant a tidier appearance. When the withered blossoms are on the head it should be carried out carefully, ensuring that the remainder of blooms, which may be fresh or even unopened, are left intact.

When the whole head, or in some cases the single blossom, has withered, it may be shortened back to a suitable bud or growth. Often this means removing several centimetres of flower stalk with some leaves attached. This may be referred to as summer pruning, although in part it overlaps deadheading. It should not be taken to the extent that there is a considerable loss of foliage and branch growth; otherwise, the health of the bush may suffer.

Autumn pruning. In exposed situations, following a good growing season, roses may be susceptible to frost damage or winter cold and wind rock. Prior to severe winds in early autumn it is advisable to prune the plants by a third of their overall height to reduce the possibility of wind damage. If the plants have rocked, carefully re-firm around their bases after pruning.

Pruning after planting and before the first season's growth. This operation is very important, for if the bushes are left unpruned before the first season's growth they become straggly with few if any low breaks. In order to carry out the subsequent pruning properly the breaks must be low down or at ground level. To encourage this, the stems are cut back to approximately 15 cm (6 in.) high, choosing outside-facing buds. This may be carried out any time after planting and before the new season's growth begins.

CLUSTER-FLOWERED BUSH ROSES (FLORIBUNDAS)

Examples *Rosa* 'Amber Queen', 'Arthur Bell', 'Champagne Moment', 'Escapade', 'Iceberg', 'Southampton'.

As with the large-flowered bush roses (Hybrid Teas), extensive hybridisation has taken place within the Floribundas in recent years. The modern varieties are mostly vigorous growers and throw up strong shoots, often from near the base. If left unattended, the bushes become very congested with wood that is old and has lost much of its vigour.

Floribundas are pruned as for the Hybrid Teas—in the dormant period, between late

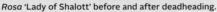
Rosa 'Lady of Shalott' before and after deadheading.

autumn and early spring, just before growth starts—for the same reasons. Firstly, the dead and diseased wood is cut out. Next remove a proportion of the older wood, if possible making the cuts low down to a suitable bud near the base. This in fact means that branch systems based on three- or four-year-old wood is removed to make way for the younger wood. Growths that remain are also cut back and, as with the Hybrid Teas, the extent of this depends upon age and condition. When the growth is very strong the pruning is light, the harder pruning being reserved for the weaker growers when as much as two-thirds or even more is removed. With moderate pruning the growths may be cut back by one-third or a half. Young growths, which are based upon any older wood which remains, are cut back harder than new shoots that spring directly from the base. Under this system the older wood supporting the weaker, exhausted, or close-growing laterals is thinned and pruned, the cuts being made above a promising shoot or buds. Thus more light and air is left for the younger material that remains, this being pruned according to vigour. Thus each branch and growth is judged upon its age and vigour, and it is only when the bushes concerned are of one variety, either in a group or bed, that uniformity is considered. Great care is needed even in this situation, for a uniform level and appearance at the time of pruning does not mean that the bushes will grow uniformly. Careful and selective pruning is a means of encouraging weaker bushes so that the planting as a whole is uniform.

Summer pruning and deadheading is of great benefit to the bushes and to their appearance and is carried out on the same principle and by the same method as for the Hybrid Teas.

OLD ENGLISH AND MODERN SHRUB ROSES

Examples *Rosa* 'Gertrude Jekyll', 'Golden Celebration', 'Graham Thomas', 'Harlow Carr', 'Kew Gardens', 'Lady of Shallot', 'Munstead Wood', 'Scarborough Fair'.

Old English shrub roses combine the forms and fragrances of old-fashioned English shrub roses with the repeat flowering and vast colour ranges of the modern large-flowered and cluster-flowered roses. They are easy to grow, healthy and reliable in most gardens, and hard to beat for sheer exuberance of flower and scent. Their natural, shrubby growth makes them the ideal candidate for large containers, traditional rose borders, or mixed (think cottage garden style) plantings. To create real impact in the border, groups of three or more of the same variety should be planted and allowed to grow together to form one dense shrub, resulting in a magnificent display of bloom. In climates with relatively mild winters, late winter is the best time to prune; however, in regions with cold winters, pruning should be delayed until spring growth is just starting.

Pruning repeat-flowering Old English shrub roses is relatively easy and straightforward. They should be reduced in height by between one-third and two-thirds, depending on their vigour, but only thinned a little as they are generally bushy shrubs. Non-repeat-flowering

Rosa 'Harlow Carr' pruned to maintain a bushy, rounded habit.

shrubs should be left alone or lightly pruned by no more than one-third and thinned very lightly.

Some of the modern shrub roses (e.g., Rosa 'Fritz Nobis', 'Nevada', 'Marguerite Hilling') make broad arching shrubs to 2 metres (6 ft.) high and wide. They should not be tip-pruned but left to maintain a natural arching form. The removal of entire old woody stems back to ground level should be carried out as needed to encourage new growths and maintain performance.

HYBRID MUSKS

Examples *Rosa* 'Buff Beauty', 'Cornelia', 'Felicia', 'Penelope', 'Prosperity'.

The hybrid musk roses, distantly related to *Rosa moschata* (musk rose), are suitable for the average shrub border and bear their flowers in large trusses like a cluster-flowered bush rose. They produce long, graceful growths, and the flower colours are very delicate with an exquisite musky scent (hence the name). They flower in profusion on new growth in early summer with some repeating later into the summer if they are deadheaded. The taller varieties are excellent plants for a low fence or wall where a rambler or climber would be too large. They are slightly tender and will not grow well in cold climates. Prune established plants in late winter/early spring; remove dead, damaged,

and diseased wood and, depending on the vigour and size of the plant, remove one to three of the oldest, woody stems. Reduce the overall height of the plant by approximately one-third, and the laterals on these by half. *Rosa* 'Buff Beauty' and other vigorous varieties can also be trained as a climber.

MINIATURE, POLYANTHA, AND PATIO ROSES

Examples *Rosa* 'Arizona Sunset', 'Ballerina', 'Miss Edith Cavell', 'The Fairy', 'Yvonne Rabier.'

This group of roses, miniature versions of the large- and cluster-flowered bush roses, are useful plants for window boxes, containers, or very small gardens, growing to a height of 35 to 45 cm (12 to 18 in.). They should be treated in the same way as their full-size counterparts. If the plants are growing well, they can be lightly pruned in late winter/early spring, but if plants are struggling and in need of some renovation, they can be cut back hard to stimulate new growths from the base. Regular deadheading will also help with repeat flowering through the summer.

RAMBLER ROSES

Examples (species) *Rosa banksiae, R. bracteata, R. brunonii, R. filipes, R. helenae, R. multiflora, R. wichuraiana*; (hybrids) 'Albéric Barbier', 'Al-

bertine', 'Dorothy Perkins', 'Félicité Perpétue', 'François Juranville', 'Kew Rambler', 'Paul's Himalayan Musk', 'Rambling Rector', 'Super Excelsa'.

These very vigorous, rampant climbing roses usually produce large sprays of flowers profusely once each year, normally in early summer, followed by decorative hips. They often flower well even without any form of formal pruning. Where a rambler rose is left to its own devices to grow up through the upper canopy of a tree, it may be totally unpractical to prune it, apart from restricting its spread to neighbouring trees; and frankly, there is no better sight than *Rosa filipes* 'Kiftsgate' pushing 12 meters (40 ft.) up through a conifer and bearing its proliferation of white flowers in early summer without any care or attention from the gardener. To encourage the rose to climb after planting it near the base of the trunk, wrap its long flexible growths around the trunk and let them spiral upward at their own will.

Immediately after planting a rambler, cut the young canes down to 20 to 25 cm (8 to 10 in.) to encourage fresh new growths from low down near to ground level. The growth habit of the majority of the rambler species and hybrids is to throw up a strong crop of shoots annually, but the new canes produced are much stronger and flexible in some species than others. Be observant and work out the required

Rosa 'Alister Stella Gray' trained against a wire fence.

training needs when pruning. Varieties that throw up long growths abundantly each year from the base are the true Ramblers, hybrids of *Rosa wichuraiana*; their young growths produce their best crop of flowers in their second year. The pruning needed, therefore, is a type of replacement pruning: each year, the complete lengths of old growths over two years old are cut out at ground level in late summer after flowering, and the new growths are tied in as replacements—and easily kept within a confined space.

CLIMBING ROSES

Examples *Rosa* 'Alister Stella Gray', 'Bantry Bay', 'Betty Sherriff', 'Climbing Cécile Brünner', 'Dublin Bay', 'Golden Showers', 'Zéphirine Drouhin'.

Unlike a rambling rose, a climbing rose will repeat-flower almost all summer and well into autumn. All the climbers produce a similar growth that makes them suitable for training over a support or on a wire system; the long growths should be tied fanwise, as near horizontally as possible, against a sunny wall or over another support, such as a fence, tripod, obelisk, or pergola. The framework or branch system is tied out and is often kept for a number of years. Prune flowering laterals produced from this framework back by two-thirds of the length to the lower healthy buds in late winter/early spring before the new growth begins. Remove any spindly or unhealthy lateral growths completely, back to the framework. From time to time young growths are produced; these may be used for extension replacements or to

further increase the growing space. Tie them carefully in with biodegradable jute garden twine and later, as they grow, use them as replacements for older and spent branch systems.

When grown up a brick pillar of a pergola system, the long, flexible growths can be trained spirally up the structure throughout the growing season, taking care not to tie in growths that are crossing over. This will add strength in support and increase the surface area of the framework.

Stems of *Rosa* 'Alister Stella Gray' tied into wires with biodegradable jute garden twine using a figure-eight knot.

Rosa 'Betty Sherriff', a hybrid of the rambling *R. brunonii*, covering a wall with little pruning.

A climbing rose trained in even spirals up the brick column of a pergola.

Rosa 'Climbing Cécile Brünner' trained and growing well on a pergola system.

Unlike most other types of roses, climbers should not be pruned after planting or during the first season's growth, unless it be to cut out any dead wood. This is an important rule to observe with the climbing cultivars in particular, for there is a danger of reversion to a bush habit if pruned back too hard.

BUSH STANDARDS

Usually these are large-flowered or cluster-flowered varieties that have been budded onto stems of *Rosa canina* or *R. laxa*, although other rootstocks are also used. Apart from the removal of suckers and the need to keep the stem clean and free from stock growths, pruning follows the same principles as for the large-flowered, cluster-flowered, or shrub roses. Likely subjects include *R.* 'Iceberg', 'Munstead Wood', and 'Silver Jubilee'. In exposed gardens it may be necessary to use a stout garden stake to support the trunk during windy periods.

WEEPING STANDARDS

These cascades of colour are often formed from ramblers, climbers, or groundcover roses (e.g., *Rosa* 'Nozomi'), the stems being trained over a hood or umbrella framework. Tie in new growths after old stems have been cut off when the blossom display is over. Remove dead, diseased, and damaged growths to a strong bud or healthy growth; otherwise, weeping standards can look very untidy. Likely subjects include *R.* 'Dorothy Perkins', 'Félicité Perpétue', 'François Juranville', and 'Super Excelsa'.

HEDGES

Rosa rugosa, *R. rubiginosa*, and several hybrids (e.g., *R.* 'Nevada', 'Roseraie de L'Hay', 'The Mayflower') make good hedges if grown and treated informally; *R. spinosissima* 'Andrewsii' makes an especially attractive, informal hedge about 1.2 metres (4 ft.) high. For those that flower throughout the summer, the withered heads may be cut back as they form in a series

of weekly operations or when time permits. Always make the cut above a suitable bud; in this way (and by feeding and watering, if necessary) a continuous display is assured. Carry out any necessary pruning in late winter/ early spring. Mechanical hedge trimmers are commonly used on hedges, but we at Kew are very shy of using these as over the long term it does damage to the bush and no dead, diseased, or dying material is removed. Bushes will also mature into old structures with few young stems coming through as successional replacement.

Rosa 'Bonica', a groundcover rose grown as a bush standard with the added support of a garden stake, in a bed of *R.* 'Eglantyne', an Old English shrub rose.

ROSMARINUS

Habit Mediterranean evergreen shrub for well-drained soil and full sun. **Attributes** Aromatic grey-green foliage used in cooking, blue flowers. **Reasons for pruning** To restrict size. **Pruning time** Early summer, immediately after flowering.

Once *Rosmarinus officinalis* (rosemary) is established, very little pruning is needed. Encourage a bushy plant by pinching out the tips at least twice during the first few months after planting. If a plant becomes straggly, cut back any untidy growths to a main branch or new growth after flowering. They do not respond well to hard renovation pruning, and old neglected plants are best removed and replaced with fresh young plants in spring. The differ-

ing habits of the several cultivars (compact, prostrate, arching, erect, pyramidal) must be taken into account before carrying out any form of pruning. Rosemary makes a good formal or informal hedge, especially if the upright cultivars (e.g., 'Miss Jessopp's Upright', 'Sissinghurst Blue') are selected; prune the hedge to shape after flowering. It also makes an ideal container plant and by regular pinching and pruning can be maintained and restricted to a pot of any size. Don't forget to save the prunings for the kitchen!

Rosmarinus officinalis grown in a container.

RUBUS

Habit Thorny, deciduous suckering shrubs with long, arching stems for any soil in full sun to partial shade. **Attributes** Showy ornamental stems. **Reasons for pruning** To encourage fresh, vigorous growths. **Pruning time** Early summer after flowering.

Personal protection Wear good thorn-proof clothing and gloves when going anywhere near these ornamental brambles and their arisings. Their thorns are vicious and have a habit of catching on everything in their way.

Rubus species flower on laterals produced

from the previous season's wood, but many will retain their long canes for three or four years, producing new laterals from buds at the base of the flowering growth. Many are actually grown for their ornamental stems; pruning out much of the old wood encourages this new growth, spurring a plentiful supply of young growths from the base during the summer months.

Rubus cockburnianus (white-stemmed bramble) is most distinctive, with pure white arching stems. The young growths are especially attrac-

tive during their first winter, but they lose their white bloom as they ripen in the second season after the flowering period. By pruning these canes down to ground level in early spring before the new growth appears, a fresh crop of canes will be produced. This is necessary and easily done with a pair of long-handled loppers to save your arms from the thorns. If the old canes were left, they would spoil the effect of these new ones.

Rubus biflorus (two-flowered raspberry) and *R. thibetanus* (ghost bramble) have a similar habit and effect and can be treated in the same way. These are hungry plants and put lots of energy into generating vigorous new growth; a good mulch and feed after pruning helps maintain a healthy stool.

Rubus odoratus (flowering raspberry) is a vigorous suckering grower with upright thornless stems and clusters of fragrant purple flowers on second-season canes in mid- to late summer. Immediately after flowering, the old canes should be cut to ground level, leaving the younger growths with more light for ripening and space to show off the mature flaking bark during the first winter.

Rubus deliciosus (boulder raspberry) is another thornless species. It does not produce enough young growth from the base to allow all the old wood to be cut out each season after flowering, so leave enough old wood to form a framework and encourage young growths from ground level. *Rubus* 'Benenden' should be treated similarly: cut away the flowering growths and some of the older wood if possible.

Rubus cockburnianus showing first-winter stem effect.

RUSCUS

Habit Low, upright evergreen suckering shrubs for dry soil in deep shade to full sun. **Attributes** Tough spine-tipped foliage, bright red fruits on false leaves (cladodes). **Reasons for pruning** To maintain a tidy plant. **Pruning time** Spring.

Personal protection Wear a pair of tough gardening gloves when pruning *Ruscus aculeatus*, as the cladodes are spine-tipped and prickly to bare skin.

Ruscus species make suitable groundcover plants and require very little pruning apart from the removal of any dead or discoloured foliage and stems in the spring. Some of the cladodes of *R. hypoglossum* (spineless butcher's broom) can discolour during the winter and look unsightly; the entire stem should be removed to ground level. Where an entire stem has died out in a clump, a sharp tug will release it from the base of the clump without the need for secateurs. Established clumps can be cut right down to ground level each spring, just before new growth begins, but such drastic action is not always successful, especially on drier and poorer soils. Normally with this species and *R. aculeatus* (butcher's broom), it is not necessary to prune out healthy stems, or even to thin out the dense clusters of erect stems as this is naturally their close and tufted habit.

RUTA

Habit Upright deciduous or evergreen sub-shrub for free-draining or droughty soil in partial shade to full sun. **Attributes** Aromatic blue-grey foliage, yellow flowers in late summer. **Reasons for pruning** To restrict size and maintain a tidy plant. **Pruning time** Mid-spring.

Personal protection All parts of this plant are poisonous in large quantities, so dispose of arisings carefully. The sap contains furanocoumarins, which when subjected to daylight cause blistering or dermatitis on the skin of sensitive individuals. Wear protective gloves and arm protection when pruning.

Despite producing some wood, *Ruta graveolens* (common rue) is seldom strong enough to reach more than 1 metre (3 ft.) high. To keep the plant compact, prune hard in mid-spring, cutting back to good growths and taking out weaker wood altogether. The corymbs of yellow flowers are interesting but usually cut off to tidy the plant up as it is mainly grown for its foliage effect. *Ruta graveolens* 'Jackman's Blue' is a more bushy compact form. Where specimens have become neglected, they can be cut back hard and will respond well.

SALIX

Habit Deciduous trees and shrubs with upright or pendulous branches for moist to wet soil in full sun; some grow successfully in dry soil. **Attributes** Various sizes and forms, some with contorted and coloured stems and foliage and attractive catkins. **Reasons for pruning** To develop a strong framework and encourage vigorous regrowth. **Pruning time** Between autumn and spring (when dormant).

Salix is a very large genus, and its diverse range of trees and shrubs can be confusing to the pruner in terms of what, when, and how to prune. To get the best out of willows in cultivation, understand the taxonomy and know the size, habit, and attributes of the species in question. There are five distinct groups of willows, each requiring a different pruning technique:

- Group 1. Upright-growing willows suitable for growing as trees.
- Group 2. Strong-growing willows suitable for growing as weeping trees.
- Group 3. Small to medium-sized willows suitable for growing as shrubs.
- Group 4. Strong-growing willows that are cut down annually for stem effect.
- Group 5. Dwarf and creeping willows.

GROUP 1

Salix alba (white willow) is typical of this first category, producing ascending branches; its leader should be retained for as long as possible. *Salix fragilis* (crack willow) forms a spreading head with wide-angled branching, which makes it difficult to retain a leader. The lower branches and main scaffolds quickly make a girth equal to or even exceeding that of the main trunk and the leading growth, which will soon lose its dominance. Unfortunately such a heavy framework is prone to damage during strong winds and heavy snow as the tree ages and declines in health. The wood of willows is soft and prone to decay, so the removal of large branches (leaving large pruning wounds) is not recommended; formative pruning (leaving small cuts) is the key to longevity where this genus is concerned.

Salix babylonica var. *pekinensis* and its selection 'Tortuosa' are smaller trees in this group. Select and train a leader from an early age to develop a strong framework; otherwise, there will be a tendency for multiple leaders to develop, particularly for 'Tortuosa'.

Salix pentandra (bay willow) makes a small to medium-sized tree, with a natural tendency toward low branching. Train a clean stem if a good height is required, but it can also be grown as a large bushy shrub or a small tree with a clean stem.

GROUP 2

Salix babylonica, *S. alba* 'Tristis', and *S. ×sepulcralis* var. *chrysocoma* all have a weeping habit. The latter is a fast grower and considered one of the best of this group of true weeping willows. Weeping willows often produce a few main branches that are large and heavy. Once the branching is left to develop on a length of clean stem, the leader is quickly lost as vigour is diverted into these main branches. The growth habit is such that the main branches arch over, additional height being built up by strong, upright shoots that in turn droop over—and so the process is repeated. The main danger is with a very old and large tree which may lean, often with considerable weight, perhaps over water, its heavy limbs vulnerable to being torn away from the trunk by strong winds. To overcome this problem, remove any branches with a tendency to lean during formative pruning, retaining the opposite branches to balance the overall canopy shape and weight.

Salix purpurea 'Pendula' forms a small but spreading tree with a head of fine, thin growths. These trees are usually grafted onto a stem of *S. purpurea* at a height of 2.4 to 3 metres (8 to 10

Salix ×*sepulcralis* var. *chrysocoma* showing typical weeping habit.

ft.). In the early years, as growths are produced on the main trunk, they should be rubbed off with the thumb while still fleshy and underdeveloped.

GROUP 3

Salix daphnoides (violet willow) produces colourful young growths and can be trained as a bushy shrub or small tree with multiple shoots for the colourful effect. Following planting, it should be left unpruned for three to four years; when the new growths become numerous and less conspicuous, the new colourful younger growths can be encouraged by pruning out sections of the older wood, while still retaining a

The decorative catkins of *Salix caprea* are produced in late winter on old wood.

Salix caprea 'Kilmarnock' grown in a container.

framework with young growths. Further pruning can be done on an annual basis in early spring, and over a period of three to five years the entire framework will be replaced.

The common *Salix caprea* (goat willow) tends naturally have low branching, often from ground level. It and some other willows in this group—*S. aegyptiaca* (musk willow), *S. irrorata* (blue-stemmed willow), *S. koriyanagi* (Korean willow)—are grown for their decorative catkins. These are produced in late winter on vigorous strong growths from the previous growing season, so maintain a strong-growing multi-stemmed shrub or small tree for the best effect. The pruning mandate is to cut out any weak or dead branches while retaining as natural a shape as possible, which is essential for aesthetic reasons: these plants draw notice during the dormant season, displaying their catkins, naked with no leaves, so outline will be important. *Salix caprea* 'Kilmarnock' is sold as a top-worked grafted weeping standard, producing a curtain of pendulous branches with showy catkins along their length. This curtain will need to be thinned annually to open up the branches; remove the dead and weak and shorten any branches that are too long for the main stem.

Others in this group (e.g., *Salix integra* 'Hakuro-nishiki') are grown for their variegation and should be treated with care as they are often less vigorous than their green counterparts. The goal with pruning will be to encourage fresh growth that will generate an abundance of variegated foliage. Mulch and feed these subjects to maintain vigour and health.

Many of the species in this group have the habit of layering naturally when a branch meets the soil surface or mulch. This layered effect may not be desirable. The larger and more spreading the plants become, the more difficult it is to access their interior, and the borders become difficult to maintain. Any layered specimens should be corrected and layers removed, or lifted and used elsewhere in the garden.

GROUP 4

A number of taxa (e.g., *Salix alba* 'Golden Ness', *S. alba* var. *vitellina* 'Britzensis', *S. alba* var. *vitellina* 'Yelverton', *S.* ×*sepulcralis* 'Dart's Snake') are grown for the ornamental effect of their colourful young stems as they ripen following the first season's growth. The method is to cut the growths hard back in the spring each year before they begin their new season's growth and lose the stem colour. This hard pruning, to within 2.5 cm (1 in.) of the older

Salix alba 'Golden Ness' grown on a short leg for winter stem effect.

wood or spur, results in a new crop of young shoots, which grow during the season to provide a display of coloured stems the following winter.

Initial pruning can be low to the ground to form a low stool or on a short trunk to 0.6 to 1 metre (2 to 3 ft.). In time, with yearly pruning, the spurs form an increasingly large head, from which a large number of coloured stems are produced annually. Any new shoots which develop on the trunk are usually wiped off to maintain a clean trunk, but one or two can be left to increase the decorative impact. The intensity of the coloured stems is more pronounced in late winter through to early spring, and the stems are therefore left as long as possible until their buds break. When grown in a bed, the stools may be over-vigorous in the early years; root prune them to restrict their size.

GROUP 5

The species in this group (e.g., *Salix helvetica*, *S. repens*, *S. reticulata*, *S. retusa*) are naturally slow growing, prostrate, or creeping and are suitable for the rock garden or sink gardening. The minimal pruning they require usually entails the removal of dead wood or restricting their spread.

SALVIA

Habit Low-spreading evergreen subshrubs for moist, well-drained soil in full sun. **Attributes** Aromatic foliage used in cooking, upright spires of blue flowers in summer. **Reasons for pruning** To develop a strong framework and stimulate fresh growth. **Pruning time** Spring.

When young, *Salvia officinalis* (common sage) forms an attractive plant, but as it grows older, patches of bare wood are exposed at the base, leaving the plant straggly and unsightly. In this condition it can be hard pruned in the spring, as buds in the older wood remain alive and develop very quickly if needed. When old

plants become too straggly and beyond renovation, they are better discarded and replaced with young plants. To delay such drastic action, plants (even the golden and variegated specimens) can be cut back after flowering almost to the base of the younger wood.

The remainder of the woody species, including *Salvia microphylla* and *S. elegans*, need the shelter and protection of a warm, sunny wall. *Salvia elegans* can build up a woody system over several years reaching a height of 0.3 to 0.6 metre (1 to 2 ft.). Species in this group should be pruned back to the older wood in

the spring, just as the new growth is about to break out. In a hard winter the growths can be killed back to near ground level. Left unpruned, these shrubs become weak and untidy. They will need some form of support in the border to keep them tidy, but they should not be trained against a wall as they are more successful when planted 30 cm (12 in.) or so away from the base and allowed to develop a bushy growth. Sucker-like growths are often produced as the shrub spreads; a covering of straw, fleece, or bracken will help get the plant through an average winter.

SAMBUCUS

Habit Deciduous shrubs or small trees (and some herbaceous perennials) for rich, moist, well-drained soil in partial shade to full sun. **Attributes** White flowers in late spring followed by clusters of fleshy black or red fruits. **Reasons for pruning** To develop a strong framework, remove dead wood, and encourage fresh shoots for foliage effect. **Pruning time** Between autumn and spring (when dormant).

Routine pruning of healthy elders involves removing dead wood and some of the older wood and branches during the dormant period to generate new growth. Where plants have become weak or very overgrown, they can be cut back hard to near ground level, where a number of young shoots will spring from the base. Annual hard pruning gradually weakens a plant; it will produce fewer and weaker canes and eventually die out. Follow up any hard pruning of elders with mulching, feeding, and, during dry conditions, some water. These plants have free-running stems underground, and it may be necessary to insert some form of root barrier around the clump to prevent it from running through the bed.

Some elders (e.g., *Sambucus nigra* 'Marginata', *S. nigra* f. *porphyrophylla* 'Eva', *S. nigra* f. *porphyrophylla* 'Guincho Purple') can be trained as small standards on a 1.5 to 2 metre (5 to 6 ft.) leg or as free-growing shrubs with canes from ground level, and—as they are grown purely for their foliage effect—can be pruned back hard each year to a low framework; alternatively, thin the canes evenly across the bush, retaining some canes to maintain vigour and the general wider shape.

Sambucus nigra subsp. *canadensis* 'Maxima' needs to be pruned hard down to ground level each year. It will produce strong canes and very large flower heads in late summer.

Treat *Sambucus ebulus* (Dane's elder) like an herbaceous plant, cutting it back down to ground level each year during the dormant season; flowering will occur during late summer.

Sambucus nigra growing naturally along an English road.

SANTOLINA

Habit Small, bushy Mediterranean evergreen shrubs for moist, well-drained soil in full sun. **Attributes** Aromatic grey foliage, yellow button-like flowers in summer. **Reasons for pruning** To develop a strong framework. **Pruning time** Spring and autumn after flowering.

When young, *Santolina chamaecyparissus* (lavender cotton) and *S. rosmarinifolia* should be pinched out to form close masses of leafy shoots. As they grow older the heavy branches become weighed down to the ground, and the whole appearance and shape is spoiled. If left unpruned the upright growths produced on the now horizontal branches are in their turn weighed down, until the whole plant becomes a mass of stems, dead growths, and fallen leaves; in a wet winter, this may cause the plants to die. Regular annual pruning should be carried out in the autumn; cut off the old flower heads and stalks, and cut back any tall or straggly growths so that they won't be weighed down by snow and rain, spoiling the appearance of the shrub over the winter. Eventually despite this regular pruning, plants become overgrown and tired, at which point they should be cut hard back into the old wood in the spring. Plants recover quickly from this treatment, and it may be necessary to repeat the hard prune approximately every three years. At some stage, however, it will be necessary to replace old plants with fresh new ones. Growth tends to be shorter and more compact when plants are grown in a dry and sunny position.

A young *Santolina chamaecyparissus*, pinched out to generate a multitude of new growths for a bushy shrub.

SAPINDUS

Habit Small deciduous decurrent trees with upright branching and a low, rounded vase-shaped crown for free-draining, poor soils in full sun. **Attributes** Small showy white flowers in early summer, clusters of yellow fruits, good autumn colour. **Reasons for pruning** To develop a strong framework and remove dead wood. **Pruning time** Late summer through winter (when dormant). Never prune in early spring as the wounds are prone to bleeding.

Sapindus saponaria var. *drummondii* (soapberry) and *S. mukorossi* must be grown in a sheltered, sunny garden; they will not tolerate shade. They should be grown with a central leader. Apart from the removal of dead wood and the lifting of lower branches, minimal pruning is necessary.

SARCOCOCCA

Habit Dwarf upright evergreen shrubs for any soil type, including chalk, in shade or full sun. **Attributes** Small fragrant white flowers in late winter followed by black fruits. **Reasons for pruning** To develop a strong framework. **Pruning time** Spring.

Christmas boxes are very useful evergreen shrubs for the winter border, requiring little pruning apart from the removal of dead or worn-out growths. These should be removed back to ground level, but sometimes it is better to cut back to a strong growth inside the bush. It is tempting to thin out the plant's stems as they can appear crowded, but this is the plant's natural habit and thinning should be avoided.

Sarcococca hookeriana is erect but spreads with age, as the branches extend and bend over under their own weight. This is a natural habit and should not be spoiled with pruning. It often throws out strong growths well above the remainder, and these may lose their leaves over winter and appear dead. Cutting back is best left until spring, when the dead wood is readily distinguished from the living.

Sarcococca confusa (sweet box) has a spreading habit and often develops one or two ragged growths that spoil the general appearance; these can be cut back in the spring to a growth which originates well down inside the bush or at ground level. It makes a good, low informal hedge; prune back any outward growths with the secateurs rather than hedging shears in order to keep an informal line.

Sarcococca confusa grown as an informal hedge.

SASSAFRAS

Habit Deciduous suckering trees with an irregular crown for free-draining lime-free soil in a sheltered position. **Attributes** Fissured bark, aromatic leaves with interesting individual shapes and good autumn colour, suitable for woodland plantings. **Reasons for pruning** To develop a strong framework. **Pruning time** Between autumn and spring (when dormant).

Sassafras albidum, *S. randaiense*, and *S. tzumu* can be miffy plants at the best of times, and if the growing conditions aren't perfect for them, they will sit still, sulking and refusing to grow. The best form in which to grow all three (but particularly *S. albidum*) is with a single trunk, retaining the leader through the crown for as long as possible. The branches often have an ascending habit as they grow away from the trunk, while the individual branches form loose heads of twiggy growth and foliage, which makes it distinct from all other trees. Keep the trunk clear of side branches to a height of 2 to 2.5 metres (6 to 8 ft.) to show off the attractive bark; the lower branches tend to sweep down to the ground and should be retained. The other two species are rarely seen in cultivation but should be treated in the same manner. Any suckers produced around the root plate can be left to form a natural group planting or removed to retain a single-trunked specimen.

SCHEFFLERA

Habit Evergreen trees or shrubs for free-draining soils and full sun in a sheltered position. **Attributes** Architectural, tropical-looking leaves with attractive spring colours. **Reasons for pruning** To develop a strong framework and branching. **Pruning time** Spring.

The few hardy *Schefflera* species in cultivation (e.g., *S. delavayi*, *S. rhododendrifolia*, *S. taiwaniana*) have an amazing tropical effect with their large palmate leaves (hence the common name, umbrella tree). They are very fussy growers and do not like low temperatures or cold winds; the protection of a warm, sunny wall will help them to establish. Wait until the nursery stock has produced some wood in the stem before planting them out, so they are better prepared for some winter cold. They require very little pruning, but if you are feeling daring and ambitious and would like a well-branched specimen, prune out the leading shoot to encourage side branching.

SCHIMA

Habit Bushy, stiff-branching evergreen shrubs or small trees for free-draining, lime-free soil in a sheltered position. **Attributes** Rarity value, white camellia-like flowers in late summer. **Reasons for pruning** To encourage new growth for flowering and restrict size. **Pruning time** Spring.

Schima khasiana and *S. wallichii* produce their flowers on the current season's wood. *Schima wallichii* will grow well in a sheltered woodland situation, but *S. khasiana* really needs to be grown freestanding with wall protection, or trained up close to a warm, sunny wall with its main branches and laterals spread fanwise and tied in. Keep growth close against the wall by careful pruning in spring. Any shoots that extend too far from the wall surface can be pruned back to suitable growing points where the cuts would be hidden by foliage. Both species respond well to hard pruning if damaged by inclement winter weather or to restrict the size of an overgrown specimen.

SCHISANDRA

Habit Deciduous woody climbers with twining stems for any type of soil in a sheltered, shady position. **Attributes** Hanging white or pink flowers in early summer, red berries in autumn. **Reasons for pruning** To develop a strong framework. **Pruning time** Winter.

Grow magnolia vines (e.g., *Schisandra chinensis*, *S. grandiflora*, *S. rubriflora*) against a sheltered, shaded wall or trellis. In the early years after planting, you will have to train the main branch system to cover the available space adequately. This entails tying out five to eight strong permanent growths fanwise from the plant at ground level. The laterals and extension growths from this system should be left to hang down like a curtain; short spurs that form the flowering growths develop from these. The topmost growths are very vigorous, especially if the height of the wall or trellis is limited, and it is important that these growths do not hide those that spring from lower down on the branch system, as if they are deprived of light they will die. Thin out the older and weaker of the pendulous growths during the winter before the buds break out. Some of the young wood, the extension growths that climbers naturally produce, may need to be cut away completely, leaving a limited number for replacement purposes.

Although these are naturally climbers, the branch system will need tying in, as the main means of support are the young twining growths that when grown on a wall have no means of twining to make height. Magnolia vines can also be grown on trees, poles, or tripods for supports, but they will still need some vertical and horizontal system of wire supports for the young stems to twine around, for as the weight of the plant increases, the mass of growth has a tendency to slip down to form a tangle of growth at the base. Once the climber has reached the top of the support, a pendulous habit from the top should be encouraged. Pruning with this system consists of cutting out the older wood in the winter and using the young growths as replacements. Any unneeded young growths can be cut out.

SCHIZOPHRAGMA

Habit Slow-growing deciduous self-clinging climbers for sunny to shady walls or tree trunks. **Attributes** Small creamy white flowers with large bracts, similar to those of hydrangea. **Reasons for pruning** To develop a strong framework and encourage flowering. **Pruning time** Between autumn and spring (when dormant).

Both *Schizophragma hydrangeoides* (Japanese hydrangea vine) and *S. integrifolium* (Chinese hydrangea vine) are commonly trained against a wall for support and flower best if that wall is sunny. They are self-clinging by means of adventitious aerial stem roots, which are freely produced from the young growths; however, some additional support by means of ties to a wire system is often necessary, especially to get young plants started. The main framework is trained out to cover the available space, but the habit is often ungainly and it is not always possible to space the branches out neatly. Two types of growth are produced, extension shoots and branched laterals. Extension shoots are long and self-clinging, growing more than 1 metre (3 ft.) in a single growing season with short laterals on the basal sections. Branched laterals grow from the main framework and have a semi-pendulous habit; these are the flowering growths, and during the winter the flowering buds can be found terminating the short spur systems. Prune during the dormant season to remove any long extension growths that are no longer needed for coverage of the wall space. The position of the cut should be made just above a lateral, which may also need shortening. Any weak growths that will not produce flower buds and dead wood should be removed at the same time.

Plants can also be trained to climb deciduous trees and cover old tree stumps, but under this system there needs to be a balance between flowering and growing stems; flowering branches will need to be encouraged, while at the same time a number of extension growths must be left, to allow for the pruning out of any older, unproductive branches and dead wood.

Schizophragma hydrangeoides, trained to cover a shady wall.

SCIADOPITYS

Habit Slow-growing, narrow upright conical evergreen conifer for free-draining lime-free soil in partial shade to full sun. **Attributes** Rarity value, unusual formation of needles, which resemble the spokes of an umbrella (hence the common name). **Reasons for pruning** To develop a strong framework. **Pruning time** Spring.

The monotypic *Sciadopitys verticillata* (umbrella pine) hails from Japan. In its best form it has a central leader, from which the smaller lateral branch system grows directly, but several specimens show a tendency to develop strong lateral branches, which first grow out at an angle from the main trunk and then assume an upright habit which in time will result in a specimen with one or more rival leaders. Some also develop leaders freely from the ground, making a multi-stemmed tree, while still retaining the typical conical habit. Early training is important for as rival leaders develop and reach a reasonable height, it would be unwise to remove them. A good specimen is often well furnished with dense branching down to ground level. While it may prefer a light partial shade, especially when young, this does not seem to be essential, but overshading can quickly cause the loss of needles.

A single-trunked *Sciadopitys verticillata* showing the narrow upright conical habit.

SENECIO

Habit Semi-evergreen, semi-woody scandent climber for moist, free-draining soil in a sunny, sheltered position. **Attributes** Small yellow flowers in autumn. **Reasons for pruning** To remove weak shoots and old flower heads. **Pruning time** Winter and spring.

Senecio scandens (yellow German ivy) can be grown over bushes and trees. A hard winter can cut this vigorous, scrambling climber back to the base; however, in spring it will break freely from the base. Any pruning other than cutting back dead growth after a hard winter should be to remove weak shoots or to reduce long shoots after flowering by about a third.

SENNA

Habit Erect deciduous shrubs for free-draining soil and full sun with shelter. **Attributes** Pinnate foliage, bright yellow flowers in late summer, seedpods in autumn. **Reasons for pruning** To develop a strong framework and fresh growth. **Pruning time** Autumn or spring.

Senna marilandica is one of the most commonly planted of sennas, as most are quite tender, but it will still need the protection of a sunny wall. It should be planted about 30 cm (12 in.) away from the base of the wall and treated as an herbaceous plant, the pithy shoots being cut back to within 2.5 cm (1 in.) of the base each autumn.

Senna corymbosa (flowery senna) can be grown in the shelter of a very sunny wall as a freestanding shrub to 2 metres (6 ft.) high or can be wall-trained, developing a framework of branches against the wall. Prune branches that have ripened in the summer sun back to the framework in spring, when the buds made during the previous year are active; provided summer heat is adequate, flowering will occur in late summer.

SEQUOIA

Habit Evergreen conifer, excurrent conical when young, for free-draining soil in a sheltered position. **Attributes** Stately trees with thick, soft, red-brown bark and flat sprays of green needles. **Reasons for pruning** To develop a strong framework and remove basal suckers. **Pruning time** Between autumn and spring (when dormant).

Sequoia sempervirens (coastal redwood) is a tall species, reaching heights of over 100 metres (330 ft.) in its natural habitat. It is prone to producing rival leaders; these should be

Sequoia sempervirens with basal suckers that need to be removed.

Sequoia sempervirens growing in its natural habitat, Jedediah Smith Redwoods State Park, California.

removed as early as possible, to retain a single trunk that will be stronger later in life. It needs shelter, as in exposed conditions it will become ragged and untidy in appearance with stunted growth, often losing the main leader to cold weather. There is considerable variation across the species in the growth habit of the branch systems; some produce sub-branches that trail down from the trunk for many metres, often reaching the ground. This is probably the most desirable aesthetic effect, and it should be encouraged should it develop. Given the ideal growing conditions and formative pruning, it will still reach a considerable height of up to 40 metres (130 ft.).

Coastal redwood should be planted as small as possible, about 1 metre (3 ft.) high; there is no need for staking as they grow quickly, establishing a strong anchor root system, provided they have shelter. For a time the trunk will be spindly with short horizontal lateral branching, but a strong, stately tree quickly develops, with regular even branching and a well-balanced conical habit. Suckerous growths are often produced from lignotubers that grow from around the base of the trunk; these should be removed at least annually during the autumn or winter, both as a means of improving the appearance and for the benefit of the tree, as they will take nourishment away from the crown if allowed to develop.

Sequoia sempervirens 'Adpressa', 'Cantab', and 'Prostrata' are all dwarf, bushy selections with spreading branches; they do however produce vigorous upright shoots, which if left will develop into large trees.

A mature *Sequoia sempervirens* retaining its excurrent form in cultivation.

SEQUOIADENDRON

Habit Fast-growing excurrent conical ever-green evergreen conifer for free-draining soil in a sunny, sheltered location. **Attributes** Stately trees with thick, soft, red-brown bark. **Reasons for pruning** To develop a strong framework. **Pruning time** Between autumn and spring (when dormant).

The natural habit of *Sequoiadendron giganteum* (giant redwood) is to retain its leader until the ultimate height is reached, which can be well over 30 metres (100 ft.) provided the soil is suitable and when grown in a sheltered position. Shelter in the early years of establishment is essential for a good start; a young specimen will rely on surrounding trees and other forms of effective shelter to protect it from exposure to strong winds. Once the topmost growth is reached, the tree loses vigour and further extension is reduced or stops altogether, and the canopy is taken over by strong lateral scaffolds. When in good condition, the trunk is usually well furnished with branches for almost the entire height of the tree; however, any branches that show signs of dieback or decline should be removed back to the main trunk. Other than this, there are no general pruning requirements. The blue form, *Sequoiadendron giganteum* 'Glaucum', is usually grafted and very slow to grow, so patience is a virtue.

A young *Sequoiadendron giganteum*.

Sequoiadendron giganteum showing the perfect conical shape that it retains into maturity in cultivation.

SHEPHERDIA

Habit Spiny, rounded, thicket-forming deciduous shrubs for infertile, well-drained soils in partial shade to full sun. **Attributes** Drought-resistant, silver foliage, yellow flowers in spring, bright red fleshy fruits. **Reasons for pruning** To remove dead wood. **Pruning time** Early to mid-summer after flowering.

The slow-growing *Shepherdia argentea* (silver buffaloberry) should be trained with a single stem. The spiny, twiggy growth coming away from this consists of small branches, giving the shrub a miniature tree-like appearance as it matures to 3.5 metres (12 ft.) high. No pruning is needed apart from the removal of dead wood. Occasionally multi-stemmed specimens are grown, and these are quite attractive if allowed to develop from ground level. *Shepherdia canadensis* (russet buffaloberry) is smaller and spreading, making a plant 2 to 2.5 metres (6 to 8 ft.) high and wide. These are dioecious: both male and female plants are needed to produce fruit.

SINOFRANCHETIA

Habit Deciduous climber with twining stems for fertile, free-draining soil in shade or sun. **Attributes** Small hanging flowers in late spring/early summer, purple fruits in autumn. **Reasons for pruning** To restrict growth and encourage flowering spurs. **Pruning time** Spring and summer.

Grown where it can climb a small tree, which is perhaps declining in health, or a trunk left after a large specimen has been cut back, the vigorous *Sinofranchetia chinensis* requires little or no pruning. When grown in a restricted space on a single stake or tripod, some pruning of the long climbing growths is needed once the support has been covered. Cut them back to the lowest two or three buds in the spring. Alternatively, stop the developing extension growths at six to eight leaves in midsummer, cutting these back to two buds in the spring; under this system, short spur-like growths build up, which should be encouraged. It can also be successfully wall-trained, but a system of vertical and horizontal wire supports, attached to the wall at 0.3 metre (1 ft.) intervals, will be needed to help it establish. Secure one or two of the main stems to the lowest wires so that the twining growths quickly attach to the vertical wires and begin to ascend the face of the wall. Once established, little or no pruning is necessary.

SINOJACKIA

Habit Loose, spreading deciduous shrubs or small trees for moist, lime-free, well-drained soil. **Attributes** Rarity value, starry white flowers in spring. **Reasons for pruning** To remove dead wood. **Pruning time** Between autumn and spring (when dormant).

Sinojackia rehderiana (jacktree) grows to 4.5 metres (15 ft.) high, usually with many branches growing from ground level, and just as well, because it looks quite ungainly and out of character when grown on a trunk. It also produces a considerable number of young upright branches from the older framework; these can be used as renewal stems. The two-year-old wood has a habit of shedding bark in strips during the winter, giving the shrub a ragged appearance. There is little need for pruning apart from the removal of dead wood as it is difficult, even impossible, to produce a shapely bush with so many crossing branches. The lower branches should be left to provide furnishing, as they will do almost to ground level. *Sinojackia xylocarpa* (Chinese jacktree) makes a small tree to 6 metres (20 ft.) high; it has a similar growth habit and so should be treated in the same way.

SKIMMIA

Habit Small, dense rounded evergreen shrubs for free-draining soil in partial shade to full sun. **Attributes** Shiny green leaves, terminal white flowers in spring, bright red, white, or black berries in summer and autumn. **Reasons for pruning** To maintain a healthy, well-shaped shrub. **Pruning time** Spring.

These bushy evergreens (e.g., *Skimmia anquetilia*, *S. japonica*, *S. laureola*) rarely need pruning, for informality is their character and beauty. They make good container subjects, but provided there is sufficient room, they are most effective when planted in a group and left to develop naturally, eventually growing together to form a large clump. Once established, plants sometimes throw up taller growths, well beyond the general height and

Skimmia japonica growing naturally in a border without any pruning.

outline of the foliage canopy; these should be left intact, as their development is a good sign of vigour and health. At other times, especially when grown in deeper shade, long and bare branches appear; these should be pruned back well into the shrub, leaving a well-furnished, informal surface. Don't plant them too close to an edge, for their characteristic look is spoiled by regular formal pruning.

SMILAX

Habit Spiny evergreen or deciduous scrambling climbers for full shade. **Attributes** Glossy green leaves, wiry stems. **Reasons for pruning** To restrict growth. **Pruning time** Spring.

Personal protection Wear good thorn-proof clothing and gauntlet gloves, as greenbrier stems bear very sharp, hooked spines.

The greenbriers (e.g., *Smilax aspera*, *S. pumila*, *S. tamnoides*) climb by means of tendrils, which occur at the base of the leaves; they also scramble over neighbouring bushes, helped by the hooked spines on their wiry stems, using the extensive long growths they are capable of producing in one season. Plants are best trained to grow on tall posts or tripods. In the early years it will be necessary to tie stems in so that the plant can gain height quickly; otherwise, it will slump in a pile at the bottom. Some species (e.g., *S. megalantha*) are very vigorous and should be grown in the wilder parts of the garden, where they can ramble over neighbouring shrubs or trees at will.

It is possible to restrict growth and size by pruning, but this must be very carefully carried out; otherwise, the shortened stems will look very unnatural and unsightly. The cuts should be made where they cannot be seen, and it is often better to remove complete lengths of stem by thinning rather than shortening every single one to the same level. Some thinning of the weaker stems and removal of dead growths can also be carried out in spring, especially after a harsh winter; however, given our experience with these climbers at Kew, the best advice is to plant them in the most remote part of the garden and leave well alone.

SOLANUM

Habit Vigorous semi-evergreen scrambling climbers for moist, free-draining soil in full sun. **Attributes** Fragrant white or violet-blue flowers followed by creamy white fruits. **Reasons for pruning** To restrict size. **Pruning time** Spring, before new growth develops.

Once established, *Solanum crispum* (potato tree) should be pruned hard to encourage a bushy habit; otherwise, it will arch and scramble over any form of support, such as an old tree trunk or the roof of low buildings. Either way it is an untidy grower and will need some pruning to maintain order. Cut weak wood back to strong, young growths in the spring. Do not prune after flowering, as *Solanum* species are slightly tender and more likely to suffer during a hard winter; mature wood is more likely to survive than the younger growths that would be produced. This subject can also be wall-trained. Tie in the framework of branches fanwise; the young growths should be loosely tied in to a horizontal wiring system in the autumn, and the final pruning and tidying up left until the following spring. This consists of cutting out lengths of the weaker wood and tying in the best of the young shoots as replacements, before the surplus ones are pruned out.

Solanum laxum and its cultivars need the mildest of gardens if they are to grow successfully without any form of protection. The ideal

Solanum crispum grown as a bushy wall shrub in a sunny position.

would be to train them on a large, warm, sunny wall with the aim to cover its surface with their main branches, using both horizontal and vertical wires to aid this. The thin shoots grow rapidly and are adapted for scrambling over supports, before producing a mass of shoot growth. Later some of the thinner and weaker wood should be cut out to relieve the congestion of growth; do this before the new growths develop in the spring. *Solanum valdiviense* will also need the shelter of a sunny wall; prune to encourage the growth of long summer shoots, which will flower the following spring.

SOPHORA

Habit Upright deciduous shrubs or small trees with rounded crown for well-drained soil and full sun. **Attributes** Fine pinnate foliage, small lavender-blue pea-like flowers in late spring/early summer. **Reasons for pruning** To develop and maintain a strong framework. **Pruning time** When needed.

All species and cultivars grow at their very best in full sun and will not tolerate any shade. This allows the wood to ripen thoroughly, and the plant is better able to withstand the winter.

One of the beauties of *Sophora davidii* is its stiff, woody main branch system; many of the smaller branches arch naturally, and it is difficult to prune without spoiling this habit. A branch will occasionally tear at the parent branch following strong winds and remain attached, but once removed the shrub often responds by sending up a quantity of young shoots that can be thinned out to fill in any gap.

Grow *Sophora tetraptera* (kowhai) as a free-standing tree in the shelter of a warm, sunny wall for winter protection, and give it plenty of headroom for development, as it can grow up to 10 metres (33 ft.) high and does not respond well to any form of pruning. The flower buds, formed in terminal clusters in autumn, yield showy yellow flowers the following spring.

SORBARIA

Habit Erect suckering deciduous shrubs for moist, well-drained soil in partial shade to full sun. **Attributes** Pinnate leaves, large terminal panicles of white flowers in summer. **Reasons for pruning** To encourage flowering on the current season's wood. **Pruning time** Early to mid-winter.

False spiraeas, as these shrubs are commonly known, are indeed very closely related to *Spiraea*. Provided they have sufficient nourishment and moisture they respond well to annual pruning, as vigour is directed into the production of fewer shoots, the result being better and more luxuriant foliage with an increased floral display. They form thickets and have the ability to produce new flowering growths both from the crown and the base. Often the strongest growths of all are pithy and originate from below ground level.

A general pruning policy is to shorten much of the young wood in order to reduce the number of buds which grow out to flower. Once the framework for the bush has been formed, the previous season's wood is cut back in early to mid-winter to 15 to 23 cm (6 to 9 in.), depending on the vigour of the shrub. The very strong growths, especially the ones springing from the older branches or at ground level, should be left longer, around 0.6 to 1 metre (2 to 3 ft.) and can be used to replace older wood and branches.

The species do vary in growth habit. *Sorbaria kirilowii* is one of the tallest, reaching 3 to 6 metres (10 to 20 ft.) high and suckering very freely. Remove these suckers unless space is plentiful and extensive colonization would be welcomed. *Sorbaria sorbifolia* is shorter but more erect, with pithy stems, making a shrub to 1 to 2 metres (3 to 6 ft.) high, and also suckering very easily. *Sorbaria tomentosa* has a more graceful spreading habit, reaching 6 metres (20 ft.) high, but is less hardy than the other species.

SORBUS

Habit Broadleaved deciduous trees. **Attributes** Thin lenticelled bark, simple or pinnate leaves with good autumn colour, white or cream flowers, winter berries. **Reasons for pruning** To develop a strong framework. **Pruning time** Between autumn and spring (when dormant); remove dead wood in summer.

For ease of describing the pruning techniques, the many taxa in this genus are split into three groups. All *Sorbus* species and their cultivars, particularly the rowans, are susceptible to fireblight (*Erwinia amylovora*) and are more prone to infection during or immediately after flowering. Cut the diseased portion of branches well back beyond the visible zone of infection, leaving no wood with a foxy brown stain on the plant. Any badly infected specimens should be removed totally and burned. Sterilize all pruning tools after each cut and certainly when working between individual trees.

ROWANS

Sorbus aucuparia (rowan) is typical. It and all the species in this group (e.g., *S. americana, S. esserteauana, S. poteriifolia, S. pseudohupehensis, S. sargentiana, S. scalaris, S. wilsoniana*) have pinnate leaves. All make medium-sized trees and are very popular for small gardens; however, as they grow so fast in the early years, if a weakness is not removed through formative pruning in the early stages, it will be difficult to rectify later in life. Most rowans are grown with a strong central leader on a single trunk with short evenly spaced, balanced lateral branching to form a strong framework, which will increase in strength as the tree matures and be better able to support the weight of a fully laden branch of fruiting spurs.

When planted as young feathered maidens, trees settle quickly into their new location and establish with little transplant stress. The

A well-trained *Sorbus* ×*kewensis* (Kew rowan) with strong lateral branching.

Sorbus commixta grown on a single trunk.

Sorbus aucuparia showing typical habit and form.

lower branches can be removed to the desired height as the tree develops in stature to suit the surroundings and landscape. Some cultivars (e.g., *Sorbus aucuparia* 'Beissneri') are grown for their orange trunks, so clean up the trunk as soon as possible, using secateurs, to show this off to best effect.

Some rowans can be grown as a multistemmed specimen, branching low from almost ground level and naturally producing a number of stems, which can be more attractive than a single trunk in the right situation. *Sorbus commixta* (Japanese rowan) prefers to be grown in this manner, although it can still be trained successfully on a single trunk. *Sorbus reducta* makes a small, erect suckering shrub up to 1 metre (3 ft.) high, and the only pruning needed is the removal of unwanted suckers from the ground.

WHITEBEAMS

Trees in this group (e.g., *Sorbus intermedia*, *S. pallescens*, *S. vestita*) do not respond to hard branch pruning and should be allowed to develop a crown naturally, without any interference. *Sorbus aria* (whitebeam) makes a shapely tree to 12 metres (40 ft.) high with a well-balanced rounded crown; it should be trained with a central leader for as long as possible before it branches and the crown begins to develop, taking on a decurrent form with an upright branch system. *Sorbus torminalis* (wild service tree) forms a wide-spreading tree as it loses its leader at a very early age; it should be trained on a 2 to 2.5 metre (6 to 8 ft.) clean trunk with a central leader and allowed to develop a natural crown with spreading branches. After this formative pruning very little further pruning is needed.

An unpruned *Sorbus alnifolia* with the lower permanent branches retained.

MICROMELES

The trunks of the species in this group have attractive lenticels, so it's best to lightly lift the skirt and thin the smaller lateral branches on the lower permanent scaffolds to make views into the trunk. The lower scaffolds on the upright-growing *Sorbus alnifolia* (Korean mountain ash) should where possible be retained as a permanent feature to show off the autumn colour and prolific bunches of pink-red berries. It will make a tree to 15 metres (50 ft.) high with a pyramidal crown in the early years, naturally maturing into a broad, rounded crown, which should be encouraged. *Sorbus alnifolia* 'Skyline' retains its fastigiate habit into maturity.

Sorbus caloneura is a short-lived tree with a low, wide-spreading crown and a flat top. It is one of the first trees to break into leaf in spring; however, it never seems to get frosted, meaning there's no need for corrective pruning to overcome frost-damaged tips. *Sorbus folgneri* and *S. meliosmifolia* behave similarly.

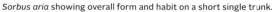

Sorbus aria showing overall form and habit on a short single trunk.

SPARTIUM

Habit Bushy deciduous shrub for free-draining soil and full sun. **Attributes** Sparse-leaved stems, yellow flowers from late summer into autumn. **Reasons for pruning** To encourage strong bushy growth. **Pruning time** Early spring.

Spartium junceum (Spanish broom) benefits from annual pruning in the early spring which leads to more compact and rigid growth. If left unpruned, the main branches build up a mass of top growth, which eventually becomes so heavy that despite staking to prevent them bending over and exposing bare lengths and patches, the whole effect is one of neglect and untidiness.

SPIRAEA

Habit Deciduous suckering shrubs with fine upright or arching branching for free-draining soil in full sun. **Attributes** Very graceful form, delicate white or pink terminal flowers, some with coloured foliage. **Reasons for pruning** To encourage free-flowering.

The shrubby species of *Spiraea* fall into two groups: those that flower on wood made during the previous season (Group 1); and those that flower on the current season's wood (Group 2).

GROUP 1

Pruning time Late spring to early summer after flowering.

Most species in this group produce short leafy twigs from growths made the previous growing season, and these terminate in a flat head or cluster of flowers usually by early summer. Several taxa, including *Spiraea gemmata* (bridal wreath), *S.* 'Arguta', *S. hypericifolia*, and *S. thunbergii*, will also flower directly from last season's wood. Many in this group also have a suckering habit, which makes them ideal for the wild garden. Any growths that spread be-

yond the intended limits should be removed with care.

The general practice for the whole of this group is to prune out a proportion of the older wood after flowering to make way for the young growths, which provide the wood for the next season's flowering. Make cuts just above a suitable growth on the general framework, and occasionally remove an old stem or branch completely to ground level. As always, the growth habit of individual species must be taken into account; for example, *S. thunbergii* produces arching growths. Strong upright growths are produced from the centre and the crown of the shrub plus new growths are produced on the older stems. The extra weight, in addition to the flowers and fruit, causes these to arch over. The horizontal portions of these arching branches then produce upright growths, and so on, until a considerable amount of dead wood builds up under the bush as it is deprived of light. Thus some of the older weaker wood should be cut out after flowering, always ensuring a plentiful supply of new growths without leaving any snags or

dead wood. Other examples of this habit include *S. canescens*, *S. gemmata*, *S. mollifolia*, *S. prunifolia*, *S. sargentiana*, and *S.* ×*vanhouttei*.

Spiraea veitchii reaches 3 metres (10 ft.) in height, with strong, arching growths and any pruning must retain this graceful habit. *Spiraea* ×*brachybotrys* is a dense bush and produces cascades of growth, making it difficult to restrict its size without spoiling the effect, so plenty of space should be given when planting; prune out entire branches of older wood after flowering in late summer. *Spiraea chamaedryfolia*, *S. longigemmis*, and *S. media* have a more upright habit with bushy tops, while *S. henryi* has a very spreading habit. *Spiraea nipponica* is a strong, dense-growing, medium-sized shrub; prune after flowering in early summer to a few shoots, leaving only the strongest.

GROUP 2

Pruning time Late winter/early spring.

The shrubs in this group put on extensive shoot growth during the summer; this growth often originates at or below ground level and produces flowers in the same season. Most

Spiraea betulifolia 'Tor' showing its rounded habit.

taxa are suckerous and spread to form a thicket of growths that, without attention, lose their vigour and become weaker in flower. If the old flower heads are removed immediately after they have faded, some of the plants in this group could give a succession of further blooms throughout the season.

Spiraea amoena, *S. corymbosa*, *S. douglasii*, *S. japonica*, *S. ×margaritae*, *S. salicifolia*, and *S. ×sanssouciana* should be hard pruned in spring, cutting out the weaker growths completely, which allows vigour to be concentrated into the fewer remaining shoots; flowering and general appearance are thus improved. The extent of this pruning depends upon vigour, but much of the oldest wood, even though it supports the young growth, should be cut out completely to ground level. Shorten the young canes that flowered during the previous summer by one-third or less, and thin them out to approximately 15 cm (6 in.) apart.

Treat cultivars grown for their coloured foliage (e.g., *Spiraea japonica* 'Goldflame') in the same way. It may be necessary to carry out renovation pruning every three to five years by cutting the entire plant hard to within 10 cm (4 in.) of the ground in late winter/early spring. The new shoots will then need to be thinned out during the following year.

Dwarf species and cultivars (e.g., *Spiraea japonica* 'Anthony Waterer') should be pruned just before growth begins in spring, cutting all the growth down to within 10 to 13 cm (4 to 5 in.) of ground level. Thus a short length of the previous year's wood is left, though very old or dead wood should be cut right down to ground level.

Spiraea japonica 'Bullata' is a close compact grower. Pruning consists of cutting over the clump or shrub in the spring with a pair of hedging shears, taking care not to cut into the old framework. Small compact growths spring up from ground level to flower later in the summer, extending the flowering display.

Spiraea betulifolia and cultivars make dwarf, compact shrubs with a rounded habit and are suitable for the front of a border or the rock garden. A few of the older stems can be pruned to the ground in the winter every year. Alternatively, cut the entire shrub back to 15 to 20 cm (6 to 8 in.) high every three or four years and allow it to regrow again.

STACHYURUS

Habit Arching deciduous shrubs for fertile, free-draining soil in partial shade to full sun. **Attributes** Pendent primrose-yellow bell-shaped flowers in late winter/early spring, before leaves appear. **Reasons for pruning** To develop a strong framework. **Pruning time** Spring, immediately after flowering.

Stachyurus species (e.g., *S. chinensis*, *S. himalaicus*, *S. praecox*) should be given adequate space to grow naturally, without any restriction to their development. They freely produce young, strong growths from the base, which allows the pruner to remove any of the old and thin growths down to ground level if necessary. Do this after flowering in the spring, although regular annual pruning is not a necessity. In colder climates they can be wall-trained, hard against the wall with the help of supporting wires, and the branches trained fanwise. Replace older branches with young growths from the base after flowering; carefully tie these in for the autumn and winter before placing them permanently after pruning. This cutting away may not be needed annually, and in some cases it may be more desirable to remove the young growths by rubbing them out, thus conserving the energy of the shrub. Freestanding plants should be left furnished to the ground.

Stachyurus himalaicus showing the arching habit.

STAPHYLEA

Habit Upright deciduous shrubs or small trees for fertile, well-drained soil in full sun to partial shade. **Attributes** Pinnate leaves, panicles of white or pink flowers in late spring, papery capsuled fruits in autumn. **Reasons for pruning** To develop a strong framework. **Pruning time** Renovation pruning between autumn and spring (when dormant); minor pruning in late spring, immediately after flowering.

Staphylea colchica is one of the most vigorous species, making an upright shrub to 3.5 metres (12 ft.) high and spreading by means of naturally layered branches and by suckerous growths, which often appear at some distance from the main plant. An overgrown shrub can be cut back to suitable growths, or the old wood can be cut down to ground level. The new growths that spring up may be thinned, the best and strongest retained for replacements. The main renovation pruning should be done in the winter, but the removal of an odd branch or light thinning of the old wood is better done immediately after flowering in early summer.

The slender branching and neat habit to 2 metres (6 ft.) of Staphylea bumalda, the compact, thick upright growth to 5 metres (16 ft.) of S. pinnata (European bladdernut), and the suckerous spread of S. trifolia (American bladdernut) are characteristics which should be taken into account when pruning. With S. trifolia, train the strongest and most centrally placed suckers for renewal purposes, removing the remainder. Staphylea holocarpa has a permanent stem system and a well-balanced crown; train it into a large multi-stemmed shrub or a small tree on a single trunk to 5 metres (16 ft.) high. When S. holocarpa var. rosea is in flower, it gives the cherries a run for their money.

STAUNTONIA

Habit Evergreen climber with strong twining stems for well-drained soil in a sheltered position with partial shade to full sun. **Attributes** Shiny palmate leaves, small bell-shaped pink-tinged white flowers, purple egg-shaped fruits. **Reasons for pruning** To develop a strong well-furnished framework. **Pruning time** Spring.

Stauntonia hexaphylla is a vigorous twining shrub that has a very similar habit to and is often mistaken for Holboellia species. It is slightly tender and in some localities needs a wall with horizontal wires. The addition of vertical wires will help the young growths to cover the available space in the early years. Encourage branching as close to ground level as possible for even coverage of the wall; once the full height of the wall has been reached, allow the growths to hang down like a curtain. Thin out weaker stems in the spring, wherever possible cutting out complete lengths rather than shortening back stems, thus avoiding a congestion of poor material.

STEPHANANDRA

Habit Dense, suckering, arching deciduous shrubs for light, moist, free-draining soil in full sun to partial shade. **Attributes** Small greenish white flowers in early summer, good autumn colour, brightly coloured canes in winter. **Reasons for pruning** To develop strong growths and healthy foliage. **Pruning time** Late summer after flowering.

Stephanandra incisa and S. tanakae are grown for their foliage and for the coloured stems, which shine brightly in winter light after the leaves have fallen. Pruning is therefore aimed at maintaining vigour, thus ensuring healthy foliage and strong growth for winter colour. Annually, in late summer after flowering, cut back a number of the old flowered growths either to healthy side branches growing from lower down on this old wood, or to ground level, still leaving a well-furnished shrub. Take care to preserve the natural habit; these plants are graceful, and hard pruning would spoil the effect of their arching canes.

Plants have a stool-like habit and with good culture and plenty of mulch, strong, young canes will be generated from the base each year as replacements. The annual thinning allows sun and air into the plant to ripen the new growths, which means they will have good winter colour. Once established, clumps have a suckerous habit and form a thicket. Stephanandra incisa 'Crispa' makes a good groundcover shrub, forming dense mounds.

STEWARTIA

Habit Deciduous shrubs or trees for moist, acidic, free-draining soil in full sun to partial shade. **Attributes** Flaking bark, white camellia-like flowers, good autumn colour. **Reasons for pruning** To develop a strong framework. **Pruning time** Between autumn and spring (when dormant).

Stewartias grow best in a sheltered position, with plenty of surrounding space for the natural spread of their branch system. Ideally, the position will highlight the attractive bark of the trunk during the winter. Plants should be allowed to grow naturally; no attempt should be made to restrict their size. Prune neighbouring plants if more space is needed to accommodate their good free growth.

It is better to plant small than too large to reduce transplanting shock. Don't prune young plants too early. Allow them to settle into their new home and produce good top growth with a natural leader. A young specimen that is checked rarely makes a good tree. When conditions are ideal, some of the larger growers naturally develop small trunks as the strong, extending branches develop in the upper part of the crown. The smaller lower branches and twig growth near ground level can be removed to expose the bark, but again, don't do this too early. Wait until lack of light causes them to dieback.

The different species show varied habits, some being stronger and more tree-like than others, such as Stewartia monadelpha (tall

A multi-stemmed *Stewartia pseudocamellia*.

stewartia), which in its native habitat reaches 20 metres (65 ft.) in height. *Stewartia malacodendron* (silky stewartia) is a large shrub with a slender branch system, and the stout *S. pseudocamellia* (Japanese stewartia) makes a medium-sized tree with upright branching and a vase-shaped crown. *Stewartia sinensis* (Chinese stewartia) is best grown on a low trunk and allowed to multi-branch from a low height. It begins to show its beautiful bark effect very early in life, before it reaches 60 cm (2 ft.) high, but be patient. Do not remove the lower feathers too soon, or growth will be checked.

Stewartia monadelpha growing in the forests of Yakushima, Japan.

Stewartia sinensis grown on a low, single trunk.

STYPHNOLOBIUM

Habit Large deciduous decurrent tree with a wide-spreading, rounded crown for free-draining soil and full sun. **Attributes** Fine pinnate foliage, pea-like cream flowers in late summer. **Reasons for pruning** To develop a strong framework. **Pruning time** Late summer to avoid the risk of bleeding from the pruning cuts.

Styphnolobium japonicum (pagoda tree) is quick off the starting blocks after planting. There is a tendency for the lowest branches to put on a larger proportion of growth in comparison to the remainder of the tree and as a result they become unduly heavy, which may cause weakness at a later stage. It is important therefore to retain a central leader for as long as possible, preferably with a trunk clear to 2 to 2.5 metres (6 to 8 ft.). If the tree grows extremely quickly, it may be necessary to restrict the leader and form a crown soon after planting to prevent a whippy trunk incapable of supporting the wide-spreading crown. The lower branchlets often sweep low to the ground, making it a very beautiful tree that is ideal as an isolated lawn specimen. Old trees do not respond well to crown reduction; formative pruning is key.

A mature *Styphnolobium japonicum* showing low, wide-spreading crown.

STYRAX

Habit Deciduous shrubs or small trees for free-draining soil and a sheltered position. **Attributes** Fine foliage, pendent white bell-shaped flowers. **Reasons for pruning** To develop a strong framework. **Pruning time** Between autumn and spring (when dormant).

Styrax species generally do not like being pruned. These large, graceful plants need to be trained with a single leader from the nursery stage and their form maintained once established. Styrax japonicus (Japanese snowbell) makes a small tree with horizontal branching and fine twiggy growth; apart from some encouragement to stay in tree form and the removal of cluttered branches that restrict the view of the beautiful flowers, very little pruning is needed, as pruning can spoil the plant's natural effect. Styrax dasyanthus makes a small tree to 6 metres (20 ft.) high; it too can be trained to form a leader, but the lower branches may eventually die back, needing removal, showing off a clean trunk to 1.2 metres (4 ft.). Styrax hemsleyanus branches from low down at ground level, producing ascending branches with a more rigid branch system, but it is still advisable to produce a leader to encourage a small tree. Styrax wilsonii makes a large shrub to 3 metres (10 ft.) high with a dense habit, whereas S. obassia (fragrant snowbell) will form a small upright tree to 9 metres (30 ft.) with a rounded crown and flowers in midsummer. The young growths on all the snowbells are prone to damage from late spring frosts and may require some corrective pruning to train out damage and reshape.

SYCOPSIS

Habit Dense, upright evergreen shrub or small tree for free-draining soil in partial shade to full sun with shelter from cold winds. **Attributes** Rarity value, small flowers in early spring. **Reasons for pruning** To develop a strong framework. **Pruning time** Spring.

Sycopsis sinensis (Chinese fig hazel) is free-branching from the base. A clear foreground encourages growth to develop on the lower branches, thus allowing the small flowers to be seen easily. The thick, bushy habit is natural and no pruning is necessary, apart from the removal of dead twiggy growth that forms inside the bush. Heavy snowfalls may cause extensive damage, so do remove snow on the branches at the earliest opportunity. If damage is such that hard cutting back is required, regeneration occurs freely, even from the main branches.

SYMPHORICARPOS

Habit Deciduous suckering shrubs for moist, free-draining soil in shade or full sun. **Attributes** Small white or pink flowers, white or purple fleshy berries that persist into winter. **Reasons for pruning** To restrict size. **Pruning time** Between autumn and spring (when dormant).

Snowberries are strong-growing bushy shrubs that produce a thicket of growth even in poor soils and shaded conditions. Care with positioning will reduce the need for pruning: certain species sucker vigorously from underground rhizomes and spread extensively, making them useful for erosion control but difficult to control.

Symphoricarpos albus (common snowberry) is an upright grower with slender lateral branches that droop heavily, especially when laden with fruit. There is little need for pruning apart from removing dead branches and restricting spread by removing suckering growths from the roots. When grown as a hedge, it will invade neighbouring ground, and it is difficult to confine without a hard edge to act as a boundary. Symphoricarpos occidentalis (western snowberry) has a similar habit.

Symphoricarpos orbiculatus (coral berry) produces arching growths when it gains height, and these eventually shade out shorter branches, causing them to die. When grown as a clump, it is difficult to prune this dead growth out. Plants are best left to form a thicket.

SYRINGA

Habit Deciduous shrubs to medium-sized trees for moist, fertile, free-draining soil in a sheltered position with full sun. **Attributes** Flowers, usually fragrant, in spring, ranging in colour from yellows and whites to pinks and purples, some with coloured foliage. **Reasons for pruning** To develop and maintain a strong framework. **Pruning time** Late spring after flowering.

There are two distinct growing habits in the genus Syringa: the majority of species throw strong shoots, often from low down in the bush, which eventually replace the older ones as they become weaker, while a few (including S. vulgaris) build up a permanent framework of twiggy, compact growth. All lilacs are subject to bacterial blight of lilac (Pseudomonas syringae), a serious disease linked to wet, cold, humid conditions and frosty nights, with shoots wilting and browning suddenly. To reduce the risk of infection, keep an open centre in the bush, to help with air circulation; avoid pruning on wet, humid days; and as always, disinfect all tools between pruning cuts.

SERIES PINNATIFOLIAE

The white-flowered Syringa pinnatifolia (pinnate-leaved lilac) is a small shrub to 3 metres (10 ft.) high with pinnate leaves, the only such lilac. It needs no pruning, apart from the occasional removal of dead wood and some light pruning to restrict its growth.

SERIES PUBESCENTES

All the shrubs in this series (e.g., Syringa pubescens and its various subspecies) make graceful medium to large shrubs and will flower with minimal pruning. Syringa meyeri and its selection 'Palibin' are slow-growing compact shrubs; both make good hedges and can be lightly clipped annually to maintain dense growth. If left, they will naturally form a compact plant.

SERIES SYRINGA

Syringa vulgaris and *S.* ×*hyacinthiflora* and their many cultivars flower from large buds that have been formed on the previous season's wood. Generally, as the flowers open, the growth buds directly beneath them develop and extend rapidly, so that by the time the blossoms fade they are often several inches long. This habit can be directly related to the pruning. It is beneficial to remove the old flower heads to prevent wasted energy in seed production, but it is important in doing this to cut them off without injury to the developing growths. If these are injured, or if the growths are cut hard back, the plant will have to open up the season again with dormant buds. Valuable time will be lost, and it is seldom that such late shoots are sufficiently mature to flower in the following season. However, the pruning of misshapen specimens may be necessary, in which case it should be carried out after flowering.

Some of the height can be pruned off the shrub, to keep flowering stems at eye level. If the loss of bloom is unimportant, pruning or even a hard cutting back to renovate may be done in winter. It is a mistake to plant these lilacs too close, as the canopies of strongly growing varieties will meet after a few years even if they are planted at 4.5 metres (15 ft.) apart. Under crowded conditions, most flowering occurs on the top of the bush where there is more light. With sufficient light even the low branches produce a few blossoms, though the best flowering heads are in the crown.

When used for hedging purposes, pruning should be carried out by cutting each shoot away individually, aiming to remove a portion each year back to a general line. A hard pruning over the entire surface will result in no flower the following year. For the cultivars grown for their coloured foliage (e.g., *Syringa vulgaris* 'Aurea'), plants should be

pruned on a four- to five-year cycle to encourage healthy vegetative shoots.

In former days lilac varieties were frequently grafted onto *Syringa vulgaris*, but the practice is a bad one owing to the free production of suckers. Remove these as they appear, albeit they may not be easy to distinguish from the cultivated parts of the plant. The use of privet (*Ligustrum*) as a stock overcomes this problem but may lead to difficulty, unless the shrubs are planted with the union well below the soil level to encourage scion rooting. Planting with the union above ground level leads to poor growth, and cutting back as a means of renovation will only aggravate the position.

It is best, if possible, to grow these lilacs on their own roots and to encourage the production of suckers. These should be thinned out to the strongest canes, creating multi-stemmed bushes that can eventually be used to replace the older stems, maintaining a smaller bush. In areas where the lilac borer (*Podosesia syringae*) is active, the encouragement of many stems also allows for the opportunity to prune out stems that are infested with the larvae, without losing the whole plant.

Syringa laciniata and *S. persica* produce slender, arching growths, which may even trail on the ground as they become longer and heavier over the years. Occasional shaping is therefore necessary, cutting back to upright growths or even down to ground level, provided there are plenty of replacement shoots. Leave these

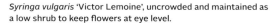

Syringa vulgaris 'Victor Lemoine', uncrowded and maintained as a low shrub to keep flowers at eye level.

A well-branched and -furnished *Syringa laciniata*.

small shrubs well furnished to the ground. *Syringa* ×*chinensis* can be treated in the same way.

Syringa oblata forms weak branches that bend over as they extend and branch; these should be cut back to upright growths after flowering.

SERIES VILLOSAE

This group flowers on terminal buds, but the growth is often distinctive, and the free production of young shoots allows some older wood to be cut out as the blossoms fade. *Syringa emodi* is grown for the stem effect as well as the flower, so some cleaning up of the main stems may be carried out to expose the lenticelled bark. *Syringa josikaea*, *S. komarowii*, *S. tomentella*, *S. villosa*, *S. yunnanensis*, and *S. wolfii* should be grown to keep their natural habit with little pruning, apart from some stem renewal. The many hybrids (e.g., *S.* ×*pres-*

toniae, *S.* ×*henryi*, *S.* ×*josiflexa*, *S.* ×*swegiflexa*) make medium to large shrubs and must be given the space to develop or be pruned regularly to keep them to a reasonable size.

SUBGENUS LIGUSTRINA

These are the tree lilacs, reaching 9 metres (30 ft.) high, and all have wonderful cherry-like bark. *Syringa reticulata* and *S. reticulata* subsp. *pekinensis* have the form of a sizable apple tree, but new shoots will break out readily from old wood if it needs to be cut back. They can be trained to a single stem, which is how to grow them if a definite tree habit is desired. Apart from this, no pruning is needed.

Syringa reticulata subsp. *amurensis* is an upright grower, preferring to grow with many main stems, but the crowded clusters of weak young wood generated in the centre of the bush should be thinned out.

The cherry-like bark on the main branching of *Syringa reticulata* subsp. *pekinensis*.

A cultivar of *Syringa vulgaris* grown with multiple stems providing an opportunity to prune out infected stems while still retaining a healthy specimen.

TAIWANIA

Habit Sparsely branched excurrent conical evergreen conifer for moist, well-drained soil, shelter, and full sun. **Attributes** Rarity value, blue-green *Cryptomeria*-like foliage, long, drooping branches. **Reasons for pruning** To develop a strong framework. **Pruning time** Spring and late summer.

Taiwania cryptomerioides (coffin tree) naturally forms a graceful tree with a definite strong leader and, with a straight trunk running up through the centre of the tree, a pyramidal outline, very similar to *Cryptomeria* and *Sequoia* in

The graceful, blue form of *Taiwania cryptomerioides*.

appearance. This tree needs space and light for development, which will also encourage the sparse, slender lower branching. The spread of this tree is very fine, and it makes an attractive specimen, the perfect Christmas tree, particularly in a lawn setting. It will require some shelter in a warm location but is hardier than most people believe. This tree needs no pruning, except for the removal of competing leaders or dead growth following a cold winter.

TAMARIX

Habit Arching deciduous or evergreen shrubs or small trees for any soil types in a sheltered position and full sun. **Attributes** Small scale-like leaves, plumes of white or pink flowers in spring or summer. **Reasons for pruning** To develop a strong framework and encourage flowering. **Pruning time** Spring and early summer.

Tamarisks are often found growing naturally in coastal regions with almost constant winds, poor soils, and intensive sunshine, which all goes to make a sturdy, shortened growth habit. Under garden conditions, which are usually sheltered with a fairly rich soil, growth often tends to be longer and stronger, with the result that a straggly bush is produced. Extensive top growth is usually produced without the spread, resulting in a dome-shaped bush and eventually to a loss of stability; the shrub may be weighed down by snow or blown out of the ground by the wind. Pruning and some form of support will help to give extra stability, and in the first two or three years after planting, a sturdy framework should be built up by hard pruning.

The species and cultivars that flower in late summer and autumn (e.g., *Tamarix gallica, T. ramosissima*) do so on the young shoots that are produced during the spring and summer, so a sturdy frame can be developed by pruning annually in the spring before growth starts. Prune these growths back to within 5 to 8 cm (2 to 3 in.) of the old wood. These species make ideal candidates for growing as an informal hedge, with hard trimming carried out each year in the spring.

The spring-flowering species (e.g., *Tamarix parviflora, T. tetrandra*) flower on growths made the previous season and may be pruned back after the flowers have faded in early summer. The long and straggly growths are shortened and any weak growths can be pruned right back into the bush. An overgrown bush can be cut back hard, taking away much of the old wood; however, flowering will be missed for a year or two afterward.

Tamarix chinensis needs a warm, sheltered position and rarely flowers, but it has beautiful foliage. Any pruning should be carried out in late spring or early summer after the possibility of it flowering in spring.

TASMANNIA

Habit Upright broadleaved evergreen shrub or small tree for moist, fertile, free-draining lime-free soils in partial shade. **Attributes** Rich red stems, aromatic green leaves, cream flowers (pink in bud), black berries. **Reasons for pruning** To encourage a bushy plant. **Pruning time** Late spring or early summer after flowering.

Tasmannia lanceolata (mountain pepper) does not like to be transplanted. It pays to be patient and plant it as a small container-grown shrub. Mulch with organic matter to help maintain good growing conditions. It rarely needs but will tolerate pruning, which will encourage a bushy plant. Any damaged branches should be cut back to suitable growths as they break out in the spring.

Tasmannia lanceolata showing the bushy branch system.

TAXODIUM

Habit Upright, dense, columnar deciduous conifers for most soil types, including very wet soil, and full sun. **Attributes** Fine, feathery foliage, dark rusty red autumn colour. **Reasons for pruning** To develop a strong framework and remove dead wood. **Pruning time** Between autumn and spring (when dormant).

The natural habit of *Taxodium distichum* (bald cypress) is to form a strong leader and to maintain this until the tree has reached a considerable height. Plant a single-trunked tree with a strong leader; if conditions are right, it will quickly make height and develop a symmetrical conical crown without any formative pruning.

Taxodium mucronatum by water, showing its broad crown.

Once the tree makes maturity and is near to maximum height, strong upright branches are thrown out, usually from the upper half of the trunk system. This too is a natural growth habit; a mature tree has a flat-topped look, and no attempt should be made to correct this. Where trees have developed multi-branching in the upper canopy, they can be prone to branch failure during storms but will send out new corrective growth from the pruning wounds.

When grown next to or in water, the roots send up "cypress knees" (pneumatophores), which are believed to provide oxygen for the roots in anaerobic conditions; they do not send them up when grown on dry sites. The columnar *Taxodium distichum* var. *imbricarium* (pond cypress) grows to 18 metres (60 ft.) high; it has a narrow crown with spreading branches and upright branchlets.

The uncommon *Taxodium mucronatum* (Montezuma cypress) needs a sheltered position to be successful but should be treated in the same way as *T. distichum*. It has a broad crown and when grown next to water it does not produce "knees."

A young *Taxodium distichum* grown on a clean trunk.

Taxodium distichum at maturity, the one on the right showing multiple branching in the upper crown.

TAXUS

Habit Slow-growing symmetrical evergreen trees and shrubs for any free-draining soil, including chalk, in partial shade to full sun. **Attributes** Red-brown peeling bark, shiny dark green needles, bright red or yellow fruits (arils), suitable for hedging and topiary. **Reasons for pruning** To restrict size and renovate. **Pruning time** Late spring or early summer.

Personal protection All plant parts are highly poisonous if ingested by humans and pets. Wear gloves and wash your hands following pruning. Dispose of arisings safely; don't leave them for pets to forage on.

Taxus baccata (English yew) makes a medium to large tree, often as wide as it is high, with a dense, upright, multi-branched crown. It is a good tree for a hedge or screen but also makes a fine single specimen in a lawn or informal setting, provided it has the space to develop freely. English yew responds so well to pruning that a flat hedge-like surface is soon built up if cuts are made to a regular line over time. To restrict the plant's size or spread and yet retain a natural look, prune very carefully in early summer: an informal effect is achieved only by varying the position of the cuts, taking some branches back to parent branches into the centre of the plant while simultaneously removing entire branches back to the main trunk. This operation should be carried out gradually over a period of two or three years. Alternatively, it can be done in one drastic pruning in late spring, making the cuts back to a framework of main branches over the entire bush or tree, but attempt this only if the specimen is badly overgrown. Fastigiate forms, including *T. baccata* 'Fastigiata' (Irish yew), have very upright branching and are often grown as specimens. If the erect branches are left to grow naturally, a loose habit will develop. Alternatively, the branches can be tied into a tight columnar shape with green wire, allowing any subsequent growth from these branches to hide the wire.

English yew is more frequently seen in gardens as topiary and as a hedging plant. Indeed, few evergreens can rival the effect of a good, well-manicured yew hedge. Once established, a yew hedge will need to be clipped once a year in summer, but for an exceptionally sharp and crisp appearance it will need to be clipped at least twice a year in late spring and summer with a fine mechanical hedge cutter or sharp hand shears. Where a hedge has been neglected and is need of renovation, yew can be cut back hard to bare stems, and it will respond with new growth from dormant buds in the bark. Renovation of a yew hedge is best carried out in spring, over a period of three years: in the first year, reduce the top to 15 cm (6 in.) below the overall desired height; in year two, cut back one face of the hedge; and in the third year cut back the other face. *Taxus ×media* 'Hicksii', another popular hedging plant, has a tight upright habit.

A mature *Taxus baccata*, given the space to develop a wide, round crown.

The dense compact habit of *Taxus baccata* 'Fastigiata'.

Trimming an established yew hedge with a mechanical hedge cutter.

TETRACENTRON

Habit Small to medium-sized deciduous tree with a broad, round crown and arching branches for fertile, well-drained acid or neutral soil and a sheltered position in full sun to partial shade. **Attributes** Rarity value, unusual bark, heart-shaped leaves borne on short spurs, small yellow flowers in summer. **Reasons for pruning** To develop a strong framework. **Pruning time** Between autumn and spring (when dormant).

Providing it is grown in the ideal conditions, *Tetracentron sinense* (spur leaf) will develop into a tree similar in appearance to the katsura with little or no training. It is best trained on a short clean trunk to show off the lacily reptilian bark and allow the low-spreading branches to develop freely, which will bear the unusual alternate spur-growth along the young stems. Late spring frosts may be damaging, especially to young growths on small trees.

Tetracentron sinense showing the unusual bark on a clean trunk.

TETRADIUM

Habit Rounded, spreading, fast-growing deciduous trees for free-draining soil in partial shade to full sun. **Attributes** Architectural form, smooth grey bark, large pinnate leaves, corymbs of white flowers in late summer. **Reasons for pruning** To develop a strong framework. **Pruning time** Between autumn and spring (when dormant).

These trees do not branch extensively and should be trained with a definite leader for as long as possible and well after planting in the permanent position. If vigour is maintained, a clean trunk of 1.2 to 2 metres (4 to 6 ft.) can be formed, the leader extending through the crown to a height of 4.5 to 6 metres (15 to 20 ft.). As the tree mature the outer branches are weighed down by extension growths, flowers, and fruits. This habit should be encouraged as it allows the flowers to be seen to perfection. *Tetradium daniellii* (Korean evodia) is the common species, forming a wide-spreading tree with horizontal branching. This tree is better grown in full sun, where it will develop a well-balanced crown; when it is grown in partial shade, the crown tends to become one-sided and irregular in shape.

Tetradium ruticarpum makes a small, shrubby tree to 9 metres (30 ft.) with aromatic leaves. The branches should be allowed to develop naturally from low down the stem without too much effort to encourage a leader.

TEUCRIUM

Habit Bushy evergreen shrubs for light, well-drained soil in full sun. **Attributes** White-felted stems, aromatic grey-green foliage, blue flowers. **Reasons for pruning** To remove dead wood. **Pruning time** Spring and summer.

In some gardens *Teucrium fruticans* (shrubby germander) needs to be grown in the shelter of a sunny wall, either freestanding or trained fanwise against the wall. Bamboo canes will be needed to assist the wall training; tie them to the wire support system first. Long growths that are not required for extension should be pruned back to suitable shoots in the spring (but not before new growth breaks out), so that it is easy to tell what wood has been killed over the winter period.

Teucrium chamaedrys is a low-growing shrub that can be used as a groundcover; over time it forms an untidy mass of growths with erect heads of flowers. It will respond to pruning back with secateurs in spring, but with a large-scale planting, hedging shears can be used successfully.

Both these Mediterranean species make a good informal hedge when grown in a warm climate and can be lightly clipped to remove dead growth and maintain a dense shrub in spring and after flowering in late summer.

THUJA

Habit Random-branched pyramidal excurrent evergreen conifers for deep, moist soil in full sun. **Attributes** Shaggy bark, flattened sprays of aromatic scale-like leaves, reddish brown winter colour. **Reasons for pruning** To develop a strong framework. **Pruning time** Summer.

Thuja plicata (western red cedar) is the strongest grower of this genus of characterful trees, producing a definite leader that runs up through its centre. Provided the tree has sufficient space around it, the branches will spread extensively, providing good furnishing to the ground; when grown in a woodland situation with limited space, by contrast, it will develop a clean straight trunk.

Encourage any strong growths that the tree produces after planting. This tree is very long-lived in its natural habitat on the west coast of North America, where it grows to 70 metres (230 ft.) with a massive trunk; but despite this height and girth it makes one of the best conifer hedges, provided it is regularly clipped to a formal surface.

Thuja standishii (Japanese arborvitae), which makes a tree to 30 metres (100 ft.) high, is sim-ilar in habit to *T. plicata*, forming a definite leader with a spreading crown.

Thuja occidentalis (arborvitae, eastern white cedar) makes a columnar tree of 10 to 20 metres (33 to 65 ft.) high; it is not as vigorous as its western cousin and has a more open habit and fewer lower branches.

Thuja koraiensis (Korean arborvitae), one of the most attractive ornamentals in this genus, has a bright silvery underside on the flat sprays of foliage. If a leader is developed, it should be encouraged to make a pyramidal tree, 3 to 10 metres (10 to 33 ft.) high.

A well-furnished *Thuja plicata* with branches down to ground level.

Thuja koraiensis with a clear leader and well furnished to the ground.

THUJOPSIS

A young *Thujopsis dolabrata* showing a good, pyramidal, multi-stemmed habit.

Habit Random-branched pyramidal evergreen conifer for moist, free-draining soil and full sun. **Attributes** Flattened sprays of glossy green foliage. **Reasons for pruning** No pruning required. **Pruning time** Summer.

Thujopsis dolabrata (hiba), when raised from seed, shows considerable variation of form. Some trees will form a definite leader; others will be shrubby and untidily spreading. Some will grow out of this shrubby habit to produce rival leaders, resulting in a tree with several slender upright trunks with supporting branches. Despite this multi-stemmed growth, these still form an overall pyramidal habit and a strong specimen tree. The foliage of *T. dolabrata* 'Variegata' has splashes of white on the flattened sprays but quickly reverts to the green form.

TILIA

Habit Large broadleaved deciduous excurrent shade trees for moist, fertile, free-draining soil and full sun. **Attributes** Stately street trees, various leaf forms, scented flowers attractive to bees. **Reasons for pruning** To develop a strong framework. **Pruning time** Winter or summer to prevent pruning wounds from bleeding.

Personal protection Take care when pruning limes (lindens) in full flower, as the flowers of some (e.g., *Tilia cordata*, *T. ×euchlora*, *T. oliveri*, *T. platyphyllos*, *T. tomentosa* 'Petiolaris') are said to be narcotic and can cause drowsiness in some people.

In former days the vigorous *Tilia ×europaea* (common lime/linden), 25 to 32 metres (82 to 105 ft.) high, was widely planted as a street tree; no doubt this is connected to its being easily propagated by layering. It is frequent in tree collections, represented by its various clones, each with its own shape and habit. *Tilia ×europaea* 'Pallida' (Clonal Group A) makes a beautiful tree with a congested lower crown that would be difficult to keep clear if this form is not wanted. Typically, the trunk divides into three to five almost vertical main scaffolds, with burrs and suckers common on the trunk and lower crown.

Tilias generally do not like too dry a soil, and given good conditions this hybrid will develop into a noble tree. The leader should be retained up through the crown but, as the tree matures, the upper branches may rival the main leader, which appears to be a natural habit. The main lower branches are often nearly horizontal in character, but occasionally a strong upright growth develops along their length, often as a response to extra light on this part of the tree. A careful watch should be kept on any such growths and if need be, they should be checked or removed at an early stage.

Old and mature trees having large, upright branches that have developed on a mature branch system also need regular inspection, and it may become necessary to remove such pieces in order to reduce excessive weight.

Tilia ×*europaea* grown as a standard with a straight clean trunk to 2 metres (6 ft.), showing the horizontal lower branching.

A mature *Tilia ×euchlora* showing the dense, congested canopy, which has been allowed to develop to the ground.

Tilia tomentosa 'Petiolaris' showing graceful branching.

Normally the tree should be raised as a standard with a 2 to 2.5 metre (6 to 8 ft.) trunk, but it may be planted as a feathered tree, to be trained as the specimen develops with a lower crown skirt. Large burrs often occur on the trunk and these develop masses of epicormic growths which should be pruned back hard to the trunk each winter, preferably with a sharp handsaw. These unsightly burrs and the extra work they involve, coupled with the fact that infestations of aphids frequently occur during the summer months and cause heavy deposits of honeydew, have made this hybrid an unpopular planting choice. Certainly there are better alternatives, and many other species and forms have similarly characterful growth habits.

Tilia ×euchlora (Caucasian lime/linden) has a thick crown and the outer branches are semi-pendulous, forming a dense, almost matted canopy. This may be allowed to develop down to ground level when planted as a lawn specimen. Often there is a considerable amount of wood to cut out from the underside of the crown, caused by dieback through lack of light. It is planted extensively as a street tree and with a good leader and a dense crown with well-spaced branches, it is rightly considered to be a safe tree. This species has no aphis attack and is free from honeydew.

Tilia americana (basswood), although it has fine, large leaves, often forms a stunted crown with dieback that needs attention. The slow-growing *T. cordata* (small-leaved lime/linden) has a fine twig and branch system; several of its selections, with upright forms to 20 metres (65 ft.) high, are suitable for street planting and small spaces (e.g., 'Greenspire', 'Rancho', and 'Swedish Upright', the latter an introduction from the Arnold Arboretum).

Tilia oliveri forms an elegant small tree with a wide but strong branch system that is semi-pendulous at its ends; these branches should be allowed to develop to near ground level. The dense, upward-branching habit of *T. platyphyllos* (large-leaved lime/linden), with tight crotches, is quite distinctive, and it can easily make 40 metres (130 ft.) in height in perfect growing conditions, rarely producing suckers on the trunk like *T. ×europaea*; selections include 'Pendula' (with wide-spreading branches and pendent branchlets) and 'Rubra' (with bright reddish winter twigs).

One of the most distinctive trees to plant and train is *Tilia tomentosa* (silver lime/linden). The crown is very thick, being formed of long, upright branches that are heavy and impressive. *Tilia tomentosa* 'Petiolaris' (weeping silver lime/linden) has beautiful downward-sweeping branches that will spoil if pruned in any

Tilia ×europaea 'Pallida' planted as a single parkland tree before 1750.

Tilia platyphyllos, about 100 years old, making a perfect narrow-domed shade tree.

way, so leave it to grow into a natural shape. Most trees are grafted onto *T. ×europaea*, and any suckers from the rootstock should be removed as soon as possible.

Tilia henryana (Henry's lime/linden) is a medium-sized tree with bristle-tipped leaves. It is slow to establish and tends to be loose and shrubby. Best to leave it to its own devices; it struggles to develop a leader and would be very difficult to train as an upright specimen.

For all tilias, young nursery stock often grows rapidly once planted and produces a heavy head of foliage. Encourage a strong central leader, using a cane and soft, plastic tying tube when necessary. Frequently, side growths that have been stopped produce sub-laterals a week or so later; these should also be stopped at two leaves.

All taxa have a very stringy inner bark or bast, and a twig or branch will rip or tear easily unless a high-quality saw or secateurs are used. Many form cavities very readily behind old pruning wounds that fail to occlude; exposed wood must be inspected regularly and appropriate action carried out when necessary. Pruning work on mature trees should be carried out in mid- to late summer in order to reduce the danger of bleeding and to promote rapid healing of the cuts.

When trees are crown reduced heavily, they rapidly produce epicormic growth along the trunk and entire scaffold and sucker profusely from the stubs of the pruning cuts, creating a shaving brush effect, which after approximately five years must be thinned as a form of crown renovation or renewal.

All limes/lindens lose large quantities of small twigs and branches during gales; these are usually dead epicormic growths no longer needed by the tree.

TOONA

Habit Vigorous upright deciduous trees for fertile, free-draining soil in full sun. **Attributes** Longitudinally flaking bark, paripinnate leaves that smell of onions when crushed, large terminal panicles of blowsy white flowers in summer. **Reasons for pruning** To develop a strong framework. **Pruning time** Between autumn and spring (when dormant).

Toona sinensis (Chinese cedar) makes a large tree at maturity and is best grown with a long clean trunk. Train and maintain a strong central leader after planting and encourage this by providing good growing conditions. Unfortunately the tree wants to produce twin leaders and as one is removed, another one is formed naturally. As the tree matures and develops lateral branching, the lower branches should be removed to reveal the attractive hickory-like bark. The main branching is heavy but sparse; and often there is an even spread of smaller lateral branching from these, which should be left.

The selection 'Flamingo' wants be a multistemmed suckering tree, which makes life difficult if you want it to be grown on a single trunk. As well as being grown as an ornamental tree, where it will need lots of initial training to keep it single-stemmed, it can also be grown in the herbaceous border, where it can be left to sucker freely, producing many upright stems with bold pink foliage. It may be necessary to thin the colony of suckers regularly to keep it in control and restrict its growth.

TORREYA

Habit Evergreen conifers with rounded, spreading crown for moist, free-draining soil in a sheltered position in deep shade to full sun. **Attributes** Shiny, yew-like foliage with longer needles, aromatic fruits. **Reasons for pruning** No pruning required. **Pruning time** Between autumn and spring (when dormant).

Torreya californica (California nutmeg) should be encouraged to develop and retain a leader, producing a straight trunk. The lateral branches, which are pendulous at the ends, will occur in whorls. Nurse the leader from an early age; a sheltered position will help this, as a weak or dead leader is quickly overtaken by the vigour of the laterals and the shape will be spoiled. *Torreya grandis* (Chinese nutmeg) always forms a definite leader and makes a strong tree to 25 metres (82 ft.) high, whereas *T. nucifera* (Japanese nutmeg) forms a large shrub, usually branching strongly from ground level. Normally all three species need very little pruning.

TRACHELOSPERMUM

Habit Slow-growing woody evergreen climbers with strong twining stems for free-draining soil in partial shade to full sun. **Attributes** Shiny foliage, fragrant white flowers in summer. **Reasons for pruning** To restrict size. **Pruning time** Early spring.

Personal protection Wear gloves and wash hands after pruning. The milky sap that exudes from pruning wounds is not poisonous but can cause a skin reaction.

These beautiful climbers grow best on a wall, which also provides shelter and protection

Trachelospermum asiaticum with a furnishing of a close mass of foliage.

from the cold. Both *Trachelospermum jasminoides* (star jasmine) and *T. asiaticum* (Asiatic jasmine) produce twining extension growths to climb naturally, but they still need a wire system on the wall. Tying the young growths in helps them stay firm against the surface of the wall until they begin to twine and helps the plant gain height. Once the allotted space is covered, the growths will keep hard up against the wall, and eventually this will be covered by a close, dense mass of stems and foliage. Any growths that do extend out from the wall can be tucked behind the horizontal supporting wires. The jasmine-like flowers are produced on small laterals from the old wood. Pruning in early spring consists of cutting back any small dead pieces and the weaker growths so that the stronger ones take their place. Any extension growths that go beyond the wall or the space allocated, and which are surplus, can be cut back to a point just above a shorter, flowering growth.

Trachelospermum jasminoides neatly trained between two large windows.

TRIPTERYGIUM

Habit Scandent deciduous climber with strong twining stems for deep, rich, free-draining soil in full sun. **Attributes** Rarity value, small white flowers, three-winged seeds, similar to an elm fruit. **Reasons for pruning** To restrict spread.

Pruning time Late winter.

For the best effect, *Tripterygium wilfordii* (thunder god vine) needs to be trained hard against a large wall that can accommodate its height and spread. This vigorous vine will need to be tied in to a wire system and should be fan-trained to cover the wall evenly. Each year in late winter before new growth begins, remove the laterals to leave a framework of woody stems.

Tripterygium wilfordii trained against a south-facing wall.

TROCHODENDRON

Habit Slow-growing broadleaved evergreen tree or shrub for deep, rich, well-drained soil in full sun to partial shade with some shelter from strong, cold winds. **Attributes** Rarity value, distinctive growth habit, leathery dark green foliage, yellow-green flowers in early summer. **Reasons for pruning** No pruning required. **Pruning time** Late summer after flowering.

Trochodendron aralioides (wheel tree) grows to 20 metres (65 ft.) high. Usually it branches freely from the base, but it will retain a leader quite readily. The main branching off the strong single trunk that runs up through its centre is horizontal or slightly upright in whorls; even the laterals have an ascending habit, but the branchlets on the lower part of the tree are pendulous, almost making the

ground, giving the plant a well-furnished skirt. There is no need for any pruning. In fact, the head of foliage that terminates each branchlet is quite large, making it very difficult to do so effectively, even if it is necessary to reduce size. Better to site this choice ornamental with ample space all around in the first place. The leading growths should never be pruned.

TSUGA

Habit Evergreen conifers, some with a pyramidal or irregular crown, for moist, free-draining soil in partial shade to full sun. **Attributes** Graceful form, with drooping growing tips and fine, shiny needles, suitable for hedging. **Reasons for pruning** To develop a strong framework. **Pruning time** Late summer.

Tsuga heterophylla (western hemlock) is the most common species. It is a rapid grower in the right conditions, making a large tree to 60 metres (197 ft.) with branches drooping at the tips, including the spire-like leader. The young leader bends over and appears to have been lost, but it will straighten itself as it grows: don't be tempted to cane it as a means of encouragement. This tree must have sufficient space and a clear foreground to be fully appreciated, and as many of the lower branches as possible should be retained and kept in a good healthy condition, so that the shapely outline and low skirt can be continued down to ground level. If the leader is lost in the early stages, rival ones will quickly develop; reduce these to one before their second season of growth.

Tsuga canadensis (eastern hemlock) often produces a number of upright stems from near ground level and is often more irregular in outline, with a broader upper crown, than *T. heterophylla*.

Many of the other species (e.g., *Tsuga caroliniana*, *T. chinensis*, *T. diversifolia*, *T. mertensiana*, *T. sieboldii*) may be no more than large shrubs in cultivation. These smaller growers should still be given sufficient space to form a leader and spread out their branch systems, which are often horizontal and low.

Hemlocks respond well to regular pruning and make very effective hedging plants. Space young plants at 1 metre (3 ft.) intervals, and let the leaders grow until they are 15 to 30 cm (6

Tsuga mertensiana growing in its natural habitat.

to 12 in.) above the final desired height. Then make the cut to the first branches about 15 cm (6 in.) below this line; this results in rival leaders developing, which in due course are also cut, forming a top surface at the required height. The sides are later formed by clipping along the line decided upon, and it is surprising how the surface develops as the laterals extend after the leading growths have been cut on the branch systems. In turn these laterals are also pruned, and thus a compact surface is built up. Clipping should take place in late summer, although a young hedge will need a mid- to late spring pruning as well.

UGNI

Habit Upright evergreen shrubs for fertile, moist, free-draining soil in partial shade to full sun. **Attributes** Fragrant white flowers in early summer, dark red berries in autumn. **Reasons for pruning** To maintain a neat appearance.

Pruning time Summer after flowering.

Ugni molinae (Chilean guava) and its selections 'Butterball', 'Flambeau', and 'Ka-pow' have no special pruning needs, except for the removal of dead or damaged branches and the reduction of the long upright-growing shoots, which may spoil the overall appearance of these small to medium-sized shrubs.

ULEX

Habit Lax evergreen shrubs for thin, free-draining soil and full sun. **Attributes** Prickly foliage, yellow pea-like flowers from early spring to early summer. **Reasons for pruning** To restrict size and encourage a bushy plant. **Pruning time** Late spring to early summer after flowering.

The gorses are similar in habit, with the exception of *Ulex minor*, which is dwarf and compact. Young plants should be encouraged to bush out at an early stage, and, if necessary, prune may be resorted to in early spring before growth begins. As the shrubs develop they will also respond to cutting back every two to three years after flowering in late spring. Provided the growth is reasonably compact and the bush shapely, there is no need to go hard back into the old wood; however, growths will break out freely from the older parts of the plant, so do not hesitate to cut back straggly, bare-stemmed shrubs, almost down to ground level, including *U. europaeus* (common gorse), which will soon become leggy if not clipped over regularly after flowering has finished. Do this in spring, just as growth is about to start, and within a year or two the shrubs will be tidy. Gorse makes a useful, tight hedgerow plant or informal hedge if pruned annually.

Ulex europaeus growing naturally and unpruned.

Ulex europaeus pruned annually by a flail cutter to produce a tight surface.

ULMUS

Habit Upright excurrent deciduous shade trees with rounded, billowing crowns for any soil type, full sun, and exposed situations. **Attributes** Majestic stature and form, interesting bark. **Reasons for pruning** To develop a strong framework. **Pruning time** Between autumn and spring (when dormant).

Many of the elms are tall growers; however, some of the species are small to medium-sized trees with wide-spreading crowns. You must have a good understanding of the habit and size of the various species and forms before trying to train or prune one. With the taller-growing species (e.g., *Ulmus procera, U. minor, U. plotii, U. glabra*), the main leader should be encouraged for as long as possible and the tree trained as a standard tree on a trunk 2 to 3 metres (7 to 10 ft.) high. Once this trunk is formed, they require very little pruning until they are mature specimens, when in full leaf they may require crown thinning to reduce the wind-sail effect.

By the time Tony Kirkham embarked upon his career in forestry in the 1970s, *Ulmus procera* (English elm) had all but disappeared from the British landscape. This was due to the infamous Dutch elm disease (*Ophiostoma novo-ulmi*) spread by two vectors (the elm bark beetles *Scolytus scolytus* and *S. multistriatus*), and as a result its numbers have been reduced to a handful in gardens. *Ulmus parvifolia* (Chinese lacebark elm) and *U. pumila* (Siberian elm) make medium-sized, decurrent shrubby trees to 15 metres (50 ft.) high and wide and are reputed to be resistant to Dutch elm disease, but we have lost several established trees at Kew to it. It will be difficult to retain a leader and once a low trunk to 1 metre (3 ft.) has been formed, the trees needs very little pruning apart from keeping the pendulous branchlets growing from the long scaffolds off the ground by crown lifting.

Ulmus glabra (Wych elm) in its typical form makes a large tree to 30 metres (100 ft.) high and produces large branches, so the leader should be left for as long as possible in order to spread the branches and weight evenly. This species is non-suckering, in contrast to *U. ×hollandica* (Dutch elm) and its forms and varieties, which are suckering but produce even larger trees to 40 metres (130 ft.) high.

Ulmus americana (white elm) also makes a large tree to 40 metres (130 ft.) high with a high, wide-spreading crown and pendulous branchlets. Train it as a standard specimen with a strong central leader, and retain the leader for as long as possible. The only pruning needed should be to remove epicormic growth from the trunk as it appears. Its selection 'Princeton', smaller, to 30 metres (100 ft.) high, is grown for its upright form, very dense, vase-shaped crown, and moderate resistance to Dutch elm disease.

Ulmus villosa (Marn elm, cherry-bark elm) has a most distinctive habit: it sheds twigs each autumn, with its leaves, and forms callused and healed scars where the twigs have been shed. The tree and the bark are best appreciated if a central leader is retained for as long as possible before a head is formed. The lower lateral branches should be removed to reveal the trunk as soon as possible; this tree is a quick grower and if a season or two of formative pruning is missed, it will be too late to lift the canopy without leaving any large, ugly pruning wounds. Leave the branchlets to gracefully

A young *Ulmus americana* 'Princeton' showing the upright vase-shaped crown.

sweep down to the ground or eye level, so that the attractive flowers can be easily seen. Like many elms, this species produces large roots near the surface of the soil; as they grow in diameter, they can be a particular nuisance, as they protrude well above the ground and inter-fere with access. If this is a problem, mulch the soil surface to avoid damaging the roots with mowing machinery.

Several popular elms are grown for their resistance to Dutch elm disease: *Ulmus* 'Lobel' has a small fastigiate crown on a tall straight trunk, and *U.* 'Sapporo Autumn Gold' produces a broad, rounded crown on a short trunk. *Ulmus* 'Dodoens' is another tree with some degree of disease resistance, making a tree to 20 metres (65 ft.) with upright branching.

UMBELLULARIA

Habit Dense medium-sized broadleaved evergreen for moist, fertile, free-draining soil in a sheltered position in full sun. **Attributes** Very pungent leaves, small yellow flowers followed by green fruits. **Reasons for pruning** To develop a strong framework. **Pruning time** Spring or summer.

Personal protection The leaves of this tree contain a volatile oil that can cause sneezing and headaches if inhaled and skin irritations upon contact. Limit the amount of time you spend inside the crown pruning and get plenty of fresh air at regular intervals during the operation.

Umbellularia californica (headache tree) should be sited with ample space for the crown to develop freely and trained with a central leader if possible, but this is no easy task, as it naturally wants to grow with several rival leaders, which have a very upright habit. Thus the narrow angles between them at the point of junction may prove to be a weakness in later years, especially during periods of heavy snow. The slightest crack in the wood and outer bark lets in air and water, and this will quickly set up a rot, especially as this monotypic tree's natural habitat in the western United States is sunnier and drier. With a single leader, the laterals are usually quite slender and well placed on the trunk. The inside growths on the branches and the main trunk should be left. The lower branches should be left to sweep down to eye level, as the foliage is quite interesting, giving off a strong pungent smell when crushed. When mature, they rarely need any pruning.

VACCINIUM

Habit Upright deciduous to compact, ground-covering evergreen shrubs for fertile, acid, moist, free-draining soil in partial shade to full sun. **Attributes** Small leathery box-like leaves, the deciduous species with white to red bell-shaped flowers in late spring/early summer, good foliage colour, and edible red or blue berries in autumn. **Reasons for pruning** To maintain vigour and remove dead wood.

The various *Vaccinium* species vary considerably in growth but have much in common where cultivation is concerned. Normally they require very little pruning, apart from the removal of dead and weak growths, but here they are divided into the two key types, deciduous and evergreen.

DECIDUOUS SPECIES
Pruning time Between autumn and spring (when dormant).

Most deciduous species and cultivars are erect in habit. Following planting, they should be pruned to encourage bushiness, taking out any damaged growths and tipping back the remaining growths by about a half of the height. The pruning positions of these growths will be easy to determine, as there are often strong growths springing from the older wood, and any cuts should be made back to these growths. For the following two years, no pruning is necessary. Leave them to develop into a strong bush. *Vaccinium angustifolium* (lowbush blueberry) makes a compact bush to 60 cm (2 ft.) high and will not require much pruning, compared to *V. corymbosum* (highbush blueberry) and *V. cylindraceum*, which are variable in habit but make erect bushes to 3.5 metres (12 ft.) high, with many branched canes. The flowers are produced on second-year wood, so excessive pruning should be avoided; however, following the establishment of a bushy plant, it will be necessary to thin out the taller, weaker unproductive canes and prune out old stems that have stopped producing fruit back to about 15 cm (6 in.) from ground level. This encourages the free development of new growths from the base, to retain a young framework.

EVERGREEN SPECIES
Pruning time Spring.

The evergreen species (e.g., *Vaccinium oxycoccus*, *V. ovatum*) tend to be more compact and ground-spreading than the deciduous species, are more susceptible to frost damage, and require far less pruning. *Vaccinium vitis-idaea* (cowberry), only 15 cm (6 in.) high and wide, has creeping rhizomes that constantly send up renewing shoots from below ground level. No pruning is needed until after five years, when they can be clipped over with hedging shears. *Vaccinium macrocarpon* (American cranberry) also spreads by creeping, wiry rhizomes, which produce upright shoots bearing flowers and fruit in early summer. No pruning is necessary apart restricting the spread of the creeping shoots.

VIBURNUM

Habit Small to large deciduous and evergreen shrubs for fertile, free-draining soil in partial shade to full sun. **Attributes** Showy specimens for the shrub border with scented flowers, colourful fruits, and some autumn colour. **Reasons for pruning** To maintain a well-balanced framework and encourage new stems.

In general viburnums have a very characteristic growth, being mostly stool-like and often producing new shoots freely from the base, which makes it easy to prune out older wood if it becomes necessary. Many species

A mature *Viburnum tinus* 'Eve Price' showing the dense habit.

Viburnum davidii grown as a mound-forming bush with minimal pruning.

will respond to hard pruning, even if there is no young replacement wood at the time of pruning. There is little difference between the species where pruning is concerned, but for timing's sake, *Viburnum* is here split into two groups, evergreen and deciduous.

EVERGREEN SPECIES

Pruning time Late spring to early summer.

As always, the various growth habits of the evergreen species, from low-growing, mound-forming bushes to large, fast-growing upright shrubs, should be taken into account when pruning. *Viburnum tinus* (laurustinus) and its selection 'Eve Price' have dense habits; some formative pruning following planting may be needed to develop a strong framework, but once established, all that is required is pruning overextended shoots back into the plant's surface. Plants will respond vigorously to hard pruning even when cut down into old wood near the ground. Renovation pruning is ideal for shrubs that have grown too large for their position or have become old and tired; if

An overgrown *Viburnum tinus* in need of renovation.

An overgrown *Viburnum tinus*, pruning in progress.

needed, it should be carried out in late spring.

Viburnum ×*rhytidophylloides* and *V. rhytidophyllum* (leatherleaf viburnum) have long leathery leaves and make strong upright shrubs. They should be treated in the same way as *V. tinus*, but carefully prune branches back to the parent branch or to a strong bud or side shoot. If hard pruning or renovation pruning is carried out, these will miss at least a year of flowering, as they flower on wood made the previous year. They will also send upright growths from the base, which will grow through the centre of the bush; these can be used for replacements of tired old woody branches.

Viburnum davidii makes a small spreading mound and is the ideal groundcover plant, needing minimal pruning to maintain a neat plant.

Viburnum odoratissimum and its var. *awabuki* are slightly tender and need the protection of a sunny wall to do well, but they should be grown as freestanding shrubs rather than being formally wall-trained. Any pruning should be carried out to maintain a natural shape and to remove frost-damaged growths and dead wood. The remaining evergreen species and cultivars (e.g., *Viburnum* ×*burkwoodii*, *V. cylindricum*, *V. henryi*) can be treated in the same way.

DECIDUOUS SPECIES

Pruning time Spring or summer, immediately after flowering.

As with the evergreen species, growth habit varies across this group. The key to correct pruning is to know the habit of the subject; in general, however, if the shrub is healthy and fits its position, there is little need for pruning. If it is needed, cut out older wood after flowering, but a caveat: the fruiting display of many species is a strong attribute, and for these, pruning should be left until winter. Sometimes specimens become large and woody with bare branching near the base and with the flowers and foliage well above eye level, where they cannot be appreciated; shortening of the branch systems to suitable growing points will encourage the lower parts of the shrub to furnish up and develop.

Viburnum plicatum (Japanese snowball) and its f. *plicatum* (the sterile form) are wide-spreading shrubs, so give them plenty of space to develop; the horizontal growths from the main upright branches are tiered, and the effect is quite distinctive. Little pruning is required, although the strong canes, which often grow up through the centre of the bush from the base, may either be cut out at an early stage or used as replacements for old or damaged branches. Hard renovation pruning is not advised as it spoils the plant's architectural effect.

This *Viburnum* ×*bodnantense* needs some older stems removed and a light thinning of the remaining stems.

Viburnum plicatum showing the tiered effect.

Viburnum farreri and *V. ×bodnantense* have stool-like branching and produce abundant young wood from ground level. They grow to a height of 1.2 to 2 metres (4 to 6 ft.), and their general outline is erect and vase-shaped, opening out to a rounded head. If the oldest branches become too old and weak for good flowering, they can be cut out at ground level to make way for the younger canes, as general tipping of the bush would produce too formal an effect and spoil the natural appearance of the bush. The lower and shorter branches near the base should be left for furnishing; if you are lucky, they can root where they touch the soil, providing a source of new plants. This method of pruning can be adopted for many other species that are similar in growth, such as *V. lantana* (wayfaring tree), *V. opulus* (Guelder rose), and *V. carlesii*, even though they may flower in the early to mid-summer period.

Viburnum betulifolium (birch-leaved viburnum) is one of the best fruiting species, retaining its red fruits well into the winter, and at least three should be planted in a group. Give it plenty of space and a clear foreground, in order that the heads of flower and the heavy bunches of fruit can be displayed to the full as they bend over under their own weight. Once fully grown, the long centrally placed branches can grow through neighbouring trees and shrubs for self-support.

VINCA

Habit Semi-procumbent or prostrate evergreen shrubs that creep and root for free-draining soil in full sun or shade. **Attributes** Green-leaved or variegated groundcover with white, blue, or purple flowers. **Reasons for pruning** To restrict spread. **Pruning time** Spring.

Vinca major (greater periwinkle) is a semi-procumbent shrub. The stems are soft and upright when they first spring from the parent plant. Later they loop over and root at the tips, continually producing new vegetative growing points. Growth quickly becomes matted, forming excellent cover against weeds, but it can soon spread beyond its bounds. No pruning is needed apart from occasionally cutting the matted growth back to the growth points, so that the border can be tidied up. This should be carried out in spring before new growth begins. When restricting the size of a planting along an edge, it is better to leave an informal rather than a formal, straight clipped line; use secateurs and randomly reduce the size of the plants to avoid the latter.

Vinca minor (lesser periwinkle), a smaller grower with a more prostrate habit, cannot be pruned in the same way; however the whole area can be cut back occasionally to remove unwanted growth and weeds without extensive damage to the vinca.

VITEX

Habit Upright-spreading medium-sized deciduous shrubs for fertile, free-draining soil in full sun and a sheltered position. **Attributes** Aromatic foliage, fragrant violet or white flowers in late summer. **Reasons for pruning** To develop a strong framework and encourage flowering wood. **Pruning time** Early spring.

Both *Vitex agnus-castus* (chastetree) and *V. negundo* (Chinese chastetree) can be tender and are best grown with the protection of a sunny wall, either as a freestanding shrub close to the wall or formally trained against the wall's surface. The terminal flowers are produced on wood produced in the current season, so they respond well to annual pruning in early spring.

When grown as a freestanding shrub very little pruning is required in the early years, but as it matures, some reduction of the previous year's wood will help to maintain the quality of the growth and flowers. Regular pruning to defined levels and spurs will in time produce a rather unsightly appearance, and care must be taken to preserve the natural outline of the shrub. The free production of young growths from the base and on the branch system should be encouraged, so that older pieces of wood can be removed and the plant refreshed.

When trained against a wall, a strong framework must be built up and wired in fanwise, hard against the surface of the wall. From this framework the growths with the old flower heads growing away from the wall are pruned back to within 2.5 to 5 cm (1 to 2 in.) of their bases. Over time a system of spurs will gradually build up along the entire length of the branches to give a complete furnishing. Any tired main branches in the framework can be replaced with strong, new shoots growing from the base.

VITIS

Habit Vigorous deciduous climbers with coiling stem tendrils for poor, free-draining soils in partial shade to full sun. **Attributes** Large leaves, edible or ornamental fruits, rich autumn colour. **Reasons for pruning** To restrict spread and control vigour. **Pruning time** Early to mid-winter (when dormant) to prevent bleeding, and in summer to restrict extension growth.

The stronger ornamental grapes are capable of producing growths at least 2 metres (6 ft.) long, which makes vigorous vines like *Vitis coignetiae* ideal for climbing over old stumps or even up large trees. If grown in this situation, little attention is needed beyond the first pruning following planting, and the vine can be left to its own devices with maybe a little encouragement to climb. If pruning is attempted, it must be done very carefully to avoid cutting through living stems that may appear dead. One mistake of this nature might sever a large portion of the crown.

Vines that are grown in a restricted space can be pruned back each winter to a framework, which is trained to cover a wall or pergola. Any pruning must be done in early to mid-winter, as once they become active there is a danger

Vitis coignetiae loosely wall-trained on a wire system.

that they will bleed from the cut surfaces. The young wood that has finished growing is cut back to one or two buds. This results in the buildup of spurs, which are twisted, gnarled and quite attractive. So is the bark, which becomes flaked as the age of the rod increases.

When grown on a pergola, the stiffer growths do not hang down as freely as those of *Ampelopsis* or *Parthenocissus*; however, some stopping may be necessary when they are grown in a restricted space as the strong shoots, which often grow out extensively, become a nuisance. This stopping or summer pruning should be done in that season, as the growths begin to ripen on the basal half. Make the pruning cut just above a node at five or six leaves. Sub-laterals are usually quickly produced, but these are attractive in their own right against the older foliage.

Vitis vinifera showing the summer growth that will be cut back to one or two buds in early winter.

The same vine after pruning back to spurs.

Vitis amurensis evenly wall-trained with the young wood pruned back to spurs, one or two buds from the main framework.

WEIGELA

Habit Medium-sized upright-arching deciduous shrubs for free-draining soil and full sun. **Attributes** Tubular white to pink flowers in late spring/early summer; *Weigela middendorffiana* has yellow flowers. **Reasons for pruning** To refresh the plant and encourage flowering. **Pruning time** Early to mid-summer after flowering.

Weigela is very closely related to *Diervilla* but don't confuse the two: *Weigela* flowers on laterals from the previous year's wood, whereas *Diervilla* flowers on the current season's wood. Weigelas should be pruned after flowering in early to mid-summer to prevent seed formation and conserve the plant's energy. Well-trained mature bushes with a good balance of old and new wood may need thinning as growth extends and thickens; cut out a proportion of old wood at or near ground level. The rule is to leave the shrub well furnished, which will make it easy to decide just where the cuts should be made. Often the branches arch over from the point of flowering, and the new canes are produced on the more upright part of the growth, below the portion that bends over. When a stool becomes overgrown and weak it can be cut back hard in the spring and it will regenerate freely; the crop of shoots produced is often so thick that they must be thinned in midsummer. If this is done too early, any secondary growth will be too soft and not ripen before winter.

Keep those that produce coloured foliage (e.g., *Weigela florida* 'Foliis Purpureis', *W.* 'Looymansii Aurea') growing freely and encourage plenty of good growth. Unlike the flowering forms, they produce the best effects from young wood, so a considerable amount of the older wood should be pruned out in late summer. Occasionally a growth of pure green without any variegation will break out on *W.* 'Florida Variegata'; remove the reversion as early as possible, cutting back into a portion of the older wood to which it is attached.

A compact, bushy *Weigela* 'Florida Variegata'.

A well-furnished *Weigela florida*.

WISTERIA

Habit Vigorous deciduous climbers with twining stems for free-draining soil and full sun. **Attributes** Pendulous flowers in various shades of purple or white in late spring. **Reasons for pruning** To encourage flowering wood and restrict growth. **Pruning time** Late winter and summer.

All wisterias have similar requirements, and with their natural climbing habit they lend themselves to training over pillars or pergolas, up trees, or against walls. The fact that it is possible to restrict their size without impairing flowering means they may also be trained as freestanding bush to be grown as a lawn specimen.

For pillar, pergola, or wall training, the main growths are tied in or placed to cover the allocated space. Initially these growths may be trained to approximately 23 cm (9 in.) apart, but as compound spurs build up under a summer and winter pruning system on the laterals, some thinning may be necessary to increase the spacing. It is desirable to control the growths that are to form the framework in order to prevent their becoming twisted together, as it is impossible to correct this later. As you train and twine the long growths around a support, keep in mind that the direction of twisting depends on the species: *Wisteria sinensis* and *W. brachybotrys* twine in an anti-clockwise direction; *W. floribunda* twines in a clockwise direction.

The lateral growths produced on the main stems are spur-pruned annually, but in order to promote freer and better flower bud formation, this should be carried out in two stages. The first stage, summer pruning, can be carried out in one operation, or extended over a period of several weeks in midsummer; prune the long trailing growths back to approximately five buds or 15 cm (6 in.) as they begin to harden and ripen at the base. In the second stage, carried out in late winter, shorten these growths again, to two or three buds. This pruning regimen, similar to the one carried out on cordon apples, maintains a satisfactory balance of growth and flowers. It also keeps the climbers neat and tidy and allows you to keep their size manageable. All this means that there is a considerable amount of ladder work at least twice a year on a large specimen, which may easily reach 9 metres (30 ft.) high against the wall of a house.

When grown as a freestanding bush, the branches, although thickened, are not capable

Wisteria floribunda 'Alba' grown as a standard.

A very well- and wall-trained *Wisteria sinensis*.

Wisteria floribunda 'Multijuga' trained as freestanding bush with the help of stakes.

of supporting their own weight, and as the growths radiates out, they will need to be tied to upright stakes. This can be done quite simply by using strong tree ties, which will allow for expansion. Under this system wisterias may reach a height of 2 to 2.5 metres (6 to 8 ft.). The branching will have a twisted, almost deformed appearance, but this is the natural habit and no attempt should be made to correct it, provided the branches radiate from the centre. Summer and winter pruning should be carried out in the way just described.

The stems of *Wisteria floribunda* twining clockwise.

Summer pruning *Wisteria sinensis*, taking the laterals back to five buds.

Reducing the summer-pruned growths on *Wisteria floribunda* to three buds in late winter.

WOLLEMIA

Habit Conical multi-stemmed evergreen conifer for free-draining, acid soil in a sheltered position in full sun. **Attributes** Rarity value, interesting bark resembling bubbling chocolate, Jurassic-like foliage. **Reasons for pruning** To remove dead branches. **Pruning time** Spring.

In its natural habitat in Australia, *Wollemia nobilis* (Wollemi pine) makes a large tree to 45 metres (150 ft.), but as it was only discovered in 1994, we have yet to see how it performs in the garden. All plants in cultivation are vegetatively propagated from several known clones. They have a strong terminal bud with apical dominance and naturally want to be multi-stemmed. When more than one stem is produced, they should not be pruned out to make a single-trunked tree, as the tree becomes moody, sulks, and tends to die back. After a harsh winter, the lower lateral branches brown and die back; these can be removed back to the trunk in spring. Wollemi pines will respond to coppicing should they outgrow their growing space or suffer from winter damage.

A young *Wollemia nobilis* with a fresh flush of growth.

A multi-stemmed Wollemi pine, newly planted at Kew.

XANTHOCERAS

Habit Upright deciduous shrub or small decurrent tree for fertile, free-draining soil and full sun. **Attributes** Rowan-like leaves, horse-chestnut-like flowers. **Reasons for pruning** To develop a strong framework and reduce the end weight of extending branches. **Pruning time** Autumn.

Xanthoceras sorbifolium (yellowhorn) should be trained on a very short leg of 0.3 metre (1 ft.) with four to six main branches. With older specimens the extending branches often bend down with their increasing weight, especially in an exposed position. This problem can be corrected, if necessary, by carefully pruning the branch ends back to the smaller lateral branches. This plant throws out young growths very freely from old wood should there be any need for hard pruning; however, the central growths should not be thinned as this is the plant's natural habit. It can be wall-trained, the main branches tied into a wire support system and the extension growths tied in annually. Any growths coming away from the wall are pruned back in autumn.

Xanthoceras sorbifolium grown on a short leg.

XANTHOCYPARIS

Habit Fast-growing upright evergreen conifers with drooping branches for moist, free-draining soil and full sun. **Attributes** Shapely specimen trees with scale-like, aromatic leaves in flattened sprays. **Reasons for pruning** To control size and vigour. **Pruning time** Winter.

Xanthocyparis nootkatensis (Nootka cypress) makes a handsome tree with a strong leading shoot and horizontal branching. It should be left to develop naturally and requires very little pruning. The branchlets have a distinct drooping habit from an early age. Mature specimens often have a cluster of rigid branches at the base and on one side. This is a type of juvenile foliage and branching, left behind as extensive and mature growth develops. Do not mistake it for stock growth from grafting. In the wild, *X. vietnamensis* makes a tree to 15 metres (50 ft.), but it was discovered only in 1999 and we have yet to see how it does in cultivation. It seems to have attributes similar to those of *X. nootkatensis*.

A young *Xanthocyparis vietnamensis* showing mature and juvenile foliage.

Xanthocyparis nootkatensis 'Pendula' showing the very pendulous habit.

XANTHORHIZA

Habit Low-growing suckering deciduous shrub for moist, sandy soil in partial shade. **Attributes** Fine foliage, reddish purple flowers. **Reasons for pruning** No pruning required.

Pruning time Autumn.

The straggly *Xanthorhiza simplicissima* (yellowroot) spreads slowly by suckers from its woody yellow roots, and as the growth extends on the older branches, they are weighed down to the ground. Its naturally untidy look cannot be corrected by pruning.

ZANTHOXYLUM

Habit Spiny, untidy deciduous trees and shrubs for most free-draining soils and full sun to partial shade. **Attributes** Aromatic foliage, black or red fruits. **Reasons for pruning** To remove dead wood. **Pruning time** Spring.

Personal protection Wear good thorn-proof clothing and gloves when pruning prickly ashes, as both branches and leaves have sharp, broad spines.

Zanthoxylum (prickly ash) is a genus of stoutly branched shrubs or small trees that retain very broad spines on even the oldest wood. Normally the various species (e.g., *Z. ailanthoides, Z. americanum, Z. armatum, Z. piperitum, Z. schinifolium*) require very little pruning, but the crowns often develop considerable amounts of dead wood as the buildup of extension growths deprives others of light.

This dead wood is prone to coral spot (*Nectria cinnabarina*) and should be cut out in spring as new growth breaks out. The main beauty of these shrubs is their heavy branching and unbalanced crowns when they reach maturity, which cannot be corrected by pruning. Avoid pruning to restrict size as well, even though they do respond by breaking out from old wood if cut back hard.

ZELKOVA

Habit Deciduous trees with upright branching for free-draining soil and full sun. **Attributes** Flaking bark, small elm-like leaves, good autumn colour. **Reasons for pruning** To develop a strong framework and remove dead wood. **Pruning time** Between autumn and spring (when dormant).

The zelkovas are of great interest to the arborist, as the species, few as they are, have distinctive yet contrasting habits of growth and outline. They are members of the elm family but show resistance to Dutch elm disease. Apart from formative pruning and the removal of dead wood, no regular pruning is necessary for zelkovas. *Zelkova abelicea* (Cretan zelkova), a wide-spreading shrubby species from Crete, is difficult to train into a formal, straight specimen.

Zelkova carpinifolia (Caucasian elm) forms a crown with a large number of ascending branches that originate at one level as soon as laterals develop from the main leader. They are unruly when young, and you need to be firm with them during formative pruning. Train a leader up to form a clean stem of 2 to 2.5 metres (6 to 8 ft.), as this enables the trunk's bark and the main branching to be seen to best effect as the tree reaches maturity. Without training, the tree will branch low, even at ground level; these lower branches will naturally take on the role of dominance, the main leader is quickly lost, and the crown becomes wider than higher, with the lower scaffolds spreading

The lower branching of *Zelkova carpinifolia* with no early formative pruning.

A mature *Zelkova carpinifolia* showing the almost vertical ascending habit of branching.

A young *Zelkova serrata* showing the unruly habit.

out horizontally. If the removal of any one of these lower scaffolds is later needed, it is often difficult to make a clean final cut because of the density and close positioning of the many branches.

Zelkova serrata (Japanese zelkova) forms a rounded, vase-shaped crown with heavy, spreading but upright branching; however, in the first five to ten years, young plants look so unruly, it is difficult to see how a uniform trunk or crown can ever develop. Maintain the leader for as long as possible; a clean trunk of 2 to 2.5 metres (6 to 8 ft.) is preferable. Use a stake or stout cane and soft, plastic tying tube to ensure the trunk will be as straight as possible. The outer lateral branches that grow from the main upright scaffolds sweep down to produce a low, graceful skirt. *Zelkova sinica* (Chinese zelkova) should be treated in the same way.

A full round-crowned *Zelkova serrata* growing in its natural habitat in Japan.

ZENOBIA

Habit Loose, deciduous (occasionally semi-evergreen) suckering shrub for neutral or acid soil and partial shade. **Attributes** Glaucous foliage, pendent white bell-shaped flowers in summer. **Reasons for pruning** To encourage flowering growths and renovate tired plants. **Pruning time** Early summer after flowering.

Zenobia pulverulenta (honeycup) develops into a vigorous, bushy shrub, the new extension growths being freely produced each season both from the base of the plant and along the length of many of the branches. By pruning out the old flowering pieces to suitable growths after the plant has flowered, the energy can be directed into better and more vigorous growths, which will improve flowering the following season. Occasionally a whole branch may be removed completely to ground level, but care should be taken not to cut out too much, spoiling the natural habit. If growth is very poor, all the old wood can be pruned out, provided the shrub is mulched and watered well.

Organizations
and
Products

Organizations

ARBORICULTURAL ASSOCIATION
The Malthouse, Stroud Green
Standish, Stonehouse
Gloucestershire GL10 3DL
United Kingdom
trees.org.uk

BROGDALE COLLECTIONS HOME OF
THE NATIONAL FRUIT COLLECTIONS
Brogdale Farm, Faversham
Kent ME13 8XZ
United Kingdom
brogdalecollections.org

INTERNATIONAL SOCIETY
OF ARBORICULTURE
Box 3129
Champaign, IL 61826
United States
isa-arbor.com

ROYAL BOTANIC GARDENS, KEW
Kew, Richmond
Surrey TW9 3AB
United Kingdom
kew.org

ROYAL HORTICULTURAL SOCIETY
80 Vincent Square
London SW1P 2PE
United Kingdom
rhs.org.uk

WEST DEAN GARDENS
West Dean, Nr. Chichester
West Sussex PO18 0QZ
United Kingdom
westdean.org.uk

Products

ARBORTIE
deeproot.com

ARS PRUNING EQUIPMENT
ars-edge.co.jp/world/index.html
sorbus-intl.co.uk/ars-range/ars-pruning-saws

FANNO SAWS
fannosaw.com

FELCO PRUNING TOOLS
felco.com

SILKY FOX SAWS
silkyfox.co.uk

SILKY SAWS
silkysaws.com

References
and
Further Reading

American National Standards Institute. 2008. "Pruning". Part 1 of *Tree Care Operations* A300. ANSI.

Bean, William Jackson. 1970. *Trees and Shrubs Hardy in the British Isles*, 8th ed. 4 vols. John Murray. Online (courtesy International Dendrology Society): beanstreesandshrubs.org.

Bird, Richard. 2006. *How to Prune Fruiting Plants*. Southwater.

Bradley, Steve. 2005. *The Pruner's Bible*. Reader's Digest.

Brickell, Christopher, and David Joyce. 2011. *RHS Pruning and Training*. Dorling Kindersley.

British Standards Institute. 1992. *Nursery Stock: Specification for Trees and Shrubs* BS 3936-1. BSI.

———. 2010. *Tree Work: Recommendations* BS 3998. BSI.

———. 2014. *Trees: From Nursery to Independence in the Landscape* BS 8545. BSI.

Dirr, Michael. 2002. *Dirr's Trees and Shrubs for Warm Climates*. Timber Press.

———. 2011. *Dirr's Encyclopedia of Trees and Shrubs*. Timber Press.

Flanagan, Mark, and Tony Kirkham. 1995. "Tree Planting at the Royal Botanic Gardens Kew and Wakehurst Place." *New Plantsman* 2(3):142–151.

Gardiner, Jim. 2012. *The Timber Press Encyclopedia of Flowering Shrubs*. Timber Press.

Gilman, Edward F. 2011. *An Illustrated Guide to Pruning*, 3d ed. Delmar Cengage Learning.

———. 2015. *Pruning: Landscape Plants*. University of Florida/IFAS. Online: hort.ifas.ufl.edu/woody/pruning.shtml.

Grimshaw, John, and Ross Bayton. 2009. *New Trees: Recent Introductions to Cultivation*. Royal Botanic Gardens, Kew.

Harris, Richard. 1991. *Arboriculture: Integrated Management of Landscape Trees, Shrubs, and Vines*, 2d ed. Prentice Hall.

Hillier, John, and Roy Lancaster. 2014. *The Hillier Manual of Trees and Shrubs*. Royal Horticultural Society.

International Society of Arboriculture. 2008. *Best Management Practices: Tree Pruning*, 2d ed. ISA.

———. 1993–2002. *Tree Maintenance: A Collection of CEU Articles*. ISA.

Johnson, Owen. 2011. *Champion Trees of Britain and Ireland*. Royal Botanic Gardens, Kew.

Shigo, Alex. 1991. *Modern Arboriculture*. Shigo and Trees Associates.

Watson, Bob. 2007. *Trees: Their Use, Management, Cultivation and Biology*. The Crowood Press Ltd.

Photo

and

Illustration Credits

All photos by Andrea Jones / Garden Exposures Photo Library, except for the following.

Photos on pages 16, 17 (top left, top right, bottom right), 21 (bottom right), 23 (top right), 28, 29, 31, 33 (bottom), 35, 37 (bottom right), 41 (top left, top right), 42 (top left, top right), 43, 45 (bottom right), 53, 54, 55 (top left), 62 (top left), 64 (left), 67 (bottom right), 70 (bottom left), 72, 73 (top left), 74 (top), 76 (top left), 78 (top, bottom left), 83 (bottom), 87, 92, 94 (bottom left), 97 (bottom), 98 (top left, bottom), 99 (bottom left), 103 (right), 104 (bottom), 106 (bottom), 108 (top right, bottom), 109, 110, 111 (right), 112 (bottom), 113, 115, 116, 117 (right), 118 (bottom), 119 (top left), 122 (top), 123 (bottom left, bottom right), 127, 129 (top left), 130 (bottom), 131 (top right, bottom), 132, 133 (top left, bottom), 134, 135 (top), 136, 137 (top), 139 (left), 140 (top), 142, 144, 145 (bottom right), 146, 147, 153, 154 (top, bottom right), 156 (top), 159 (top left, bottom), 160 (top, bottom left), 161 (top left), 162 (top), 164, 166 (bottom), 167 (top), 168, 169 (bottom left), 171, 173, 174, 176 (top four), 179 (top), 180 (bottom), 185 (bottom), 186, 187 (right), 188, 190, 191, 192, 194 (bottom left, bottom right), 195 (bottom right), 196, 197 (right), 200, 205 (bottom right), 209 (top left, bottom), 210 (left), 211 (top), 212, 213, 215, 216 (top, bottom right), 217, 219 (bottom), 223, 224, 225, 231, 236 (middle, bottom), 244 (left), 248, 251, 253 (top, bottom right), 258 (bottom), 260 (left), 261, 263, 266 (top), 268, 270, 271, 272, 281 (top right), 285 (left), 286, 292 (left), 293 (right), 294 (bottom), 298, 299, 300, 301, 302, 311, 312, 313, 314, 325 (left), 326, 327, 328, 331, 332, 333, 334, 336, 337, 341 (right), 342, 346, 347, 350 (top), 351, 352, 353, 354 (left), 355 (bottom right), 356, 357, 359, 360, 361, 364, 365, 366, 368 (top), 372, 374 (right), 375, 377 (bottom left, bottom right), 378, 379, 381, and 383 by Tony Kirkham.

Illustrations on pages 19, 26, 29, 36, and endpapers by Chas Shine; illustrations on pages 31, 32, and 33 by Tony Kirkham.

Index

A

Abelia, 52
Abelia chinensis, 52
Abelia ×*grandiflora*, 52
Abelia parvifolia, 52
Abelia umbellata, 52
Abeliophyllum, 52–53
Abeliophyllum distichum, 52
Abies, 23, 53–55
Abies concolor, 53, 55
Abies fraseri, 53
Abies grandis, 53
Abies koreana, 55
Abies magnifica, 53
    var. *shastensis*, 53
Abies nordmanniana, 53
Abies pinsapo, 53
Acacia, 55
Acacia baileyana, 55
Acacia longifolia, 55
Acacia melanoxylon, 55
Acer, 24, 56–67
Acer campestre, 45, 56, 58, 59, 61
Acer capillipes, 65
Acer cappadocicum, 59
    var. *sinicum*, 56
Acer caudatifolium, 65
Acer cissifolium, 67
Acer crataegifolium, 65
Acer davidii, 63
Acer ×*freemanii*, 65
Acer griseum, 15, 67, 270
Acer grosseri, 65
Acer henryi, 67
Acer hyrcanum, 61

Acer japonicum, 63
Acer longipes, 59
    subsp. *amplum*, 59
Acer macrophyllum, 61–63
Acer maximowiczianum, 67
Acer miyabei, 59
Acer monspessulanum, 61
Acer negundo, 44, 67
Acer opalus, 61
Acer palmatum, 62, 63
Acer pectinatum, 65
Acer pensylvanicum, 29, 63, 64
Acer pictum, 59
    subsp. *mono*, 59
Acer platanoides, 56, 57
Acer pseudoplatanus, 59–61
Acer rubrum, 65, 66
Acer rufinerve, 64, 65
Acer saccharinum, 64, 65
    f. *laciniatum*, 65
Acer saccharum, 61, 65
Acer sempervirens, 61
Acer sterculiaceum subsp. *franchetii*, 63
Acer tegmentosum, 65
Acer truncatum, 59
Acer tschonoskii, 65
Actinidia, 67–68
Actinidia arguta, 67, 68
Actinidia deliciosa, 67–68
Actinidia kolomikta, 68
Actinidia polygama, 68
acute oak decline (AOD), 290
Adam's laburnum, 192
Aesculus, 68–70

Aesculus californica, 69–70
Aesculus ×*carnea*, 69
Aesculus chinensis, 70
    var. *wilsonii*, 70
Aesculus flava, 70
Aesculus hippocastanum, 18, 68–69, 70
Aesculus indica, 13, 70
Aesculus parviflora, 70
Aesculus pavia, 69
Aesculus turbinata, 69, 70
aftercare, 17, 35
Agrilus anxius, 85
Ailanthus, 71
Ailanthus altissima, 44, 71
Ailanthus vilmoriniana, 71
Akebia, 71–72
Akebia quinata, 71–72
Akebia trifoliata, 71–72
Albizia, 72
Albizia julibrissin, 72
    f. *rosea*, 72
alders, 72–74
Algerian oak, 289
almond, 275–276
almond-leaved pear, 287
Alnus, 72–74
Alnus cordata, 72
Alnus firma, 74
Alnus glutinosa, 72–73
Alnus hirsuta, 72
Alnus incana, 74
Alnus japonica, 74
Alnus maritima, 74
Alnus nitida, 72

Alnus orientalis, 72
Alnus pendula, 74
Alnus rubra, 72
Alnus subcordata, 72
Alnus tenuifolia, 74
Alnus viridis, 74
alpine bottlebrush, 92
alternate buds, 25
Amelanchier, 74–75
Amelanchier alnifolia, 75
  var. *semiintegrifolia*, 75
Amelanchier amarckii, 75
Amelanchier asiatica, 75
Amelanchier canadensis, 74
Amelanchier ×*grandiflora*, 75
Amelanchier humilis, 74
Amelanchier laevis, 75
Amelanchier sanguinea, 75
Amelanchier spicata, 74
American bittersweet, 107
American bladdernut, 344
American chestnut, 101
American cranberry, 367
American persimmon, 141
American sycamore, 267
American witch hazel, 168–169
Ampelopsis, 75, 373
Ampelopsis brevipedunculata, 75
Amur cork tree, 248
Amur honeysuckle, 208
anchor plant, 121
antarctic beech, 232
anvil secateurs, 21
aphids, 250, 306
apple, 35–41, 220–222
apple rose, 311
apricot, 22, 275
apricots, 274–275
aquiboquil, 196
Aralia, 75
Aralia bipinnata, 75
Aralia chinensis, 75
Aralia elata, 75
Aralia spinosa, 75
Araucaria, 76–77
Araucaria araucana, 76, 77
Araucaria heterophylla, 76, 77
arborvitae, 357
Arbutus, 77–78
Arbutus andrachne, 77, 78
Arbutus ×*andrachnoides*, 77
Arbutus menziesii, 78

Arbutus unedo, 77, 78
  f. *rubra*, 77
Arctostaphylos, 79
Arctostaphylos manzanita, 79
Arctostaphylos uva-ursi, 79
Argyrocytisus, 79
Argyrocytisus battandieri, 79
Aristolochia, 80
Aristolochia macrophylla, 80
Aristolochia sempervirens, 80
Aristotelia, 80
Aristotelia chilensis, 80
Armenian oak, 289
Aronia, 81
Aronia arbutifolia, 81
Aronia melanocarpa, 81
ash dieback, 161
Asimina, 81
Asimina triloba, 81
Atlantic ninebark, 254
Atlantic white cypress, 114
Aucuba, 81
Aucuba japonica, 81
Aucuba omeiensis, 81
Austrian briar, 310
Austrian pine, 261, 265
autumn pruning, roses, 316
avocado, 247
Azara, 82
Azara lanceolata, 82
Azara microphylla, 82
Azara petiolaris, 82

B

backfill, 17
bacterial canker of cherry, 23, 274
bald cypress, 352
Balearic box, 90
Balearic Jerusalem sage, 251
balsam poplars, 272
bamboos, 82–83
Banksian rose, 313
barbed wire plant, 121
basswood, 360
bastard senna, 125
bay laurel, 198
bay willow, 323
bead tree, 224
beautybush, 192
beech hedge, 41

Bentham's cornel, 123
Berberidopsis, 83
Berberidopsis corallina, 83
Berberis, 21, 22, 83–84, 218
Berberis buxifolia, 84
Berberis candidula, 84
Berberis chitria, 83
Berberis darwinii, 84
Berberis dictophylla, 83
Berberis gagnepainii, 84
Berberis julianae, 84
Berberis ×*lologensis*, 84
Berberis ×*media*, 84
Berberis ×*ottawensis*, 83
Berberis sieboldii, 83
Berberis ×*stenophylla*, 84
Berberis temolaica, 84
Berberis thunbergii, 83
  f. *atropurpurea*, 84
Berberis valdiviana, 84
Berberis vulgaris, 83
Berberis wilsoniae, 83
besom heath, 149
Betula, 24, 85–86
Betula albosinensis, 19, 86
Betula davurica, 86
Betula ermanii, 86
Betula luminifera, 85
Betula maximowicziana, 85
Betula nigra, 86
Betula papyrifera, 85
Betula pendula, 85, 86
Betula utilis var. *jacquemontii*, 86
Bhutan pine, 263–264, 265
Bignonia, 87
Bignonia capreolata, 87
Billardiera, 87
Billardiera longiflora, 87
birch, 19, 24, 85–86
birch-leaved viburnum, 371
bird cherry, 281
bitternut, 99
black chokeberry, 81
black mulberry, 228, 230
black poplars, 272–274
blackthorn, 275
black walnut, 184
"bleeding", 23–24
bleeding pruning cut, 184
blue spiraeas, 100
blue-stemmed willow, 325
bog myrtle, 230

Boston ivy, 243–244
boulder raspberry, 322
box, 41
box elder, 67
box-leaved honeysuckle, 210
Brachyglottis, 87
Brachyglottis elaeagnifolia, 87
Brachyglottis greyi, 87
Brachyglottis hectori, 87
Brachyglottis laxifolia, 87
Brachyglottis monroi, 87
bracket fungus, 65
branch bark ridge, 28
branch collar, 28
bridal wreath, 342
broadleaved mock privet, 250
bronze birch borer, 85
Broussonetia, 87
Broussonetia papyrifera, 87
buckeye, 35
Buddleja, 24, 88–89
Buddleja alternifolia, 88–89
Buddleja colvilei, 89
Buddleja crispa, 88
Buddleja davidii, 14, 88
Buddleja fallowiana, 89
Buddleja forrestii, 88
Buddleja globosa, 89
Buddleja nivea, 88
Buddleja salviifolia, 88
buffalo currant, 306
bullbay, 216–217
Bupleurum, 89
Bupleurum fruticosum, 89
burnet rose, 310
burr rose, 314
bush honeysuckle, 141
bush standard roses, 320
bush trees, 36
Buxus, 34, 89–90
Buxus balearica, 90
Buxus sempervirens, 41, 46, 90, 201
    var. *japonica*, 90
bypass secateurs, 21

C

cabbage rose, 310
Caesalpinia, 91
Caesalpinia decapetala, 91
Calceolaria, 91

Calceolaria integrifolia, 91
California buckeye, 69–70
California coffeeberry, 160
California nutmeg, 362
California privet, 201
California walnut, 185
California wax myrtle, 228
Callery pear, 289
Callicarpa, 91
Callicarpa americana, 91
Callicarpa bodinieri, 91
    var. *giraldii*, 91
Callicarpa dichotoma, 91
Callicarpa japonica, 91
Callistemon, 92
Callistemon citrinus, 92
Callistemon linearis, 92
Callistemon pallidus, 92
Callistemon salignus, 92
Callistemon sieberi, 92
Callistemon subulatus, 92
Calluna, 92
Calluna vulgaris, 92
callus, 29
Calocedrus, 92–93, 201
Calocedrus decurrens, 92–93
Calycanthus, 93
Calycanthus chinensis, 93
Calycanthus floridus, 93
Calycanthus occidentalis, 93
Calycanthus ×*raulstonii*, 93
Camellia, 93–95
Camellia cuspidata, 94, 95
Camellia japonica, 93–95
Camellia reticulata, 95
Camellia sasanqua, 95
Camellia ×*williamsii*, 95
Campbell's magnolia, 214
Campsis, 95–96
Campsis grandiflora, 95
Campsis radicans, 95
Campsis ×*tagliabuana*, 95
canker stain of plane, 21, 267
canyon live oak, 298
Cappadocian maple, 59
Caragana, 96
Caragana arborescens, 96
Caragana frutex, 96
Caragana microphylla, 96
Caragana sinica, 96
Carolina snowdrop tree, 168
Carpenteria, 96

Carpenteria californica, 96
Carpinus, 96–98
Carpinus betulus, 16, 41, 42, 43, 45, 46, 97, 98
Carpinus caroliniana, 98
Carpinus coreana, 98
Carpinus fangiana, 98
Carpinus turczaninowii, 97
Carrierea, 98
Carrierea calycina, 98
Carya, 24, 99
Carya cordiformis, 99
Carya illinoiensis, 99
Carya ovata, 99
Caryopteris, 100
Caryopteris incana, 100
Caryopteris ×*landonensis*, 100
Caryopteris mongholica, 100
Cassiope, 100
Cassiope tetragona, 100
Cassiope wardii, 100
Castanea, 100–101
Castanea dentata, 101
Castanea sativa, 43, 45, 100–101
Castanopsis, 102
Castanopsis chrysophylla, 102
Castanopsis cuspidata, 102
Casuarina, 102
Casuarina equisetifolia, 102
Catalpa, 103–104
Catalpa bignonioides, 44, 103–104, 104, 115
Catalpa fargesii, 103
Catalpa speciosa, 103
Cathaya, 104
Cathaya argyrophylla, 104
Caucasian elm, 380–383
Caucasian lime/linden, 360
Caucasian wingnut, 284–285
Ceanothus, 105
Ceanothus arboreus, 105
Ceanothus rigidus, 105
Ceanothus thyrsiflorus, 105
    var. *repens*, 105
Ceanothus velutinus, 105
cedar, 35
Cedrus, 105–107
Cedrus atlantica, 107
Cedrus deodara, 106, 107
Cedrus libani, 105–106, 107
    var. *brevifolia*, 107
Celastrus, 107

Celastrus orbiculatus, 107
Celastrus scandens, 107
Celtis, 107–108
Celtis australis, 108
Celtis choseniana, 108
Celtis glabrata, 108
Celtis jezoensis, 108
Celtis laevigata, 108
Celtis occidentalis, 108
Celtis pumila, 108
Celtis tournefortii, 108
Cephalotaxus, 108–109
Cephalotaxus fortunei, 109
Cephalotaxus harringtonia, 109
    var. *drupacea*, 110
Cephalotaxus wilsoniana, 109
Ceratocystis fagacearum, 23, 296
Ceratocystis fimbriata f. *platani*, 21, 267
Ceratostigma, 109–110
Ceratostigma griffithii, 109–110
Ceratostigma willmottianum, 109–110
Cercidiphyllum, 110–111
Cercidiphyllum japonicum, 110–111
    f. *pendulum*, 110, 111
Cercidiphyllum magnificum, 110
Cercis, 111–112
Cercis canadensis, 112
Cercis chinensis, 112
Cercis racemosa, 112
Cercis siliquastrum, 111–112
Chaenomeles, 15, 112–113
Chaenomeles cathayensis, 113
Chaenomeles japonica, 49, 113
Chaenomeles speciosa, 49, 112–113
Chaenomeles ×*superba*, 113
chain-flowered redbud, 112
chalara dieback of ash, 21
Chamaecyparis, 23, 43, 113–114, 134
Chamaecyparis lawsoniana, 113–114
Chamaecyparis pisifera, 114
Chamaecyparis thyoides, 114
Chamaerops humilis, 240
chastetree, 371
checkerberry, 164
Cherokee rose, 313
cherry, 18, 22, 276–281
cherry-bark elm, 366
cherry laurel, 281–282
cherry plum, 275
cherry prinsepia, 274
chestnut blight, 101
chestnut oak, 290
Chilean bellflower, 196

Chilean guava, 365
Chilean jasmine, 223
Chilean lantern tree, 130
Chilean laurel, 198
Chilean myrtle, 211
Chilopsis linearis, 115
Chimonanthus, 114
Chimonanthus praecox, 114
China rose, 313
Chinese cedar, 362
Chinese chastetree, 371
Chinese cork oak, 293
Chinese fig hazel, 348
Chinese fir, 132
Chinese fringe flower, 211
Chinese fringetree, 115
Chinese gooseberry, 67
Chinese hydrangea vine, 330–331
Chinese jacktree, 336
Chinese lacebark elm, 366
Chinese money maple, 142
Chinese mulberry, 230
Chinese necklace poplar, 272
Chinese nutmeg, 362
Chinese parasol tree, 158
Chinese pear, 287
Chinese pearl-bloom tree, 269
Chinese pistache, 266
Chinese plumbago, 109–110
Chinese privet, 201
Chinese quince, 113
Chinese redbud, 112
Chinese silver fir, 104
Chinese stewartia, 346
Chinese swamp cypress, 166
Chinese tulip tree, 206
Chinese wingnut, 284
Chinese yellow wood, 212
Chinese zelkova, 383
chinquapins, 102
Chionanthus, 115
Chionanthus retusus, 115
Chionanthus virginicus, 115
×*Chitalpa*, 115
Chitalpa ×*tashkentensis*, 115
Choisya, 115–116
Choisya arizonica, 116
Choisya ×*dewitteana*, 116
Choisya ternata, 116
Chondrostereum purpureum, 22, 274
Christmas berry, 172
Christ's thorn, 240
Chusan palm, 240–241

Cistus, 116
Cistus ladanifer, 116
Cistus monspeliensis, 116
Cistus pulverulentus, 116
Cistus purpureus, 116
Cladrastis, 117
Cladrastis kentukea, 117
"cleaning out a canopy", 15
clematis, 48, 117–119
Clematis, 117–119
Clematis alpina, 118
Clematis aristata, 118
Clematis armandii, 118, 119
Clematis ×*cartmanii*, 118
Clematis chrysocoma, 118
Clematis cirrhosa, 118
Clematis macropetala, 118
Clematis montana, 117, 118
    var. *rubens*, 118
Clematis orientalis, 119
Clematis rehderiana, 118
Clematis tangutica, 118, 119
Clematis terniflora, 118
Clematis tibetana, 119
clematis wilt, 119
Clerodendrum, 120
Clerodendrum bungei, 120
Clerodendrum trichotomum, 120
Clethra, 121
Clethra acuminata, 121
Clethra alnifolia, 121
Clethra barbinervis, 121
Clethra monostachya, 121
Clethra tomentosa, 121
cliff bush, 181
climbers, 47–48
climbing hydrangea, 259
climbing roses, 47, 319–320
cloud-pruning, 90
clump-forming bamboos, 82–83
cluster-flowered bush roses, 316
coastal redwood, 332–334
coast live oak, 297
Cocculus, 121
Cocculus orbiculatus, 121
coffin tree, 350
coigue, 232
Colletia, 121
Colletia hystrix, 121
Colletia paradoxa, 121
Colutea, 121
Colutea arborescens, 121
Colutea orientalis, 121

common almond, 275
common ash, 160–161
common gorse, 365
common hackberry, 108
common privet, 201
common sage, 326
common snowberry, 348
compost, 16, 17
composted woodchip, 35
conifers, 23
coppicing, 43–45
coral bead, 121
coral berry, 348
coral spot, 16, 65, 86, 99, 111, 175, 216, 302, 380
cordon tree form, 36, 39–40
cork oak, 295
cornelian cherry, 122
Cornus, 122–125
Cornus alba, 34, 44, 45, 124, 125
Cornus alternifolia, 124
Cornus angustata, 123
cornus anthracnose, 21, 123
Cornus capitata, 123
Cornus controversa, 123–124
Cornus elliptica, 123
Cornus florida, 122, 124
Cornus kousa, 123, 124
  var. *chinensis*, 123
Cornus mas, 122
Cornus nuttallii, 122, 124
Cornus officinalis, 122
Cornus racemosa, 124
Cornus rugosa, 124
Cornus ×rutgersensis, 124
Cornus sanguinea, 124
Coronilla, 125
Coronilla valentina, 125
corrective formative pruning, 13–14
Corsican heath, 148
Corylopsis, 125
Corylopsis glabrescens, 125
Corylopsis sinensis, 125
Corylus, 125–126
Corylus avellana, 43, 44, 45, 126
Corylus chinensis, 125
Corylus colurna, 125
Corylus maxima, 126
Corylus tibetica, 126
coryneum canker, 134
Cotinus, 127–128
Cotinus coggygria, 127–128
Cotinus obovatus, 127

Cotoneaster, 128–129
Cotoneaster adpressus, 129
Cotoneaster apiculatus, 129
Cotoneaster ascendens, 129
Cotoneaster bullatus, 128
Cotoneaster conspicuus, 129
Cotoneaster dammeri, 129
Cotoneaster divaricatus, 129
Cotoneaster franchetii, 128
Cotoneaster frigidus, 128
Cotoneaster horizontalis, 129
Cotoneaster insignis, 128
Cotoneaster lacteus, 128
Cotoneaster lucidus, 129
Cotoneaster multiflorus, 128
Cotoneaster salicifolius, 128, 129
Cotoneaster simonsii, 128
Cotoneaster ×suecicus, 129
Cotoneaster ×watereri, 128
cowberry, 367
crab apple, 220, 222
crack willow, 323
crape myrtles, 195
Crataegus, 42, 129–130
Crataegus laevigata, 18
Crataegus monogyna, 43, 129
Crataegus submollis, 130
creeping wire vine, 230
Cretan zelkova, 380
Crinodendron, 130
Crinodendron hookerianum, 130
Crinodendron patagua, 130
cross-leaved heath, 149
crown lifting, 12, 31
crown reduction, 32–33
crown renovation/renewal, 33
crown thinning, 32
Cryphonectria parasitica, 101
Cryptomeria, 130–131, 350
Cryptomeria japonica, 130–131
cultivation, 16–17
Cunninghamia, 132
Cunninghamia konishii, 132
Cunninghamia lanceolata, 132
Cupressus, 23, 43, 132–133
Cupressus arizonica, 133
Cupressus cashmeriana, 133
Cupressus macrocarpa, 132–133
Cupressus sempervirens, 133
×*Cuprocyparis*, 134
×*Cuprocyparis leylandii*, 134
cut-leaved crab apple, 222
Cydonia, 134–135

Cydonia oblonga, 134–135
Cytisus, 135–136
Cytisus ×beanii, 136
Cytisus ×kewensis, 136
Cytisus multiflorus, 135
Cytisus nigricans, 136
Cytisus praecox, 135
Cytisus scoparius, 135
cytospora dieback of cherry laurel, 282
Cytospora laurocerasi, 282

D

Dahurian birch, 86
Dahurian buckthorn, 299
Daimio oak, 290
damaged branches, 15–16, 23, 31
damask rose, 310
Dane's elder, 327
Daphne, 136
Daphne bholua, 136
Daphne blagayana, 136
Daphne cneorum, 136
Daphne mezereum, 136
Daphne petraea, 136
Daphniphyllum, 137
Daphniphyllum macropodum, 137
Dasiphora fruticosa, 137
date plum, 141
Davidia involucrata, 138
dawn redwood, 226–227
dead branches, 15–16, 23, 31
deadheading
  Grevillea, 166
  Kalmia, 188
  Lagerstroemia, 195
  rhododendrons, 300
  roses, 315–316, 318
dead man's fingers, 139
deadwood removal, 31
Decaisnea, 139
Decaisnea fargesii, 139
decurrent tree, 11, 18
Delavay privet, 201
denatured alcohol, 22
Deodar cedar, 107
desert willow, 115
Desfontainia, 139
Desfontainia spinosa, 139
Deutzia, 139–140
Deutzia coreana, 140
Deutzia gracilis, 140

Deutzia ×*lemoinei*, 140
Deutzia monbeigii, 140
Deutzia pulchra, 139
Deutzia purpurascens, 140
Deutzia ×*rosea*, 140
Deutzia scabra, 139
Deutzia setchuenensis, 140
devil's club, 237
diamond sharpener, 21, 22
dieback, 24, 289–290, 292
Diervilla, 141, 373
Diervilla lonicera, 141
Diervilla rivularis, 141
Diervilla sessilifolia, 141
Diervilla ×*splendens*, 141
Diospyros, 141
Diospyros kaki, 141
Diospyros lotus, 141
Diospyros virginiana, 11, 141
Dipelta, 142
Dipelta floribunda, 142
Dipelta ventricosa, 142
Dipelta yunnanensis, 142
Dipteronia, 142
Dipteronia sinensis, 142
Disanthus, 142
Disanthus cercidifolius, 142
Discaria chacaye, 143
Discaria toumatou, 143
Discosporium populeum, 274
Discula destructiva, 21, 123
diseased branches, 15–16, 23, 31
diseases, 15–16, 22–23
Distylium, 143
Distylium racemosum, 143
dog hobble, 200
dog rose, 311
dogwood, 122–125
Dorset heath, 148
Douglas fir, 283
dove tree, 138
Drimys winteri, 143
Dutch elm disease, 366, 367
dwarf Russian almond, 276
dwarf suckering rose, 311
dying branches, 15–16, 23, 31

E

early flowering clematis, 118–119
eastern hemlock, 364
eastern white cedar, 357

Edgeworthia chrysantha, 144
Ehretia, 144
Ehretia acuminata, 144
Ehretia dicksonii, 144
Elaeagnus, 145–146
Elaeagnus angustifolia, 145
Elaeagnus ×*ebbingei*, 146
Elaeagnus glabra, 145
Elaeagnus macrophylla, 145
Elaeagnus multiflora, 145
Elaeagnus ×*reflexa*, 145
Elaeagnus umbellata, 145
Eleutherococcus, 146
Eleutherococcus lasiogyne, 146
Eleutherococcus sieboldianus, 146
elm bark beetles, 366
Embothrium, 146
Embothrium coccineum, 146
Emmenopterys henryi, 146
English holly, 179–180
English lavender, 199
English oak, 289
English walnut, 184
English yew, 354–355
Enkianthus, 147
Enkianthus campanulatus, 147
Enkianthus deflexus, 147
Enkianthus perulatus, 147
epaulette tree, 285
epicormic shoots, 33–34
Erica, 147–149
Erica arborea, 147–148, 149
Erica australis, 148
Erica canaliculata, 148
Erica carnea, 148
Erica ciliaris, 148
Erica ×*darleyensis*, 148
Erica erigena, 148
Erica lusitanica, 148
Erica mackayana, 148–149
Erica scoparia, 149
Erica terminalis, 148
Erica tetralix, 149
Erica vagans, 149
Erica ×*veitchii*, 148
Eriobotrya, 149
Eriobotrya japonica, 149
Erwinia amylovora, 15, 129, 253, 287, 289, 338
Escallonia, 49, 150
Escallonia illinita, 150
Escallonia rubra var. *macrantha*, 150
Escallonia virgata, 150

espalier tree form, 36, 40–41
Eucalyptus, 150–151
Eucalyptus pauciflora, 150
  subsp. *niphophila*, 150
Eucommia, 151
Eucommia ulmoides, 151
Eucryphia, 151
Eucryphia ×*nymansensis*, 151
Euonymus, 151–152
Euonymus alatus, 151–152
Euonymus bungeanus, 151
Euonymus europaeus, 152
Euonymus fortunei, 152
Euonymus grandiflorus subsp.
  morrisonensis, 152
Euonymus japonicus, 152
Euphorbia, 152
Euphorbia characias subsp. *wulfenii*, 152
Euptelea, 153
Euptelea pleiosperma, 153
Euptelea polyandra, 153
European beech, 153
European bladdernut, 344
European hornbeam, 97
European larch, 196
European nettle tree, 108
Eurya, 153
Eurya japonica, 153
evergreen laburnum, 265
Exbury azaleas, 300
excurrent tree, 11, 18
Exochorda, 153
Exochorda giraldii, 153
Exochorda korolkowii, 153
Exochorda ×*macrantha*, 153
eye protection, 22

F

Fagus, 11, 153–155
Fagus grandifolia, 155
Fagus japonica, 155
Fagus sylvatica, 16, 41, 42, 43, 45, 153–154
Fallopia, 155–156
Fallopia baldschuanica, 155–156
false acacia, 307, 308
false castor oil plant, 156
fan tree form, 36, 39
Fargesia murielae, 82
Fargesia nitida, 82
fastigiate tree, 18

Father David's maple, 63
Father David's rose, 312
Father Hugo's rose, 308
×*Fatshedera*, 156
Fatshedera ×*lizei*, 156
Fatsia, 156–157
Fatsia japonica, 156
feathered tree, 18
fern tree, 208
feverbush, 202
Ficus, 157–158
Ficus carica, 157–158
field maple, 59
filbert, 126
fireblight, 15, 129, 253, 287, 289, 338
Firmiana, 158
Firmiana simplex, 158
Fitzroya, 158
Fitzroya cupressoides, 158
flowering currant, 304–306
flowering quince, 112–113
flowering raspberry, 322
flowery senna, 332
flush cutting, 29
folding saws, 21
forked/twin leaders, 11–12
formal hedges, 41–42
formative pruning, 11–13
Forsythia, 14, 24, 158–159
Forsythia ×*intermedia*, 159
Forsythia suspensa, 159
    f. *atrocaulis*, 159
    var. *sieboldii*, 159
Fothergilla, 159
Fothergilla gardenii, 159
Fothergilla ×*intermedia*, 159
Fothergilla major, 159
fountain butterfly bush, 88–89
fragrant snowbell, 348
fragrant sumach, 304
Frangula, 160
Frangula californica, 160
Franklinia, 160
Franklinia alatamaha, 160
Franklin tree, 160
Fraxinus, 161
Fraxinus americana, 160, 161
Fraxinus angustifolia, 160
    subsp. *syriaca*, 161
Fraxinus dipetala, 161
Fraxinus excelsior, 160–161
Fraxinus latifolia, 160
Fraxinus mandshurica, 161

Fraxinus ornus, 160, 161
Fraxinus pennsylvanica, 161
French lavender, 199
French rose, 310
fruit trees
    cordon tree form, 36, 39–40
    espalier tree form, 36, 40–41
    fan tree form, 36, 39
    forms, 35–36, 39–41
    pruning established, 37–39
    pruning over-vigorous fruit trees, 38
    pyramid tree form, 36, 39
    renovation pruning, 38–39
    stepover tree form, 36, 41
    summer pruning, 38
    training, 36–37
    winter pruning, 37–38, 40
Fuchsia, 162–163
Fuchsia magellanica, 34, 162–163
Fuji cherry, 280–281
fungal diseases, 21, 22–23, 274, 276

G

Ganoderma applanatum, 65
garden plum, 275
Garrya, 163
Garrya elliptica, 49, 163
Garrya ×*issaquahensis*, 163
Garrya laurifolia subsp. *macrophylla*, 163
Garrya ×*thuretii*, 163
Gaultheria, 164
Gaultheria hookeri, 164
Gaultheria mucronata, 164
Gaultheria procumbens, 164
Gaultheria shallon, 164
Gaultheria ×*wisleyensis*, 164
Genista, 164
Genista aetnensis, 164
Genista cinerea, 164
Genista horrida, 164
Genista lydia, 164
Genista monspessulana, 164
Genista sagittalis, 164
Genista tenera, 164
Georgia oak, 297
ghost bramble, 322
giant filbert, 126
giant redwood, 335
Ginkgo, 164–165
Ginkgo biloba, 18, 164–165
Gleditsia, 165–166

Gleditsia caspica, 166
Gleditsia delavayi, 166
Gleditsia japonica, 166
Gleditsia sinensis, 166
Gleditsia triacanthos, 165–166
    f. *inermis*, 166
    var. *nana*, 166
glory flower, 120
Glyptostrobus, 166
Glyptostrobus pensilis, 166
goat horn tree, 98
goat willow, 325
golden chain tree, 195
golden larch, 282
golden-leaved Jerusalem sage, 251
golden oak, 293
grape vines, 24
greater periwinkle, 371
Grevillea, 166
Griselinia, 166–167
Griselinia littoralis, 43, 167
Griselinia racemosa, 167
Guelder rose, 371
Gymnocladus, 167
Gymnocladus dioicus, 167

H

hackberries, 107–108
Halesia, 168
Halesia carolina, 168
Halesia diptera, 168
Halesia macgregorii, 168
×*Halimiocistus*, 168
×*Halimiocistus sahucii*, 168
×*Halimiocistus wintonensis*, 168
Hamamelis, 168–170
Hamamelis ×*intermedia*, 169
Hamamelis virginiana, 168–169
hand-hedging shears, 42
handkerchief tree, 138
handsaws, 13, 15, 21, 26–27
hard pruning, 34–35
hardy rubber tree, 151
harlequin glorybower, 120
harsh downy rose, 311
hawthorn, 18, 42
hazel, 126
headache tree, 367
healthy nursery stock, 16
heather, 147–149
Hebe, 170

Hebe albicans, 170
Hebe brachysiphon, 170
Hebe cupressoides, 170
Hebe ×*franciscana*, 170
Hebe odora, 170
Hebe pinguifolia, 170
Hebe salicifolia, 170
Hebe speciosa, 170
Hedera, 156, 170–171
Hedera colchica, 171
Hedera helix, 47, 170, 171
hedge renovation, 43
hedge roses, 320
hedges, 41–43
Helianthemum, 171
Helichrysum, 171
Helichrysum italicum, 171
Helwingia, 171
Helwingia chinensis, 171
Helwingia himalaica, 171
Helwingia japonica, 171
Hemiptelea, 171
Hemiptelea davidii, 171
Henry's emmenopterys, 146
Henry's lime/linden, 361
Heptacodium, 172
Heptacodium miconioides, 172
herbaceous bamboos, 83
Heteromeles, 172
Heteromeles arbutifolia, 172
hiba, 358
Hibiscus, 172–173
Hibiscus syriacus, 172–173
hickory, 24
highbush blueberry, 367
Himalayan honeysuckle, 200
Hippophae, 173
Hippophae rhamnoides, 173
Hippophae salicifolia, 173
Hoheria, 173–174
Hoheria glabrata, 173–174
Hoheria lyallii, 173–174
Hoheria populnea, 174
Hoheria sexstylosa, 174
Holboellia, 174, 344
Holboellia coriacea, 174
Holboellia latifolia, 174
holly, 41, 43, 179–180
holly-leaved sweetspire, 181
holly osmanthus, 237
holm oak, 293
Holodiscus, 174
Holodiscus discolor, 174

honeycup, 383
honey locust, 165–166
honey rose honeysuckle, 208
hop hornbeam, 238
hop tree, 284
hornbeams, 96–98
horse-chestnut, 68–69
horsetail tree, 102
houmapara, 283
Hovenia dulcis, 175
huckleberry oak, 298
Hungarian oak, 289
hybrid musks, 318
Hydrangea, 175–178
Hydrangea anomala subsp. *petiolaris*, 48, 177
Hydrangea arborescens, 175
Hydrangea aspera, 176
Hydrangea heteromalla, 176–177
Hydrangea macrophylla, 176
Hydrangea paniculata, 175
Hydrangea quercifolia, 176
Hydrangea seemannii, 178
Hydrangea serrata, 176
Hydrangea serratifolia, 177
Hymenoscyphus fraxineus, 21, 161
Hypericum, 24, 178
Hypericum androsaemum, 178
Hypericum beanii, 178
Hypericum calycinum, 178
Hypericum forrestii, 178
Hypericum ×*hidcoteense*, 178
Hypericum hookerianum, 178

I

Idesia, 179
Idesia polycarpa, 179
igiri tree, 179
Ilex, 179–180
Ilex aquifolium, 41, 43, 46, 179–180, 198
Ilex crenata, 46
Ilex ×*koehneana*, 180
Ilex verticillata, 180
Illicium, 180
Illicium anisatum, 180
Illicium simonsii, 180
incense cedar, 92
incense rose, 310
Indian bean tree, 103
Indian horse-chestnut, 70
Indigofera, 181
Indigofera heterantha, 181

Indigofera kirilowii, 181
Indigofera pendula, 181
Indigofera potaninii, 181
industrial methylated spirits, 22
infection, 21–22
informal hedges, 41–42
insects, 23
interior live oak, 297
invasive species, 107
Irish yew, 109
ironwood, 238
irrigation, 17
Italian maple, 61
Itea, 181
Itea ilicifolia, 181
Itea virginica, 181
ivy, 170–171

J

jacktree, 336
Jamesia, 181
Jamesia americana, 181
Japanese apricot, 275
Japanese arborvitae, 357
Japanese blue oak, 298
Japanese cedar, 130–131
Japanese cornel dogwood, 122
Japanese dogwood, 123–124
Japanese flowering cherry, 276
Japanese honeysuckle, 210
Japanese hop hornbeam, 238
Japanese horse-chestnut, 69
Japanese hydrangea vine, 330–331
Japanese larch, 196–197
Japanese mallotus, 219
Japanese maple, 63
Japanese nutmeg, 362
Japanese orixa, 237
Japanese persimmon, 141
Japanese plum yew, 109
Japanese raisin tree, 175
Japanese rose, 189, 312
Japanese rowan, 340
Japanese silver tree, 232
Japanese snowball, 369
Japanese star anise, 180
Japanese stewartia, 346
Japanese tallow tree, 232
Japanese walnut, 184–185
Japanese wingnut, 285
Japanese zelkova, 383

L

Jasminum, 182
Jasminum beesianum, 182
Jasminum fruticans, 182
Jasminum humile, 182
Jasminum mesnyi, 182
Jasminum nudiflorum, 48, 182
Jasminum officinale, 182
Jerusalem sage, 250–251
jet bead, 302
Judas tree, 111–112
Juglans, 24, 182–185
Juglans ailantifolia, 184–185
Juglans californica, 185
Juglans mandshurica, 184–185
Juglans microcarpa, 185
Juglans nigra, 183, 184
Juglans regia, 184
Juniperus, 185–187
Juniperus chinensis, 186, 187
Juniperus communis, 185, 187
Juniperus occidentalis, 186
Juniperus osteosperma, 185, 187
Juniperus ×pfitzeriana, 185
Juniperus virginiana, 185

K

Kalmia angustifolia, 188
Kalmia latifolia, 188
Kalopanax septemlobus, 189
  f. *maximowiczii*, 189
katsura, 110
Kentucky coffeetree, 167
kermes oak, 293
Kerria, 189
Kerria japonica, 189, 302
koda, 144
Koelreuteria, 190–191
Koelreuteria bipinnata, 191
Koelreuteria paniculata, 190
Kolkwitzia, 192
Kolkwitzia amabilis, 192
Korean arborvitae, 357
Korean evodia, 356
Korean fir, 55
Korean forsythia, 52
Korean hornbeam, 98
Korean mountain ash, 341
Korean willow, 325
kousa dogwood, 123
kowhai, 338
Kurume azalea, 300–301

+*Laburnocytisus*, 192
Laburnum, 193–195
Laburnum anagyroides, 194, 195
Laburnum ×watereri, 195
lacebark pine, 265
Lagerstroemia, 195
Lagerstroemia fauriei, 195
lancewood, 283
Lapageria, 196
Lapageria rosea, 196
larch, 196–197
Lardizabala funaria, 196
large-flowered bush roses, 314–316
large-leaved lime/linden, 360
large-leaved poplars, 272
Larix, 196–197
Larix decidua, 196, 197
Larix kaempferi, 196–197
late flowering clematis, 119
latex gloves, 22
Laurelia, 198
Laurelia sempervirens, 198
Laurus, 198
Laurus azorica, 198
Laurus nobilis, 46, 198
laurustinus, 368
Lavandula, 10, 199
Lavandula angustifolia, 199
Lavandula stoechas, 199
Lavatera, 200
Lavatera ×clementii, 200
lavender, 199
lavender cotton, 328
Lawson cypress, 113–114
leather gloves, 22
leatherleaf viburnum, 369
Lebanon cedar, 105–106, 107
Leptospermum, 200
Leptospermum myrtifolium, 200
Lespedeza, 200
Lespedeza bicolor, 200
Lespedeza kiusiana, 200
Lespedeza thunbergii, 200
lesser periwinkle, 371
Leucothoe, 200
Leucothoe fontanesiana, 200
Leycesteria, 200
Leycesteria formosa, 200
Leyland cypress, 134
Libocedrus bidwillii, 201
Libocedrus plumosa, 201
Ligustrum, 42, 201, 349
Ligustrum delavayanum, 46, 201

Ligustrum japonicum, 201
Ligustrum lucidum, 201
Ligustrum ovalifolium, 201
Ligustrum quihoui, 201
Ligustrum vulgare, 201
lilac, 348–350
lily of the valley tree, 130
lime/linden, 358–361
Lindera, 201–202
Lindera benzoin, 202
Lindera megaphylla, 202
Lindera praecox, 201–202
Liquidambar, 203–205
Liquidambar acalycina, 205
Liquidambar formosana, 205
Liquidambar orientalis, 203–205
Liquidambar styraciflua, 18, 203–205
Liriodendron, 206
Liriodendron chinense, 17, 21, 206
Liriodendron tulipifera, 206, 207
Lomatia, 208
Lomatia ferruginea, 208
Lomatia hirsuta, 208
Lomatia tinctoria, 208
London plane, 267
long-armed secateurs, 14
long-handled loppers, 21
Lonicera, 208–211
Lonicera acuminata, 210
Lonicera ×americana, 210
Lonicera ×brownii, 210
Lonicera caprifolium, 210
Lonicera etrusca, 210
Lonicera fragrantissima, 209
Lonicera henryi, 210
Lonicera hildebrandiana, 210
Lonicera japonica, 210
Lonicera korolkowii, 208
Lonicera maackii, 208
Lonicera nitida, 43, 46, 210
Lonicera periclymenum, 48, 210
Lonicera pileata, 210
Lonicera purpusii, 209
Lonicera quinquelocularis, 208
Lonicera sempervirens, 210, 211
Lonicera standishii, 209
loquat oak, 297
Loropetalum, 211
Loropetalum chinense, 211
  var. *rubrum*, 211
lowbush blueberry, 367
Luma, 211
Luma apiculata, 211

Lycium, 211–212
Lycium barbarum, 211–212
Lycium chinense, 211–212
Lydian broom, 164
Lyonia ligustrina, 212

M

Maackia, 212
Maackia amurensis, 212
Maackia hupehensis, 212
Mackay's heath, 148–149
Maclura pomifera, 213
Maclura tricuspidata, 213
macqui, 80
Magnolia, 213–217
Magnolia campbellii, 214, 215
Magnolia compressa, 217
Magnolia delavayi, 217
Magnolia doltsopa, 216
Magnolia figo, 217
Magnolia grandiflora, 216–217
Magnolia macrophylla, 216
Magnolia rostrata, 216
Magnolia sieboldii, 216
Magnolia ×*soulangeana*, 214
Magnolia stellata, 216
Magnolia ×*thompsoniana*, 216
magnolia vines, 330
Magnolia virginiana, 217
Magnolia wilsonii, 216
×*Mahoberberis*, 218
Mahonia, 218–219
Mahonia aquifolium, 218
Mahonia bealei, 218
Mahonia fortunei, 219
Mahonia japonica, 218
Mahonia lomariifolia, 218
Mahonia ×*media*, 218
Mahonia napaulensis, 219
maidenhair tree, 164
maleberry, 212
Mallotus, 220
Mallotus japonicus, 219
mallow, 200
mallow ninebark, 254
Malus, 15, 220–222
Malus baccata, 220, 221
Malus domestica, 36, 39, 40, 41
Malus floribunda, 221
Malus hupehensis, 220
Malus ×*moerlandsii*, 221

Malus toringo, 222
Malus toringoides, 222
Malus trilobata, 221, 222
Malus tschonoskii, 222
Malus yunnanensis, 220
Malus ×*zumi*, 220
Manchurian cherry, 281
Manchurian walnut, 184–185
Mandevilla, 223
Mandevilla laxa, 223
manna ash, 161
many-flowered rose, 312
maple, 24, 56
Marn elm, 366
matagouri, 143
mechanical hedge cutter, 355
medlar, 226
Melaleuca, 223
Melaleuca gibbosa, 223
Melaleuca squarrosa, 223
Melia, 224
Melia azedarach, 224
Meliosma, 224–225
Meliosma beaniana, 224
Meliosma dilleniifolia, 224
Meliosma myriantha, 224
Meliosma parviflora, 224
Meliosma veitchiorum, 224, 225
memorial rose, 312
Menispermum canadense, 226
Mespilus, 226
Mespilus germanica, 226
Metasequoia, 226–227
Metasequoia glyptostroboides, 226–227
Metrosideros, 227
Metrosideros diffusa, 227
Metrosideros excelsa, 227
Metrosideros robusta, 227
Metrosideros umbellata, 227
Mexican oak, 297
Microbiota decussata, 228
midseason flowering clematis, 119
Mimulus, 228
Mimulus aurantiacus, 228
mineral turpentine, 22
miniature roses, 318
mock orange, 249–250
modern shrub roses, 318
monarch birch, 85
Montpelier broom, 164
Montpelier maple, 61
moonseed, 226
moosewood, 63

Morella, 228
Morella californica, 228
Morus, 24, 228–230
Morus alba, 44, 229, 230
Morus cathayana, 230
Morus nigra, 228, 229, 230
mountain laurel, 188
mountain ninebark, 254
mountain pepper, 352
Mount Etna broom, 164
Mount Omei rose, 310
Muehlenbeckia, 230
Muehlenbeckia complexa, 230
mulberry, 24
mulch, 17, 35
multi-stemmed tree, 19
musk rose, 312, 318
musk willow, 325
Mutisia, 230
Mutisia decurrens, 230
Mutisia ilicifolia, 230
Mutisia oligodon, 230
Mutisia spinosa, 230
mycorrhizae, 16
Myrica gale, 230
myrtle, 230
myrtle beech, 232
myrtle teatree, 200
Myrtus communis, 230
    subsp. *tarentina*, 230
Mysore thorn, 91

N

Nandina, 231
Nandina domestica, 231
narrow-leaved ash, 160
narrow-leaved mock privet, 250
natural root plate mulching, 35
Nectria cinnabarina, 16, 65, 86, 99, 111, 175, 216, 302, 380
Neillia, 231
Neillia ribesioides, 231
Neillia thibetica, 231
Neolitsea, 232
Neolitsea sericea, 232
Neoshirakia, 232
Neoshirakia japonica, 232
Nerium, 232
Nerium oleander, 232
New Zealand broadleaf, 167
New Zealand lacebark, 174

New Zealand pittosporum, 266
Nikko maple, 67
nonclimbers, 49
Nootka cypress, 378–379
North American dogwoods, 122–123
northern spicebush, 202
Norway maple, 56
Norway spruce, 254, 256
Nothofagus alpina, 232
Nothofagus antarctica, 232
Nothofagus betuloides, 232
Nothofagus cunninghamii, 232
Nothofagus dombeyi, 232
Nothofagus menziesii, 232
Nothofagus obliqua, 232, 233
Notholithocarpus densiflorus, 234
Nyssa, 234
Nyssa sylvatica, 18, 234

O

oak, 289–298
oak-leaved hydrangea, 176
oak wilt, 23, 296
oceanspray, 174
Oemleria cerasiformis, 235
oil stone, 21
Old English shrub rose, 316–318, 321
Olea, 235–236
Olea europaea, 235
Olearia, 237
Olearia avicenniifolia, 237
Olearia haastii, 237
Olearia phlogopappa, 237
olive, 235–236
Ophiostoma novo-ulmi, 366
Oplopanax horridus, 237
opposite buds, 25
Oregon ash, 160
Oregon grape, 218
Oregon maple, 61–63
organic compost, 17
organic matter, 16
oriental bittersweet, 107
oriental plane, 267
Oriental sweetgum, 203
Orixa japonica, 237
Osage orange, 213
Osmanthus, 237–238
Osmanthus ×burkwoodii, 238
Osmanthus decorus, 238
Osmanthus delavayi, 46, 237

Osmanthus heterophyllus, 237
osoberry, 235
Ostrya, 238–239
Ostrya carpinifolia, 238
Ostrya japonica, 238
Ostrya virginiana, 238
Oxydendrum arboreum, 239
Ozothamnus, 239

P

Pacific madrone, 78
Pacific ninebark, 254
Paeonia, 240
Paeonia delavayi, 240
Paeonia ludlowii, 240
Paeonia suffruticosa, 240
pagoda dogwood, 124
pagoda tree, 346
Paliurus, 240
Paliurus spina-christi, 240
palms, 240–241
paperbark maple, 67, 270
paper birch, 85
paperbush, 144
"parrot bills", 21
Parrotia, 241–242
Parrotia persica, 241–242
Parrotia subaequalis, 242
Parrotiopsis, 243
Parrotiopsis jacquemontiana, 243
parterre hedge, 90
Parthenocissus, 243–244, 373
Parthenocissus henryana, 244
Parthenocissus quinquefolia, 243
Parthenocissus tricuspidata, 47, 243–244
Passiflora, 244–246
Passiflora caerulea, 244–246
passion flower, 244–246
Patagonian cypress, 158
patio roses, 318
Paulownia, 246–247
Paulownia tomentosa, 18, 44, 246
peach, 275–276
peach leaf curl, 276
pear, 35–41, 287–289
pea shrubs, 96
pecan, 99
pergola, 72
Perovskia, 247
Perovskia atriplicifolia, 247
Persea, 247–248

Persea americana, 247
Persea borbonia, 247
Persea palustris, 247, 248
Persian ironwood, 241–242
Persian ivy, 171
personal protection, 22
pests, 15–16
petrol hedge cutter, 42
Phellodendron, 248
Phellodendron amurense, 248
Phellodendron chinense, 248
Phellodendron sachalinense, 248
Philadelphus, 14, 24
Philadelphus coronarius, 250
Philadelphus microphyllus, 250
Philadelphus purpurascens, 249
Phillyrea, 250
Phillyrea angustifolia, 250
    f. *rosmarinifolia*, 250
Phillyrea latifolia, 250
Phlomis, 250–251
Phlomis chrysophylla, 251
Phlomis fruticosa, 250–251
Phlomis italica, 251
Phlomis longifolia, 251
Phoma clematidina, 119
Photinia, 251–253
Photinia beauverdiana, 251–253
Photinia davidiana, 253
Photinia ×fraseri, 253
Photinia glabra, 253
Photinia serratifolia, 253
Photinia villosa, 251–253
Phygelius, 254
Phygelius aequalis, 254
Phygelius capensis, 254
Phygelius ×rectus, 254
Phyllodoce, 254
Phyllodoce breweri, 254
Phyllodoce caerulea, 254
Phyllodoce empetriformis, 254
Phyllodoce ×intermedia, 254
Phyllostachys aurea, 82
Phyllostachys nuda, 82
Phyllostachys viridiglaucescens, 82
Physocarpus, 254
Physocarpus capitatus, 254
Physocarpus malvaceus, 254
Physocarpus monogynus, 254
Physocarpus opulifolius, 254
Phytophthora ramorum, 21
Picea, 23, 254–257
Picea abies, 254, 256

Picea jezoensis, 257
Picea omorika, 254, 257
Picea orientalis, 257
Picea smithiana, 255
Picrasma, 258
Picrasma quassioides, 258
Pieris, 258
Pieris floribunda, 258
Pieris japonica, 258
Pileostegia, 259
Pileostegia viburnoides, 259
pine, 23, 260–265
pineapple broom, 79
pine resin, 22
pinnate-leaved lilac, 348
pin oak, 296
Pinus, 11, 260–265
Pinus bungeana, 265
Pinus nigra, 261, 265
Pinus pinea, 260, 262, 265
Pinus sylvestris, 265
Pinus thunbergii, 260
Pinus wallichiana, 263–264, 265
Piptanthus, 265
Piptanthus nepalensis, 265
Pistacia, 266
Pistacia chinensis, 266
Pistacia terebinthus, 266
Pittosporum, 266
Pittosporum patulum, 266
Pittosporum tenuifolium, 266
plane, 267
planting depth, 17
planting hole, 16
planting operation, 16–17
Platanus, 45
Platanus ×hispanica, 267
Platanus occidentalis, 267
Platanus orientalis, 267
Platycarya, 268
Platycarya strobilacea, 268
Platycladus, 269
Platycladus orientalis, 269
pleaching, 45–46
Pleioblastus, 83
Pleioblastus auriocomus, 83
Pleioblastus chino, 83
Pleioblastus linearis, 82
Pleioblastus simonii, 82
Pleioblastus variegatus, 83
plum-fruited yew, 274
plums, 22, 274–275

plum yew, 108–109
Podocarpus, 269
Podocarpus lawrencei, 269
Podocarpus nivalis, 269
Podocarpus salignus, 269
pole pruners, 21
pole saws, 14
Poliothyrsis, 269
Poliothyrsis sinensis, 269
pollarding, 45
polyantha roses, 318
Polylepis, 270
Polylepis australis, 270
pomegranate, 286
Poncirus, 270–271
Poncirus trifoliata, 270–271
pond cypress, 354
poplar canker, 271
poplar dieback, 274
Populus, 271–274
Populus alba, 272
Populus balsamifera, 272
Populus ×berolinensis, 272
Populus ×canadensis, 272
Populus ×canescens, 271
Populus deltoides, 272
Populus ×generosa, 272
Populus grandidentata, 271
Populus ×jackii, 272
Populus lasiocarpa, 272
Populus nigra, 18, 273, 274
Populus remula, 272
Populus tomentosa, 271
Populus tremuloides, 272
Populus trichocarpa, 272
Populus wilsonii, 272
Portugal heath, 148
port wine magnolia, 217
posts, 72, 75
potato tree, 337
prairie white rose, 311
prickly ash, 380
prickly castor oil tree, 189
prickly heath, 164
pride of India, 190
Prinsepia, 274
Prinsepia sinensis, 274
Prinsepia uniflora, 274
Prinsepia utilis, 274
privet, 42, 349
protective wound sealants, 31
Prumnopitys, 274

Prumnopitys andina, 274
pruning
    aftercare, 17, 35
    back to a bud, 25
    coppicing, 43–45
    corrective formative pruning, 13–14
    crown lifting, 31
    crown reduction, 32–33
    crown renovation/renewal, 33
    crown thinning, 32
    dead, dying, diseased, and damaged branches, 15–16, 23
    epicormic shoots, 33–34
    established fruit trees, 37–39
    for flowers and fruit, 14–15
    formative pruning, 11–13
    fruit tree forms, 35–36
    hard pruning, 34–35
    healing response of pruning cuts, 24
    hedge renovation, 43
    hedges, 41–43
    main reasons and objectives for, 10
    mature tree, 31–33
    pleaching, 45–46
    pollarding, 45
    position of pruning cuts, 24–25
    removing a branch with a handsaw, 26–27
    removing a branch with secateurs, 26
    to restrict plant growth, 15
    reversions, 33
    shortening branch end, 31
    shortening larger branch using pruning saw, 30
    shortening small branch using secateurs, 30
    suckers, 13, 34
    target pruning, 27–31
    timing of operations, 22–24
    topiary, 46
    training fruit trees, 36–37
pruning saws, 13, 15, 21, 30
pruning shears, 21
Prunus, 15, 18, 274–282
Prunus armeniaca, 275
Prunus avium, 276, 279
Prunus cerasifera, 275
Prunus domestica, 39, 275
Prunus dulcis, 275
Prunus incisa, 280–281
Prunus jamasakura, 276
Prunus laurocerasus, 281–282
Prunus lusitanica, 281
Prunus maackii, 281

Prunus mume, 275
Prunus padus, 281
Prunus persica, 275, 276
Prunus sargentii, 279, 280
Prunus serrula, 279–280, 281
Prunus serrulata, 276, 277
Prunus speciosa, 276
Prunus spinosa, 275
Prunus tenella, 276
Prunus triloba, 49, 276
Pseudolarix, 282
Pseudolarix amabilis, 282
Pseudomonas syringae, 348
Pseudomonas syringae pv. *morsprunorum*, 23, 274
Pseudopanax crassifolius, 283
Pseudopanax ferox, 283
Pseudopanax lessonii, 283
Pseudotsuga, 11, 23, 283
Pseudotsuga macrocarpa, 283
Pseudotsuga menziesii, 11, 283
Ptelea, 284
Ptelea trifoliata, 284
Pterocarya, 284–285
Pterocarya fraxinifolia, 34, 284–285
Pterocarya hupehensis, 284
Pterocarya macroptera, 284
Pterocarya ×*rehderiana*, 34, 284–285
Pterocarya rhoifolia, 284, 285
Pterocarya stenoptera, 284
Pterostyrax, 285
Pterostyrax corymbosa, 285
Pterostyrax hispida, 285
Punica, 286
Punica granatum, 286
purple appleberry, 87
purple cherry plum, 275
Pyracantha, 286–287
pyramid tree form, 36, 39
Pyrus, 15, 287–289
Pyrus amygdaliformis, 287, 289
Pyrus calleryana, 289
Pyrus communis, 38, 40, 287
Pyrus nivalis, 287, 289
Pyrus salicifolia, 287–289
Pyrus ussuriensis, 287

Q

quaking aspens, 271–272
Quercus, 289–298
Quercus agrifolia, 297, 298

Quercus alnifolia, 293
Quercus bicolor, 290
Quercus canariensis, 289
Quercus castaneifolia, 293, 294
Quercus cerris, 293
Quercus chrysolepis, 298
Quercus coccifera, 293
Quercus coccinea, 23, 296
Quercus crassifolia, 297
Quercus dentata, 290, 292
Quercus frainetto, 289
Quercus georgiana, 297
Quercus glauca, 298
Quercus ×*hispanica*, 293, 294
Quercus ilex, 45, 289, 293–295
Quercus macranthera, 289
Quercus marilandica, 296–297
Quercus montana, 290
Quercus morii, 298
Quercus myrsinifolia, 298
Quercus nigra, 12
Quercus palustris, 23, 296, 297
Quercus petraea, 289, 290
Quercus phellos, 296
Quercus phillyreoides, 295
Quercus pontica, 289
Quercus pubescens, 289
Quercus pyrenaica, 289
Quercus robur, 18, 28, 289–290, 291, 292
Quercus ×*rosacea*, 290, 292
Quercus rubra, 23, 296
Quercus rysophylla, 297
Quercus sessilifolia, 298
Quercus suber, 295
Quercus ×*turneri*, 296
Quercus vacciniifolia, 298
Quercus variabilis, 293
Quercus velutina, 23, 32, 296
Quercus wislizeni, 297

R

rambler roses, 318–319
rauli beech, 232
red buckeye, 69
redbud, 112
red chokeberry, 81
red currant, 304
red horse-chestnut, 69
red oaks, 18, 23, 296–297
Rehderodendron, 299
Rehderodendron macrocarpum, 299

reversions, 33
Rhamnus, 299
Rhamnus alaternus, 299
Rhamnus davurica, 299
Rhaphiolepis ×*delacourii*, 299
Rhaphiolepis indica, 299
Rhaphiolepis umbellata, 299
Rhododendron, 10, 299–301
Rhododendron augustinii, 300
Rhododendron davidsonianum, 300
Rhododendron rex, 299
Rhododendron sinogrande, 299
Rhododendron yunnanense, 300
Rhodotypos, 302
Rhodotypos scandens, 302
Rhus, 302–304
Rhus aromatica, 304
Rhus glabra, 304
Rhus trilobata, 304
Rhus typhina, 34, 302–304
Rhus verniciflua, 302, 303
Ribes, 304–306
Ribes alpinum, 306
Ribes laurifolium, 306
Ribes odoratum, 306
Ribes rubrum, 304
Ribes sanguineum, 304–306
Ribes speciosum, 305, 306
ring cup oaks, 298
rival leaders, 11–12
river birch, 86
Robinia, 307–308
Robinia ×*ambigua*, 308
Robinia pseudoacacia, 307, 308
roble beech, 232
Rosa, 10, 21, 22, 24, 308–321
Rosa ×*alba*, 310
Rosa arkansana, 312
Rosa banksiae, 313, 318
Rosa bracteata, 318
Rosa brunonii, 318
Rosa canina, 311, 320
Rosa carolina, 311
Rosa ×*centifolia*, 310
Rosa chinensis, 313, 314
Rosa corymbifera, 311
Rosa damascena, 310
Rosa davidii, 312
Rosa ecae, 310
Rosa elegantula, 310
Rosa filipes, 318
Rosa foetida, 310
Rosa foliolosa, 311

S

Rosa gallica, 310
Rosa glauca, 311
Rosa helenae, 318
Rosa laevigata, 313
Rosa laxa, 320
Rosa maximowicziana, 312
Rosa micrantha, 311
Rosa mollis, 311
Rosa moschata, 312, 318
Rosa moyesii, 309, 312
Rosa multiflora, 312, 318
Rosa nitida, 311
Rosa ×*odorata*, 308, 313, 314
Rosa primula, 310
Rosa pulverulenta, 311
Rosa roxburghii, 314
Rosa rubiginosa, 311, 320
Rosa rugosa, 312, 320
Rosa sericea, 310
    subsp. *omeiensis* f. *pteracantha*, 310
Rosa soulieana, 312
Rosa spinosissima, 310, 320
Rosa stylosa, 311
Rosa tomentosa, 311
Rosa villosa, 311
Rosa virginiana, 311
Rosa wichuraiana, 308, 312, 318, 319
Rosa willmottiae, 312
Rosa xanthina f. *hugonis*, 308
rose of Sharon, 172–173
Rosmarinus, 322
Rosmarinus officinalis, 322
rosy dipelta, 142
rowan, 338–340
rubber-coated canvas gloves, 22
rubber gloves, 22
Rubus, 21, 22, 322
Rubus biflorus, 322
Rubus cockburnianus, 22, 322
Rubus deliciosus, 322
Rubus odoratus, 322
Rubus thibetanus, 322
rum cherry, 281
Ruscus, 323
Ruscus aculeatus, 323
Ruscus hypoglossum, 323
russet buffaloberry, 336
Ruta, 323
Ruta graveolens, 323

sacred bamboo, 231
safety glasses/goggles, 22
salal, 164
Salix, 45, 323–326
Salix aegyptiaca, 325
Salix alba, 323, 326
    var. *vitellina*, 43, 45, 325
Salix babylonica, 323
    var. *pekinensis*, 323
Salix caprea, 325
Salix daphnoides, 324–325
Salix fragilis, 323
Salix helvetica, 326
Salix integra, 325
Salix irrorata, 325
Salix koriyanagi, 325
Salix pentandra, 323
Salix purpurea, 323–324
Salix repens, 326
Salix reticulata, 326
Salix retusa, 326
Salix ×*sepulcralis*, 325
    var. *chrysocoma*, 19, 323
Salvia, 326
Salvia elegans, 326
Salvia microphylla, 326
Salvia officinalis, 326
Sambucus, 327
Sambucus ebulus, 327
Sambucus nigra, 327
    subsp. *canadensis*, 327
    f. *porphyrophylla*, 327
Santolina, 328
Santolina chamaecyparissus, 328
sap, 22
Sapindus, 328
Sapindus mukorossi, 328
Sapindus saponaria var. *drummondii*, 328
"sap leakage", 23–24
Sarcococca, 329
Sarcococca confusa, 329
Sassafras, 329–330
Sassafras albidum, 329
Sassafras randaiense, 329
Sassafras tzumu, 329
saucer magnolia, 214
sausage vine, 174
scarlet willow, 43, 45
scented paperbark, 223
Schefflera, 330
Schefflera delavayi, 330
Schefflera rhododendrifolia, 330
Schefflera taiwaniana, 330

Schima, 330
Schima khasiana, 330
Schima wallichii, 330
Schisandra chinensis, 330
Schisandra grandiflora, 330
Schisandra rubriflora, 330
Schizophragma, 330–331
Schizophragma hydrangeoides, 47, 48, 330–331
Schizophragma integrifolium, 330–331
Sciadopitys, 331
Sciadopitys verticillata, 331
Scolytus multistriatus, 366
Scolytus scolytus, 366
Scots pine, 265
sea buckthorn, 173
secateurs, 13, 21, 22, 26, 30
Semiarundinaria fastuosa, 82
Senecio, 332
Senecio scandens, 332
Senna, 332
Senna corymbosa, 332
Senna marilandica, 332
Sequoia, 332–334, 350
Sequoiadendron giganteum, 335
Sequoia sempervirens, 34, 332–334
Serbian spruce, 254
Seridium cardinale, 134
sessile oak, 289
seven son flower of Zhejiang, 172
shagbark hickory, 99
sheep laurel, 188
Shepherdia, 336
Shepherdia argentea, 336
Shepherdia canadensis, 336
shrubby cinquefoil, 137
shrubby germander, 356
shrubby musk, 228
shrub pruning, 24
Siberian crab, 220
Siberian cypress, 228
Siberian elm, 366
Sierra juniper, 186
silky stewartia, 346
silver beech, 232
silver birch, 85
silver leaf, 22, 274
silver lime/linden, 360
silver maple, 65
Sinofranchetia, 336
Sinofranchetia chinensis, 336
Sinojackia, 336
Sinojackia rehderiana, 336
Sinojackia xylocarpa, 336

Skimmia, 336–337
Skimmia anquetilia, 336
Skimmia japonica, 336
Skimmia laureola, 336
skirt lifting, 12
skunkbush, 304
small-leaved lime/linden, 360
Smilax, 337
Smilax aspera, 337
Smilax megalantha, 337
Smilax pumila, 337
Smilax tamnoides, 337
snow pear, 287
soapberry, 328
soft downy rose, 311
soil ameliorants, 16
Solanum, 337–338
Solanum crispum, 337
Solanum laxum, 337
Solanum valdiviense, 338
Sophora, 338
Sophora davidii, 338
Sophora tetraptera, 338
Sorbaria, 338
Sorbaria kirilowii, 338
Sorbaria sorbifolia, 338
Sorbus, 338–341
Sorbus alnifolia, 341
Sorbus americana, 338
Sorbus aria, 340, 341
Sorbus aucuparia, 338, 340
Sorbus caloneura, 341
Sorbus commixta, 340
Sorbus esserteauana, 338
Sorbus folgneri, 341
Sorbus intermedia, 340
Sorbus ×kewensis, 339
Sorbus meliosmifolia, 341
Sorbus pallescens, 340
Sorbus poteriifolia, 338
Sorbus pseudohupehensis, 338
Sorbus sargentiana, 338
Sorbus scalaris, 338
Sorbus torminalis, 340
Sorbus vestita, 340
Sorbus wilsoniana, 338
sorrel tree, 239
sourwood, 239
southern bush honeysuckle, 141
southern rata, 227
Spanish broom, 341
Spanish heath, 148
Spartium, 341

Spartium junceum, 341
Spiraea, 342–343
Spiraea amoena, 343
Spiraea betulifolia, 343
Spiraea corymbosa, 343
Spiraea douglasii, 343
Spiraea gemmata, 342
Spiraea hypericifolia, 342
Spiraea japonica, 343
Spiraea ×margaritae, 343
Spiraea ×sanssouciana, 343
spreading juniper, 185
spruce, 254–257
spur leaf, 356
spur pruning, 246
Stachyurus, 343
Stachyurus chinensis, 343
Stachyurus himalaicus, 343
Stachyurus praecox, 343
"stag-headed", 33
stag's horn sumach, 302–304
staking systems, 17
standard trees, 36
Standish's honeysuckle, 209
Staphylea, 344
Staphylea bumalda, 344
Staphylea colchica, 344
Staphylea pinnata, 344
Staphylea trifolia, 344
star magnolia, 216
Stauntonia, 344
Stauntonia hexaphylla, 344
Stephanandra incisa, 344
Stephanandra tanakae, 344
stepover tree form, 36, 41
sterilizing tools, 21–22
Stewartia, 344–346
Stewartia malacodendron, 346
Stewartia monadelpha, 344–346
Stewartia pseudocamellia, 345, 346
Stewartia sinensis, 346
St. John's wort, 178
stone pine, 262, 265
stooling, 43–45
Styphnolobium, 346–347
Styphnolobium japonicum, 346, 347
Styrax, 348
Styrax obassia, 348
Styrax wilsonii, 348
suckers, 13, 34
sudden oak death, 21
sugar hackberry, 108
sugar maple, 61

sugi, 130
summer pruning, roses, 315–316
support systems, 17, 46, 47–49
swamp bay, 247
swamp white oak, 290
sweet bay, 217
sweet box, 329
sweet briar, 311
sweet chestnut, 100–101
sweetgum, 203
sweet olive, 238
sycamore, 59–61
Sycopsis sinensis, 348
Symphoricarpos, 24, 348
Symphoricarpos albus, 348
Symphoricarpos occidentalis, 348
Symphoricarpos orbiculatus, 348
Syringa, 24, 348–350
Syringa ×chinensis, 350
Syringa ×henryi, 350
Syringa ×hyacinthiflora, 349
Syringa ×josiflexa, 350
Syringa josikaea, 350
Syringa komarowii, 350
Syringa laciniata, 349
Syringa oblata, 350
Syringa persica, 349
Syringa pinnatifolia, 348
Syringa ×prestoniae, 350
Syringa pubescens, 348
Syringa reticulata, 350
  subsp. *amurensis*, 350
  subsp. *pekinensis*, 350
Syringa ×swegiflexa, 350
Syringa tomentella, 350
Syringa villosa, 350
Syringa vulgaris, 348, 349, 350
Syringa wolfii, 350
Syringa yunnanensis, 350

T

Taiwania, 350–352
Taiwania cryptomerioides, 350, 351
tall stewartia, 344–346
Tamarix, 352
Tamarix chinensis, 352
Tamarix gallica, 352
Tamarix parviflora, 352
Tamarix ramosissima, 352
Tamarix tetrandra, 352
tanoak, 234

Taphrina deformans, 276
target pruning, 27–31
Tasmannia, 352
Tasmannia lanceolata, 352
Taxodium, 352–354
Taxodium distichum, 352, 354
   var. *imbricarium*, 354
Taxodium mucronatum, 353, 354
Taxus, 34, 108, 354–355
Taxus baccata, 41, 43, 46, 109, 354–355
Taxus ×media, 355
tea rose, 313
Tetracentron, 356
Tetracentron sinense, 356
Tetradium, 356
Tetradium daniellii, 356
Tetradium ruticarpum, 356
Teucrium, 356
Teucrium chamaedrys, 356
Teucrium fruticans, 356
Texas walnut, 185
Thamnocalamus spathiflorus, 82
"3-cut method", 26–27
Thuja, 23, 43, 357
Thuja koraiensis, 357
Thuja occidentalis, 357
Thuja plicata, 357
Thuja standishii, 357
Thujopsis, 358
Thujopsis dolabrata, 358
thunder god vine, 363
Tibetan cherry, 279–280
Tibetan hazel, 126
Tibetan neillia, 231
Tilia, 34, 45, 358–361
Tilia americana, 360
Tilia chinensis, 12
Tilia cordata, 358, 360
Tilia ×euchlora, 358, 360
Tilia ×europaea, 358, 359, 361
Tilia henryana, 361
Tilia oliveri, 358, 360
Tilia platyphyllos, 358, 360, 361
Tilia tomentosa, 358, 360
tool maintenance, 21–22
tools, 20–21
Toona, 362
Toona sinensis, 45, 362
toothed lancewood, 283
topiary, 46
Torreya, 362
Torreya californica, 362
Torreya grandis, 362

Torreya nucifera, 362
Trachelospermum, 362–363
Trachelospermum asiaticum, 362
Trachelospermum jasminoides, 362
Trachycarpus fortunei, 240–241
tree anemone, 96
tree forms and shapes, 18–19
tree heath, 147–148
tree of heaven, 71
tree paints, 31
tree peonies, 240
tree-watering bags, 17
trellis, 75
tripods, 67
Tripterygium, 363
Tripterygium wilfordii, 363
Trochodendron, 364
Trochodendron aralioides, 364
trumpet creeper, 95–96
trumpet honeysuckle, 211
Tsuga, 364–365
Tsuga canadensis, 364
Tsuga caroliniana, 364
Tsuga chinensis, 364
Tsuga diversifolia, 364
Tsuga heterophylla, 364
Tsuga mertensiana, 364
Tsuga sieboldii, 364
tulip tree, 206
tupelo, 234
Turkish hazel, 125
Turner's oak, 296
turpentine tree, 266
two-bud spur system, 194
two-flowered raspberry, 322
two-winged snowdrop tree, 168

U

Ubame oak, 295
Ugni, 365
Ugni molinae, 365
Ulex, 365
Ulex europaeus, 365
Ulex minor, 365
Ulmus, 366–367
Ulmus americana, 366
Ulmus glabra, 366
Ulmus minor, 366
Ulmus parvifolia, 366
Ulmus plotii, 366
Ulmus procera, 366

Ulmus pumila, 366
Ulmus villosa, 366
Umbellularia, 367
Umbellularia californica, 367
umbrella pine, 331

V

Vaccinium, 367
Vaccinium angustifolium, 367
Vaccinium corymbosum, 367
Vaccinium cylindraceum, 367
Vaccinium macrocarpon, 367
Vaccinium ovatum, 367
Vaccinium oxycoccus, 367
variegated dogwoods, 125
varnish tree, 302
Viburnum, 367–371
Viburnum betulifolium, 371
Viburnum ×bodnantense, 369, 371
Viburnum carlesii, 371
Viburnum davidii, 368, 369
Viburnum farreri, 371
Viburnum lantana, 371
Viburnum odoratissimum, 369
   var. *awabuki*, 369
Viburnum opulus, 371
Viburnum plicatum, 369, 370
   f. *plicatum*, 369
Viburnum ×rhytidophylloides, 369
Viburnum rhytidophyllum, 369
viburnums, 34, 367–371
Viburnum tinus, 13, 368, 369
Vinca, 371
Vinca major, 371
Vinca minor, 371
violet willow, 324–325
Virginia creeper, 243
Virginia sweetspire, 181
Vitex, 371
Vitex agnus-castus, 49, 371
Vitex negundo, 371
viticellas, 119
Vitis, 24, 371–373
Vitis amurensis, 373
Vitis coignetiae, 371, 372
Vitis vinifera, 373

W

walls
  climbers, 47–48
  nonclimbers, 49
walnut, 24, 182–185
wandering heath, 149
wavyleaf silktassel, 163
waxyleaf privet, 201
wayfaring tree, 371
weeping ash, 161
weeping forsythia, 159
weeping standard, 19
weeping standard roses, 320
Weigela, 373–374
Weigela florida, 374
western catalpa, 103, 104
western hemlock, 364
western snowberry, 348
wheel tree, 364
whitebeam, 340–341
white elm, 366
white mulberry, 230
white oaks, 289–292
white poplars, 271–272
white rose of York, 310
white spirit, 22
white-stemmed bramble, 322
white willow, 323
wild cherry, 276
wild Irishman, 143
wild service tree, 340
willow, 323–326
willow-leaved podocarp, 269
willow-leaved sea buckthorn, 173
willow oak, 296
Wilson's honeysuckle, 210
winged rose, 310
winterberry, 180
winter hazel, 125
winter heath, 148
winter honeysuckle, 209
winter's bark, 143
winter sweet, 114
Wisteria, 374–377
Wisteria brachybotrys, 374
Wisteria floribunda, 374, 375, 376
Wisteria sinensis, 48, 374, 376
Wollemia, 377
Wollemia nobilis, 377
Wollemi pine, 377
woodbine, 210
Wych elm, 366

X

Xanthoceras, 378
Xanthoceras sorbifolium, 378
Xanthocyparis, 134, 378–379
Xanthocyparis nootkatensis, 378–379
Xanthomonas populi, 271
Xanthorhiza, 380
Xanthorhiza simplicissima, 380

Y

Yeddo hawthorn, 299
yellow buckeye, 70
yellow German ivy, 332
yellowhorn, 378
yellow poplar, 206
yews, 41, 108
Yushania anceps, 82

Z

zabala fruit, 196
Zabelia triflora, 52
Zanthoxylum, 380
Zanthoxylum ailanthoides, 380
Zanthoxylum americanum, 380
Zanthoxylum armatum, 380
Zanthoxylum piperitum, 380
Zanthoxylum schinifolium, 380
Zelkova, 380–383
Zelkova abelicea, 380
Zelkova carpinifolia, 380–383, 381
Zelkova serrata, 18, 382, 383
Zelkova sinica, 383
Zenobia, 383
Zenobia pulverulenta, 383

About
the
Authors

George E. Brown (1917–1980) was Assistant Curator at the Royal Botanic Gardens, Kew, a founding member of the Arboricultural Association, and a recognized authority on trees and shrubs. *Photo courtesy Sally Annett.*

Tony Kirkham is Head of the Arboretum, Gardens, and Horticultural Services at RBG Kew, where he has worked since 1978. He lectures regularly internationally and lives in Middlesex. *Photo by Andrea Jones.*